NATURAL BODYBUILDING FOR MEN AND WOMEN

PETER NEFF

AVON
PUBLISHERS OF BARD, CAMELOT, DISCUS AND FLARE BOOKS

I would like to give special thanks to the following gyms for use of their facilities for the training photos:

East Coast Health Club, West Islip, N.Y.
Gold's Gym, Fairfield, N.J.
Ultimate Fitness Health Club, Port Chester, N.Y.
West Harrison Fitness Center, Inc., White Plains, N.Y.
Northeast Fitness Center, Mahopac, N.Y.

AVON BOOKS
A division of
The Hearst Corporation
1790 Broadway
New York, New York 10019

Library of Congress Cataloging in Publication Data
Neff, Peter.
  Natural bodybuilding.
  1. Bodybuilding. 2. Exercise. I. Title.
GV546 .5.N44 1985   646.7'5   84-45584

First Avon Printing, September 1985

This book is dedicated to Bob Gruskin for his guidance, patience and selfless giving. Without his support I could not have achieved such a high level of success as a natural bodybuilder nor have been able to make this book as comprehensive and complete as it is.

Acknowledgments

The following individuals have made significant contributions in two important areas. Some have contributed to the success of my body-building career and others have supplied me with information which aided me in writing this book. I extend my thanks and heartfelt appreciation to each one of these individuals: Mike Adelman, Sal Barracca, Geoff Cohen, Carl Colker, Ralph Eannace, Dave Franze, Karla Major, Charles Malfetti, Mike Mayers, Nancy Mayers, Walter Meade, David Patt, Carlos Sotolongo, Diane Terazakis, Greg Valentino, my parents (Peter and Regina Neff), my sisters, Karla and Erika, Edward Christiansen and family, Josephine Neff, Marion Childs, Peg and Gus Carayas, Tom and Linda Bleasdale, and Harvey Stern.

Book design by Design Image, Inc.

Contents

1

INTRODUCTION

Bodybuilding is quickly becoming the activity of the 1980s. The fitness craze is sweeping America and people are looking for the best way to get in shape. There is no question in my mind that bodybuilding is the answer. No other activity allows you to effect such splendid changes on your body. Bodybuilding is exactly what the name implies: It gives you the power to build and mold your body exactly the way you want it to look. Progressive resistance weight training lets you decide just how far you want to go with it.

You may just want to tone up, get a little stronger, and lose a little fat or you may want to put in the many hours of hard training and make the sacrifices necessary to develop a competitive physique. The choice is yours. No matter how far you decide to take it, one thing is for sure: Bodybuilding will have a positive effect on you both physically and psychologically. Watching your body improve is an exciting experience and it almost always has a positive affect on your self-image. It's a personal challenge. Your body and mind work together to benefit both.

In the following chapters you will find all aspects of bodybuilding covered, including training, diet, mental approach and competition. However, they will be explored in a unique way for this book, unlike others, is based upon and extols the virtues of the natural bodybuilding philosophy.

Is bodybuilding a sport?

The answer is yes. Bodybuilding is a demanding and competitive sport. There are bodybuilding contests held weekly across the country and all are fiercely competitive. However, while organized contests legitimize it as a sport to the average layman, the real sport of bodybuilding goes much deeper. It is first and foremost a struggle to improve oneself. It's you against the weight in an effort to force the body to conform to the desire of the mind, and the struggle and ultimate accomplishment of something so difficult and so personal is perhaps the greatest demonstration of a sport there is. After all, aren't the most important characteristics of any true sport competitiveness and the challenge to excel—to be the

best that one can be? Bodybuilding comes under the classification of individual sports, not team sports.

Besides being a sport itself, bodybuilding is now used as a training aid in almost all other sports. Prime examples are football, hockey, and track and field. In today's extremely competitive sports world, the added strength, flexibility, and coordination provided by bodybuilding training can often mean the difference between being good and being great. Those athletes who do heavy training with weights generally seem to have fewer injuries and longer careers than those who don't. More coaches see these obvious benefits and are including bodybuilding exercises in the training routines of their athletes. Within a few years it's quite possible that athletes from every sport will be using bodybuilding to improve their athletic performance.

Bodybuilding as an art form

In bodybuilding, the emphasis is placed on creating and presenting a certain visual image. Because of this, bodybuilding is considered by many to be an art form as well as a sport. A bodybuilder is a living piece of sculpture. The tools he uses to mold and create his masterpiece are pieces of equipment in the gym. Like the sculptor who uses a chisel. And make no mistakes about it, a well-developed physique is indeed a masterpiece. The Greeks used to consider a muscular, well-developed physique to be a thing of extreme beauty and many statues were sculpted in reverence of the male form. This continued through the Roman Empire and was best epitomized in Michelangelo's sculpture of David. The modern bodybuilder is, in effect, the ancient sculpture brought to life.

Bodybuilding myths

Bodybuilding, because of its egocentric nature, has been plagued by many uncomplimentary myths, which serve to limit the acceptance of bodybuilding as a sport by the general public. The most prevalent myth is the old one that "all that muscle will turn to fat." Muscle and fat consist of entirely different physiological structures and neither can change into the other. Muscle can be broken down into its basic components, converted to glucose, and burned away as energy, but it cannot be converted to fat. Some bodybuilders

do get fat as they get older and train less or stop training altogether, but this happens for a totally different and very basic reason. Normally, bodybuilders in heavy training consume extremely large quantities of food, which they require to replenish the enormous energy drain caused by heavy training. When a bodybuilder cuts back on his training, but does not cut back on his food intake, he will gain excess fat as would any average human being who eats more than he requires. In terms of the muscles themselves, when a bodybuilder cuts down drastically on his training or completely terminates it, his muscles begin to atrophy, to shrink down in size and lose tone.[1] If he cuts down on his food intake accordingly, he will actually become slender in appearance, the total opposite of the myth.

The second most prevalent myth is that "all bodybuilders are musclebound." People tend to assume that if a man is massively muscular, he must also be clumsy, slow, and uncoordinated. While there are a few bodybuilders who could be classified as musclebound, this is the exception rather than the rule. Most bodybuilders are, in fact, extremely quick, agile, coordinated, and even flexible. The more a bodybuilder trains, the more control he gains over his muscular system. Bodybuilding has actually been found to increase speed, mainly because highly trained and unusually strong muscles can contract harder and faster than those that have not been trained.[2]

The final myth I want to clarify—the most ridiculous of all—is that all bodybuilders are stupid. Most people seem to be under the impression that all bodybuilders do is go to the gym, lift some weights, and put on pounds of muscle. It is not that simple. Bodybuilding is an extremely complex science. An in-depth understanding of muscle kinesiology, bodybuilding training principles, nutrition, correct dieting techniques, the power of the mind, and the ability to apply all this information to your own body is imperative if one is to succeed in the sport. It requires above average intelligence as well as simple common sense.

What's the best age to start bodybuilding?

You're never too young or too old to start bodybuilding training and once you start, there's no reason to ever stop.

There's no other activity like it for retarding the aging process and maintaining muscle strength and tone, and a healthy appearance well into old age.

In terms of training for high levels of muscular development or competition there are, however, certain peak years during which the potential to gain muscle is at a maximum. The generally accepted prime of bodybuilding are the years between 18 and 45. Before age 14 or 15 the body is not mature enough nor does it have the proper hormone balance to gain an optimum amount of muscle tissue. After age 45, the body begins aging too quickly to allow maximum results.

In general, bodybuilders must begin training by their late teens in order to reach their ultimate muscular potential, which takes about 20 years to attain. An exception to this rule is Chris Dickenson, who began training at age 24 and went on to become the top money-winning pro in bodybuilding history in his early forties.[3] Unlike most other athletes, bodybuilders tend to improve with age. It takes many years of hard training to develop a muscularly mature, perfectly sculpted physique and most of today's top pros are in their late thirties and early forties, fulfilling the approximate 20-year period necessary to reach the upper limit of muscular potential.

Advantages and disadvantages

There are five drawbacks in bodybuilding. The most important of these is that bodybuilding does not promote cardiovascular fitness. Bodybuilding exercises exert short, intense, muscular contractions on localized muscle groups. Since the stress on the muscle does not last for more than a few seconds at a time, the increased heart rate resulting from intense exertion is not maintained consistently enough or long enough to promote cardiovascular fitness. Because of this, bodybuilders should supplement their training with some sort of activity such as long distance running, cycling or swimming at least three times a week in order to build a strong, healthy heart and increase endurance. Anyone who does both bodybuilding and endurance training on a regular basis will obtain the highest level of overall physical fitness possible.

The second disadvantage is that bodybuilding training can become boring because of the repetitive nature of the exercises. However, as you progress in the sport, you'll be changing your routines from time to time and the training will become more individualized and scientific. This should keep you from becoming stale. If that's not enough, the excitement of watching your body improve should definitely do the trick.[4]

The difficulty of finding clothes that fit is the third disadvantage. Even worse is the fact that if you train in order to develop to your full muscular potential, you will almost definitely need to have your clothes custom tailored, which can be very expensive. They just don't make clothes for bodybuilders! Of course, while they are expensive, custom-tailored clothes will dramatically enhance your physique. Nothing looks more impressive than a well-tailored bodybuilder.[5]

The fourth disadvantage is that the higher you go in the sport, the more committed you must become in order to continue improving. This is especially true for those who compete, as preparing for a contest requires attention to an incredible number of details. Those who desire high levels of success in the sport must be committed to train consistently for years, as well as to gather and implement scientific information on both training and diet. All of this takes time. However, it's probably the best time investment you can make in terms of benefits received.

The final drawback is expense. Gym memberships, training equipment, and food supplements such as vitamins and protein all cost money. Then there are always the travel expenses and extras associated with competition. I must stress, however, that this is an investment in one's health—and what better thing is there to spend one's money on?[6]

As I've already shown, almost every disadvantage of bodybuilding can be seen from another perspective as being an advantage. But that's not convincing enough in itself. Fortunately, bodybuilding has so many straight-out advantages that the drawbacks mentioned pale in comparison.

Of the six benefits I will discuss, the health benefit received from bodybuilding as it is presented in this book—natural and without any artificial aids to training—has to be the most important. The natural bodybuilding life style consisting of hard and consistent training, good nutrition, and proper rest will do wonders to improve your overall health. Natural bodybuilders very rarely get sick and are unusually full of energy. They treat their bodies right, and their bodies are more than happy to reciprocate.

The second advantage of bodybuilding is the dramatic effect it can have on your appearance. After all, most people first take up bodybuilding not for its health benefits, but for the dramatic effect it has on improving physical appearance. As mentioned previously, bodybuilding gives you the power to mold your body as you desire.

Another benefit closely related to appearance is the improvement in self-image that most bodybuilders experience. In general, as a bodybuilder improves his body to how he wants it to look, he becomes positive about the body image he is presenting to others. This results in an improved self-image and greater confidence which is, in turn, conveyed to those around him.

The fourth advantage, also closely related to appearance, is that bodybuilding training combined with a sensible diet allows you to gain and lose weight almost at will with little or no discomfort.[7]

The fifth advantage is that heavy bodybuilding training will make you exceedingly strong. It's not unusual to triple or quadruple your strength. You never know when a situation will come up where some extra strength will come in handy. Everyday things are easier when you're super-strong. In relation to this, the extra strength that your tendons, bones, and ligaments gain from heavy training and proper nutrition make you less vulnerable to severe injury and has saved many bodybuilders' lives. A prime example of this is Steve Michalik whose car was run over by a garbage truck three days before the Mr. Olympia contest. Steve was critically injured, almost beyond repair. It was only the reserve strength he had acquired from bodybuilding that saved his life and he readily admits this. Today he is fully recovered and back in competition.

Bodybuilding's final major advantage is that the increasing demands of the sport as you strive for higher levels of development enables you, over time, to develop more self-discipline. Discipline is an essential prerequisite of bodybuilding success. It also happens to be essential for obtaining success in all other fields. For this reason, the ability to discipline oneself is exceedingly valuable. Many bodybuilders have held down full-time jobs, gone to school full-time, and have still been able to train hard—all because they have mastered the ability to discipline themselves.[8]

2

NATURAL BODYBUILDING

Natural bodybuilding is the purest form of a sport that, like almost every sport, has been slowly permeated by the use of substances which artificially enhance performance. It is a problem which has now reached epidemic proportions. Bodybuilding has the potential to be one of the healthiest sports a person can engage in. It is unfortunate that the improvement of one's health does not even seem to be a consideration of many who take up bodybuilding and of most who compete.

The prevalent reason that many young men take up bodybuilding is to increase muscular mass. The desire of a young man to impress and gain the respect of his peer group, and especially girls, is in most cases, a deep-seated and powerful one. A sure way of gaining this attention is by developing a muscular, powerfully built physique. Those who are totally obsessed with developing one are often willing to try anything that might help them, including potentially dangerous drugs. This type of thinking obviously reflects immaturity, insecurity, and narrow-mindedness. It's inconceivable to me that anyone would risk their health and possibly their life in order to impress others. However, it does happen and is, in fact, very common.

The obsession to get big constitutes one major reason why bodybuilders will risk ruining their health. The desire to win constitutes the second reason. Competitive people, as a rule, love to win. Some cannot stand to lose, and most will do anything within their power to maximize their chances of success. In terms of bodybuilding, this often consists of taking drugs that are believed to enhance muscular development.

The most prevalent class of drugs used by bodybuilders are anabolic steroids. Most members of the bodybuilding community believe steroids enhance the level of muscular development one can achieve, and do so at an accelerated rate.

Definition of a natural bodybuilder

Simply stated, a natural bodybuilder is one who has never used any artifical means whatsoever in his entire life to enhance muscular development. This pertains especially to the use of steroids which have invaded the sport like the plague. Just to give you an idea of how serious the drug problem is, I've heard of young kids being told the day they walk into the gym that the only way they'll get anywhere is if they take steroids. One national physique judge with a deep knowledge of the competing scene has informed me that upward of 99 percent of competing bodybuilders take steroids. And the talk in today's modern bodybuilding gyms centers around what drugs to take and in what dosage to take them instead of how to train. Now that the situation has become so bad that everyone in the sport has come to believe that the only way to become a great bodybuilder is take steroids, and hard work doesn't count for anything, it's time to set the record straight and separate myth from reality. It's a real shame that things are so bad that a natural bodybuilding book has to be written, but the use of steroids and other drugs has simply gone too far. Almost all of today's bodybuilding books and magazine articles are being written by bodybuilders who use or have used bodybuilding drugs. Therefore, the training, diet, and psychological differences necessary to develop a championship physique naturally are not covered.

Natural bodybuilding life style

Natural bodybuilding is both an activity and a sport. More than that, it is a life style concerned with promotion of a high degree of physical health simultaneously with a high level of muscular development. It is based on the premise that a championship physique can be built while the health of the individual is maintained and, in fact, promoted to higher levels. While today's bodybuilder seems convinced that risking his health is a necessary sacrifice to obtain bodybuilding success, it is overlooked that a healthy, highly fit body also has the potential to reach an exceedingly high level of muscular development.

One element critical to achieving bodybuilding success naturally involves keeping all aspects of the natural bodybuilding life style in perfect balance. In bodybuilding if you don't pay as much attention to getting enough rest, or eating correctly or any number of other factors as you do to your training, you will be hindered from rising to the top. If training hard was all that was necessary to be great, every gym would have hundreds of champions. Since reaching the top is even harder without chemical aid, the proper balance of all factors supportive of muscular growth becomes even more important. To compete successfully as a natural against those who use drugs requires a flawless implementation of all aspects which make up the natural bodybuilding life style. It is a life style requiring discipline and sacrifice, but nobody ever said being a natural bodybuilding champion was going to be easy.

What exactly are the factors that make up this life style? First of all, a natural bodybuilder must train consistently and correctly, or everything is for naught. Next, he must make sure he provides his body with the nutrients it requires to function at optimum efficiency. The nutrients should come from eating as much wholesome and natural, unprocessed food as possible. Good nutrition is essential for good health and optimum muscle growth. Another important aspect of the natural bodybuilding life style is rest and recuperation. Without adequate rest, the body and mind will not be able to function optimally and recovery from workouts will be hindered.

Since we are talking here about a life style concerned with promoting good health as well as enhancing muscular development, let me say that cardiovascular conditioning should be a part of every natural bodybuilder's training routine. I have included an in-depth section on cardiovascular fitness later on in this book.

There is no place in the serious natural bodybuilder's life for so-called recreational drugs such as alcohol, marijuana or cocaine. These drugs are abusive to the body and there is no faster way to slow down your progress than to indulge yourself in them. Alcohol is an all-too-common culprit. The pressure to go out and "have a good time" is great.

Unfortunately, while there's certainly nothing wrong with going out and socializing, having a good time is often equated with getting high on alcohol. When the body breaks down alcohol, it uses up large quantities of vitamin C, vitamin B-complex, and other important nutrients. Once in the body, alcohol is treated like a poison. Eliminating it from the system puts a tremendous strain on the liver and kidneys specifically and the body in general. All the energy put into metabolizing alcohol could be better spent on recovering from your last workout. Of course, the depletion of nutrients vital for rebuilding muscle hinders your progress and affects your health negatively. It often takes a couple of days for the body to function optimally after assimilating large doses of alcohol, and even small amounts can have a noticeably negative effect on the body. Abstaining from overindulgence in alcohol and other recreational drugs is one of the sacrifices necessary to succeed in natural bodybuilding and to maintain optimum health.

Since the natural bodybuilding life style is dedicated to enabling the body to function at maximum efficiency, the potential of preventive medicine as a positive aid to achieving this must be discussed. In terms of bodybuilding, probably the best known and most beneficial of the preventive medicine fields is chiropractic. The chiropractic philosophy contends that optimum functioning of the central nervous system is of utmost importance in obtaining and maintaining good health.

Chiropractors use special manipulations called adjustments to align the spine and relieve the pressure on nerves originating from the spine. With maximum nerve transmission the body functions at its utmost efficiency. When the nerve transmissions are reduced by pressure from spinal misalignment, the area not receiving the transmission is weakened, and, in the case of a vital area, this can cause injury and illness. The science of chiropractic is dedicated to preventing any breakdown in efficient bodily functioning from occurring and to restoring maximum functioning to those already afflicted by such a condition.

Chiropractic is especially valuable for natural bodybuilders for two reasons. First, its health-promoting benefits make it a valuable part of the natural bodybuilding life style. Remember, the more efficiently your body functions, the easier it will be to gain muscle. Secondly, bodybuilding training by its very nature puts a tremendous amount of pressure on the spine and sooner or later something's going to go out of alignment. This can eventually lead to back and shoulder injuries. Regular chiropractic adjustments will correct any misalignments that occur and help keep you strong and moving free. Obviously, chiropractic has many benefits for the natural bodybuilder. I highly recommend a continuing program of regular chiropractic adjustments to all natural bodybuilders serious about keeping their health intact and achieving a high level of success in the sport.

Finally, we come to the most important aspect of the natural bodybuilding life style—total abstinence from all arti-

ficial substances believed to enhance muscular development, particularly steroids. These drugs pose a serious threat to your health and totally distort the image of the healthy sport that bodybuilding is supposed to be. Let the natural bodybuilding life style make you the healthy, strong, well-muscled, and physically fit person a bodybuilder should be. It is a life style that demands some sacrifice and discipline, but it is an investment in yourself that will pay dividends until the day you die.

How far can I go naturally?

Now we come to the big question asked by every bodybuilder serious about the competitive aspect of the sport. How far can I go naturally? Can I win against guys who have the advantage of taking drugs? There is no definitive answer to this question. Some natural bodybuilders can compete successfully against drug users and some never will. There are many factors involved.

Remember, first of all, that in any field very few ever make it to the top. This is especially true in bodybuilding. It is a rare individual who has all the capabilities and determination necessary to develop a championship physique and it is even more difficult naturally. But it can and has been done. Several natural-for-life bodybuilders have won local, state, and regional steroid contests. And a couple are capable of competing at the national level without chemical aid. There is no question that natural bodybuilders are at a disadvantage against steroid users. It takes an abundance of genetic potential and a total commitment to maximizing that potential to be a competitively successful natural bodybuilder capable of defeating the druggies. It seems, unfortunately, that very few naturally gifted bodybuilders are willing to make the sacrifices necessary to achieve the level of success that could be theirs.

Genetic potential

Genetic potential is that which you were born with. Its components include your body type, the type of muscle fibers you have, and your metabolism. Everybody has some good genetic traits and some poor ones. Those with more favorable genetic characteristics tend to progress faster and achieve higher levels of development than those with serious genetic

flaws. However, many bodybuilders, through sheer persistence, have been able to overcome such flaws and develop championship physiques. Even if your genetic potential is so poor as to prevent you from being able to compete successfully, you can still develop a healthy muscular physique. The following information will help you assess your potential correctly. It is then up to you to work within your genetic limitations and to make the most of what God has given you.

Body type

The most common body-type classification system used today for assessing bodybuilding potential was developed by a man named W. H. Sheldon.

Sheldon believed that the relative amounts and distribution of muscle, bone, and fat in conjunction with body shape are mainly responsible for one's body build and genetic potential. Based upon these factors Sheldon classified three different general body types. They are the ectomorphic type, which tends to be small boned and frail; the mesomorphic type, which tends to be muscular and athletic; and the endomorphic type, which tends to be fat and roundish-looking.

According to Sheldon, no physique can be classified as being totally one type or another. These three body-type classifications were developed as general guidelines. While one body type tends to predominate in each individual, everyone has certain characteristics from each of the other two types. Because of this Sheldon devised a system in which the degree of dominance of each body type is measured on a scale of 1 to 7, with 1 denoting a small degree of dominance and 7 a high degree. Therefore the bodybuild, otherwise known as somatotype of an individual, is denoted by three numerals, such as 4-5-3, etc., in which the endomorphic number is given first, the mesomorphic second and the ectomorphic last.[1]

In order to help you classify your physique as accurately as possible, an in-depth list of the characteristics of each of these general body types follows. As you'll soon see, 1-7-3 probably denotes the perfect bodybuilding somatotype. A bodybuilder with a perfect mesomorphy of 7 and a moderate degree of ectomorphy would be heavily muscled with a relatively light bone structure and have the ability to become muscularly defined for contests with ease.

A. Endomorphic type

Rotund; thick-boned; wide hips and shoulders; short, thick neck; predominance of weight in the center of the body; thick, fat torso; short arms; and short, heavy legs.

Because of their thick bones and slow metabolism endomorphs tend to gain muscle and strength fast. However, they also gain fat easily and tend to appear short. Their disproportionately short arms and legs coupled with extreme difficulty in achieving low levels of body fat and a high degree of muscular density severely limit their ability to win high-level bodybuilding shows.[2]

B. The ectomorphic type

Long and slender in build; appears frail; light overall bone structure; narrow rib cage, shoulders, and hips; small wrists and ankles; muscles tend to be long and slender and hard to develop; susceptible to injury.

Ectomorphs find it extremely difficult to gain muscular body weight and increase strength because of their unusually high metabolism, long, thin muscles, and light bone structure. They do, however, find it extremely easy to lose body fat and achieve the hard muscular look necessary to win contests. However, their lack of muscle mass is a severely limiting factor to making it big in bodybuilding.[3]

C. Mesomorphic type

Medium bone; shoulders wider than hips; small knees and ankles; large chest; slender waist and hips; strong neck; massive arms and legs; proportionate bone structure; low percentage of body fat. This is the ideal body type for bodybuilding. Mesomorphs have the ability to gain both muscle mass and strength at an exceedingly fast rate. Their metabolism tends to be neither too slow nor too fast. They find it relatively easy to become muscularly defined. Their proportionate bone structure and muscle distribution enable them to develop the massively muscular proportionate and perfectly balanced physique necessary to become a natural bodybuilding superstar.[4]

Muscle types

First of all, it should be stated that an individual muscle group's ability to gain size is directly proportional to its length. The circumference of a muscle measured at its thickest point can never exceed the length of that muscle. So the longer a muscle is, the bigger it can become. Also of importance is the degree of neuromuscular efficiency. A person with a high neuromuscular efficiency can stimulate more muscle fibers to contract under stress, and can contract the muscles with greater force. This enables the muscles to grow stronger and bigger more quickly than they would in a case where neuromuscular efficiency was low.

It has been found that there are two different types of muscle fibers. The first type are white fibers, otherwise known as fast twitch muscle fibers, since they contract quickly and powerfully. These fibers are used mainly in the performance of movements requiring strength and power. In bodybuilding this usually constitutes the first six repetitions of an exercise. They tend to grow and expand quickly under heavy stress. White fibers function anaerobically, which means they do not need a continuous oxygen supply.

The second type of fibers are red fibers, otherwise known as slow twitch muscle fibers. These fibers function aerobically which means they require a sustained oxygen supply. They are stringier than white fibers and do not grow as fast. These fibers can be classified as endurance fibers and are used during sustained, low-intensity activities such as long-distance running. In bodybuilding they come into play after the first 15 repetitions of an exercise.[5]

Obviously, bodybuilders whose muscles contain a large amount of white fibers will grow bigger and at a quicker rate than those whose muscles contain a predominance of red fibers.

Carrying this even further, most bodybuilders have certain body parts that tend to lag behind the rest, which further demonstrates the unlikelihood of being a pure mesomorph. This is often due to an uneven distribution of white and red muscle fibers throughout one's physique. Those muscle groups in which white fibers predominate will grow faster than those muscle groups higher in red fibers.

Another reason for lagging body parts has to do with muscle length. As previously mentioned, a short muscle simply does not have the capacity to grow as big as a long one and, as in the case of uneven muscle fiber distribution, it is not unusual to have one or two muscle groups that are unusually short in length, thus limiting the ability of that muscle to gain size. Persistent training will usually bring a lagging body part up to par. However, if you are unfortunate enough to be born with a muscle group that is both short in length and high in red fiber count as well as low in neuromuscular efficiency, you will find your chances of developing a championship physique greatly hindered. Everything else on your physique could be perfected, but one lousy, unresponsive body part is all it takes to hold you back from reaching the top, and in such a case using bodybuilding drugs is of no value. You'll just develop your stronger body parts to an even greater degree and make the difference that much more obvious. There's only so much you can do and so far you can go.

After three or four years of heavy training, if you find yourself with just such a lagging body part, it might be worth your while to have a muscle biopsy done. A muscle biopsy will determine whether you have a predominance of red or white fibers in that particular muscle. This will at least will give you some idea where you stand and you'll get a good idea exactly how much you can get that body part to come up.

As you can see, there are a lot of factors which determine one's genetic potential. Some people are more blessed genetically than others, but everybody has strong and weak points. Your ultimate goal with natural bodybuilding should not be to win top bodybuilding titles, but to develop your own physique to its fullest natural genetic potential. You do this by making the most of your strengths and working diligently to overcome your weaknesses. Always remember that many bodybuilders have overcome almost insurmountable weaknesses in their physiques to become champions. While favorable genetics certainly plays a major role in achieving bodybuilding success, there are other factors of at least equal importance. There are dozens of bodybuilders with fantastic genetic potential who will never win a local show, and there are many others with somewhat less than perfect genetics who will rise to the top.

Positive mental attitude

The power of the mind is incredible and it is my opinion that your mental attitude is the single most important aspect of developing a championship physique naturally. As mentioned previously very few individuals have the potential necessary to become a natural bodybuilding champion, but even fewer have the desire, intelligence, and mental discipline necessary to realize that potential. It is exceedingly rare to find an individual who has both. Intelligence and total commitment can therefore enable many natural bodybuilders with somewhat less than perfect bodybuilding genetics to eventually overcome their faults and become natural champions.

Keep in mind, however, that you still must have above average genetic potential to start with. Before mentally committing yourself to becoming a natural bodybuilding champion, realistically assess your bodybuilding potential with the information presented in the section on genetics. If you find out you just don't have what it takes to be a natural champion, don't even consider taking bodybuilding drugs as a means of overcoming your limitations. This will disqualify you from ever competing in natural bodybuilding contests in the future. It will also put you in a position where you must compete against many bodybuilders with superior genetics who are already taking drugs, creating a disadvantage that you can never hope to overcome. You should, in such a case, be more concerned with following the natural bodybuilding life style and developing a muscular, physically fit body for your own personal satisfaction.

If, on the other hand, you find yourself to have favorable genetic potential and you have the right mental attitude, you may very well be on your way to becoming a natural bodybuilding champion capable of winning regional contests against steroid users—and maybe even capable of winning the Natural Mr. America. Assuming you are somewhat gifted genetically, what exactly are the mental qualities necessary to realize your full genetic potential and become a champion?

The most important quality is definitely desire. You must have a burning desire to be a natural champion. You have to want success so badly you can almost taste it. You have to believe that becoming a natural champion is worth all the sacrifices involved and, believe me, you'll have to make a lot of sacrifices. As previously mentioned, this natural bodybuilding life style is one of sacrifice and discipline, but success in bodybuilding is impossible without

such sacrifice. If you truly have a burning desire to be a natural champion, you won't be concerned with how many sacrifices you must make to achieve your goal.

Intense desire is the catalyst that enables you to develop almost all of the other mental qualities necessary to be a champion natural bodybuilder including persistence, patience, discipline, and consistency of effort.

A prospective natural champion must be disciplined enough to follow all aspects of the natural bodybuilding life style, including training when he doesn't want to, and sticking to a rigid diet when preparing for a contest. He also must train consistently and persistently to achieve an outstanding physique. A prize-winning physique isn't built overnight. It takes many years of hard, consistent workouts to develop. Muscle gains often come very slowly, necessitating a patient, persistent approach to training.

Two things are imperative if you intend to make it in natural bodybuilding. No matter what happens, you must maintain a positive mental attitude at all times. And once you've been found to have relatively good genetic potential you must never doubt your ability to become a champion. No matter what happens, you must believe in yourself completely. When a workout goes poorly, you can't let it bother you. Remember, they can't all be perfect. When you lose a contest, use it as a learning experience for future successes, not as an excuse to quit. This type of thinking turns every potentially negative experience into a positive learning experience.

Another vital mental aspect involves setting goals. In order to stay motivated and committed to your natural bodybuilding, you must constantly have a goal to shoot for and strive to achieve your desire. Goals are usually divided into three categories: short-term goals, medium-range goals, and long-term goals.

Short-term goals can be daily, weekly, or monthly. Examples of short-term goals are putting a half-inch on your arms in a month, or going up five pounds on your bench press during a workout. Medium-range goals usually are goals set six months to a year in advance. Examples of medium-range goals include adding fifty pounds to your bench press in a three-month period, and winning a local bodybuilding show eight months away. Long-range goals usually include your ultimate goals in a chosen activity and can span

many years. Winning the Natural Mr. America in less than ten years of serious training is an excellent example of a long-range goal.

Constantly set goals of each type and write them down. Read them every day and set out to achieve them. It is important that the goals you set be realistic. If you constantly set unrealistic goals, your attempts to achieve them can only end in failure. Enough failures will eventually lead to frustration. You can lose confidence in your ability to achieve what you want and you might even quit bodybuilding. That's why setting unrealistic goals can have a cumulative negative effect.

On the other hand, setting reasonable goals, especially short-range goals, and obtaining them can have a dramatic positive effect. As you continue to set short-term goals, achieve them, and set new ones, you'll gain positive reinforcement of your ability to succeed. This leads to a progressive increase in confidence and belief in oneself, and is instrumental in establishing a success pattern.

The final mental factor necessary for natural bodybuilding success is intelligence. Few people realize how scientific bodybuilding really is. Bodybuilding training is based on scientific principles, muscle kinesiology, biomechanics, exercise physiology, psychology, and nutrition. Every bodybuilder is a unique individual and while there are general training and nutrition guidelines to follow, no two bodybuilders react in exactly the same way to the same exact nutrition and training programs. It takes above average intelligence to figure out through research and experimentation exactly what works best for your own body. All other things being equal, the man who has the intelligence necessary to discover what works best for his own body will triumph over those who don't have the intelligence necessary to do this.

Is it really worth staying natural?

Only you can answer that question. Most of you reading this book probably don't even want to become natural bodybuilding champions. I'm sure most of you are much more concerned with improving your health and physical fitness. One of the major goals of this book is to convey to the average person who wants to get in shape the value of following the natural bodybuilding life style.

This life style is, more than anything

else, a holistic approach to health and fitness. However, the information presented in the following chapters will enable you to go as far as you wish in natural bodybuilding, within your genetic limitations. This can include the competitive level.

One of the best reasons to abstain from bodybuilding drugs is for personal satisfaction. In bodybuilding anybody can take the easy way out and use drugs as an artificial aid to developing a contest-winning physique. But how many have enough guts and belief in themselves to do it on their own the hard way? Very few indeed. It takes an exceptional individual to resist using chemical aid. No matter how far a bodybuilder goes naturally, there's always the nagging question, "What if I took the drugs; how much further could I go?"

Drugs may enable you to get huge and win some contests you might otherwise not win. But how can you be proud of yourself and your accomplishments in the sport knowing that you needed artificial means to reach that level? One of the major reasons competing natural bodybuilders, including myself, stay natural, is because we get extreme personal satisfaction knowing that what we present onstage is a real physique consisting of natural muscle, developed purely from honest hard work. I want it to be "me" up on stage, not a blown-up pharmaceutical factory. I feel that a bodybuilder who takes drugs is, in effect, giving up his identity and becoming a sort of robot, programmed to win at any cost. An individual's physique is a reflection of his beliefs, values, convictions, and self-image. It is really a part of his identity.

A second reason to stay natural is for the challenge that succeeding totally on your own merit presents. Natural bodybuilding champions, as a rule, love a good challenge. We know we're at a sizeable disadvantage compared to the druggies, but we get a tremendous amount of satisfaction working to overcome that disadvantage. We believe in ourselves and we believe in our ability to compete equally with the drug users at a high competitive level. We may never go quite as far as we would with drugs, but there is no greater satisfaction in the sport of natural bodybuilding than to win a steroid show, even a local one—knowing, as you're handed the winner's trophy that you won solely by your own honest hard work while everyone else had artificial aid. This gives you an incredible feeling of accomplishment and pride in yourself, as

well it should. It's an unbelievable high I wish all natural bodybuilders could experience.

A large percentage of natural bodybuilders can win at least local steroid shows even if their genetic potential isn't that great. It's just a question of being committed to the natural bodybuilding life style and being extremely patient. Your gains will take longer than the drug users', but they will come with time. Just bide your time and you'll eventually get where you're going. Remember, almost everybody is impatient in today's society. Ours is a society of instant gratification. You must resist taking the easy way out. Even with drugs, it takes many years to develop a championship physique. It just takes a couple of years longer naturally.

In terms of competition, there is one major benefit of staying natural. Drug users, in general, can only compete in top shape two or three times a year because they have to take the drugs in cycles. Natural bodybuilders, on the other hand, can usually remain very close to competitive condition for long periods of time if they so desire. It's normally just a case of watching your diet. This ability enables natural bodybuilders, as a rule, to be able to compete in top contest condition almost at will. You just have to know when to take a break so you don't burn out.

So how much of an advantage is this? Well, for a natural bodybuilder who has developed his physique to the point where he can win steroid shows it's a big one. Obviously, the more contests you can enter in top shape, the greater is your chance of winning. The law of averages is on your side. Sooner or later, if you're good, you're gonna win. It's as simple as that.

In addition, if you learn to use this ability wisely, you can make quite a name for yourself in the sport without ever taking drugs. I always believed that if you don't quite have what it takes to win that one big title like Mr. U.S.A. or Mr. America, the next best thing is to win a large number of titles at a slightly lower level. As you start racking up the wins, your name will appear in more and more muscle magazines as a contest winner, and you will gain an increasing amount of notoriety. Your name can, in fact, come to be as well known as a Mr. America winner's name if you win the right shows and appear in the right magazines repeatedly.

The big trick to doing this successfully involves picking your contests very carefully. You don't want to compete in contests in which you'll be over

your head.

As you progress in natural bodybuilding make sure always to appraise your physique honestly and realistically. When you feel you're good enough to compete, test yourself in a local show. If you win, try a state level show; if you win that enter a small regional. And so on. Once you reach the level where you no longer can win or place near the top you should do one of two things. The first is to compete at the next lower level since you would have already proven your ability to win at that level. For example, if you had already proven yourself capable of winning state level shows, but then you entered a couple of regional shows and didn't even place, it would be wise to go on competing at the state level until you made such improvements in your physique that you knew you could move up to the regional level successfully.

The second alternative is simply not to compete until you've made the improvements necessary to move up to the next level successfully.

As a teenager, I used this ability to compete almost perpetually to its full advantage. By the time I was 19½, I had developed a physique capable of winning local, state, and regional teenage shows. Being natural prevented me from acquiring the development necessary to win the drug Teenage U.S.A. and America, so I didn't even bother to enter them. But I did feel I was capable of winning just about any other contest I decided to enter. Picking and choosing my contests carefully, I won thirteen contests out of fifteen I entered during my last six months as a teenager. Most of them were regional-level wins and all were steroid shows. These successes resulted in my name and picture appearing in over thirty bodybuilding magazines during the next few months. As a result I came to be extremely well known in bodybuilding circles and considered a force to be reckoned with in any contest I entered. Altogether, I've won twenty drug shows as a natural, a feat that will not soon be forgotten by the many who know of it.

From competition many of you can have similar success as naturals if you're willing to make the many sacrifices necessary to compete in top shape repeatedly. The hardest sacrifice is probably sticking to a rigid diet for a long period of time. But in my opinion, it's worth it. After you've won a fair share of titles and built a nice little trophy collection, what will you remember? The sacrifices you had to make or those great moments of glory when you were declared the best? In my case I feel my success was worth the price I paid. The titles I've won will always serve to remind me that at one point in my life, I was truly great at something.

However, those individuals blessed with the ability to make a name for themselves in the sport of bodybuilding as naturals all must decide for themselves whether the sacrifices are worth the benefits.

Is winning worth your life?

In the last section I discussed three excellent reasons why it's worth staying natural. But by far the most important thing to consider when trying to decide whether it's worth staying natural is the answer to this question. Is winning a contest really worth risking your health and possibly your life? There is absolutely no question in my mind that the answer is no. Winning is an incredible high, no question about it. It brings with it a feeling of extreme satisfaction and accomplishment. It can also bring a good deal of recognition from one's peers and others in society. These are nice benefits indeed, but how can you justify risking your life for them? Remember, a moment of glory is just that, a moment. Champions come and go, and people quickly forget them. I mean, how many people remember who won Mr. America ten years ago or even five? Believe me, not many, and who really cares anyway? The guy who won, his family, the men he beat and maybe a few friends. That's about it. As should be obvious to any rationally thinking bodybuilder, it isn't worth risking your life for the recognition bodybuilding provides because it just doesn't provide that much. Your successes will be forgotten with the passage of time. And all you'll be left with is the distinct possibility of developing liver and kidney problems, cancer and any number of other life-shortening health problems.

What about the personal satisfaction and feeling of accomplishment that winning provides? Is it worth risking your life for that? Well, let me ask you this: Compared to the length of a normal life span and all the hundreds of exciting events that occur during such a lifetime, how significant can a few moments of contest glory be?

At the time an individual decides he wants to be a bodybuilding champion

those few moments of glory could easily be distorted to the point of taking on an all-consuming importance. Many prospective champions exaggerate the importance of winning a contest to such an extent that it becomes the only thing of importance in their life. This, of course, is a gross distortion of reality. Once again that moment of glory can, at best, be described as fleeting. As time passes, all achievements become fond memories and the trophies of the steroid users become tarnished with the years. Concern and fear over just how much damage a bodybuilder may have done to his body tends to increase progressively. Any time a health problem develops he wonders whether the bodybuilding drugs he used during his competitive career are responsible. In many cases they are.

If you're one of those bodybuilders determined to win at any cost, take a couple of minutes, look at yourself in the mirror and honestly ask yourself whether it's worth wondering for the rest of your life whether the bodybuilding drugs you're taking or planning on taking could drastically shorten your life. All for a moment of glory!

What happens if you take bodybuilding drugs and risk your life, then never win a contest and have that moment? Remember, only one man can win a contest. There are thousands of bodybuilders using bodybuilding drugs who don't have the potential to win a local show even with chemical aid. It might take a while, but eventually the individuals who fall into this category must admit to themselves how foolish they were. They have to go through life with the risk of a premature death with absolutely nothing to show for it. Such a realization has the potential of having a profoundly negative psychological effect. Such individuals often experience anything ranging from mild disappointment in themselves to intense self-hatred for having needlessly and foolishly risked their lives. The potential for self-hatred is especially high in those individuals who experience severe side effects from the bodybuilding drugs they have taken, probably because the manifestation of these side effects blatantly points out to them the error of their ways. Stay away from bodybuilding drugs. As I hope I've been able to illustrate clearly in this section, the potential benefits they provide pale in comparison to the potential destruction they can cause.

How long does it take to develop a contest-winning physique naturally?

The answer to this question varies with the individual. The more potential you have and the more committed you are to realizing that potential, the faster you'll progress. Assuming you have reasonably good potential and are totally committed to realizing it, you should be able to win a local natural show within two to three years after you start training. After about three or four years you should be able to win local drug contests. And after a half-dozen years of training you should be able to win most of the big natural regional contests and a good portion of the drug regionals as well. By the time you've been training ten years, there's no reason why you shouldn't be a top natural bodybuilder with the capability of placing at or near the top at the Natural Mr. America, and also be able to win almost any regional drug contest you choose to enter in top shape.

What about improvement in terms of an increase in muscular body weight? More specifically, how much muscle can you expect to gain in a year, assuming you have good genetics and strong mental commitment?

In order to answer this question thoroughly, let me first point out that muscle mass and strength gains in bodybuilding follow the law of diminishing returns. In other words, the further you go, the harder it becomes to continue improving. When you first start training, improvement comes quickly. It's not unusual for a natural bodybuilder to gain five to ten pounds of muscle during his first month of training and 20 to 25 pounds of muscle during the first year. However, as the years go by and you come closer and closer to achieving your ultimate natural muscular potential, the muscle gains come more and more slowly.

After training consistently for about four years you will find it extremely difficult to gain more than eight pounds of solid muscle mass per year. After eight years of training up to four pounds of added muscle mass per year is considered to be a good improvement. While that may not seem like a lot of muscle, it really is. Just go down to your neighborhood grocery store and pick up a four-pound roast. Then just imagine adding that to your physique.

The reason it is so difficult to reach a high level of muscular development is that it is an unnatural state for the body to be in. Large quantities of muscular tissue are not considered essential for survival by the human body. Therefore, it tends to conserve its energy for other tasks, the most important of which involves maintaining healthy body functioning. Also, the human body tends to maintain a state of equilibrium and to resist change. The more you try to change it, the more it resists. So it stands to reason that the more muscle you attempt to gain, the more the body will resist. As you progress through your bodybuilding career, finding ways to continue putting on muscular body weight will become an increasingly difficult challenge. While no one has ever been able to develop themselves to their ultimate muscular potential because of the body's staunch resistance to such an endeavor, the information presented in this book will enable you to make the best natural muscle gains possible—to come as close as humanly possible to reaching your full potential.

3

DRUGS IN BODYBUILDING

As mentioned previously, the influx of drugs used to artifically enhance muscular development has reached epidemic proportions in bodybuilding. The five major classes of drugs used by today's competitive bodybuilder are: anabolic steroids, growth hormones, thyroid preparation, amphetamines, and diuretics. While amphetamines and diuretics can hardly be considered healthy or natural, it is the first three classes of drugs that we are mainly concerned with because of their potentially dangerous effects on the hormone balance and metabolism of the human body.

Benefits of anabolic steroids

Anabolic steroids are by far the most prevalent and popular class of drugs used by bodybuilders for the purpose of artificially enhancing muscular development. Virtually all of today's competing bodybuilders take them, and the common belief in bodybuilding circles is that you can't gain significant muscle mass without them. While steroids definitely seem to help, they certainly are not all they are cracked up to be. Contrary to common belief, everyone who takes anabolic steroids does not become a bodybuilding champion. Drugs do not make champions. Excellent genetic potential, proper training and diet, and total mental commitment do. Drugs like anabolic steroids are just the icing on the cake. Without the other factors drugs are of absolutely no value and, even with all the other factors in perfect balance, there is no guarantee that anabolic steroids will give you the kind of gains that some bodybuilders get from them. Every body is different and therefore everybody who takes steroids responds a little bit differently to them. So how much do they help? At this time there's no definitive answer to that question. Since most of the studies on steroid effects have thus far been done on animals and hospital patients and not on serious bodybuilders, there is not enough scientific data to draw conclusions on just how much of an effect these drugs have on muscular development.[1]

Until recently, medical authorities and groups such as the American College of Sports Medicine claimed that steroids do little if anything to enhance athletic ability. However, unofficial evidence to the contrary is overwhelming. Thousands of athletes from all fields including swimming, track and field, weightlifting, and of course bodybuilding have reported achieving a dramatic improvement in their athletic performance and muscular development from the use of these drugs.[2] Let's face it; if they didn't work you wouldn't find such large numbers of athletes in almost all sports taking them, including over 99 percent of competing bodybuilders.

The general consensus is that anabolic steroids increase the potential to gain lean body mass by anywhere from 5 to 20 percent over an individual's natural potential, with the average being about 15 percent. This translates into an average gain of between 10 and 20 pounds of muscle over what can be achieved naturally. Anabolics also seem to have a positive effect on the quality of muscles; the muscles of steroid users tend to gain density and become harder and fuller looking than those of a natural bodybuilder. The skin of many steroid users also undergoes changes, appearing tighter and thinner than usual, thus giving the illusion of increased muscle density. Besides this, anabolic users tend to be a lot more vascular than their natural counterparts. Ropelike veins crisscrossing the various muscle groups also tend to make the steroid users appear more muscular.

One big disadvantage of anabolic steroids is their tendency to retain water. Most bodybuilders who take anabolic steroids find it exceedingly difficult to obtain the degree of muscularity necessary to win bodybuilding contests, because of the water retention properties of these drugs. Many bodybuilders who were able to obtain peak muscularity before going on the drugs have never been able to get into top contest condition again because of this side effect, and this includes many of the pros. It takes a lot of trial and error to overcome this side effect and most steroid users never figure out how to do it.

Since it is impossible to win today's bodybuilding shows without being in peak muscular condition, steroids can do more harm than good for your bodybuilding career. This one side effect has the potential to neutralize all the positive effects the drugs provide. After all, what's the point of adding 20 solid pounds of muscle to your frame if you can't display it to full advantage because of water retention? Being big doesn't win contests anymore. You're better off never using the drugs to gain added muscle mass and instead retaining the ability to get into peak muscular condition. That's what wins. I myself have beaten a lot of massive steroid users who just couldn't get muscular looking because I as a natural had no such water retention problems. All things being equal it is definitely true that a steroid user who overcomes this problem will appear much bigger and more muscular than his natural counterpart; however, the odds are stacked against your being one of the few to do this.

One very interesting point about anabolic steroids is that the percentage of muscle mass gains they provide over your ultimate muscular potential also seems to have a direct correlation with how much muscle you've developed naturally at the time you take them. For example, using the average 15 percent benefit steroids provide, an individual who put on 30 pounds of muscle naturally from the time he started training would tend to gain 15 percent more than this from proper steroid therapy, or 4½ pounds of muscle. The more muscle you gain naturally before taking them, the higher tends to be the proportion of benefits they provide. This is by no means a rule, but it does tend to hold true in most cases.

For a number of reasons the benefits anabolics provide also seem to increase in proportion to the number of years you've been training naturally at the time you take them. While this is mainly because of the increasing amount of muscle you gain over time (as just outlined), it also has been found that high-quality muscle tissue developed from years of training is much more sensitive to anabolic steroid stimulation than muscle tissue that's only been trained for a year or two. Besides this, someone who's only been training a couple of years does not have the understanding of or control over his body that someone who's been training for five or six years has developed. After training for this length of time, the mind and body of the serious bodybuilder are literally programmed to gain muscle. These factors enable him to utilize steroid therapy much more effectively than someone who hasn't been training long and therefore does not have near the degree of muscle mass, muscle maturity, and control over his mind and body that the veteran bodybuilder has developed.

For this reason alone, teenagers,

novice bodybuilders, and those body-builders who find it impossible to gain 40 to 50 pounds of muscle naturally due to genetic limitations or other factors should not even consider taking anabolic steroids. I know of many bodybuilders who fall into these categories who have gotten absolutely no benefits from steroids. These individuals simply do not have the capacity to utilize the drugs anywhere near their full potential.

Physiology of steroids

The term steroid comes from the Greek word meaning solid or firm.[3] They are classified as one of a large group of powerful endocrine compounds called hormones. Hormones are mainly responsible for coordinating the chemical reactions that occur in all the cells of the human body. Many hormones are proteins. Steroids, however, which are manufactured in the male testes and in the adrenal cortex and ovaries of the females are special types of lipids or fat-based compounds.[4]

In terms of bodybuilding, the most important hormone in the steroid group is testosterone, which is produced in the testicles of the male.[5] Testosterone has two important effects in the human body. First, it is responsible for stimulating the development of secondary male sex characteristics during puberty, such as the maturation of the male sex organs, deepening of the voice, an increase in body and facial hair, etc. These are known as androgenic effects.[6]

Secondly, by aiding in the retention of the dietary protein nitrogen necessary for the formation of the amino acids from which new muscle tissue is built, while simultaneously minimizing the amount lost through chemical breakdown, testosterone has been found to have a profound effect on the stimulation of the tissue-building processes of the human body resulting in greatly accelerated tissue growth and repair. This is known as an anabolic effect.[7]

More specifically, the creation of such a nitrogen reserve, otherwise known as a positive nitrogen balance, indirectly results in the increased anabolism (repair) of protein while simultaneously minimizing protein catabolism (breakdown).[8]

Since muscle tissue is mainly composed of protein, and normal testosterone levels have been shown to exert a strong anabolic effect on the development of skeletal muscle tissue during puberty,[9] it would stand to reason that unusually high levels of testosterone would, under the proper conditions, promote an unusually high level of muscular development. It was only a matter of time before someone decided to test this idea out.

In 1954 John B. Ziegler, team physician for the U.S. weightlifters at the World Championships in Vienna, was informed by the Russian team physician that certain members of the Russian weightlifting team were using testosterone to improve their performance.[10]

Ziegler returned to the U.S. to further research testosterone. He discovered that this hormone had first been isolated in 1935 and that an increasing number of contraindications to its use had accumulated as more and more studies involving both animals and humans had been done over the years.

Nevertheless, in spite of the potential danger, Ziegler decided to conduct very limited case studies on himself and several other people, some of whom were competitive weightlifters. As a result, he found that although there was an increase in strength levels from testosterone, there were also strong side effects, including an increase in the size of the prostate gland.[11]

In the late 1950s, in response to medical need for a substance with a high anabolic, low androgenic effect in the treatment of debilitating diseases and severe accidents which involved the breakdown of body protein, Ciba Pharmaceutical Company, with Ziegler's help, developed Dianabol, the first of a class of drugs known as anabolic steroids.[12]

Simply stated, anabolic steroids are synthetic derivatives of testosterone[13] chemically manipulated to maximize their anabolic growth stimulating properties while minimizing the androgenic properties which are mainly responsible for testosterone's side effects.[14]

In 1960, Ziegler decided to try Dianabol in combination with the newest system of strength building techniques known as isometric contraction, which consisted of straining against an immovable object, on a few of the top U.S. lifters. At the time, anabolic steroids were a big secret. Very few athletes knew about them and they were hard to obtain. However, as the elite lifters started making incredible progress with the addition of Dianabol to their training regimen, news began to spread. As access to anabolic steroids became easier, and more and more athletes proved to their own satisfaction that they worked, the strength-building drug scene exploded.[15] During the past few years the use of anabolic steroids to improve athletic performance in sports has reached epidemic proportions. The use of these drugs has now spread so far that athletes in almost every sport use them.

Besides having a large amount of muscle tissue, and the ability to obtain peak muscular condition, a competitive bodybuilder must also be well-proportioned in order to be successful. All of the muscle groups must be developed as evenly as possible. It can be disastrous to let one or more muscle groups become either too developed in proportion to the rest of the body or to lag noticeably behind.

Keeping this in mind, it is an unfortunate fact that not all muscles are equally responsive to steroids. All bodybuilders have muscle groups that grow easily and others that respond with difficulty. Unfortunately, the muscle groups most responsive to steroid therapy tend to be those that grow most easily without them. Therefore, taking steroids can cause these muscle groups to grow way out of proportion in relation to the rest of the body, thus totally destroying your symmetry.[16] A smaller, well-proportioned physique will always beat a much more massively muscular but disproportioned physique, all other factors being equal. No amount of steroid-induced muscle gains is worth the sacrifice of excellent muscle proportion and symmetry of development.

Besides the competitive disadvantage of having disproportionate development, there's also the fact that a disproportioned physique simply doesn't look good. A big chest and small arms or any number of other disproportionate combinations can appear laughable. Since one of the major reasons most people bodybuild in the first place is to improve their appearance and gain the admiration of their peers, developing a large but ridiculous-looking physique is the last thing you want to do.

Steroids also increase muscle strength. Since muscles increase in size as an adaptive response to progressive resistance training, it follows that the stronger you are, the more resistance you can place upon the muscles, and the faster they'll grow. It's no coincidence that almost all of the really massive bodybuilders are also exceedingly strong. Bodybuilders are always looking for ways to get stronger as a means of getting bigger. It so happens that anabolic steroids appear to have tremendous strength-building potential. While research reported in *Sports Medicine* magazine acknowledges that high doses of steroids combined with training will result in increases in maximal voluntary or static strength compared to placebo controls,[17] they do not know to what extent this is true.

All of my bodybuilding sources have reported receiving dramatic strength increases from anabolic therapy. Many of them have reported a 100- to 150-pound increase in their bench press and up to a 200-pound increase in their squat over a six-week period of steroid usage. As is the case of muscle gains from steroids, strength gains from anabolics appear to be proportional to how strong an individual is prior to taking them. The average strength increase from anabolics over what one can achieve naturally appears to be anywhere from 20 to 30 percent. As an example, an individual capable of bench pressing 300 pounds naturally can expect to do around 400 pounds after utilizing proper steroid therapy.

While rapidly increasing strength at first appears to have major benefits for the serious bodybuilder, most notably in terms of facilitating a dramatic increase in muscular size, it does have one major disadvantage that can more than outweigh these potential benefits.

A rapid and dramatic increase in muscle strength such as that produced by steroids can put a tremendous amount of pressure on the tendons and ligaments connecting the muscles to the bones. Under heavy stress, this can often result in serious injuries such as partial or complete tendon tears. A torn rotator cuff in the shoulder and partial or complete bicep tendon tears are particularly common injuries incurred by unusually heavy training. Either one of these injuries can easily keep you from training for at least six months, and according to the severity of the injury, you may never be able to train at peak capacity again. In other words, a serious injury of this sort could very easily result in the end of your bodybuilding career. In my opinion the risk of injury from steroid-induced strength increases is simply too high in relation to the amount of added strength-producing muscle gains they provide. After all, is the risk to your bodybuilding career really worth an extra 100 pounds on the bench press and five pounds of strength-produced muscle mass?

Another indirect effect of steroids, in terms of promoting unusually rapid muscle growth, is their ability to dramatically enhance both individual muscle recuperative ability and, to a lesser degree, systemic recuperative ability. This is mainly a function of the combined increased anabolic and decreased catabolic effect that steroids cause in all the tissues of the body, although, as previously mentioned, anabolic steroid effects are more pronounced in the skeletal muscle system than in most of the other tissues of the body.

In terms of gaining muscle, enhanced muscle recuperative ability is a big advantage. It enables a bodybuilder to train more frequently and more intensely than is possible training naturally. Simultaneously it minimizes the possibility of overtraining, which is a persistent curse for the natural bodybuilder.

The improved systemic recuperative benefits of steroids include a higher overall level of energy which enables a bodybuilder to put more energy into his workouts and to train more intensely than is normally possible without exhausting himself completely. He often finds he requires less sleep than usual and his ability to recover quickly from excessive energy-draining activities such as bodybuilding borders on the remarkable. As mentioned previously, building muscle is not considered a priority by the body and only excess energy is used to build muscle tissue. Under normal circumstances, the energy required by the average natural bodybuilder for such things as normal body growth and repair, a full-time job, recreational activities, and training itself, leaves very little for muscle recuperation. The increased systemic recuperative abilities provided by steroids creates an energy surplus which enables a substantially increased amount of energy to be put into muscle recuperation. Thus the rate at which muscle can be gained is accelerated.

A third indirect physique enhancement effect of steroids is a mild fat-burning effect. Anabolics have been found to lower body fat levels in two ways. First, they promote rapid growth and repair, which has the effect of stimulating an increase in metabolic activity. They encourage the body to burn fat as an energy source to be utilized for this purpose. Secondly, they stimulate the thyroid gland to produce unusually high amounts of thyroxin, which further stimulates an increase in the metabolic rate. These two effects combined have enabled many bodybuilders on steroids to lose significant amounts of body fat. This enables them to diet less strictly than they normally would have to for a contest, while actually getting their body fat levels to a point lower than they could achieve naturally. This, of course, can enable the steroid user to become more muscular than his natural counterpart, assuming he is able to overcome the water retention problem discussed previously. The reason the steroid user has the potential to get his body fat level lower than is possible naturally is that the increased release of thyroid hormones enables him to overcome the body's natural tendency to hoard its last traces of body fat. This enables him to burn away practically every last ounce of muscle hiding subcutaneous fat, so that the skin is right against the muscle. This gives the skin the appearance of being paper-thin and allows every muscular detail to show through.

One final way in which anabolic steroids indirectly promote muscle growth involves the powerful effects that steroids, particularly testosterone, have on the central nervous system. This effect manifests itself in terms of pronounced behavioral changes in the athletes who use them.[18]

Potentially, the most beneficial of these effects in terms of bodybuilding is that of increased aggression and energy, which tends to encourage the bodybuilder to train heavier and more intensely than he normally would naturally. This, of course, results in increased muscle growth stimulation and accelerated progress.[19]

Unfortunately, this one potentially positive psychological effect of anabolic therapy is totally overshadowed by so many deleterious effects that it warrants discussing them separately to show how dangerous they can ultimately be to your physical and psychological health and well-being.

The first of these deleterious effects involves the fact that the increased aggressiveness produced by steroids, especially pure testosterone, appears to be a major reason for the widespread increase in muscle and tendon injuries among strength athletes.[20] This is in addition to the increased threat of injury caused by their rapid strength development properties. As previously discussed, the reason increased aggressiveness appears to make strength athletes prone to injury is that it causes them to train hard when they should take it easy. The body has ways of telling an athlete when to back off, but the impulsive desire to train hard and dominate the weights, as a result of the steroids' aggressive effect, overrides these messages. The result is often severe injury,[21] and we already discussed what a serious injury can do to your bodybuilding career.

Many of the psychologically deleterious effects of steroids stem from the fact that people given extra male hormones react in many of the same ways as people given amphetamines. Along with increased alertness and reduced feelings of fatigue, which can be considered positive effects, there are frequent and often extreme mood swings with a predominance of mood elevation.[22]

These mood swings, in combination with an aggressive behavior pattern, can cause the steroid user a great deal of difficulty in terms of effectively carrying on meaningful interpersonal relationships. People don't want to be around moody, overly aggressive individuals. These drastic changes in behavior have resulted in the end of more than a few bodybuilders' marriages and long-term relationships with serious girlfriends, because of the inability of the partner to cope with these personality changes.[23]

Just imagine sacrificing your personality and your marriage for some muscle, and maybe a few titles. It hardly seems worth the trade-off.

Perhaps the greatest psychological danger of steroids is the strong tendency they have to cause psychological dependence.

There are two aspects of steroid therapy which tend to cause psychological dependence. The first of these involves the fact that although there are wide mood swings while on the drugs, an elevated mood tends to predominate.[24] The elevated mood, combined with the increase in aggression, creates the effect of being on a kind of high. In this state, the athlete feels strong, energetic, and confident of his ability to train and compete successfully. He also feels positive and happy about things in general.

When the athlete goes off steroid therapy, this positive feeling is often replaced by a depressed state. This occurs because of the loss of both the physical and psychological benefits of the drugs, combined with the fact that the suppression of the individual's own testosterone level, which increases progressively during the length of anabolic therapy, continues for at least a few weeks after the drugs are discontinued. So the individual coming off the drugs suddenly goes from a very high testosterone level to a very low one, which throws the body's hormone level out of balance and creates a number of undesirable physical and psychological effects, including decreased libido.

In fact, the second reason steroid users find it difficult to stay off the drugs is due to a loss of a portion of their physical benefits. According to the individual, a bodybuilder can lose anywhere between 10 and 70 percent of the muscle and strength gains he obtained while on the drugs. The degree of loss depends partly on how hard the individual trains while on the drugs, whether he uses them correctly, and how many weeks it takes for his own testosterone level to return to normal. Fortunately for most steroid users, they tend to have a rebound effect from going off the drugs in which their own testosterone level temporarily returns to a point higher than normal for a period of a few weeks before dropping back down to the level which was normal prior to the period in which the drugs were taken. This enables most steroid users to get back some of the muscle and strength they lose during the period immediately after going off the drugs. In fact, the length this rebound effect lasts is the primary factor in determining how much of the muscle and strength gains that an individual receives from anabolic therapy he will be able to retain.

While muscle and strength losses can be minimized to a certain degree by the factors just mentioned, it is a fact that, in all cases, some of the benefits of the drugs will definitely be lost after going off them. Most bodybuilders cannot psychologically handle watching themselves get smaller and weaker. This, combined with the loss of a psychological high, is often too much for the steroid user to cope with. He either goes back on the drugs without giving his body a long enough break from them, or simply stays on them as close as possible to year-round in order to preserve their effects, often taking larger doses as the body refuses to respond to the normal dose. This is how the anabolic user becomes an anabolic abuser, and it is most assuredly the greatest psychological danger of taking steroids.

Side effects of anabolic agents

Before anyone decides to take steroids, it's critical that he know the potential health destruction properties of these drugs. Some of the side effects are minor, but others can be catastrophic. Before getting into the actual side effects, let's first discuss the way in which bodybuilders use and abuse the drugs and why they do so, so we can get a good idea of just how much potential for serious damage there really is.

Practically all steroid side effects depend upon the dosage you take, and the length of time you use the drug. According to the American College of Sports Medicine, some side effects, including a decrease in testicular size and a decrease in sperm production, appear to be reversible when small doses of steroids are used for short periods of time. However, the reversibility of the side effects caused by taking large doses over extended periods of time is unclear.[25]

Unfortunately, most bodybuilders take exceedingly large doses of steroids for prolonged periods of time. This is partly because of the psychological dependency fostered by the drugs (as previously discussed), and partly because of the philosophy that if some is good, then more is better. While this may be true to a small degree, it certainly does not warrant an individual taking 10 times or more the minimal dose of steroids he finds effective in promoting muscle growth. You can only gain so fast, no matter what you do.

The fact is that laboratory studies have found the relationship between the dose of steroids and the muscle growth response to be logarithmic. That means you must take 10 times a given dose to get twice the muscle and strength gains and 100 times that dose to get a response four times greater than the original.

Side effects, however, appear to increase in more direct proportion to the increase in dosage. Taking 10 times as much as necessary results in approximately 10 times the incidence and severity of side effects.[26]

The length of time an individual is on anabolic therapy also plays a major role in determining the extent to which side effects will manifest themselves. Bodybuilders, like most athletes, take steroids in cycles. Most bodybuilders who know what they are doing go on steroids for two to three cycles a year, each cycle ranging in length from 6 to 12 weeks. While this is bad enough, it is unfortunate that many others stay on drugs almost all year long, because, as previously mentioned, they are either psychologically dependent on them, or can't handle losing some of their gains when they go off them, or both.

It is as difficult to specify the maximally effective and relatively safe number of cycles per year as it is to specify the dosages. However, it is definitely advisable for an individual on anabolic therapy to correspondingly reduce the number of cycles used per year as the dosages increase. Also, under no circumstances should a steroid user be on the drugs for a longer period of time during the course of a year than he's off them.[27] He must be off them at least 50 percent of the time and preferably a lot longer, or serious side effects, such as irreversible suppression of the individual's own testosterone production can result.

Another factor responsible for an increased risk of side effects involves the way in which steroids are ingested, otherwise known as the route of administration. There are two classes of anabolic steroids, oral and injectable. The orals are in the form of various pills. They are swallowed, digested, and assimilated by way of the digestive tract. Injectable steroids are administered by intramuscular injection, usually into the gluteal muscle. Oral steroids are metabolized by the liver before being released into the body tissues. This puts a tremendous amount of stress on the liver, similar to the way alcohol does, although much more severe. Long-term use of oral steroids is almost guaranteed to result in any of a number of serious liver disorders, damage, or even death. Injectable steroids, on the other hand, bypass the liver, which tends to make them relatively safer than orals, at least in terms of this side effect.

One potentially dangerous aspect of injectable steroid use is that most bodybuilders either administer these drugs to themselves or have someone who isn't medically qualified, such as their wife or training partner, give them the injections. This can result in injury or disease. When giving an injection into the buttocks, it is quite possible to hit the sciatic nerve if you don't know what you're doing. This is the major nerve running down both legs, and damaging it can result in permanent paralysis. Then there's the ever-present threat of hepatitis from using an unsterile needle, and believe me, it's very easy to break sterility if you don't know what you're doing. Anyone who takes injectable steroids would be wise to have them administered by their doctor.

The fourth factor which has a direct effect on the severity of steroid-induced side effects involves the proportion of anabolic properties to androgenic properties in the steroids any given individual chooses to take. These are called anabolic and androgenic indexes. Since it is the androgenic properties of the steroids which are responsible for most of their side effects, it follows that the higher the androgenic index of any particular steroid, the greater its potential to cause side effects. Pure testosterone is often used as an anabolic agent. However, since it has not been chemically manipulated to reduce its androgenic index, it has the most potential to cause side effects. There are so many steroids around with high anabolic and relatively low androgenic indexes, which have at least as much benefit in producing muscle and strength gains as testosterone without the risk of side effects, that I find it difficult to understand why so many bodybuilders continue to use it. Those who do are really asking for trouble.

The final factor influencing the severity of side effects involves the way your own particular body reacts to anabolic therapy. Everyone is an individual and it's impossible to determine exactly how a particular bodybuilder will respond to the drugs until after he takes them. Some people are able to get away with abusing the drugs while having only mild side effects. Others have taken minimal doses under a doctor's supervision and have suffered severe consequences. While it's true that the more you abuse your body with these drugs, the greater the chance you'll severely damage yourself, this rule does not always hold true. There are no guarantees when it comes to taking anabolic steroids. It's like playing Russian roulette; you may get through the first few rounds. But sooner or later, if you don't quit while you're ahead, you'll blow your brains out. The question is: Are you willing to go through life never knowing when or if the effects of the steroids you took during your bodybuilding career are going to catch up with you? While a few individuals may get off scot-free, problems will eventually catch up to the overwhelming majority. Should you decide to use Decadurabolin, Anavar, *Primabolin*, Dianabol, Maxibolin, or any of a number of other anabolic steroids, I will next outline the ways in which most of you will ultimately pay for your indulgence, in terms of side effects.

Anabolic steroid side effects

The following is a description of the side effects most common with anabolic steroids. You can find a list of these side effects in both the *Physician's Desk Reference* and on the drug description sheets which accompany each and every anabolic steroid dispensed. Many of these side effects are self-explanatory, others I will elaborate upon. While some of these side effects are more apt to occur with certain anabolic steroids and not with others, most of them are common to the group as a whole.

1. Nausea and vomiting[28]

2. Excitation and sleeplessness[29]—
Many bodybuilders have reported increased sleeping difficulties and general restlessness while on the drugs. This is due to both the psychological high the drugs give combined with the increased energy they tend to give the athlete. Since sleep is vital to muscle recuperation this can hinder your progress.

3. Acne [30]—It is not uncommon to find bodybuilders on steroids, especially teenagers, to have severe cases of acne all over their body, especially on the back and shoulders. Not only does this look horrible, but it can actually cost you a contest, since overall general appearance is part of the judging criteria at contests.

4. Inhibition of testicular function[31]

5. Testicular atrophy[32]

6. Decreased sperm count[33]

7. Impotence[34]—Side effects 4 through 7 are a direct result of the suppression of the steroid user's natural testosterone level during the course of anabolic therapy. They are especially apt to occur during the period of time immediately following the termination of anabolic therapy up until the individual's own testosterone level returns to normal. This is because the testosterone level is so low during this time. Depending upon the intensity of steroid therapy, this period can last as long as ten weeks after a steroid cycle. While these effects do appear to be 100 percent reversible with steroid therapy of

low dose and short duration, prolonged steroid abuse could lead potentially to a permanent testosterone shutdown and lifelong impotence.

8. Gynecomastia[35]—Otherwise known as "bitch tits" in bodybuilding circles. This involves the development of enlarged nipples and swelling in the surrounding tissue, giving the appearance of small breasts.[36] Though still rare, this condition is becoming increasingly common in bodybuilding circles. Those bodybuilders who take pure testosterone are most susceptible to this condition. Obviously, "bitch tits" do not enhance the appearance of one's physique and are, in fact, quite unsightly. Cosmetic surgery is often required to remove them.[37]

9. Premature balding—Many bodybuilders on anabolic therapy have complained of hair loss.

10. High blood pressure—There are two factors responsible for this condition. The first of these involves the fact that steroids increase sodium and water retention.[38] This has the effect of increasing blood volume which results in an increase in blood pressure. This is usually a short-term reversible side effect as the blood pressure drops once anabolic therapy is stopped and sodium is no longer being retained.

Unfortunately, anabolic steroids can also cause a long-term, permanent increase in blood pressure. By depressing alkaline phosphatase and HDL cholesterol levels, they tend to promote arteriosclerosis[39] which results in progressively increasing blood pressure.

11. Coronary disease—Coronary disease is a very serious side effect. It can eventually lead to a heart attack and possibly death. A prime example of a strength athlete developing this condition involves nine-time world powerlifting champion, Larry Pacifico. At the age of 35, he barely escaped death from advanced arteriosclerosis! It was found that one of his coronary arteries was 70 percent blocked and a second was 99.9 percent blocked. He was immediately scheduled for a triple bypass. First they decided to try an angioplasty and, fortunately for him, it worked. Pacifico and his doctor are both convinced his steroid use contributed to his coronary

heart disease. He said he should have realized it was happening because every time he went on a cycle of heavy steroid use he would develop high blood pressure and an increased pulse rate.[40] Larry Pacifico's case is not an isolated one. Thousands of steroid users have developed high blood pressure and arteriosclerosis without even knowing it. Little do they realize that these drugs greatly increase their risk of premature death from heart disease.

12. Premature closing of the epiphyses of the bones—This side effect is applicable to individuals who have not completed their developmental growth and reached physical maturity, which basically means all bodybuilders under the age of 21 or 22. Simply put, this side effect can result in stunted or retarded growth since the bones are not able to grow to full length.[41] This is the major reason why teenagers should absolutely, positively not take steroids. For those who feel they must take them, at least wait until you've reached physical maturity, or irreparable structural damage may result.

13. Liver dysfunction and liver cancer—The liver is one of the most important organs in the body. It is the main line of defense against poisons and invading organisms. It is also responsible for the metabolism of carbohydrates, the storage of glycogen, the conversion of nitrogenous wastes into urea, the metabolism and storage of fatsoluble vitamins, and many other functions.[42] Proper liver function is essential for growth and repair. The liver is one organ you cannot afford to live without. Unfortunately, steroid therapy puts a tremendous strain on this vital organ and seriously disrupts normal functioning. Many studies have been done on the effects of steroids on the liver, none of them with positive results.

In some cases of steroid use, dosages as low as 10 to 15 mg./day taken for only three or four months have caused liver complications. Alterations of normal liver function have been found in as many as 80 percent of one series of patients treated with oral anabolic steroids.[43] The fact is some 19-year-old bodybuilders have been found to have the livers of 75-year-old men.[44] And this isn't the worst of it.

Five reports document the occurrence of toxic hepatitis in 17 patients who had no previous evidence of significant liver disease after they were

treated with oral anabolic agents. Peliosis hepatitis is a liver disease which causes massive hemorrhaging and bursting of cellular tissue resulting in the formation of blood pools or lakes. This often leads to liver necrosis, which is a fancy term for liver death. The fact is, seven of these patients died of liver failure.[45] That's a staggering death rate.

In terms of liver cancer, the first case of hepato-cellular carcinoma associated with taking anabolic steroids was reported in 1965. Since then at least 13 other patients on oral steroid therapy have developed hepato-cellular carcinoma.[46] The more that individuals continue to abuse oral anabolics, the more drastic the increase in the number of reported cases of this and other forms of liver cancer.

14. Kidney damage—The kidneys find the waste products of anabolic therapy hard to handle. The increase in the amount of nitrogenous waste in the form of urea is especially stressful as high levels of urea can irritate and ultimately damage the nephrons of the kidney. Prolonged steroid use can therefore ultimately cause irreversible functional impairment of the kidneys which will severely hinder normal body functioning and potentially shorten your life.

15. Enlarged prostate and cancer of the prostate—As previously mentioned, anabolic steroids have been found to enlarge the prostate gland. This condition is known as benign prostatic hypertrophy. If used or abused for extended periods of time, especially in instances in which benign prostatic hypertrophy is already present at the time anabolic therapy is started, steroids have the potential to cause prostatic carcinoma. In fact, steroid use is specially contraindicated by the medical literature in such a situation, because of the high risk of cancer.[47]

16. All forms of cancer—The human body is a precisely balanced organism. Proper regulation of the various hormones in our body happens to be one of the most important internal aspects of maintaining this balance. Any disruption of this hormone regulation system can therefore have severe consequences. This is especially reflected in a dramatically increased risk of cancer. Cancer, simply stated, is the unchecked reproduction of mutated

cells that have no function. Normally, the body is able to destroy the mutated cells that it occasionally produces, thanks to a carefully balanced, hormonally influenced defense mechanism. As previously stated, anabolic steroids totally disrupt the body's hormone balance and lower the body's defenses in general, thus weakening its ability to keep the reproduction of these cells in check. This can enable almost any type of cancer to develop at any time. Therefore, the more an individual disrupts his hormone balance with anabolic therapy, the more he increases his risk of developing cancer somewhere down the road. This is especially true of individuals who already have a genetic predisposition to develop cancer. In such cases, anabolic therapy can be the final straw.

Besides disrupting hormone balance, there is one other way in which anabolic steroids can cause cancer. Certain anabolic steroids have been found to actually cause changes in the structure of DNA, the material which makes up our genetic code, and determines the physical and mental characteristics and capacities of each individual. It just so happens that drug-induced changes in DNA structure are believed by medical authorities to be one of the mechanisms responsible for causing cancer.[48]

One example of a bodybuilder who developed cancer from anabolic steroids is Bill Ashpaugh. Bill was a competing bodybuilder who took Dianabol intermittently for a number of years. During that time he managed to achieve a fairly high level of success in the sport, winning such titles as Mr. Detroit, Mr. Indianapolis, and runner-up as Mr. Indiana. He was on the verge of achieving a national title-winning physique, when he developed a painful mass in his abdomen. He was diagnosed as having a malignant teratoma, which means that it was technically three types of tumors in one. One of the types, choriocarcinoma, is a highly malignant form of cancer with a great propensity to spread rapidly by way of the bloodstream. After the main tumor was removed, he was given four years to live if he underwent a form of protective surgery known as retroperitoneal node dissection and only six months to live without it.[49] Bill became a born again Christian while in the hospital and came to believe that Jesus Christ would heal him of cancer. He also knew only a miracle could save his life. So he refused further treatment. During the month following his release from the hospital, the cancer ravaged

Bill Ashpaugh's body. He progressively lost body weight, energy, and strength at a rapid rate. One month after his release from the hospital, Bill reported being healed at a Youth for Christ tent meeting.[50] A couple of days later the results of a test known as a 24-hour lymphangiogram showed Bill to be totally free of cancer.[51] Bill's only hope of surviving the life-destroying side effects of steroids had been a miracle. Whether or not you believe that Bill was healed by God, or by the power of his own mind, there is no question that it was indeed a miracle that saved his life. Two months later, Bill went on to win the Mr. Indiana title. He did not take steroids for the contest, yet he was better than he had been at any time previously while on the drugs.[52] This serves as an excellent example of what you can do naturally, if you commit yourself totally. Today Bill resides in Noblesville, Indiana, with his wife Nancy and their three sons. Bill is lucky to be alive today and he thanks God for being so fortunate.[53]

Unfortunately, many other bodybuilders have not been so fortunate. Cancer is an ever-present threat to anyone who chooses to disrupt their body chemistry with anabolic steroids. As steroid use in sports continues to increase, more and more cases of cancer in athletes will be diagnosed as attributable to their use.

17. Accelerate the aging process—

This is the 17th and final major side effect of anabolic use as it applies to athletes. Many bodybuilders who use steroids appear much older than they really are. In fact, it is not unusual to find anabolic users with internal organs at the same level of degenerative function as normal, healthy individuals 20 or more years older than they are. This is mainly due to the fact that anabolics speed up the bodily functions of those who use them to an alarming degree, in essence, burning out the individual and aging him beyond his years.[86] Since the purpose of bodybuilding is to maintain a youthful appearance and inhibit the aging process, rather than promote it, this defeats the original purpose of bodybuilding. Besides this, speeding up the aging process has the obvious effect of shortening the life span, and if that's not a serious side effect, I don't know what is.

Growth hormone—STH

Growth hormones, otherwise known as STH (Somatotropic Hormone) is produced by the anterior portion of the pituitary gland. It is used by the body to promote normal growth and development during the formative years[55] and to regulate the processes of cellular and tissue growth and repair throughout adult life, once physical maturity is realized. It therefore has strong anabolic properties.

For many years, the only use for growth hormone was in the treatment of children with definite medical evidence of delayed growth. STH gave hope for near normal growth and development for these children.

Since the only source of growth hormone is the pituitary glands of cadavers, and the amount of available cadaveric pituitary material has always been limited in this country, the STH derived from these cadavers was used exclusively for the treatment of these children. The supply was, in fact, so limited that candidates for STH therapy had to demonstrate good medical evidence of short stature and even then, treatment was halted when the child reached a certain predetermined height.[56]

Strength athletes have long been aware of the ability of STH to induce anabolic conditions in the body. However, they were unable to obtain any human STH because of the short supply. Because of this, some athletes turned to Europe for an STH derived from the pituitary glands of rhesus monkeys. This turned out to be a terrible mistake. It so happens that STH is species specific. In other words if you want to develop big monkeys, you give them rhesus monkey STH, but if you want to create a larger, stronger human, you have to give him human STH. As a result, the indiscriminate use of rhesus monkey STH resulted in horrible skeletal deformities in many of the athletes who used them. Those deformities occurred in the skull, wrists and hands, and resulted in these individuals looking like freaks.[57] Athletes finally realized the dangers of monkey STH and its use declined.

Within the last year, a new source of human STH was obtained from Scandanavia[58] where autopsies are more routinely performed and organs can be removed without the complications we have in this country.[59] This made it possible to increase the supply of STH in the U.S. to the point where athletes could get their hands on it. In my opinion, this is most unfortunate.

The result of this increased availability of STH was predictable. It is currently the new rage in bodybuilding because of its strong anabolic effects.[60] Many bodybuilding authorities consider STH to be superior to anabolic steroids when considering the ratio of benefits received as opposed to side effects experienced. What they fail to consider, however, is that since growth hormone has only been available to bodybuilders for a year, it is difficult to determine what the long-term side effects will be. However, when the information presently available on STH is thoroughly analyzed, it becomes clear that the predisposition for serious long-term detrimental effects is much greater than these so-called authorities would lead us to believe. This will be covered in detail later, but first I will examine the specifics of how STH has been found to be of benefit to bodybuilders, as well as more detail on exactly what it does.

Benefits of STH

New information and ongoing research indicate that adults can utilize STH not only for growth of tissue size and the maintenance of existing cells, but also for the development of new cells.[61] This is especially important to bodybuilders in terms of potentially increasing the number of muscle cells they have. This is one benefit anabolic steroids do not provide. Growth hormones affect nearly every cell in the body except the brain and eye tissues.[62] STH also causes the thickening and strengthening of connective tissue such as tendons and ligaments, which reduces the chance of incurring serious injury. However, muscle tissue is the area most affected by STH therapy.[63] And that makes it especially beneficial to bodybuilders.

STH has many of the same anabolic effects as steroids. Like steroids, it promotes the uptake of amino acids by the cells. It also helps maintain a positive nitrogen balance in the cells, the importance of which was previously explained. Also, because STH promotes the uptake of amino acids by the cells, protein synthesis increases when G.H. levels rise, resulting in an increase in the development of lean body mass.[64]

STH has also been shown to induce a strong fat-burning effect. It exerts this lipolyzing effect by causing many of the same metabolic conditions normally found during periods of fasting. In fact growth hormone levels are known to increase during fasts. This appears to be the body's natural method of maintaining body protein stores and promoting glycogen stores during periods of low food intake while simultaneously burning fat.[65] This quality of growth hormone has made it a favorite anabolic agent among bodybuilders for use during precontest training, at which time the individual is attempting to maintain as much muscle mass as possible while simultaneously stripping away all subcutaneous body fat.

In terms of increases in muscle mass and strength, almost all documented reports of individuals taking STH indicate greatly enhanced gains beyond what you would be expected to achieve from anabolic steroids. Many bodybuilders have reported these gains while being on STH for as little as three to six weeks. Some studies indicate that, unlike anabolic steroids in which a large portion of the gains are lost once the athlete goes off them, the gains from STH seem to persist for up to 12 months or more, thus reducing the need to take steroids.[66]

One final beneficial or detrimental effect—according to how the individual looks at it—is that STH can cause an increase of height in some individuals of up to 1 inch.

One study of a group of strength athletes on STH therapy reports that one out of six individuals registered some gain in height. They were all adult males ranging in age from 29 to 52. Generally, the younger the athlete, the greater the chance of becoming taller.[67]

A major negative feature of STH that is not a side effect is the cost. While there is now enough of a supply of STH to make it available to those who are not necessarily in medical need of it, supplies are still very limited. Because of this it is very expensive, costing as much as $85 for a one-week supply.

However, work is being done to develop a synthetic STH which works the same as the human-derived substance for a fraction of the cost.[68] This could happen within the next couple of years, in which case the use of this substance would probably become at least as widespread as the use of anabolic steroids.

Side effects

1. Acromegaly—Acromegaly is the medical name for an abnormal condition characterized by excessive growth of the skull, jaw, elbows, and feet as a result of an abnormally high level of human or monkey STH resulting in a neanderthal facial appearance.[69] As mentioned previously, this condition commonly occurred in strength athletes who took rhesus monkey STH. Until recently there has been no mention of acromegaly occurring from taking human STH. However, let me warn you right now, it has been medically proven for a number of years that those individuals whose bodies produce an abnormally high level of human growth hormone once they reach adulthood develop a progressively severe condition of acromegaly during the course of their lifetime. Medical treatment can now restore the STH level in these individuals to normal levels, but the skeletal deformities which have occurred up to the point this is done are largely irreversible. Remember, there are documented medical cases of this occurring. So it's a fact that abnormally high levels of human growth hormone in the body, whether naturally or artificially induced, will result in acromegaly.

Recently, the inevitable has started to happen, and as a result of G.H. use several bodybuilders have developed acromegaly. It's happening with enough frequency that even the muscle magazines are starting to report its occurrence. While it stands to reason that the higher the level of STH a bodybuilder artificially induces, the greater his chance of developing acromegaly, characteristics of acromegaly have been noted in bodybuilders taking low dosages regularly for only a six- to 10-week period. So the danger is a very real one.[70]

2. Can aggravate or promote diabetes—STH tends to increase the blood sugar and antagonize insulin, giving it the potential to either cause diabetes or to aggravate an already present diabetic condition.[71] Prolonged administration of growth hormones has already been found to produce diabetes in laboratory animals.[72] There has not as yet been any research done on humans for obvious reasons. Any athlete with any degree of hyperglycemia at all should not take STH under any circumstances. Because of its effects on blood sugar and insulin, there is a good possibility that STH therapy could be the final factor necessary to produce diabetes under such conditions. Of course, it goes without saying that any diabetic who decides to go on STH borders on the insane, and is most definitely risking his life.

3. Kidney and cardiovascular system damage—According to Hans Seyle, the world's preeminent expert on stress physiology, STH can damage the kidneys and cardiovascular system only in the presence of the adrenals. Since those who have not yet reached physical maturity do not have fully functioning adrenal glands, they are not at risk of these side effects, even in the presence of above normal growth hormone levels. However, mature adults do have fully functioning adrenal glands and would therefore seem to be at risk of damaging these organs if they take STH.[73]

4. Cancer—The most serious consideration of STH therapy is that high concentrations of the hormone can foster conditions for the growth of cancerous cells, making even short-term administration a danger, and constant use a definite hazard.[74]

Remember, the human body is an extremely complex organism maintained by a precarious balance of forces. When, all of a sudden, one of its truly eminent forces, the endocrine system, is tampered with to any significant degree, disintegration can most definitely occur.

To suddenly increase the amount of one of the regulating hormones in the body could have disastrous effects on tissues which, for an individual's entire life, have adapted to and functioned in the presence of a far different level of that hormone.[75] That's why anabolic steroids and STH have such potential to cause cancer.

5. Unknown?—As I previously mentioned, young bodybuilders tend to take too much of everything. At this time we cannot predict what will happen when overdoses of STH interact with overdoses of other drugs. Certain bodybuilders obsessed with winning will use and abuse everything at their disposal in order to develop a champi-

onship physique. This has resulted in many of their bloodstreams containing a potpourri of powerful chemicals. How this mixture of anabolic steroids, amphetamines, thyroid, and now STH, combined with who knows what else, will ultimately affect the body no current research can possibly predict,[76] but logic dictates that the effect will not be a beneficial one. Evidence, in fact, suggests that it could be disastrous.

Thyroid preparations

The generic term "thyroid" refers to a preparation of synthetic or desiccated animal thyroid gland containing active thyroid hormones. Thyroid preparations are prescribed by doctors for a condition known as hypothyroidism, in which the thyroid gland is underactive.[77]

This gland, which is part of the endocrine system, is located in the back of the throat. The release of hormones from the thyroid is controlled by the pituitary gland, which releases TSH (Thyroid Stimulating Hormone) and subsequently stimulates the release of additional thyroid hormones, the most important of which is thyroxin.[78]

The thyroid gland and its hormones have many functions. The most important of these is the regulation of the basal metabolic rate, which consists of the rate of protein, carbohydrate, and fat metabolism, oxygen consumption, respiratory rate, body temperature, cardiac output and blood volume.[79] As you can see, proper thyroid function is essential for proper body function.

So what do thyroid preparations have to do with bodybuilding? In recent years bodybuilders have used these drugs increasingly as part of their precontest preparations in the hopes of speeding up their metabolisms for the purpose of burning off stored body fat more readily. As it turns out thyroid preparations do burn fat and help the individual taking them to appear more muscular and get into contest shape more quickly than would be possible without them. This is one drug, however, in which the disadvantages and side effects associated with taking it so far outweigh this one benefit that they just aren't worth the risks they produce. I'll explain why.

First, there's the fact that by taking thyroid preparation and putting his body into a state of hyperthyroidism (abnormally high thyroid hormone level) a bodybuilder causes his thyroid

gland to shut down its own hormone production, much the same way the introduction of anabolic steroids into the body shuts down the production of testosterone.[80] This has the effect of putting the body in a severe state of hypothyroidism immediately following the discontinuation of thyroid supplementation. As a result some bodybuilders balloon drastically in weight during this period[81] and find it impossible to normalize their weight to any degree until their own thyroid hormone levels return to normal. This often takes a number of weeks, and it is not uncommon for the individual's own thyroid production never to return to its previous level. This makes it even more difficult and often necessitates taking even more thyroid preparations to gain an acceptable degree of muscularity for future contests.[82] It is a vicious cycle that will ultimately burn you out and end your bodybuilding career.

The biggest and most relevant disadvantage to bodybuilders of taking thyroid preparations is that thyroid supplements are indiscriminate in what they burn. While they do burn fat, they also burn significant amounts of muscle[83], and muscle is the one commodity a bodybuilder can not afford to be without.

The reason for this is that too much thyroid puts the body in a catabolic state as opposed to having the right amount which is anabolic. So while you can lose fat by putting yourself in a hyperthyroid state, you cannot possibly build significant muscle mass, or even keep what you already have. This results in your ending up lean, but with no appreciable mass, by the time contest day rolls around.[84]

Thyroid preparations provide no benefit that any bodybuilder can't achieve on his own. A proper contest diet will burn off all subcutaneous fat while simultaneously preserving one's muscle mass. So the bodybuilder who is willing to diet for a couple of weeks longer without taking thyroid will end up being a lot more massive than, and just as muscular as, the bodybuilder who uses these drugs. Thyroid is guaranteed to hurt your appearance more than help it. Plain and simple, thyroid preparations are a cop-out for those bodybuilders who are too undisciplined to stick to a contest diet. Maybe when they see enough of their hard-earned muscle wasting away, they'll wise up. If that's not enough, here's a nice list of side effects to think about.

Side effects

The following side effects can occur as a result of the inducement of a hyperthyroid state from thyroid preparation therapy.

1. Insomnia

2. Spontaneous perspiring resulting from heat intolerance

3. Nervousness

4. Tremor

5. Hyperglycemia—As with STH, thyroid should under no circumstances be taken for bodybuilding purposes by anyone who is either already hyperglycemic or diabetic.[85]

7. Arrythmia[86]—Irregular heartbeat. This could be a sign of an impending heart attack.

8. Tachycardia—This can lead to a heart seizure[87] and possibly death.

If for no other reason, thyroid preparations should be avoided because of their deleterious effects on the heart. Any bodybuilder who has an unknown weakness in his heart such as a congenital defect could potentially induce a heart attack.

Amphetamines

The use of amphetamines, like steroids, is widespread among bodybuilders today. They are most commonly abused by bodybuilders because they produce an elevation of mood, a reduction of fatigue, a sense of increased alertness and invigorating aggressiveness, and a suppression of appetite.[88] These effects enable the athlete to train harder, eat less, and burn more body fat.[89] This makes amphetamines particularly appealing to competitive bodybuilders prior to a contest as they allow the user to get muscularly defined in a shorter period of time while simultaneously enabling him to continue to train hard on a restrictive diet without feeling exhausted. In many ways their effects are similar to those of thyroid preparations.

It must be noted that amphetamines do not actually create extra physical or mental energy; rather they promote expenditure of present resources at an accelerated rate[90], thus giving the feeling of increased energy.

In fact, it is now generally believed by researchers that amphetamines may only suppress the sensations of fatigue rather than eliminating fatigue itself or the toxins it produces in the body. In other words, when you take amphetamines you don't feel tired, because the drug blocks the usually perceived signs of fatigue so that physiological changes, even those of measurable damage, can occur without your being aware of them.[91]

In this way, amphetamines seriously interfere with the body's natural fatigue alarm system and thus pose possibly the greatest danger of all to the bodybuilder, who is stressing his system with hard training.

Besides this, amphetamines have a number of other major disadvantages to the serious bodybuilder. The first of these involves the fact that while amphetamines temporarily promote a feeling of increased energy, the stress they put on the body by speeding up normal body processes results in the individual physically "burning out." When the effect of the drug wears off, the user sleeps for long periods of time. Upon awakening, the individual often feels hungry and extremely lethargic.[92] It is impossible to train effectively in such a state so while you may have a couple of good workouts when you're taking amphetamines, this benefit will be neutralized by the fact that you'll have lousy workouts when you discontinue their use until such time as you recover your energy reserves. This neutralizes any positive energy-producing effects these drugs may have initially.

Another big disadvantage of amphetamines is that they promote loss of muscle mass in much the same way as thyroid preparations do. The stress they put on the system encourages the body to burn its muscle mass as a source of energy. Once again, this is one thing any serious bodybuilder cannot afford to let happen.

Finally, amphetamines are known for their tendency to cause psychological dependence mainly because of the elevation in mood they produce. In fact, withdrawal from the drug often leaves the user profoundly depressed, and in certain instances, suicidal.[93] Amphetamines are also said to be psychotomimetic drugs since heavy users may develop psychosis characterized by delusions of persecution, paranoia, and fully formed visual and auditory hallucinations either as a direct effect of the drugs themselves or as a result of the effects of sleep deprivation from prolonged amphetamine abuse.[94] Either way, this type of psychological effect can do nothing but damage your bodybuilding career, perhaps irreparably.

As in the case of thyroid preparations, amphetamines do not provide any benefits that cannot be matched or bettered by a little extra concentration and mental commitment. Their strong tendency to cause both physical and mental burnout makes them inappropriate for use by the bodybuilding community. Besides this, amphetamines have many side effects similar to those of thyroid preparations.

Side effects

1. Dry mouth

2. Insomnia—Discussed previously.

3. Irritability

4. Impotence and a change in libido—This can occur with prolonged use.[95]

5. Cardiorespiratory effects—The stimulant properties of the amphetamines can cause dramatic cardiorespiratory side effects such as tachycardia, dypsnea, and chest pain.[96] Not to mention a significant elevation of the heart rate. It doesn't take a genius to figure out that this stress on the cardiovascular system, combined with that exerted by exercise, could result in overstimulation and possibly irreparable damage[97] to the heart and blood vessels.

Diuretics

Diuretics are used by both male and female bodybuilders as just one of a number of methods of dehydration prior to competition. The reason competitive bodybuilders use diuretics to dehydrate prior to competition is that they consider their use an effective means of removing subcutaneous water from under the skin, resulting in a more muscular appearance. While this is true to a certain degree, bodybuilders tend to ignore the fact that the muscle tissue and internal organs lose water first, before the subcutaneous water is lost.[98] Since muscles are 70 percent water, and depletion of water from the body's tissues decreases the volume of each muscle,[99] the use of potent diuretics, while slightly enhancing muscular definition, will also give a flat and depleted look to the muscles,[100] thus negating any benefit they provide.

Besides this, the loss of electrolytes such as sodium, chloride, calcium, magnesium,[101] and especially potassium that results from taking potent prescription diuretics causes such untoward effects as fatigue, thirst, irritability, muscular weakness, and muscular cramping[102] as well as more serious adverse effects which I will discuss later. The extreme fatigue and muscle weakness, combined with the flat and depleted look of the muscles caused by diuretics, result in those bodybuilders who take them appearing unhealthy and drained of energy onstage. Besides this, these individuals do not have either the energy or muscular strength necessary to pose effectively and present their physique to the best possible advantage. In a close contest, this can mean defeat. So in terms of appearance and performance, diuretics do a lot more harm overall than they do good. In my opinion, they have no place in any bodybuilder's contest preparations.

Besides this, overdosing on diuretics can cause a list of side effects a mile long, many of them very serious, and some potentially deadly.

Many bodybuilders have gotten dizzy and fainted at contests as a direct result of the use of diuretics. The reason for this is that diuretics quickly deplete the circulating blood volume to such a low level that there simply isn't enough blood in the vascular system to fully oxygenate the brain when a rapid change of body position occurs. This results in a dizzy feeling when the bodybuilder gets up quickly from a seated or lying position,[103] and according to just how dehydrated the individual is, fainting can result.

Besides this, tests on dehydrated athletes have demonstrated impaired renal function that could possibly be permanent as a result of a lack of significant blood supply to the kidneys.[104]

Also, sitting in a sauna or training in a hot gym while severely dehydrated from the use of diuretics will knock out the normal thermostatic mechanism that controls the body. This results in the impairment of the function of the thermoregulation system making heat stroke and circulatory collapse a distinct possibility. If this occurs, the major organ systems of the body will not receive an adequate blood supply and may be damaged.[105] All of these side effects are even more pronounced when salt and fluid intake are also restricted. If blood volume is decreased sufficiently from the addition of these two stresses, circulatory collapse can occur, resulting in permanent organ damage and death. Also the possibility of heat stroke occurring increases[106], with the potential for the same result. If this isn't enough, the loss of the electrolyte, potassium, as a result of taking potent diuretics such as Lasix can cause heart arrythmias. This can result in the occurrence of heart seizures and death.[107] Some bodybuilders take supplemental potassium in an effort to counteract the loss of potassium, but it's impossible to determine how much to take, and too much potassium can also cause side effects. In case you think I'm exaggerating the risks presented by diuretics, let me tell you that there are documented cases of bodybuilders dying as a result of their use.

For example, early in 1982, Heinz Salzmayer, the 1980 IFBB Lightweight Mr. Universe, died of a heart attack while preparing for a professional competition. An autopsy revealed a minor congenital heart malformation, but the cause of death was excessive use of diuretics, which led to heart arrythmia and the heart attack. A few weeks later, an 18-year-old Swedish bodybuilder also suffered a fatal heart seizure as the result of massive dehydration from using potent diuretics.[108] Diuretics and other means of dehydrating the body excessively are just too dangerous to play games with. They are usually used by bodybuilders who haven't dieted long enough to appear really muscular as a last-ditch effort to achieve a high degree of muscularity, and they just don't do the job. If you're planning to compete, make sure you diet long enough to get into top shape, restrict your sodium intake for a few days, since salt retains water, and you'll end up in top shape. Stay away from diuretics. Your life may depend on it.

The five classes of drugs I have just discussed are the ones most commonly used by the bodybuilders of today, both male and female, competitive and noncompetitive. There are other drugs used by bodybuilders, but their use is much more limited. This book doesn't have the space to go into each one of these drugs in detail. New and suppos-edly better drugs are coming out every year, anyway. However, the five classes I discussed will be around for quite a while.

I tried to be as objective as possible in the presentation of my information. While I acknowledge that each of the drugs do have certain benefits, these benefits can only be obtained by serious, intelligent bodybuilders who have been training for a number of years and have a clear idea of what they're doing. Remember, these individuals will still experience some or all of the side effects previously listed. Since everybody is an individual and no drug combination works exactly the same way for any two people, nobody who uses them can predict the effect they will have. I honestly believe that the disadvantages and dangers of taking any of these drugs far outweigh any potential benefit they provide. This is especially true in the case of thyroid preparations, and amphetamines, which have no real benefits to the bodybuilder whatsoever when analyzed objectively.

While I hope that none of you reading this book will ever take bodybuilding drugs of any kind, I know that this is unrealistic, and that some of you will. For those of you who are determined to take bodybuilding drugs no matter what, at least be as sensible as possible in your use of them.

First of all, wait until you've gone as far as you can naturally, for all of the reasons I outlined previously, including the fact that they don't work effectively until you've reached a certain level. Secondly, always take them in the lowest dosages and for the shortest amount of time possible that provides good gains, keeping in mind that in this case more isn't better. You can only speed up your progress so fast. Remember that ridiculously high levels of steroids will not make you grow any faster than moderate doses, but that your risk of side effects will increase dramatically. I will not list recommended dosages of steroids or the other bodybuilding drugs for obvious reasons. If you want that information badly enough, there are a number of books by doctors associated with the sport on how to take them. Finally, make sure you're under the care of a medical doctor in case some unforeseen medical problem should develop.

Psychological characteristics of the drug user

During the past few years as I've gotten to know bodybuilders who use bodybuilding drugs, especially anabolic steroids, as a means of artificially enhancing their muscular development, I've discovered certain common psychological traits that they all possess to some degree.

Almost all of the psychological characteristics which the drug-using bodybuilder possesses are a function of one common denominator—a low self-image. Individuals with a low self-image usually do not like themselves very much. More importantly, they also normally do not believe in themselves or in their ability to accomplish anything worthwhile, at least not without outside help, either from someone else or, in the case of bodybuilding drugs, something else.

Specifically, any bodybuilder who does not believe in himself cannot possibly believe that he has the ability to achieve a superior level of muscular development totally on his own merit. He automatically concludes that if so many other bodybuilders had to take steroids or any of the other drugs in order to achieve a massively muscular physique, then there is no reason for him to believe he can achieve a similar level of development naturally. He won't even give himself the chance to find out by training naturally for a few years. The fact is many of the bodybuilders who have taken steroids soon after they started training would have been surprised at the level of muscular development they could have achieved on their own if they had just given themselves a chance. Who knows, maybe some of these individuals would have been so proud of what they had accomplished on their own merit that they would never have taken the drugs. Of course, then they wouldn't have to go through life worrying about the consequences of their lack of belief in themselves either. So have some faith in your ability and give yourself a chance. You'd be amazed at the level of physical development you can achieve naturally with a little hard work and determination. Not everyone can keep up with the druggies, but I truly believe that if I was able to do it, then many of you can, too. And as I said previously, nothing can beat the feeling of self-pride and accomplishment you'll get from knowing that the physique you developed was built purely by the sweat of your brow.

Another reason bodybuilders take steroids, which also is a function of a lack of self-image, is that they crave recognition. Individuals who don't think much of themselves often seek reassurance from others that they are worthwhile individuals. Being noticed, recognized and respected by their peers for some kind of achievement or special ability is an extremely effective means by which such individuals can obtain the reassurance of their worth that they so desparately need. For certain individuals, bodybuilding is the vehicle chosen as a means of obtaining this reassurance. These individuals often become so obsessed with becoming as big and muscular as possible in order to impress others, and hopefully gain their respect, that they will often use any means at their disposal to achieve such development in the shortest period of time possible. This, of course, includes using anabolic agents. Because of their obsession, these individuals are strong candidates to abuse these drugs without any concern for their potential side effects. Even more unfortunate is the fact that because of the desire they have to impress their peers, a great number of these individuals are teenagers. I already mentioned how disastrous steroid abuse can be to youths.

Narrow-mindedness is also demonstrated by steroid-using bodybuilders by the fact that they seldom consider the consequences taking drugs today will have on their lives tomorrow. Bodybuilding success is often considered so important by these individuals that they just don't think about the consequences their drug use will have in the future. As I mentioned previously, however, bodybuilding success is only a temporary thing, and today becomes tomorrow before you know it.

Another characteristic of bodybuilders who take drugs to speed up the development of a superior physique is impatience. As discussed previously, the longer you train, the harder it becomes to make appreciable gains in muscle size and strength. At times progress can come to a complete halt. This can be extremely frustrating for the hard-training bodybuilder, but it is a normal occurrence. You just can't develop a super physique overnight. Many bodybuilders are too impatient to give their body the time it needs to reach superior development naturally, so instead of sticking it out, they take steroids. Once again, teenagers are especially notorious for this because they tend as a rule to be extremely impatient

and don't fully realize that certain things like bodybuilding success don't happen overnight.

Incredibly, some individuals take bodybuilding drugs simply because they are too lazy to put in the hard work it takes to develop a superior physique. They feel that the drugs will make it easier to gain the muscle they desire. This is, in my opinion, absolutely the most foolish reason there is to take bodybuilding drugs. What these fools fail to realize is that you actually have to train much harder when you're on steroids than when you're natural, in order for them to work effectively. So these individuals who aren't willing to train hard in the gym won't get any further with steroids than they'll get without them. If you're not totally serious about bodybuilding, taking steroids absolutely cannot be justified in any possible way whatsoever. Anyone who would take them because he's too lazy to train hard is beyond crazy, he borders on insane.

Many bodybuilders have been known to develop a syndrome which can be considered the opposite of anorexia nervosa. Anorexia is a syndrome common to teenaged girls in which they see themselves as being fat when they are really thin. Individuals with this condition often refuse to eat for long periods of time or vomit up what they do eat in order to lose the fat they think they have. This results in severe emaciation and the individuals can literally starve to death if they do not receive the psychological help necessary to enable them to see themselves realistically.

Well-developed bodybuilders, on the other hand, often have a distorted image of themselves in which they think they look smaller than they really are. One Mr. Universe I know constantly wears baggy clothes to hide his physique because he doesn't consider it good enough to be on public display. This guy weighs 230 pounds of solid muscle at 5 feet 10½. To other bodybuilders he appears huge and to the general public he's totally awesome. However, he sees himself as being too small. And this isn't an unusual case. If this guy isn't happy with the way he looks, just imagine how the average bodybuilder must feel. Such an unrealistic assessment by many bodybuilders of their own physiques often leads to discouragement and disappointment even when totally unwarranted. It can ultimately lead to steroid use as a last resort by these individuals attempting to achieve their own unrealistic ideal.

The irony is that no matter how much these individuals gain, even with drugs, they are almost never happy with what they achieve. In the mind of the supercritical bodybuilding perfectionist, nothing less than a perfect physique is acceptable. Unfortunately, the perfect physique has never been built. So learn to assess your physique realistically and work within your limitations. Steroids are not the answer to correcting a distorted, unrealistic, and disappointed view of your own physique. The answer is a change in your thinking from a perfectionist's attitude, in which every minor flaw in your physique appears to be a major fault, to one of acceptance and realistic appraisal of such flaws followed by a scientific training approach to overcome them as much as realistically possible.

Then of course, we have competitive bodybuilders, a group of athletes, who as a rule, are obsessed with winning at any cost. Competitive bodybuilding requires more dedication and sacrifice than almost any other sport, and no one likes to lose a contest after putting so much work into preparing for it. The fact is that many bodybuilders simply can't handle defeat. Usually because of a low self-image, these athletes take defeat to mean they are failures. It is considered a negative reflection on themselves, in essence a verification of their own worthlessness. Such an individual believes he must win at all costs. He needs contest victories to verify his worth. Such a person has no qualms about taking steroids or anything else that might hurt him. All that matters is that he win.

Finally there are the competitive bodybuilders who point out that since everybody else is taking steroids, they'd be crazy not to take them if they hope to win. While I've already verified that this is to a great extent true, I've also pointed out that many natural bodybuilders can compete successfully against drug users if they give themselves a chance. But independent of this, that kind of thinking shows total lack of character. I mean, would you jump off a bridge and kill yourself just because everybody else was doing it? Hopefully you'd have more guts and think for yourself. Always weigh your alternatives. Make your decision based on *your* needs and values, not on what everyone else is doing.

4

PREREQUISITES FOR TRAINING NATURALLY

Why are you training?

Before you ever walk into a gym you should know exactly why you are going to start training. This is critical if you plan on successfully implementing a natural bodybuilding training program. Some of you may want to get into better shape or lose a few inches off your waist, while others may want to become competitive natural bodybuilders.

Once you've decided to start a program of progressive resistance natural bodybuilding training, and you have in mind a clearly defined goal to train for, you should definitely analyze your physique, using the information presented in the genetics chapter as a means of determining just how realistic your goal is.

It's almost impossible to accurately assess the potential an individual has for developing a championship natural physique until he's been training a couple of years and has laid a solid foundation of muscle. However, a good general assessment of how close the individual can come to achieving his natural bodybuilding goal can be made according to which body type he possesses. It can then be determined with a good degree of accuracy whether the goal is reasonable or must be compromised.

By using the information on genetic potential and body type in an earlier chapter and by being totally honest with yourself about which category you fit into, you too can accurately assess whether the goal you have set for yourself is reasonable or not. If you find it difficult to be totally objective about your own physique, try asking a competitive bodybuilder for his opinion. Most competitive bodybuilders, especially title winners, are well versed in analyzing the potential of an individual to achieve whatever level of development he desires from his training.

Get a physician's checkup

If your are over the age of 25, it is wise to have a medical checkup before commencing a natural bodybuilding training program, or any other form of strenuous physical exercise for that matter. If you are over the age of 40 it's a good idea to have an electrocardiogram (EKG) done along with your checkup to make sure your heart is strong enough to handle the introduction of regular strenuous physical activity into your life style. Chances are excellent that your doctor will give you the go-ahead to begin your training program. If he does find anything wrong with your health, he will prescribe effective treatment to correct your problem. Also, if you have a condition he feels will prevent you from safely following the training programs as outlined in this book, chances are he will have some useful suggestions on how to work around your problem in the most effective way possible. By modifying your training routine in a way that best takes into consideration your physical limitations you can, with your doctor's help, develop a training routine that best suits *your* needs and provides the maximum benefit possible for you.[1]

Besides making sure your heart is strong enough to handle the stress of a strenuous training program, a thorough medical checkup can identify conditions such as hypo- or hyperthyroidism, an unusually fast or slow metabolism, and vitamin deficiencies to name a few, which can severely impair the benefits you can obtain from your training. You can be eating right, training correctly, and sleeping plenty, but fail to progress satisfactorily because of the way such conditions can abnormally affect the way you gain or lose weight, both fat and muscle.

If you have a history of being physically active and in relatively good health, you should be able to handle the full beginner's program presented in this book with relative ease. You may suffer minimal muscular and cardiovascular discomfort during the first few workouts, but you should adapt quickly. If, on the other hand, you have a history of poor health and physical inactivity you should start off slowly and easily and gradually work your way up to the full training program as you feel strong enough and comfortable enough to advance.[2]

Choosing a gym

Once you've decided to train and gotten the okay from your physician to go ahead, the next step is to choose the type of facility which best suits your purposes and personality. Your choices include training in either a home gym, YMCA, a school weight room, a Nautilus gym, a fitness center, a health spa, or a hard-core bodybuilding gym.

Home gym

The most common place to begin any type of bodybuilding training is at home, although the recent explosion of fitness centers and gyms has resulted in many more individuals beginning their training in commercial facilities.

Training in a home gym provides many advantages. The most obvious of these is that a person who trains at home can work out anytime he wants to, day or night. For an individual who has a busy or unusual work schedule, this type of convenience is helpful and often critical.

Another advantage of training at home involves the privacy it provides. This is of particular importance to those individuals who are self-conscious about their appearance because they are either exceedingly skinny or fat.[3]

Training at home can also be of benefit because it provides an atmosphere which is generally much less distracting than that of a commercial training facility. This results in an increased ability to concentrate on workouts and the feel of the muscles under stress.[4] This increased concentration can also result in a decreased risk of injury because of the greater awareness of how the muscles are responding.

A final advantage of training at home is that once you buy the equipment for your gym, it is yours. Commercial gyms, on the other hand, charge yearly membership rates, and you definitely don't get to bring home the equipment at the end of the year. If you like training at home and don't plan on advancing past the beginner or intermediate levels of training, you could equip a home gym with all the equipment necessary for progressing to this level for just a few hundred dollars, and you would save a large amount of money over the cumulative cost of training at a commercial gym. At the end of this section I'll discuss exactly how to equip a home gym.

Now that I've presented the advantages of training at home, let's discuss the disadvantages. First of all, there is another side of the coin when considering whether it's more expensive to train at home or at a gym. While it is generally more expensive to train at a commercial gym than at home, you must consider the fact that a commercial gym provides you with a much wider variety of equipment than you can possibly equip a home gym with unless you are prepared to spend tens of thousands of dollars. Even then, you still won't be able to match the many equipment options provided by a well-equipped commercial gym. A complete Nautilus line alone can cost upward of $100,000. Then there's the expense of heavy-duty power racks, leg press machines, benches, pulleys, etc. Besides this, the solid dumbbells and barbells found in commercial gyms are very convenient and result in minimal time being spent between sets changing weights.

Ultimately, you can progress only so far training at home. If you are either a serious natural bodybuilder whose goal is to reach his ultimate natural potential or simply an individual who likes a lot of variety in his workouts, you will find yourself graduating to the world of the commercial gym. I myself had a very well-equipped home gym and was able to reach an unusually advanced level of development while training there, but eventually I simply outgrew it. I needed the heavy-duty equipment provided by a commercial gym.

Training at home alone presents a serious threat of injury and even death to those individuals who train heavy. It is all too common for an athlete training heavy by himself without a spotter to be pinned under a heavy bench press or squat because of a slight miscalculation in how much weight he thought he could handle. Such pinnings can result in severe muscle and joint tears. Besides this, there are numerous reports of weight trainers suffocating as a result of being pinned under a heavy bench press. I strongly suggest that you either find a steady training partner or someone who can spot you when you want to go heavy.

The final disadvantage of training at home is that it can often be difficult to stay motivated to train. Dragging yourself out to your garage or basement day in and day out usually requires an incredible amount of discipline. Training all by yourself is lonely and the workouts seem to drag along because there's nothing to do between sets except pace back and forth. It's very easy to become bored with training.

If you can find a training partner who is willing to work with you at your home gym on a consistent basis, you can, to a large degree, minimize this problem. However, it is unlikely you will be able to find such a person. It is an unfortunate fact that dedicated weight athletes are few and far between and chances are that anyone you find to train with you will soon quit. Constantly looking for someone to train with can be a frustrating experience, and if you don't thoroughly enjoy training alone, you're better off joining a commercial facility where finding someone to train with is never a problem.

Nautilus clubs

For anyone who is into progressive resistance training for any purpose other than just toning up, Nautilus centers are not recommended. These centers, which normally have one or two complete lines of Nautilus equipment consisting of one or two exercises per muscle group, provide too limited a variety of exercises to stimulate an adequate muscle and strength response. Some of the individual machines are themselves superb, but Nautilus training in general is only slightly more than minimally effective unless it is either used in combination with, or as an adjunct to, training with free weights. Since Nautilus centers are concerned only with selling the Nautilus concept as the ultimate method of shaping up, they rarely have free weights, or any other training equipment for that matter.[5] This makes them totally inadequate for any individual serious about developing significant increases in either strength or muscle mass, or both. Even for those just interested in toning up, I consider free weights to be far superior to Nautilus machines. Doing the same Nautilus routine day in and day out can quickly lead to boredom. However, the variety of exercises and directed stress on the muscles that training with free weights affords results in being able to shape and tone the muscles more quickly and effectively than the Nautilus machines while simultaneously maintaining a high degree of interest in your training.

YMCA's

Many YMCA's have well-equipped, heavy-duty free weight rooms and many bodybuilders have made excellent progress training in them. A big advantage of training at a YMCA is that the cost is usually much less than that of other commercial training facilities. One disadvantage of YMCA's is that the weight room is usually tucked away in some dark corner of the basement floor, resulting in a dark, dingy, somewhat uninspiring atmosphere. Besides this, most YMCA weight rooms are known for having an inherent lack of qualified training personnel and many have no supervision whatsoever. As a result, you'll have to rely on the advanced bodybuilders training there to help you with any training problems you may encounter.[6] And since practically all advanced bodybuilders are on drugs, chances are a lot of the advice you receive will not be applicable to your own natural bodybuilding training regimen.

Health spas

Health spas tend to gear their equipment and personnel toward low-intensity fitness training as a means of becoming physically fit. The free weights these establishments provide aren't very heavy. As a result almost all natural bodybuilders reaching the intermediate level of training will find they quickly outgrow the usefulness of such a facility.

Also, since spas are generally high dollar volume businesses, primarily interested in individuals who are willing to pay for the right to do very low-intensity workouts, the general atmosphere of such a facility will be somewhat less than inspiring. Working up anything more than a light sweat in such a place is considered unusual. Even if you can get motivated to train hard in such a lackadaisical atmosphere, chances are your attempts at generating a high level of training intensity will be discouraged by the club's personnel.[7]

If your purpose is simply to tone up, and you like to swim and maybe play racquetball or tennis, a health spa may be the perfect place for you. If you don't let the lackadaisical "let's do as little as possible" attitude of the majority of members influence you negatively, you will reach your fitness goals. Anyone who plans on advancing past beginner and on to the intermediate or advanced levels of natural bodybuilding should join a spa only if no other training facilities are accessible.

High school and college weight rooms

Many high school and especially college weight rooms are exceedingly well equipped for heavy weight training. However, because of the number of school teams using them, they tend to be overcrowded. This can result in interference with your workout because of difficulty obtaining the equipment you require for various parts of your workout at the time you need it. Also, excessive numbers of people, combined with worrying whether you'll be able to get the piece of equipment you require, can create a very high-pressure, distracting environment. You may find it too uncomfortable to train there. Inadequate supervision also tends to be a problem at these facilities. Now we come to the two best facilities for the serious natural bodybuilder to train in.

Hard-core bodybuilding gyms

Bodybuilding gyms are not without certain disadvantages to the athlete whose intent it is to stay natural. The first of these involves the fact that an exceedingly large number of serious bodybuilders, mainly steroid users, develop ego problems. They walk around the gym as if they own the place. Many of them tend not to be friendly and some have even been known to literally take whatever piece of exercise equipment they want without any regard for the person who was using it or wants to use it. I personally find this kind of behavior to be repulsive. I like to be able to carry on a friendly conversation with the other members of the facility where I am training, and it's always nice to have a few people to call on either to spot you or motivate you in the particularly tough portions of your workout. In hard-core bodybuilding gyms, the self-centeredness of most of the clientele makes friendliness extremely hard to find.

The most important disadvantage however, is that by training in a hard-core bodybuilding gym, you are putting yourself in a position where you, as a natural bodybuilder, will be constantly tempted to take steroids. Chances are that you will either give in eventually to this temptation, or lose enthusiasm for your training as a result of seeing everyone else in the gym gain markedly faster than you.

While some of you may find it motivating to try and keep up with these drug users while staying natural and may, in fact, be able to do so in terms of developing a competitive physique, it's a fact that you will never be able to gain muscle as quickly as the steroid user. Even the most determined natural can't help but become discouraged from constantly fighting to gain in an environment where everyone else is growing with ease. I have been in a number of hard-core bodybuilding gyms in my life, just for the purpose of taking a workout and checking out the environment. I found the atmosphere to be depressing because of the unfriendliness of most of the bodybuilders training there, combined with the overwhelming size of many of them, which constituted a degree of muscular mass that I could not hope to achieve naturally. Even though I knew I could beat most of these guys in a contest because of superior shape, proportion, and definition, just seeing how much bigger they were than me was something I couldn't handle. I knew that if I had to train with such monsters for any length of time that I almost definitely would give in to the steroid temptation—either that or I would become so frustrated that I would quit training. Fortunately, I found what I consider to be the perfect facility for the hard-training natural bodybuilder.

The modern fitness center

As far as I am concerned, well-equipped fitness centers are the ultimate training facility for the serious natural bodybuilder. Fitness centers normally have both a well-equipped free weight room and a room containing a full line of machines such as Nautilus, thus making them suitable for weight training athletes at practically every level.

The free weight room at such a facility normally has all the benches, weights, pulley machines, squat racks, etc., that you'll find at any heavy-duty bodybuilding facility with a few minor exceptions. Usually the equipment is not quite as heavy-duty as that found in a bodybuilding gym, but since it isn't abused nearly as much, this really doesn't pose a problem. There also generally aren't quite as many Olympic weight sets or free weights, but once again, since very few people at fitness centers are into heavy weight training, finding enough weight is almost never a problem. The only disadvantage in terms of equipment is that the dumb-bells usually only go up to 80 or 100 pounds, not 150 and 200, as in hard-core bodybuilding gyms. But how many natural bodybuilders are strong enough to use 80-pound dumbbells in strict form for exercises such as dumbbell bench presses anyway? Not many, believe me. If you, however, happen to be one of the few exceedingly strong natural bodybuilders around, you'll be happy to know that most fitness centers have a pair of adjustable dumbbells lying around onto which you can add as much weight as you like. If they don't have them, you can bring your own.

Another advantage of modern fitness centers is that they normally allow their members to use both the free weights and Nautilus machines in any combination they want. You don't have to use the Nautilus machines in a specific order as in Nautilus centers. And the increased flexibility resulting from being able to use whatever equipment you want, when you want to use it, and in whatever order you like, can give you almost unlimited options for developing individual training routines of the most possible benefit to your own particular needs.

Besides this, modern fitness centers have the atmosphere most conducive to making rapid natural bodybuilding progress, while you simultaneously enjoy your workouts. You will encounter individuals of every age and from every background imaginable, all with different training goals. Some will be training to get in shape, others for football, and still others will be training specifically to become muscular and well developed. There is usually a certain camaraderie among the members and as long as you act friendly and down-to-earth and not like a macho, stuck-up bodybuilder, you'll have no trouble making friends. Also, bodybuilding is accepted enough in these facilities (almost every fitness center has one or two), that you'll have no trouble with management as long as you put your weights away, and don't grunt and scream too much, which is unnecessary except in rare circumstances anyway. Also, fitness centers are normally well staffed with qualified personnel, which is a big advantage to anyone starting out. Finally, and most importantly, is that very few members of fitness centers have ever heard of bodybuilders taking steroids, no less taken them themselves. So you'll have no outside pressure to take them.

For all the reasons mentioned above, I strongly advise that if you can find the type of fitness center described in this section, you should join it. If you don't have such a facility, take a trial workout at all the gyms in your area until you find one that best suits your needs and gives you the most comfortable feeling. The first workout at any facility is usually free anyway. So you might as well try them all out, and then make a logical, rational decision.

Equipping a home gym

For those of you planning on training at home, I will briefly describe what constitutes a reasonably priced, well-equipped home gym. Basically, you will require two or three standard barbells, each 5 to 6 feet in length, four pairs of adjustable dumbbells, a curling bar, at least 500 pounds of plates, and a lifting belt. As far as benches are concerned, a sturdy adjustable incline bench will serve you well, but I strongly recommend that you invest in a multipurpose bench instead.

These benches give you the option to purchase a wide variety of additional attachments, which enable you to specialize in the various muscle groups. The most useful of these are the leg-extension-leg-curl attachment, and leg press attachment for the legs, the preacher curl attachment for the biceps, and the dipping bar attachment for shoulders and chest. Most of this equipment runs between $30 and $60. If you're willing to spend an additional $100 or so you can get a lat pulldown attachment for your back. Many wholesale equipment distributors carry such benches for reasonable prices. Your best bet is to look through the muscle magazines until you find such a bench with all the available attachments at a good price, usually in the range of $400 to $600 for everything. If you're serious about equipping a good home gym as economically as possible, this type of bench can't be beat. Each of the attachments would cost at least $100 more if bought as separate units instead of attachments to the bench. Besides this, so many separate pieces of equipment would take up an excessive amount of room and since most home gyms are limited by space restrictions, this can be a big disadvantage. The attachments, however, can be stored in a relatively small area, usually right against a wall.

One virtually essential piece of equipment for the home gym of any serious natural bodybuilder is a heavy-duty squat rack or power rack for the purpose of doing squats and calf raises.

Your home gym should also include a wide-grip chinning bar mounted in the ceiling if at all possible.

There are a couple of things to avoid when buying equipment. First, you should always buy solid metal weights; stay away from the plastic-coated sand and concrete-filled ones. The plastic weights are exceedingly bulky in size which makes it impossible to fit enough of them on a standard barbell to use respectable poundages on your basic exercises. The plastic covers of these plates also tend to split and crack after a couple of years of heavy use. The concrete and sand spills out and they become useless and messy.[8] Therefore, although these weights are somewhat cheaper than the solid metal ones, they do not have near the durability and, therefore, in the long run, prove to be a poor investment. The metal plates last a lifetime.

Another thing you should avoid when buying equipment is the tubular steel-constructed benches sold at department stores. These benches tend to be somewhat unstable and aren't sturdy enough to support heavy weights continuously. They just aren't built to last. Also many of these benches are excessively wide, making it next to impossible to lower your arms sufficiently to get a full range of motion on any type of chest exercise such as bench presses.

If you don't have the money to buy new equipment put an ad in the paper stating that you're looking for weight equipment. Numerous people have old weight sets and benches sitting in their home as a result of giving the iron a try and eventually losing enthusiasm. They'll usually be more than happy to sell them to you at a cheap price. You can also attend garage sales and lawn sales and look for ads concerning people who are looking to get rid of their old equipment. However, your chances of finding a used multipurpose bench with attachments, in good condition, and at a cheap price is slim.[9] In my opinion, this is one piece of equipment you should buy new. Your best deal in used equipment is purchasing additional barbells, dumbbells, and especially extra metal weights, as you become more advanced. New metal plates usually cost between 60 and 70 cents a pound while you can pick up used ones for only 10 to 15 cents a pound. Since old plates are just as useful as new ones unless they are excessively rusted, buying them used can prove to be a great deal for anyone building a home gym. Altogether it

shouldn't cost you more than $1,000 to fully equip a home gym capable of developing your physique to at least the intermediate natural bodybuilding level.

You'd be amazed at how far you can progress with just basic equipment. Initially all you really need is the basic multipurpose bench, a squat rack, one barbell, one pair of dumbbells, a couple hundred pounds of weight, and a lifting belt. Your initial cash outlay doesn't really have to be more than $300 or $400. You can buy the additional multipurpose bench attachments, bars, and weights, piece by piece over time, as you progress to the point where you need them. Thus, your monetary investment will be over time and not all at once, which should make it much easier to handle. One thing you should always remember is that your investment in home gym equipment is one that will last a lifetime.

If you happen to have a few friends who are into bodybuilding you could conceivably combine your equipment and monetary resources. This will enable you to fully equip a home gym while laying out only a certain percentage of the investment. Another advantage of this is that with three or four partners, chances are that you will not always have to train alone, and if one of them has a schedule similar to yours you can become steady training partners. This would be a big advantage since having a training partner will enable you to overcome many of the disadvantages commonly associated with home gym training. You can motivate and supervise each other which will make your training both safer and more enjoyable.

Training attire

There are two important guidelines to follow when choosing what to wear for a particular workout. First of all, whatever clothing you wear should be unrestrictive to movement and allow full range of motion for both your arms and legs. Secondly, it is extremely important that you dress according to the temperature of your training environment. Constantly keeping your muscles warm is a major contributory factor to preventing injuries. It also helps keep blood in the muscles, thereby promoting and prolonging the pump in whichever body part you're training.[10]

So what should you wear? During the summer most bodybuilders prefer to wear either a T-shirt or tank top and shorts. However, many gyms happen to be excessively air-conditioned during the summer, and if yours is one of them, you should also wear a warmup suit (one that provides full range of motion, of course) over your other clothes. Always remember that it's better to be a little too warm than too cold, especially in an air-conditioned gym where going back and forth between the warm summer air and cold gym can result in your getting a chill.

During the colder months of the year, if you happen to be training in a commercial facility, you should be provided with a reasonable amount of heat. If this is the case, you probably will not require more than a warmup suit. If, however, either your gym is inadequately heated, or you happen to be unfortunate enough to train in an unheated garage, as I did, you will almost definitely have to wear a couple of extra layers of clothing under your sweat suit if you hope to maintain sufficient body warmth. In such cases I would recommend wearing a couple of T-shirts and a pair of long underwear under your sweat suit. Several light layers of clothing retain body heat more effectively than one or two equally thick layers of heavy clothing. This is superior to wearing another sweatsuit over the one you already have.[11]

Another topic to consider is footwear. Bodybuilders should always wear shoes while training, preferably sneakers or running shoes. Sooner or later if you don't wear shoes, you are bound to suffer the unfortunate experience of someone accidentally dropping a barbell plate on your foot. This can be an extremely painful, not to mention bone-shattering experience. Besides this, there's the ever-present danger of stubbing your toe against a barbell plate. Finally, doing heavy exercises such as squats without adequate foot support can result in compression injuries and irreversible destruction of the arches of your feet. So always make sure you wear shoes, and while you're at it, don't forget sweat socks to soak up the extra perspiration and keep your feet comfortable.[12]

It is my opinion that anyone who trains with free weights should wear a lifting belt. In fact, a lifting belt is essential to prevent back injuries. They provide a substantial amount of support to the lower back. This is especially important when performing exercises such as squats, bent-over rows, and military presses, to name a few which are notorious for putting undue stress on this area. This added support enables

you to lift heavier weights than you normally would be able to on these exercises, while simultaneously protecting your lower back against injury. I cannot emphasize their importance enough as an injury-prevention method because I can guarantee you that if you don't wear such a belt, you will eventually incur a serious back injury.

Lifting belts come in three sizes, small, medium, and large. They are adjustable and should be worn snugly, but not so tightly that they impair circulation or, more importantly, restrict your ability to breathe deeply while training.

Body wraps are generally used to support and protect an injured joint or muscle group. However, they can also be used as a preventive measure. It is common for bodybuilders to wrap their knees when performing heavy squats because of the extra support these wraps provide. And I strongly suggest you do the same. It is a good idea to give the knee joints and surrounding tissue extra support and to simultaneously keep them warm while performing squats. One of the two types of wraps I am about to discuss will provide both these benefits. There is really no need to wrap any other area on any other exercise unless that area is either temporarily bothering you or has previously been injured.

The first basic type of wrap is called a neoprene rubber body band. These wraps do not actually provide much support for the joints such as the knee or elbow joint. However, the rubber retains body heat around the joints quite effectively. As a result, they are excellent for use as a preventive injury measure when performing heavy exercises such as squats.[13] Power wraps made of heavy-duty spandex are very similar in effect to these wraps, and are the type most commonly used to give support and act as a preventive injury measure when performing squats.

The other basic type of wrap is called an elastic gauze bandage. These wraps provide significantly more support for the joints than rubber support bands do. However, they are not nearly as effective for holding in heat and keeping the area warm. Therefore, they should only be used for added support when a serious joint or muscle injury has been sustained.[14]

On exercises such as bent-over rows, shoulder shrugs, chins, and standard machine hack squats, it is common for an individual's grip to give out before the muscle has been thoroughly worked. Using lifting straps will enable you to overcome this problem.

There are various types of straps on the market, some more simple to use than others. The one thing they all have in common is that they wrap around your wrist and then, according to the type, secure your grip to the bar in various ways. The simplest type to use is in the shape of a loop. You simply put your hand through it so that it is resting around your wrist. Then you wrap the remainder of the loop around the bar until your wrist is pulled tightly against the bar. You wrap your hand around the bar on top of the part of the loop which is wrapped around the bar. This will fasten your grip to the bar securely and you'll have no trouble holding on. Some types of grips are better than others. A decent pair of straps can be made out of a material such as webbing, but the best are made out of heavy-duty cloth material.

One type of strap, the Meeko Power Grip, deserves special mention. This is a unique type of strap which was invented two years ago by a competitive bodybuilder named Joe Meeko. In the space of this brief period of time the Meeko Power Grip has come to be considered among the best straps on the market by the bodybuilding community. What separates this form of strap from all others (besides being made out of thick, heavy-duty material) is that the strap itself does not wrap around both your hand and the bar. Instead the strap has a semicircular piece of metal attached to it which is designed to slide under and around the barbell to provide maximum support. The strap itself just slides over your hand and wraps around your wrist as does any other strap. Then you just wrap your hands around the top of the bar and you'll have the most secure grip possible. Because of their heavy-duty construction, these straps are significantly more expensive than most, but they are built to last a long time and definitely worth the investment if you're serious about training.

Weight-holding belts have been designed to enable you to safely use more than your body weight on exercises such as chins and dips in which it is impossible to hold any weight in your hands because you need them for support purposes. These belts wrap around your waist and have either a chain or some kind of strap hanging down from them. The chain or strap is designed in such a way that you can safely secure a dumbbell or a couple of plates to it. The weight will hang below you at about the level of your lower thighs. When performing the exercise they are using it for, most individuals brace their inner thighs against the weight to keep it from swinging back and forth. Then they go ahead and perform the exercise as they normally would. Only now they have the additional weight safely supported which they need to make the exercise most productive.

Free weights vs. machines

When you first begin training you will find that you have a wide variety of exercise equipment to choose from. The two main classes of equipment are, first, free weights, consisting mainly of plate-loading barbells and dumbbells in combination with various benches, squat racks, etc., and second, exercise machines such as Nautilus, Universal, and Polaris. Somewhere in between are such specialized exercise units as plate-loading leg press machines, cable pull-down units, and long-range cable rows.

Every beginner invariably asks which is better to use, free weights or machines. There is no question that free weights are, by far, the superior of the two for developing muscle mass, strength, flexibility, and coordination. Machines have their place, but basic free weight exercises should form the backbone of the training program for every individual who is serious about getting the greatest benefit from his natural bodybuilding training.

From my standpoint exercise machines do serve two important purposes. First of all, a complete line of machines designed to work each individual body part can provide an excellent introduction to progressive resistance training to someone who has never done such training before. This is true for a number of reasons. First, machines require less coordination than free weights and are therefore easier for a beginner to use. Also, exercises performed on machines, in general, stress the muscles less than similar exercises performed with free weights. This means the novice is less apt to become uncomfortably sore and stiff than he would be if he immediately jumped into free weights. Finally, because of the convenience of changing the resistance provided by machines simply by moving a pin from one weight to another in a prearranged weight stack, combined with the simplicity of getting in and out of a machine, as opposed to the hassle of constantly loading and unloading a barbell, it makes it easier for the as-yet-undisciplined novice to stick

to his training program than if he immediately started out with free weights.

For all the reasons stated above, complete machine lines, the best of which is Nautilus, are excellent as both an introduction to progressive resistance training and for use as a transition from inactivity to the physical and psychological stress of training with free weights. Some individuals whose sole purpose is to tone up choose to always train only with machines. However, free weights are superior to machines even for just toning up once you have developed the ability to use them effectively. Besides this, training solely with a limited amount of machines day in and day out is extremely boring.

The second purpose machines serve is their occasional use as either a supplement to a basic free weight program, or as a temporary replacement from time to time. Reasons for this may include using machines to work around an injury incurred from training with free weights or simply training with them for a week or two occasionally as a means of providing a change of pace for your training.

Except for these two uses, machines have virtually no place in the training program of anyone even remotely serious about effecting noticeable improvement upon their physiques. The fact is, it is virtually impossible to gain substantial muscle mass or strength while training solely on machines. I don't know of any title winning natural bodybuilder or any non-natural title-winning bodybuilder, for that matter, who has developed his physique to that level with anything except a routine based almost exclusively on the use of basic free weight exercises.

There's also the fact that while it is easy to get free weight exercises to conform to your needs, machines are usually built for the average person and are of such rigid structure that you have to conform to them. If you're not of average height and build and are unfortunate enough not to fit a machine perfectly (which is usually the case) you may find the machine putting undue stress on your joints or other areas of your body. This can ultimately result in an injury.

Finally, we have the fact that free weight exercises have the benefit of dramatically improving coordination. This is a result of the fact that you always have to balance and control barbells and dumbbells. Machines, on the other hand, are already set on a specific track which cannot be altered. The

weight is already balanced and controlled for you. You just have to push the weight up. As a result, your coordination is not substantially improved from machine training. The dramatic increase in coordination in all muscle groups provided by free weight training will noticeably improve your performance in any other sport or physical activity. This, of course, is evidenced by the fact that weight training is being used by more and more athletes as a means of improving their performance.

When discussing training with free weights, there are two classes of exercises we must be concerned with. The first of these are basic exercises, otherwise known as compound exercises because they involve the use of more than one muscle group. The second group is isolation exercises, so named because they effectively isolate one particular muscle group.

Basic exercises such as the bench press, squat, overhead press, and bent-over row each work mainly one particular target muscle group. However, they utilize other muscle groups as a means of assisting in their performance. This may, at first, seem to be a negative effect since it would appear that the potential benefit of a basic exercise would be lost due to a diffusion of effort through one or more other muscle groups. An example is the bench press, whose target muscle is the pectorals, but which also involves the deltoids and triceps as assistance muscles necessary for effectively completing the movement. In reality, however, the opposite is true. While the assistance muscle groups are most definitely put under some stress, they are not involved to the point where they are being worked at anywhere near the intensity which would constitute a good workout, except in the case of the novice weight trainer for whom any muscle involvement is considered a maximum stress.

The biceps and triceps are the two most often used and involved assistance muscles, as arm strength is necessary for effectively performing every basic upper body exercise. Since beginners aren't accustomed to using their arms so much they often find that their arms give out on a basic exercise way before the target muscle group is adequately stimulated. However, as they continue training, the arms and other assistance muscle groups will gain an increasing amount of endurance so that within a few months, the target muscle will be receiving most of the stress. Once the assistance muscles gain this endurance and the athlete learns how to perform his basic exercises so he can direct the maximum amount of stress to the target muscle he will find that the only negative effect he will experience in his assistance muscle groups is slight fatigue and at times, according to how heavily he trains, a minimal degree of soreness. This situation is easily compensated for by training assistance muscle groups such as your arms and lower back with slightly less intensity than other muscle groups. In this way, you'll still derive maximum muscle mass gains for the muscle group without risking overtraining.

So now that I've established that there isn't any substantial negative effect on the assistance muscle groups, what exactly is the advantage of doing basic exercises? Simply stated, basic exercises, because of the added strength provided by assistance muscle groups, enable you to train the target muscle group with much heavier weight and therefore generate a much higher level of intensity than you could possibly derive from using isolation exercises. This enables you to stimulate many more muscle fibers including the deep muscle fibers which isolation exercises don't have the capacity to stimulate at all. Because of this, basic exercises are considered to be far superior to isolation exercises for building both muscle mass and strength. This is especially significant to the natural bodybuilder, because of the increased difficulty he has in stimulating increases in both muscle mass and strength in relation to the drug user. If you as a natural bodybuilder ever hope to develop a massive muscular physique capable of competing with the druggies, you must resign yourself to the fact that you will be training almost exclusively with basic exercises for the length of your natural bodybuilding career. This will be the case even before a contest, a time in which almost all druggies switch over almost exclusively to isolation exercises.

Due to conclusive evidence obtained from both research and personal experience, the only way to develop a competitive physique naturally is to train almost exclusively with basic exercises. All natural training routines presented in this book either totally or to a large degree consist of such exercises.

Incidentally, getting back to machines such as Nautilus, one of the reasons they are largely ineffective in providing muscle and strength gains is that they tend to be too isolating in na-

ture and are, therefore, generally equivalent to isolation free weight exercises in benefit. No matter what you see other people doing, resist the temptation to add isolation exercises to the routines presented in this book. All you'll do is waste your energy and dramatically increase your chances of overtraining.

Free weight equipment

As mentioned previously, you will be training almost exclusively with free weights. I therefore feel it is worth including some information on free weight equipment itself. One question that is always asked by beginning bodybuilders is how much the various barbells and dumbbells weigh. Standard solid metal barbells weigh anywhere between 15 and 25 pounds, depending upon their length, which ranges from 4 to 6 feet. So generally, 4-foot bars weigh 15 pounds, 5-foot bars weigh 20 pounds, and 6-foot bars weight 25 pounds. Inside and outside collars generally weigh between one-half and one pound. Metal weights, otherwise known as plates, which fit on barbells and dumbbells vary widely in weight. The weight of a specific plate is normally engraved on its side. Common weights, however, are 1¼, 1½, 2½, 5, 10, 12, 15, 20, 25, 35, and 50 pounds. These plates are always bought by the pound. Standard prices today range in the area of 45 to 60 cents per pound. Standard solid dumbbells generally weigh 5 pounds and standard E-Z curl curling bars generally weigh 25 pounds.[15]

Most well-equipped gyms also have Olympic barbells. These bars are specially machined and are known for being perfectly balanced, easier to control, and smoother in execution of all exercises than standard barbells. Naturally, they are also much more expensive. But they are worth the extra money. These bars are approximately 7 feet in length, and are capable of easily handling weights in excess of 500 pounds. Because of their balance and sturdiness they are particularly useful on such heavy basic exercises as squats and bench presses. These bars are either standardized in pounds or in kilos for use in international competition. Accordingly the unloaded bar weighs either 20 kg. or 45 lbs. The inside collars are already built into the bar. Adjustable outside collars weigh 2½ kg., or 5 lbs.

Common metric plates weigh 1¼,

2½, 5, 7½, 10, 15, and 20 kg. Common nonmetric plates weigh 2½, 5, 10, 25, 35, and 45 lbs.[16]

There are many different pieces of free weight exercise equipment which have been developed with the purpose of enabling weight trainers to better work certain muscle groups.

Here is a list of the most common pieces of equipment, what exercises they are most commonly used for, and which muscle group they are commonly used to aid in developing. If you have never used some of these pieces of equipment and you want to learn how, any knowledgeable gym instructor or serious bodybuilder will be able to show you how to use them correctly.

Much of the equipment listed here is considered essential to substantial bodybuilding progress, most notably flat and incline benches, and a squat rack. Many of the others are extremely valuable, too. However, there are a few (the best example being the cable crossover machine) which have absolutely no place in the training program of anyone but the most advanced natural bodybuilders, and then only for a few weeks before a contest. Cable crossovers are the perfect example of an isolation exercise and as such are of no value when it comes to developing muscle mass.

Importance of a training diary

It is my belief that everyone who is serious about their natural bodybuilding training should keep some sort of record of both their daily workouts and of other factors and events pertinent to monitoring their progress and furthering their bodybuilding careers. The diary should contain a daily comprehensive report of your workouts, the number of exercises, sets and reps done for each body part, as well as an assessment of how well the muscles responded. Energy levels should be included, along with any changes in training methods and diet. Furthermore, a training diary can be used to record your progress. Every few months, you should measure your arms, legs, and chest to see if you have had an increase. While these measurements are useful for finding out about muscle growth, it will also measure gains in fat.

Equipment	Muscle Group Trained	Exercises
1. Flat bench	Pectorals	Dumbbell and barbell bench presses
2. Incline bench	Upper pectorals	Incline dumbbell & barbell bench press
3. Decline bench	Lower pectorals	Decline dumbbell & bench press
4. Seated press behind neck bench	Deltoids	Seated barbell press behind neck & seated barbell front press
5. Lat pulldown machine	Latissimus dorsi	Lat pulldowns behind & in front of neck
6. Long range cable row machine	Latissimus dorsi	Cable rows
7. Cable crossover machine	Pectorals, rear delts	Cable crossovers, bent-over cable laterals
8. Preacher curl bench	Biceps	Preacher curls
9. Dipping bars	Triceps & chest	Dips
10. Tricep cable pressdown	Triceps	Tricep pressdowns
11. Chinning bar	Latissimus dorsi	Close grip & wide grip chins
12. Triceps bomber	Triceps	Standing & lying tricep extensions
13. Power rack	All major muscle groups	Squats, deadlifts, presses over head, bench presses, clean & jerk, snatch
14. Squat rack	Quadriceps & deltoids	Squats & overhead presses
15. Smith machine	Deltoids	Military press & press behind neck
16. Leg extension machine	Quadriceps	Leg extensions
17. Leg curl machine	Hamstrings	Leg curls
18. Standing calf raise	Calves— gastrocnemius muscle	Standing calf raises
19. Seated calf raise	Calves— soleus muscle	Seated calf raises
20. One-legged leg curl	Hamstrings	One-legged leg curls
21. T-bar row	Lower lats	T-bar rows
22. Lying leg press	Quadriceps	Leg presses
23. Hack squat	Quadriceps	Hack squats
24. Roman chair	Lower back, abdominals	Hyperextensions, Roman chair situps
25. Incline situp boards	Abdominals	Incline situps & leg raises

Injury prevention—safety precautions

During the course of his bodybuilding career almost every natural bodybuilder suffers at least one injury of some sort. Injuries can range in severity from a muscle strain whose only deleterious effect might be hindering your training for a couple of days to a herniated disc which could end your natural bodybuilding career. Almost all bodybuilding injuries are a result of carelessness, a miscalculation of ability to handle a heavy weight, or simply pushing too hard when you shouldn't. The following are safety precautions, which, if always taken, should practically eliminate your chances of incurring an injury.

The first precaution involves making sure you always wear a weightlifting belt when performing any exercise which puts any pressure whatsoever on your lower back, even when using light weights. The lower back is the weakest link in the human skeletal structure. It's exceedingly easy to injure, and once you do injure it, you'll be severely limited when it comes to training with heavy weight on practically every exercise, particularly squats and bent-over rows. Always remember that unless you're able to train with relatively heavy weights on the basic exercises, you'll never be able to develop your physique to its fullest natural potential. So protect your lower back at all costs, and make wearing a lifting belt a steady habit.

Secondly, and of equal importance, is to thoroughly warm up your entire body in general and the muscle group or groups you plan on training during a particular workout before training heavy. Such a thorough warmup will practically eliminate your chances of incurring an injury while training. This is particularly true when it comes to muscle strains, tears, or pulls.

The third precaution involves always making sure you have someone spotting you when you train heavy. Every so often the best of us make a miscalculation and put more weight on the bar than we can handle for the prescribed number of repetitions we are shooting for. Without a spotter, you can get pinned under the barbell. This can be especially dangerous on exercises such as squats and especially bench presses. There are quite a large number of documented cases of people dying as a result of being pinned under a heavy bench press. Having a spotter who knows when to lend a hand will virtually eliminate any danger of being pinned under a heavy weight. With the worry of being pinned removed, you can train with heavier weights than you would normally be willing to risk while training on your own. So be safe and make sure you don't train heavy without a spotter.

Another precaution involves the use of adjustable collars. During the course of a set of an exercise it is not uncommon for the bar you are using to tilt slightly to one side. This is an especially common occurrence for beginners because they have not yet developed the coordination necessary to perform their exercises in a smooth and controlled manner. Another common cause of uneven lifting is that most people have one arm stronger than the other, usually according to whether they are right- or left-handed. It often takes a few months for your weak arm to approximately match the stronger one in strength, and until that time you can have all kinds of problems keeping your arms even and the bar balanced while performing upper body exercises. Besides this, many lifters have been known to tilt to one side or the other without realizing it while performing such exercises as squats.

The result of all this uneven lifting is that the weights can go sliding off one end of the bar in the middle of a set unless you have outer adjustable collars locked tightly in place. This can be disastrous. When the plates slide off one end of a bar, the dramatic imbalance created by the weight still on the other side of the bar will cause a tremendous jolt on the now-empty side of the bar, pulling it from your grasp. According to how heavy the weight is, the heavy side will either collapse on top of you or slide off as a result of the lighter side being pulled up into the air. This will cause another severe jolt on your muscles and joints. Either way, you are risking severe injury by not using outer adjustable collars in exercises in which you don't have 100 percent control. Even on those you can normally control, you never know when you might make a miscalculation or get careless and suffer such an experience. I therefore suggest that you always use outer collars when going heavy on any exercise. Also, for those of you who use adjustable dumbbells, always securely tighten and double check the outside dumbbell collars, to prevent a similar experience from occurring on your dumbbell exercises.

In relation to keeping the bar as balanced as possible, it is always a good idea to double check both sides of a barbell and both dumbbells to make sure that the weight on both sides is exactly even. It's not uncommon to accidentally put a 10-lb. plate on one side of a bar, thinking it was a 5-lb. plate, or to add weight to one side of a bar and simply forget to add it to the other. This can be more dangerous than one might think. Even a difference of only 2½ or 5 lbs. can create a significant imbalance capable of totally throwing off your form and putting enough uneven pressure on certain muscles or joints so you can be severely injured. And, of course, if you don't have outside collars on, the weights can go flying and then you're really in trouble.

Never using more weight than you can safely control was already discussed in detail. Remember that if you can't control a weight, it will control you. Training with ridiculously heavy weight far beyond your capacity, besides providing absolutely no benefit, puts tremendous strain on your tendons, ligaments, and joints and is one of the surest ways of suffering a severe injury.

Finally, it is not advisable to train when you are overtired or unusually fatigued. Safe and effective training requires a high level of concentration. If you're so tired that you can't maintain that concentration, you greatly increase your chances of suffering an injury, while simultaneously diminishing the benefit you can receive from your workout. Good workouts don't just happen, you have to make them happen, and that takes conscious effort which a tired mind cannot generate.

Breathing patterns

Most beginning bodybuilders are concerned with how they should breathe while performing their training routine. Normally you should breathe in while lowering the weight on each repetition of an exercise and breathe out while raising the weight. You'll probably find yourself exhaling the most air at the point of greatest exertion, and you may find that this actually makes you feel stronger while pushing up the weight. Often one breath per repetition is not enough, especially on strong oxygen-depleting exercises such as squats. In such instances you'll find yourself unconsciously establishing a compensatory breathing pattern which will enable you to obtain all the oxygen you need. Between sets it is a good idea to take a few deep breaths as a means of facilitating the intake of oxygen and normalizing the somewhat heavy breathing you will experience after each set.

Under no circumstances should you ever hold your breath at any time during the performance of an exercise. Doing so will build up intrathoracic pressure. This will substantially reduce the blood flow to and from your brain, ultimately causing you to faint. Technically, this is called the vasalva effect. If you black out while doing a heavy bench press you could conceivably be killed as the bar crashes downward.[17] So always make sure you breathe regularly on all your exercises. Since there's always the possibility that you still may unconsciously hold your breath while concentrating on lifting a very heavy weight, it's a good idea to enlist a spotter for such situations as well as for those discussed previously.

5

FUNDAMENTALS OF NATURAL BODYBUILDING

Physiology of muscle growth and training

Before we get involved with the particulars of natural bodybuilding training, it is important that we first know what makes a muscle grow. This will help to clarify the reasoning behind the training program and principles.

Contrary to the predominant belief of a few years ago that muscle cells and fibers increased in number in response to physical stress put upon them (thus accounting for increases in muscle size), it has now come to be generally accepted by physiologists and bodybuilders alike that the individual muscle cells and fibers themselves increase in mass and size in a process known as muscle hypertrophy[1] and this accounts for muscle growth.

It is a physiological fact that strength and muscle size can be increased only by the muscle contracting against a resistance that calls forth effort. In general, the degree of increase depends upon the degree of resistance. Muscles are extremely adaptable to the stress put upon them. As a result, you will have to progressively increase the resistance placed upon your muscles as you continue to train in order to register continued increases in both muscle size and strength. This is known as the overload principle.[2] The most effective way of implementing it is with progressive resistance training.

There are numerous ways of progressively increasing the intensity of effort applied to a particular muscle. The best way is to continue adding weight to your exercises. Since the strength of a muscle is roughly proportional to its physiological cross-sectional area, the larger the muscle, the stronger the muscle, all other things being equal, and vice versa. So if you continue to progressively increase your muscle strength on all your exercises, it follows that you should ultimately gain muscle size. Another benefit of continuously striving to increase the weights on all your exercises for the prescribed number of repetitions involves the fact that individual muscle fibers either contract

to their fullest capacity or they don't contract at all.[3] It's all or nothing; there's no in between. Therefore, when a muscle composed of many fibers contracts against a light weight, only a few of the fibers are called into play. However, a maximum weight requires that all available fibers contract. Consequently, more of the muscle is exercised and muscle hypertrophy takes place more rapidly.

Other ways of increasing intensity include increasing the number of repetitions done with a particular weight, taking less rest between sets, doing forced reps (an advanced training principle which will be discussed later on), or combining any two of these methods or more for a real intensity shock. All of these intensity boosters will be discussed in detail later on.

It is the emphasis placed on gaining strength as a means of gaining muscle that causes many bodybuilders to become overly concerned with using exceedingly heavy weights. They think that if they can't bench 300 lbs. or squat 500 lbs., they'll never get big, and they'll often struggle with weights which are so far beyond their strength capacity that they perform the exercise with terrible form. As a result, they derive no benefit from it while simultaneously risking injury. This is totally unnecessary, not to mention counterproductive and dangerous. The amount of weight against which the muscle works is of absolutely no consequence as long as the resistance or load is sufficient to make the muscle exert maximum tension.[4] In other words, if you are benching only 200 lbs. for six reps and someone else can bench 300 lbs. for six reps, and you're both using the maximum amount of weight you can handle in good form, you will both derive the same maximum benefit from the weight you are using. Some people don't have the capacity to be as strong as others due to such factors as a weak bone structure or disadvantageous leverage, but as long as you use a weight which is heavy for you—no matter how light it is to someone else—you will stimulate maximum muscle growth. Just train sensibly and don't let your ego rule you. Remember, you're a bodybuilder, not a powerlifter. Throwing around heavy weights as a means of impressing your peers has no place in the training regimen of a serious natural bodybuilder.

One thing you will never want to do is attempt to increase the intensity of your training by adding large numbers of extra sets to your training program.

Doing this will actually have the effect of lowering intensity. As I will soon demonstrate, muscles can exert maximum contractile force for only very brief periods of time. Therefore, if you hit your muscles with maximum intensity they will quickly become exhausted, within the space of a few sets. Since short, maximally intense workouts have been shown to promote stimulation of the maximum amount of muscle fibers possible, this type of training is most productive for maximizing increases in muscle mass and strength.

If you start adding extra sets to your routine, above the minimum number necessary to work a muscle with maximum intensity, you will have to reduce the overall level of intensity generated on each set if you hope to complete the additional sets. While a couple of extra sets are often necessary to work a muscle thoroughly because it is virtually impossible to generate top muscular intensity on each set, and you need a couple sets to warm up, doing an excessive number of sets is totally nonproductive, and in the case of the natural bodybuilder, counterproductive. Doing so many sets (generally more than 12 on large muscle groups and more than 8 on small muscle groups) for advanced natural bodybuilders, forces you to reduce the level of intensity generated on each set to a point where the number of muscle fibers stimulated to contract on each set is so low that it is inadequate for the purpose of stimulating muscle growth. Besides this, doing so many sets puts an enormous stress on your energy reserves and recuperative ability. Keeping this in mind, stick to the training routines outlined in this book and resist the temptation to do more than necessary for maximum results. More isn't always better, and nowhere is this more true than in terms of natural bodybuilding training.

After taking all this time to emphasize the importance of generating maximum intensity, I must warn you just as vehemently against training with maximum intensity too often. Training intensity puts a tremendous amount of stress on the body. After being throroughly worked, it takes between 72 and 96 hours for the muscles to recover fully, depending upon the individual. As previously discussed, the muscles of steroid users generally recover faster than those of naturals because of the effects of the drugs, often in as little as 48 hours. After the muscles are fully recovered they can be trained again. However, they cannot handle the stress of being trained to exhaustion every workout. They will eventually lose the ability to recover from the consistent brutal beatings and they will either stop growing or actually lose mass. Also, the stress that maximally intense training places on both the nervous system and the body's energy reserves will, if carried on too long, lead to a state of total physical exhaustion. It is also impossible to sustain the mental energy necessary to generate this type of intensity for any length of time. If you persist in doing so, you will lose enthusiasm for your training and ultimately suffer total mental burnout as well. All of these negative effects are symptoms of the condition known as overtraining, the condition most responsible for hindering natural bodybuilding progress and causing sticking points.

For the steroid user the threat of overtraining is always present, but for the natural bodybuilder it is practically a curse. It is so easy to overtrain and unless you learn how to prevent it from plaguing you, you will never achieve your ultimate natural bodybuilding potential. Steroids provide a big cushion against overtraining, but as natural bodybuilders we do not have that cushion, so we have to take every precaution possible to prevent it.

For now, let me just say that while you will always be striving to increase the level of intensity generated in your workouts, you will be performing the majority of your workouts at somewhat less than 100 percent intensity. While workouts of maximum intensity must be performed on a consistent basis, they must be performed rather infrequently and at carefully chosen times for maximum results. All the particulars involved in making the proper choice of when to train hard and when to train easy will be discussed at each level of training. No matter what, always remember that it's much safer and often beneficial to undertrain than it is to overtrain.

Basic terminology

To derive maximum benefit from this book, it is essential that you be familiar with the following basic terminology:

An exercise is an individual movement performed while training (examples: bench press, barbell curls, etc.). A rep or repetition is the count of the exercise. A set is a number of reps. Several sets are the given training program.[5]

Number of sets per body part

At the beginner level of training the number of sets you will be performing for each body part will be low enough so you'll be able to train your entire body in one session without becoming overly fatigued. Your basic routine will consist of three sets of one basic exercise for each of what are termed major muscle groups. These muscle groups are so named because they are the largest muscle groups in the body.

The pectorals, latissimus dorsi, trapezius, deltoids, and quadriceps are major muscle groups. You will also be performing two sets of one exercise for each of the smaller muscle groups, namely the biceps, forearms, triceps, abdominals, and hamstrings. Because these muscle groups have less muscle tissue than the major muscle groups, hitting them with an equivalent workout is not of maximum effectiveness. They simply cannot handle such a workload without eventually becoming chronically overtrained. Although calves cannot really be considered a major muscle group because they are made up of extremely dense muscle tissue and are used every day to assist with walking, they can handle a more intense workout than most small muscle groups. Because of this and the fact that the calves tend to be the most neglected body part (and therefore lag behind the rest of the physique), I suggest that you hit them with three sets.

Abdominals and forearms also seem to be able to handle a disproportionately high workload in relation to their size because of the fact that they are used more than most other muscle groups. The abdominals are always in a semicontracted state since they have to hold in the internal organs and your forearm muscles constantly assist your hands and fingers in the performance of a variety of activities. Despite the fact that these muscle groups can handle a disproportionately high workload, they are so much smaller than the other small muscle groups that in actuality they can't handle any more sets than these muscles. I suggest you just train them with two sets. Abdominals, forearms, and calves differ in training from the other muscle groups more in terms of the number of repetitions they best respond to than in terms of the number of sets they can handle.

If you jump right in and train your muscle groups with two or three sets on the very first day, they will become extremely sore for several days. To avoid

this it is best to use at least a four- to eight-week break-in program and a longer one if necessary.

During the first two or three weeks it is advisable to train every muscle group with only one set and with very light weights. Between the third and fifth week, according to how you feel, you should increase the number of sets done for the major muscle groups from one to two. Keep doing only one set for the smaller muscle groups. After six to eight weeks you should be able to handle the two or three sets per muscle group which constitutes the full basic beginning routine.

According to how quickly you are able to progress, you will remain in the beginning phase of natural bodybuilding training for six to eight months.

The specific pattern of adding additional sets will be outlined throughout each level of training. You should perform the basic training routine for a solid two months to ten weeks before you add any additional sets. The reason for this is as follows.

As you'll remember when you started, you went from doing nothing to doing two to three sets per muscle group in the space of a two-month period. Although that increase in workload can be considered quite gradual, the fact is that the increase from nothing to two to three sets is itself quite dramatic. This dramatic increase in workload puts a tremendous amount of stress on the body. It takes the body a considerable length of time to fully adapt to this stress. This is especially true when you consider that training with weights is an entirely new experience for all the body's systems to cope with. Allowing a solid two months on the basic beginners program before further increasing the amount of the workload will give your body sufficient time to fully adapt to and absorb all the physical stress which was put on both your body's systems and the muscles themselves during that initial two-month break-in period.

Your initial increase in workload above and beyond the basic program will occur approximately 4 months after you first begin training and should consist of an increase of one set on every exercise except those for abdominals and forearms. In other words, you will now be performing four sets of one basic exercise for each of the major muscle groups and three sets of one basic exercise for each of the smaller muscle groups. At this time you will be in the advanced beginner phase of training. An excellent way of introducing this increase in workload without threatening your body's adaptive capability is to spend two to three weeks taking turns between doing two to three sets per muscle group and doing three to four sets per muscle group. After this two- to three-week period, you can just continue doing the additional set for each muscle group. This pattern can be used each time you add additional sets to your routine. At this level you should still be able to work every muscle group in one day. However, the next increase in sets (about two to three months after this, which will qualify you as an intermediate natural bodybuilder) will require your splitting your workout into two parts to perform most effectively.

How long to rest between sets

The length of time you rest between sets is crucial. If you move from set to set too quickly you will have a hard time catching your breath. Also, your muscles will not recover sufficiently from the previous set to enable you to handle anywhere near the training poundages necessary to stimulate the deep muscle fibers and produce maximum muscle growth. You simply need to allow sufficient time for enough of the waste products, especially lactic acid, to be removed from the muscle after each set so the as yet unused muscle fibers can generate enough force to contract with maximum efficiency. If you don't allow this time, you'll find your exercise poundages taking a steep drop and, as already discussed, it's virtually impossible to stimulate the deep muscle fibers with light weights.

The other problem, of course, involves taking too long a rest. Taking too long a rest gives some of the muscle fibers which have already contracted during previous sets too much of an opportunity to recover. The result of this is that when you perform your next set, you will be restimulating some of these previously used fibers. As a result you will not be recruiting near as many fresh muscle fibers as you would have had you taken a shorter rest. Also, resting too long increases the risk of injury because the body has too much of an opportunity to cool down. Besides this, too much of a rest between sets will dramatically hamper your ability to attain a deep growth-producing pump in the muscle being worked. The term "pump" is used to describe the process by which a particular muscle be-

comes increasingly gorged with oxygen and nutrient-rich blood during the time it is being trained. During the beginning phase of training most individuals do not have sufficient muscle mass, nor can they work the muscle thoroughly enough to experience a pumped feeling in the muscles. It is, therefore, not of much concern to the beginner. However, during the intermediate and advanced phases of training the consistent achievement of a full pump becomes extremely important for a variety of reasons which will be discussed in detail in the section on intermediate training. Resting too long between sets has a detrimental effect as you strive to reach increasing levels of development for all of these reasons.

So exactly how long should you rest between sets? Many bodybuilding books consider 60 to 90 seconds to be the optimum rest period between sets. But my experience has shown this to be an insufficient length of time for sufficient waste products to be removed from the largest muscles when training in a manner most conducive to stimulating the deep fibers during the beginning level of training. In order to stimulate these deep fibers you have to train with relatively heavy weights. After performing a heavy basic exercise for one of the major muscle groups, such as squats for the quadriceps or bent-over rows for the lats, you'll need a solid 100 to 120 seconds both to regain your breath sufficiently and remove enough lactic acid to get the most out of your next set. In most cases, you'll probably require the two minutes. Generally, I've found that the smaller the muscle group, the less rest required between sets. This is true because it is easier to remove waste products from a smaller muscle group than from a larger one, and because training a smaller muscle group puts less stress on the body as a whole. As already mentioned, 90 to 120 seconds between sets is optimum rest when performing basic exercises for the two largest muscle groups in the body, the lats and the quadriceps. Slightly smaller muscle groups such as the pectorals, trapezius, and deltoids respond best to approximately a 100-second rest between sets. Small muscle groups such as the biceps, triceps, hamstrings, and calves respond best to approximately an 80- to 90-second rest between sets, and the smallest muscle groups, the forearms and abdominals, seem to respond best to a 60-second rest. Wearing a watch, preferably a stopwatch, while you train is a good idea so you can tell exactly

how long you are resting between sets. Eventually, you'll be able to tell by the way the muscles feel, when it's time to do the next one.

Workouts per week

I've already mentioned that you will be training your entire body in one day during the length of time for which you are a beginner bodybuilder. Now it's time to discuss exactly how many times per week you should be performing your beginner's workout for maximum benefit. It takes anywhere between 48 and 96 hours for a muscle group to recover from a workout, depending upon both your natural recovery ability and the intensity with which you train during a particular workout.

For a number of reasons including an inability to generate maximum neuromuscular control over a working muscle, and general unfamiliarity with the biomechanics of weight training, beginners are unable to stress their muscles to near the degree that experienced natural bodybuilders are able to. The inability to train with any real degree of intensity makes it appear that the muscles of beginning natural bodybuilders would be able to recover more quickly than those of more advanced athletes. This is apparently the reason why virtually every bodybuilding book and magazine on the market recommends that beginners train their entire body on three nonconsecutive days of each week such as Monday, Wednesday, and Friday.

What these sources of information fail to consider is the fact that while beginning weight trainers cannot train with much intensity, they also are unable to cope with the stress weight training puts on their body, mind, and particularly their muscles with anywhere near the efficiency of an experienced weight trainer. Another point is that virtually every book or article which covers beginning weight training (and all other aspects of the sport for that matter) is written by individuals who are either using or have used steroids. This is almost assuredly another reason why the three nonconsecutive days a week routine is so universally recommended. These authors appear to write from the perspective of the increased recuperative abilities they received from using anabolic aids. They seem to forget that the vast majority of beginners do not use steroids. Unfortunately, some of them do, but that is the exception rather than the rule.

Conversations with other natural bodybuilders combined with my own personal experience have absolutely convinced me that there is no way a natural bodybuilder at any level can recover fully from hard workouts on a consistent basis in anything less than 72 hours. Consistently training on 48 hours' rest, even at the beginner's level, will lead quickly to overtraining. I therefore suggest that beginners perform their basic natural bodybuilding workouts once every three days on a consistent basis for maximum benefit. An example of this involves doing your first workout on a Monday, the next on Thursday, then Sunday, the following Wednesday, then Saturday, etc. The schedule will rotate so that you'll be doing each workout on a different day for a period of three weeks. So if you do your first workout on a Monday, you will not train on a Monday again until the beginning of the fourth week. You will find it unnecessary to take a 96-hour rest between workouts until at least the intermediate level of training.

Number of repetitions

The number of repetitions you perform on each one of your exercises depends on which body part you are training and what you are specifically trying to accomplish with your training. In general, low repetitions, anywhere between one and four per set, are used for the purpose of building maximum strength. For natural bodybuilders attempting to gain maximum muscle mass, the average range of repetitions will be between six and ten. Certain muscle groups such as the pectorals, deltoids, biceps, and triceps seem to respond best to repetitions in the range of six to eight. The largest muscle groups, namely the latissimus dorsi, trapezius, and quadriceps seem to respond best to repetitions in the range of eight to ten. Although not a particularly large muscle group, the hamstrings also respond best to 8 to 10 reps. In general, the legs respond better to higher repetitions than the muscle groups of the upper body. This is probably due to the fact that they are already used a great deal for just getting us around on a daily basis. Last but not least, we come to the calves, forearms, and abdominals. As I already mentioned, these muscle groups are made up of extremely dense muscle tissue compared to the muscle groups of the rest of the body. Because they are constantly being used they have a much higher percentage of red fibers (those used for endurance) than

the other muscle groups. As a result, they thrive on high repetition training. This is especially true of the abdominals which I've found respond best to repetitions in the range of 20 to 40. Calves and forearms respond best to a repetition range of between 10 and 20 per set.

Remember, these repetition ranges are the most productive for the natural bodybuilder in terms of building solid muscle mass. They will apply for your entire natural bodybuilding career after the beginning phase. Although the repetition ranges presented here are optimum for gaining muscle naturally, it's a good idea to do slightly higher or lower repetitions from time to time for a change of pace and as a means of shocking the muscles into new growth. The same thing is applicable to the number of sets done for each muscle group at both the intermediate and advanced levels. This principle will be discussed in detail later. Always remember that the muscles respond best to variety. The ways to vary your workout as a means of increasing their productivity will be covered in the sections on intermediate and advanced training at the time they are most applicable.

During the beginning phase perform the routines exactly as they are outlined. When you first begin training it is best to use slightly higher repetitions on all your exercises than you will eventually perform to gain maximum muscle mass. The reason for this is twofold. First is the fact that training with high reps for the first couple of months will work the muscles thoroughly while simultaneously increasing their endurance and conditioning the body as a whole. This is important since a high level of muscular endurance is essential for sustaining the force necessary to lock out a heavy weight. Once you have laid this foundation, performing the lower range of repetitions will maintain the muscular endurance you have developed. The second reason for doing higher than normal repetitions with the reduced poundages necessary to allow completion of these reps is that starting off with lower reps and the heavier weights necessary to make the reps productive greatly increases the risk of injury. You have to remember that the muscles, tendons, and ligaments of the beginner do not have the strength and coordination necessary to lift heavier weights for less than ten reps without dramatically increasing the risk of suffering some type of pull or tear. A couple months of high rep training will gradually accustom these tissues to the

stress of weight training and ultimately strengthen them to the point where they can handle heavier weights and lower reps safely. At the advanced beginner level, you will begin to work with heavier weights and lower reps. So my actual recommendation is to perform 12 reps on the basic exercises for the latissimus dorsi, trapezius, quadriceps, and hamstrings; 10 reps on those for the pectorals, deltoids, biceps and triceps; 20 reps on the forearm and calf exercises, and as many reps as you can do on each set of abdominal exercises up to 50 for the first couple of months during this break-in phase.

One thing that should be discussed briefly here about repetitions is the belief of most competitive bodybuilders that doing high repetitions with lighter weights during precontest training will enhance muscular definition and detail. This statement holds a certain degree of truth. However, the real key to becoming super muscular and defined is to follow an intelligent precontest diet which slowly strips away all the subcutaneous fat. What the proponents of such a high repetition scheme fail to realize is that training with very high reps (an average of five reps higher than the number recommended for each muscle group for maximum growth) for any length of time at the intermediate level and above does not allow you to stimulate the deep muscle fibers that you have previously developed with heavy training. The result in the case of the natural bodybuilder is that these deeper fibers begin to atrophy and lose mass. After only two to three weeks such training can create a marked loss in muscle size, and appreciable muscle mass is one thing a natural bodybuilder cannot afford to lose at any time, especially before a contest. I obviously never recommend that a natural bodybuilder, especially a competitive one, train with high reps for any length of time. The only ones who can get away with this type of training are, of course, the drug users. Steroids enable an individual to hold practically all of his muscle mass while training in such a manner.

Finally, I should mention that there are various repetition schemes which will be outlined at the appropriate time in this book. For now, try to perform the prescribed number of reps suggested for each exercise on every set of that exercise. At first you probably won't have the necessary endurance to do this, and the number of reps you will be able to do with the same weight will decrease on each succeeding set. If this happens, don't worry about it. Your endurance will improve dramatically as you continue to train.

Training poundages

Strength levels vary dramatically from individual to individual so it's almost impossible to suggest an optimum initial weight to use on each exercise of the beginner's routine. What I will do along with the actual routine is suggest beginning training poundages for each exercise in terms of a percentage of your own body weight. This will give you a basic guideline to follow. However, since these percentages are based on average strength levels for men and women, you will find that many of them aren't applicable to your own case as you'll tend to be either stronger or weaker than average on most exercises. For whichever exercises this proves to be the case, just raise or lower the weight accordingly over the next couple of workouts until you find the weight which feels most comfortable to you. Always remember that at the beginning level, a set done with the correct training poundage should be comfortably difficult to complete. If you must strain to complete it, or if you are unable to complete the assigned number of repetitions, the weight should be reduced accordingly.[6]

During the more advanced levels of training it will be beneficial to occasionally use a weight which provides great difficulty in completing a set, but that will be discussed at the time it is applicable. Of course, it goes without saying that if the weight is too light it should be raised accordingly. After you have been training for a month or two you will easily be able to determine your own training weights. Incidentally, when using the percentage of body weight to calculate your initial suggested training poundages, you may come up with a poundage which is not a multiple of 5, such as 57 lbs. In such a case, reduce the poundage to the next lowest multiple of 5, in this case 55 lbs.[7]

As I discussed, it will take approximately a two-month break-in period before you can handle the workload of the full beginner's program. This is true of how quickly you can handle maximum weights for the number of repetitions suggested in this program as well as for the number of sets. The rule that you should use a weight which makes a set comfortably difficult to complete applies to the full beginner's program

and also to the last few weeks of the break-in period. You will find that your strength increases rapidly during the first few weeks of training. However, if you either add weight too quickly in an effort to match this quick gain in strength or if you train with weights which give you trouble for the last couple reps of a set more than once in a while during this break-in period, your muscles will become painfully sore for a number of days. Working into the routine slowly will ensure that you experience only the mildest form of muscle soreness possible.

Exercise cadence

Exercise cadence is the rate at which you raise and lower the weight on each rep of your exercises. Raising or lowering a weight too quickly will not stimulate near the maximum amount of muscle fibers that performing your reps at a slower rate will. Raising or lowering a weight too slowly will not allow the muscles to contract with the intensity necessary to lift a heavy weight and, as a result, the deep muscle fibers will not be stimulated. You will be forced to use very light weights, and the surface muscle fibers can easily become overtrained as a result of having to sustain tension against the weight for prolonged periods of time. Lowering your weights too slowly is a form of negative resistance training, a type of training which has been found to be particularly stressful to the muscles. Negative resistance training can be very productive when used for short duration by advanced bodybuilders, who have the capacity to handle the stress it puts on the muscles. However, beginning and intermediate natural bodybuilders do not have the capacity to handle and effectively utilize such training.

The most beneficial exercise cadence for natural bodybuilders at any level involves taking approximately one second to raise the weight and another one or two seconds to lower it. The exact speed will depend on what feels best for you, but be sure to stay within these strict guidelines. After a few weeks of training you should develop a certain rhythm when performing your reps, a sort of groove. When performing your sets it is also a good idea to pause for a split second at the top and bottom of each rep. This enables you to better control the weight you are using and prevents you from using the momentum generated by the previous repetition to help you perform the following one.

Exercise form

The form you use while performing each exercise will determine how much of the resistance is actually directed to the muscles you are trying to work and how much of the effort is diffused through and absorbed by assistance muscle groups. Using sloppy exercise form will deprive the target muscle of much of the resistance it should receive. By using correct form, you transfer maximum resistance to the muscles intended to be stressed by any bodybuilding movement. Do not allow your knees to jerk, your back to bend unnecessarily, or your body to sway back and forth during the performance of any exercise. Such extraneous motion is referred to as cheating, and it robs the muscles of the benefits they should be receiving from an exercise.[8] Sloppy exercise technique will also increase your chances of suffering an injury while training. Concentrate on performing exercises exactly as described. It is extremely important to perform each repetition with the fullest range of motion possible on any given exercise. Doing anything less than full range will eventually result in the muscles becoming tight and inflexible, and the muscles themselves can actually suffer a reduced range of motion. Since the muscles tend to become somewhat tight no matter what, it is an excellent idea to do some stretching.

Warming up

Doing a proper warmup before beginning your workout provides many valuable benefits for natural bodybuilders at all levels of training. Some of them include helping to prevent training injuries, greatly improving neuromuscular coordination, and preparing the muscles to handle heavy weights. A good warmup also increases the heart rate and improves circulation. Besides this, it has been proven scientifically that warm muscles are significantly stronger than cold muscles.[9] A thorough warmup can be done in 10 to 15 minutes. If you aren't willing to invest this short amount of time, sooner or later you will suffer some kind of injury, most likely a severe one.

Your warmup should consist of a few minutes of aerobic activity both to stimulate circulation and get the muscles warm, a few minutes of stretching, and a light set or two on each of the exercises constituting your training routine.

During the first few weeks of the break-in period you will be training with light enough weight on your exercises that the one or two sets you will be performing of each will double as a warmup while still stimulating muscle growth. Once you get to the point where you are performing three or more sets of each exercise, it is strongly suggested that you use very light weight on your first set (50 to 60 percent of the heaviest weight you can handle for 10 reps). You should then add weight on each additional set until you are training with maximum weights by the third or fourth set. Make sure the increases in weight are relatively equal from set to set, as the muscles are able to handle such increases much better than if you add a large percentage of weight one set, and a small percentage of weight on another.

There are a variety of aerobic exercises and stretching exercises which you can perform as a means of warming up thoroughly. Jogging in place, jumping jacks, and squat thrusts are examples of excellent aerobic activities. Hamstring stretches, calf stretches, shoulder stretches, and hurdler's stretches are all excellent stretching exercises. Regular stretching keeps the muscles flexible, and flexible muscles are much more resistant to pulling or tearing under the stress of heavy weights than inflexible ones. It is especially important to keep both the lower back muscles and hamstrings as flexible as possible because of the high susceptibility of the lower back to sustaining injury.

Logical progression of muscle groups

The following training routines have been carefully organized so you will be able to train your body in the most productive way, with the least detrimental effects to the muscle groups.

The first muscle group you will train during your beginner's routine is the pectorals. The reason for this is that it's almost impossible to use sufficient amounts of weight on the bench press unless all the assistance muscle groups—the lats, delts, and triceps—are completely fresh. Training any one of these muscle groups before benching will result in a significant drop in exercise poundage. Because of their deep involvement in almost all chest exercises, I consider it best to train the deltoids next. After chest training they will be warmed up and perfectly primed to train, and it doesn't make sense to let

them cool down and then have to warm them up again later. Also, the deltoids combined with the shoulder joint are more vulnerable to injury than almost any other area except for the lower back, and this makes it especially wise to train them immediately after the pecs and take advantage of the fantastic warmup pec training affords them. Since the delts are involved so much in pec training, you do not have to train them with as heavy weights to stimulate maximum muscle growth as you would if you trained them separately. This is important because the ability to handle respectable weights on your shoulder presses will be limited anyway by the loss of strength in your triceps, which also comes as a result of their heavy involvement in benching. Normally a significant reduction in tricep strength would result in your having a less than optimally productive delt workout. But since benching tires and works the delts as much as it does the triceps, the reduction in capacity of the delts to handle relatively heavy weights will be equal to that which your tired triceps can no longer handle. In other words, your reduced tricep strength will not affect you detrimentally because they will have the strength to handle the reduced poundages which your tired delts can handle, and which will still provide maximum muscle growth stimulation for them.

Pec and delt training involves the latissimus dorsi and the trapezius to a certain degree so it makes sense to work these two muscle groups next. The lats, like the pecs, require a large degree of assistance from other muscle groups in order to enable them to lift the weights necessary to stimulate maximum muscle growth. The primary assistance muscle group which aids the lats in lifting weight is the biceps, which are heavily involved in all lat exercises. The rear delt, triceps, trapezius, and the smaller muscles of the upper back, the rhomboids and infraspinatus, also provide assistance. All these muscle groups, especially the biceps, must be as fresh as possible before undertaking lat training. Since the traps are needed to assist the lats in lifting heavy, and training the traps also involves the biceps to a certain degree, it simply does not make sense to train the traps before the lats. So hit the lats first.

It's interesting to note that although the traps are a slightly larger muscle group than the lats they actually require much less help from assistance muscles

than the lats when it comes to training them effectively. Shoulder shrugs are the exercise of choice, when training the traps as a beginner and, in fact, throughout your natural bodybuilding career, because they enable you to train the traps with heavy poundages while only involving the major assistance muscles to trap training, the biceps, to an almost insignificant degree. Training the pecs, delts, lats, and traps in this order will, as I've just outlined, provide maximum benefit for each one of these individual muscle groups while leaving the entire torso feeling full, tight, and thoroughly worked.

After training the torso you will proceed to train the three major muscle groups of the arms, the biceps, forearms and triceps, in that order. The first thing that should be explained is why I recommend not training the triceps immediately after the pecs and delts when they are already thoroughly warmed up. There are two good reasons for this. First, they are one of the assistance muscle groups necessary for training the lats, and although they aren't involved to the extent that the biceps are, I guarantee you the training poundages you can use for your lat training will take a noticeable drop if you train triceps first. The second and most important reason involves the fact that most tricep exercises place undue stress on the elbow joints. Training the triceps after the elbows are thoroughly warmed up from bicep and forearm training practically eliminates any chances of suffering injury to the elbow joint and surrounding tendons and ligaments. The pumped biceps and forearms act as a sort of cushion when lowering the weight, reducing the stress on the area even more.

The biceps should be trained before the forearms both because training forearms first reduces the effectiveness with which you can train your biceps and because training the back muscles warms them up sufficiently to make training them immediately after a logical choice. Training the biceps first also provides a good warmup for the forearms without negatively affecting their ability to handle heavy weights. So when training the muscles of the arms together, even at the more advanced levels, always remember to train biceps, then forearms, and then triceps in that order for the best possible results. At this point in the workout you have completed training all the muscle groups of the upper body.

Now it's time to train the legs. Leg training, more specifically training the quadriceps, puts a tremendous drain on the energy reserves of the body. Whether you train this muscle group first or last, you'll find yourself feeling extremely fatigued at the completion of three or four sets of heavy quad exercises, especially squats. Since it would be practically impossible to muster up enough energy to train all the rest of your muscle groups if you trained them early in your workout, I have set up the program so they are trained as late in the workout as possible while still providing maximum benefits.

Squats are the exercise of choice when it comes to training your quads and you will be performing various types of squats throughout the length of your natural bodybuilding career. Squats require extreme coordination. Therefore, don't train your hamstrings, and calves before squatting otherwise you will find that your legs will be weak and shaky and you will dramatically increase your risk of injury when performing this exercise. So when training legs, you will always train the quads first when following any of my programs. Since most heavy quadricep exercises warm up the hamstrings to some degree they should be trained next, then calves. It is fortunate that the hamstrings and calves are small muscle groups and therefore require very little energy to train effectively. Because of this you can still hit these muscle groups hard even after a grueling squat workout which has left you totally drained of energy. It will just take a little discipline to drag yourself through these two muscle groups and to finally finish the whole workout off with a few sets of abdominals. The reason for doing abdominals last is quite simple. It is very uncomfortable to train the rest of your body when your abdominals are tight and burned out. Your stomach often feels uncomfortable after ab training and you can even feel a little nauseous at times if you train your abs especially hard.

Beginning level training routines

This section will outline all four basic level workouts. These workouts are categorized as break-in level 1 (first two to three weeks); break-in level 2 (from the 3rd or 4th to the 6th to 8th week); basic beginning training routine (approximately from second to fourth month); and advanced beginner's routine (approximately from fifth to sixth month). These routines will all be very similar in nature. The exercises will be basically

the exact same for each routine. The only differences will be an increase of one set performed on either some or all of the exercises from one level to the next, and a progressive reduction of reps on each set performed of most of the exercises in the basic beginner and advanced beginner routines, which will allow you to lift correspondingly heavier weights. However, you will use descending reps and heavier weights during the beginner's routine, but you will not advance to the point where you are using the lowest reps and heaviest weights which are most productive until the advanced beginner level. The reason for this is that it will take until the third or fourth month before you have developed sufficient muscle and tendon strength and coordination to train with the heavier weights and lower reps which promote maximum muscle growth with minimal risk of becoming injured. You will also be so well adapted to training by this time that lifting even the heaviest weights for the prescribed number of reps will, at worst, produce only minimal muscle soreness. It is still advised, however, to resist going too heavy too quickly even at this stage because of all the reasons outlined previously.

At the advanced beginner level, an example of a suggested rep pattern for most of the exercises is four sets (10, 8, 7, 6). The first two sets of reps (10 and 8 respectively in this example) should always be performed with less than maximum weights and used to thoroughly warm up the muscles for the last two sets, which will be maximum efforts. In choosing your weights for each set use the following guidelines. During the first set choose a weight which would allow you to get five more reps than the number suggested. This ensures that you will warm up the muscles, joints, and tendons gradually without any chance of pulling or straining them. Using the example of 10 reps suggested for the first set, you would proceed to use a weight which would allow you to get 15 reps if you trained to maximum capacity. During the second set you should choose a weight which would allow you to get two or three reps above the prescribed number. Using the example of 8 reps suggested for the second set you would therefore proceed to use a weight which would allow you to get 10 to 11 reps if you trained maximally with it. After this set the particular muscle you are training will be thoroughly prepared to handle maximum weights in the repetition range, which will pro-

duce optimum muscle growth for that particular muscle. Keep in mind that the lowest number of reps of this suggested range is normally six. At the times you choose to train with lower reps such as three or two, or for increased power, you will have to do more submaximal warmup sets in order to best guard against injury.

Anyway, getting back to the advanced beginner level rep scheme, by the third set you will be ready to handle either a maximum weight for the prescribed number of reps, or a weight that is slightly less than maximum and would allow you to get maybe one rep more than the prescribed number. I personally suggest you play it completely safe and use the slightly lighter weight. Using the example of 7 reps recommended for the third set, you would therefore use a weight that would allow you to get 8 reps if you do this. By the fourth set you will definitely by ready for an all-out effort with maximum weight, with virtually no chance of ever injuring yourself, assuming you use correct exercise form. Incidentally, this three-set warmup can be used when performing 5, 6, or more sets of an exercise at the more advanced levels with total safety, as long as you don't perform less than 6 reps of any exercise.

The routine I just presented, along with the rest of the beginner-level complete-equipment programs I will present, is best performed in a commercial gym where all the equipment you require is easily available. However, if you are willing to equip your home gym exactly as outlined earlier you can perform all these complete equipment programs effectively at home. For those who have only barbells, dumbbells, squat racks, and an adjustable bench press at home, I will outline the most effective routine possible which you can perform at each of the beginner levels. Finally, since many high school and college students only have access to a Universal gym, I will outline the best possible Universal program you can perform at each of these levels. So altogether 12 training routines will be outlined in this section, three for each of the four levels. At each level the complete equipment routines will be presented first, since they consist of the most productive exercises you can perform for every muscle group and are, therefore, what I consider to be the ultimate workout for each level.

Training program No. 1—break-in—level 1 (Combined equipment program) Estimated length of workout—20-30 minutes

Muscle Group	Exercise	Sets	Reps	% Body Weight
Pectorals	Bench press	1	10	25
Deltoids	Standing military press	1	10	20
Latissimus Dorsi	Bent-over rows	1	12	25
Trapezius	Shoulder shrug	1	12	30
Biceps	Standing curls (E-Z curl bar)	1	10	20
Forearms	Wrist curls	1	20	15
Triceps	Standing tricep extensions	1	10	20
Quadriceps	Parallel squats	1	12	30
Hamstrings	Leg curls	1	12	15
Calves	Standing calf raise	1	20	35
Abdominals	Bent-knee situps	1	Up to 50	0

Training program No. 2—break-in—level 1 (Free weight routine) Estimated length of workout—20-30 minutes

Muscle Group	Exercise	Sets	Reps	% Body Weight
Pectorals	Bench press	1	10	25
Deltoids	Military press	1	10	20
Latissimus dorsi	Bent-over rows	1	12	25
Trapezius	Shoulder shrugs	1	12	30
Biceps	Standing curls (E-Z bar)	1	10	20
Forearms	Wrist curls	1	20	15
Triceps	Standing tricep extension (E-Z bar)	1	10	20
Quadriceps	Parallel squats	1	12	30
Hamstrings	Stiff-legged deadlift	1	12	20
Calves	One-legged calf raises	1	As many as possible up to 20	Body weight
Abs	Bent-knee situps	1	Up to 50	

Universal machine exercises are easier to perform than free weight exercises because of way the resistance is set up. As a result your initial poundages in terms of percentage of body weight will be higher than with free weights. I must state here that because of lack of space, I will not be able to explain how to perform the universal exercises suggested here. Your best bet is to ask the phys. ed. instructor at school how to perform each of them.

Training program No. 3—break-in—level 1   **(Universal routine)**   **Estimated length of workout—17-22 minutes**

Muscle Group	Exercise	Sets	Reps	% Body Weight
Pectorals	U. bench press	1	10	35
Deltoids	U. standing military press	1	10	30
Latissimus dorsi	U. wide grip front pulldown	1	12	40
Trapezius	U. shoulder shrugs	1	12	40
Biceps	U. cable curls	1	10	30
Forearms	U. cable wrist curls	1	20	20
Triceps	U. tricep pressdowns	1	10	30
Quadriceps	U. leg press (top step)	1	12	60
Hamstrings	U. leg curl	1	12	20
Calves	U. calf press (bottom step)	1	20	60
Abs	U. incline situps	1	As many as possible up to 30	Body weight

Training program No. 1—break-in—level 2
(Combined equipment program) Estimated length of workout—30-45 minutes

Muscle Group	Exercise	Sets	Reps	Weight
Pecs	Bench press	2	10, 10	
Delts	Military press	2	10, 10	
Lats	Bent-over rows	2	12, 12	
Traps	Shoulder shrugs	2	12, 12	
Biceps	Standing curls (E-Z bar)	1	10	
Forearms	Wrist curls	1	20	
Triceps	Standing tricep extensions (E-Z bar)	1	10	
Quads	Parallel squats	2	12, 12	
Hams	Leg curls	1	12	
Calves	Standing calf raise	2	20, 20	
Abs	Bent-knee situps	1	Up to 50	Body weight

Training program No. 2—(free weight routine)   Estimated length of workout 30-45 minutes

Muscle Group	Exercise	Sets	Reps	Weight
Pecs	Bench press	2	10, 10	
Delts	Military press	2	10, 10	
Lats	Bent-over rows	2	12, 12	
Traps	Shoulder shrugs	2	12, 12	
Biceps	Standing curls (E-Z bar)	1	10	
Forearms	Wrist curls	1	20	
Triceps	Standing tricep extensions (E-Z bar)	1	10	
Quads	Parallel squats	2	12, 12	
Hams	Stiff-legged deadlift	1	12	
Calves	One-legged calf raise	2	As many as possible up to 20	
Abs	Bent-knee situps	1	Up to 50	Body weight

Training program No. 3—(Universal routine) Estimated length of workout—25-35 minutes

Muscle Group	Exercise	Sets	Reps	Weight
Pecs	U. bench press	2	10, 10	
Delts	U. standing military press	2	10, 10	
Lats	U. wide-grip front pulldown	2	12, 12	
Traps	U. shoulder shrugs	2	12, 12	
Biceps	U. cable curls	1	10	
Forearms	U. cable wrist curls	1	20	
Triceps	U. tricep pressdowns	1	10	
Quads	U. leg press (top step)	2	12, 12	
Hams	U. leg curl	1	12	
Calves	U. calf press (bottom step)	2	20, 20	
Abs	U. incline situps	1	As many as possible up to 30	Body weight plus weight

Basic beginner's training programs

Training program No. 1—(combined equipment program)   Estimated length of workout—45 minutes to 1 hour

Muscle Group	Exercise	Sets	Reps	Weight
Pecs	Bench press	3	10, 9, 8	
Delts	Military press	3	10, 9, 8	
Lats	Bent-over rows	3	12, 11, 10	
Traps	Shoulder shrugs	3	12, 11, 10	
Biceps	Standing curls (E-Z bar)	2	10, 9	
Forearms	Wrist curls	2	20, 15	
Triceps	Standing tricep extensions (E-Z bar)	2	10, 9	
Quads	Parallel squats	3	12, 11, 10	
Hams	Leg curls	2	12, 11	
Calves	Standing calf raise	3	20, 18, 16	
Abs	Bent-knee situps	2	Up to 50	Body weight & more if necessary

Training program No. 2—(free weight routine)   Estimated length of workout—60-80 minutes

Muscle Group	Exercise	Sets	Reps	Weight
Pecs	Bench press	4	10, 8, 7, 6	
Delts	Military press	4	10, 8, 7, 6	
Lats	Bent-over rows	4	10, 9, 8, 8	
Traps	Shoulder shrugs	4	10, 9, 8, 8	
Biceps	Standing curls (E-Z bar)	3	10, 8, 6	
Forearms (outer)	Reverse wrist curls	1	12	
Forearms (inner)	Wrist curls	2	17, 13	
Triceps	Standing tricep extension (E-Z bar)	3	10, 8, 6	
Quads	Parallel squats	4	12, 10, 9, 8	
Hams	Stiff-legged deadlift	3	12, 10, 9, 8	
Calves	One-legged calf raise	4	20, 17, 17, 15	Dumbbell in hand
Abs	Bent-knee situps	3	40, 30, 20	Body weight plus weight

Training program No. 3—(Universal routine)   Estimated length of workout—40-50 minutes

Muscle Group	Exercise	Sets	Reps	Weight
Pecs	U. bench press	3	10, 9, 8	
Delts	U. standing military press	3	10, 9, 8	
Lats	U. wide-grip front pulldowns	3	12, 11, 10	
Traps	U. shoulder shrugs	3	12, 11, 10	
Biceps	U. cable curls	2	10, 9	
Forearms	U. cable wrist curls	2	20, 15	
Triceps	U. tricep pressdowns	2	10, 9	
Quads	U. leg press (top step)	3	12, 11, 10	
Hams	U. leg curls	2	12, 11	
Calves	U. calf press (bottom step)	3	As many as possible up to 20	
Abs	U. incline situps	2	Up to 30	

Advanced beginner's training program

Training program No. 1—(combined equipment program)   Estimated length of workout—60-80 minutes

Muscle Group	Exercise	Sets	Reps	Weight
Pecs	Bench press	4	10, 8, 7, 6	
Delts	Military press	4	10, 8, 7, 6	
Lats	Bent-over rows	4	10, 9, 8, 8	
Traps	Shoulder shrugs	4	10, 9, 8, 8	
Biceps	Standing curls (E-Z bar)	3	10, 8, 6	
Forearms (outer)	Reverse wrist curls	1	12	
Forearms (inner)	Wrist curls	2	17, 13	
Triceps	Standing tricep extensions (E-Z bar)	3	10, 8, 6	
Quads	Parallel squats	4	12, 10, 9, 8	
Hams	Leg curls	3	12, 10, 8	
Calves	Standing calf raise	4	20, 17, 15, 12	
Abs	Bent-knee situps	3	40, 30, 20	Body weight plus weight

Training program No. 2—(free weight routine)   Estimated length of workout—45 minutes to 1 hour

Muscle Group	Exercise	Sets	Reps	Weight
Pecs	Bench press	3	10, 9, 8	
Delts	Military press	3	10, 9, 8	
Lats	Bent-over rows	3	12, 11, 10	
Traps	Shoulder shrugs	3	12, 11, 10	
Biceps	Standing curls (E-Z bar)	2	10, 9	
Forearms	Wrist curls	2	20, 15	
Triceps	Standing tricep extensions (E-Z bar)	2	10, 9	
Quads	Parallel squats	3	12, 11, 10	
Hams	Stiff-legged deadlift	2	12, 11	
Calves	One-legged calf raise	3	As many as possible up to 20	Body weight
Abs	Bent-knee situps	2	Up to 50	Body weight & more if necessary

Training program No. 3—(Universal routine)   Estimated length of workout—60–80 minutes

Muscle Group	Exercise	Sets	Reps	Weight
Pecs	U. bench press	4	10, 8, 7, 6	
Delts	U. standing military press	4	10, 8, 7, 6	
Lats	U. wide-grip front pulldown	4	10, 9, 8, 8	
Traps	U. shoulder shrugs	4	10, 9, 8, 8	
Biceps	U. cable curls	3	10, 8, 6	
Forearms (outer)	U. reverse cable curls	1	12	
Forearms (inner)	U. cable wrist curls	2	17, 13	
Triceps	U. tricep pressdowns	3	10, 8, 6	
Quads	U. leg press	4	12, 10, 9, 8	
Hams	U. leg curls	3	12, 10, 8	
Calves	U. calf press	4	20, 17, 15, 12	
Abs	U. incline situps	3	40, 30, 20	Body weight plus weight

Summary of programs

There are a few points which must be clarified in relation to the training routines I just presented. First, all the exercises in both the complete equipment and free weight training routines at all four levels are performed with barbells unless otherwise specified. The bicep curls and tricep extensions can be performed with either a straight bar or an E-Z curl bar, according to what you feel most comfortable with, although I consider the E-Z curl bar to be more beneficial overall for reasons which will be discussed when describing the performance of the exercises.

Another thing is that the rep schemes for high rep exercises such as the various calf, forearm, and ab exercises do not have to be followed to the letter. There is room for a couple of reps leeway, without any deleterious effects to attaining maximum development from them. One major component of these training programs which deserves explanation is the fact that for each of the three different types of programs, the same exact basic exercises are used at each of the four levels. In other words, except for changes in sets and reps from

one level to the next, you'll be doing virtually the same exact program for the entire four- to six-month period constituting the beginning level of training. Normally, it is beneficial to change your training programs somewhat every two months or so and henceforth you should. However, since virtually all the basic exercises presented in this section in both the mixed equipment and free weight routines will form the backbone of your training for your entire bodybuilding career, I believe the entire beginner level should be spent performing them. This way, you perfect your form on each, and also gain the ability to use progressively heavier weights and lower reps from level to level on each of them. Mastering these exercises is so important because they are the ones most responsible for building solid muscle mass and strength throughout the body. Also, most of the other exercises you will eventually be performing are simply variations of these particular basic exercises anyway, so mastering them will make it easier to master those which you will be performing later on.

The reason the Universal programs are all outlined with the same exercises

for each level is simply that there are practically no other exercises which you can perform for the various muscle groups on the Universal which will provide any muscle development whatsoever. I must emphasize here that past the beginner level, Universal machines become virtually ineffective in building muscle, except in the special circumstances previously outlined in which various machines can be of benefit to more experienced bodybuilders.

Certain of the exercises included in the free weight routines which were designed to use only the most basic equipment will also become ineffective to a large degree after the beginner level for providing any substantial muscle development. One-legged calf raises are the prime example of such an exercise and stiff-legged deadlifts are another. These exercises are of value as supplementary exercises, but they do not compare with exercises such as standing calf raises on a free weight calf machine and leg curls respectively. If you're really serious about reaching a high level of development in bodybuilding, you have to either invest in the equipment which constitutes a well-equipped home gym or join a well-equipped commercial gym by the time you reach the intermediate level.

One thing I mentioned previously is that for those of you who have access to them, using Nautilus machines for a couple of weeks before switching over to free weights can be an excellent idea, especially if you've been sedentary for a long period of time or are middle-aged and haven't ever done progressive resistance training before. For these individuals I will now present such a program which can be performed before beginning the free weight break-in Level 1 program. The Universal program can also be used for this purpose.

The Nautilus routine I just presented is the one I consider to be the best. However, since many fitness centers with Nautilus do not have all the pieces of equipment necessary to perform the routine as outlined, you may have to substitute other Nautilus exercises according to what machines are available. Because of limited space, I do not have room to discuss how to perform the Nautilus exercises, but any qualified instructor at a facility which has Nautilus will be able to effectively put you through a Nautilus workout. Just remember to take it easy and not to train anywhere near capacity during the first couple of weeks, especially when using Nautilus as a transition from a sedentary life style to free weight training.

Intermediate level natural training

I readily acknowledge that the vast majority of people reading this book are much more concerned with toning up, adding just enough muscle tissue to maximally enhance the masculine or, in the case of women, feminine attributes of their physiques, losing excess body fat, and achieving the highest level of musculoskeletal, cardiovascular, and overall fitness possible. I realize that most of you are not concerned with developing massive amounts of muscle mass or strength, and that physique competition is the farthest thing from your mind.

On the other hand, I know for a fact that a certain percentage of you are more concerned with developing your physique to its full muscular potential and of eventually competing than with anything else.

The intermediate training section is approached in such a way that it takes the goals of both groups into consideration. It will provide a sort of crossroads

Break-in Nautilus workout

Muscle Group	Exercise	Sets	Reps	Weight
Pecs	N. bench press	1	10	
Delts	N. laterals	1	10	
Lats	N. pulldown	1	12	
Traps	N. shoulder shrug	1	12	
Biceps	N. bicep curl	1	10	
Forearms	N. wrist curl	1	20	
Triceps	N. tricep ex.	1	10	
Quads	N. leg press	1	12	
Hams	N. leg curl	1	12	
Calves	N. calf raise	1	20	
Abs	N. ab machine	1	20	

for both groups, with one group heading off in one direction and the other group in another upon completion of this level of training.

No matter what your ultimate goal from natural training happens to be, progression to the intermediate level and mastery of the training techniques and exercise programs involved at this level are imperative if you hope to derive substantial and long-lasting benefits from your natural bodybuilding training.

The workload and intensity level which is generated at the beginner level is not sufficient to add the amount of muscle mass necessary to shape and mold your physique to a point where it looks strong, supple, and shapely. You can definitely make significant gains at the basic level of training, but because of the restrictions imposed by training at this level, you are severely limited in terms of how far you can progress and how much you can accomplish with your physique.

The intermediate level both raises the intensity level and provides so much more flexibility in terms of training routines and exercise techniques that you can continue to progress almost indefinitely. Your options are virtually unlimited. Eventually you will reach a point where you won't be able to progress that quickly unless you decide to move on to the advanced level. However, if you do choose to stay at the intermediate level for the rest of

your training days, it's nice to know that you will have enough variety to choose from so you will always be able to render at least small improvements on your physique. The wide variety of exercises and training principles outlined at the intermediate level will enable you to fully develop all sections of each muscle.

For example, in terms of pec training, exercises designed to specifically work the upper and lower portions of the pecs as well as exercise techniques which will enable you to emphasize either the inner or outer pec will be outlined at this level as opposed to just using bench presses for overall but not specific development at the beginner level. Similar detail will be paid to each muscle group. As a result, you will be able to specialize on those areas of each muscle which you consider to be under par. You will be able to shape and tie together your physique and muscle development exactly the way you want it to look, taking genetic limitations into consideration of course.

The other major benefit such variety provides is that you will never get bored with your training. If you get tired of performing a certain exercise or training technique you can substitute another exercise or training technique which will provide similar benefits. Experimenting with different training options is exciting and will keep you interested in your training at all times. If you remained at the beginner level,

53

you would most likely eventually become so bored with your training that you would probably eventually quit.

In other words, the intermediate level training allows you to develop specific muscle sections. Another benefit is that the variety of exercises at the intermediate level will keep you from getting bored. A third benefit is that fully developing each muscle group and the surrounding tissue with a variety of exercises and training techniques will provide the maximum amount of muscular strength, stability, and coordination possible, and will also provide similar benefits for the surrounding and supportive tissue, mainly the tendons, ligaments, and connective tissue. These same benefits are for both the serious bodybuilder and those who wish to shape and tone their bodies.

The exercises, organization of training routines, and training principles outlined in this section will enable you to gain muscle mass at the quickest rate possible by natural methods. You will learn how to develop the most massive, symmetrical, proportional physique possible within the limits of your genetic potential and you will lay the groundwork to compete successfully if you so desire. If you commit yourself totally to your training and follow all other aspects of the natural bodybuilding life style, and you train specifically to achieve the maximum level of muscular development possible, I guarantee you that by the time you complete the advanced intermediate level you will have taken on the appearance and muscular proportions which will indisputably designate you as a well-developed natural bodybuilder.

Three phases of intermediate training

Assuming you desire to progress at the fastest rate possible, the intermediate level of training will last anywhere between 12 and 18 months. The intermediate level will be broken down into three phases. They are the beginning intermediate, intermediate, and advanced intermediate levels. As was true with the basic levels of natural training, the three intermediate levels are categorized according to how many sets you are performing for each muscle group.

At each of three levels you will be adding one set to the number performed for each of the major muscle groups and at two out of three of the levels you will be adding one set to the number performed for most of the

smaller muscle groups. Each of the levels will average four to six months in length according to how quickly you adapt to each and feel capable of moving onto the next one. According to what your goals are in terms of muscular development and musculoskeletal fitness you have the option of leveling your training program off at any one of the three levels, although I don't suggest you consider this until you have reached at least the second of the three intermediate levels.

Number of exercises per muscle group

For the torso muscle groups (i.e., pecs, delts, lats, traps, and abs) you will be performing two exercises at each of the three intermediate levels. You will continue to perform only one exercise for the biceps, triceps, quads, hamstrings, and calves until the second intermediate level. Even at this level you should often hit these muscle groups with just one exercise for the prescribed number of sets. When a major muscle group is included it is often better to do a disproportionately high number of sets of the exercise which you know provides the most benefit, such as squats for the quads. Generally, you should always do one or two sets more of the exercise which stimulates the greatest portion of the muscle and thereby provides the most potential for muscle growth.

The following chart illustrates how many sets should be done for each muscle group at all three intermediate levels in relation to the number of exercises to be performed. Also the portion or dimension of development of each muscle group in relation to the amount of attention it should receive will be noted.

In the above chart Ex 1 stands for exercise No. 1 and Ex 2 stands for exercise No. 2. In cases where you are given two or three alternatives for dividing your sets between the two exercises given for a particular muscle group, it is an excellent idea to either take turns if there are two choices or rotate if there are three choices from workout to workout so that you utilize all the set combinations when performing the actual workouts which will be outlined at the end of this section. Also, these workouts substitute actual exercises in place of the descriptions in the above chart of what dimension of development or part of the muscle group you are supposed to concern yourself with.

Number of repetitions

This topic was thoroughly discussed in the basic training section, and everything that was previously written is applicable to this section and beyond. At this level and from now on you will be training all your muscle groups consistently with the optimum range of repetitions known to stimulate optimum muscle growth. However, as I have previously discussed, training with low reps and heavy weights all the time will quickly lead to overtraining.

During the entire intermediate level you will be training each muscle group on the average of twice a week. It is a good idea to perform the first workout of each week with the lower range of reps found to be most productive in terms of stimulating gains in muscle growth. This means you will be training relatively heavy. Then, during the second workout of the week, for each muscle group, you should perform the upper range of repetitions found to be most productive, for stimulating muscle growth. This means you will be performing the second workout of the week for each muscle group with relatively light weights. By alternating heavy and light workouts you will stimulate the maximum amount of muscle growth possible while simultaneously minimizing the risk of overtraining. You will also add another dimension of variety to your workout. Of course, there are a lot more factors involved when it comes to preventing overtraining while simultaneously maximizing muscle gains and they will be discussed later on in this section at the appropriate times.

Rest between sets

At the beginner level, the optimum rest periods were rather long compared to the length of rest time which is considered optimum at the intermediate and advanced levels of training. The reason for this is that during the beginner level the body is not used to dealing with the stress each set of progressive resistance training places upon it.

Along with the stress, the body cannot efficiently cope with the buildup of lactic acid (a waste product developed by the body during exercise), pump oxygen-rich blood into the muscles rapidly or recover quickly from the intensity of the set when you first begin training. It takes time for the muscles to adapt to the rigor of the exercising, but now at the intermediate level, your

Muscle Group		Sets Beg. Int. Level	Sets Int. Level	Sets Adv. Int. Level	
Pecs	Lower Pec	3 or 2	3	4 or 3	Ex 1
	Upper Pec	2 or 3	3	3 or 4	Ex 2
Delts	Front Delt	3 or 2	3	4 or 3	Ex 1
	Side Delt	2 or 3	3	3 or 4	Ex 2
Lats	Width	2 or 3	3	3 or 4	Ex 1
	Thickness	3 or 2	3	4 or 3	Ex 2
Traps	Shrug Movement	3 or 2	3	4 or 3	Ex 1
	Other Movement	2 or 3	3	3 or 4	Ex 2
Abs	Upper Abs	2	3 or 2	3	Ex 1
	Lower Abs	2	2 or 3	3	Ex 2
Intercostals	Twists	2	3	3	Ex 1
Biceps	Heavy Basic Curls	3	4	3 or 5	Ex 1
	Other Versions of Curls			2 or 0	Ex 2
Forearms	Outer	2	2 or 2	3 or 2	Ex 1
	Inner	2	2 or 3	2 or 3	Ex 2
Triceps	Heavy Extensions	3	4	3 or 5	Ex 2
	Other Basic Exercises			2 or 0	Ex 1
Quadriceps	Squat / Other Heavy Quad Exercises	5 / 0	6 or 4 / 0 or 2	7 or 5 or 4 / 0 or 2 or 3	Ex 1 / Ex 2
Hamstrings	Leg Curls / Other Hamstring Exercises	4 / 0	5 or 3 / 0 or 2	6 or 4 or 3 / 0 or 2 or 3	Ex 1 / Ex 2
Calves	Standing Calf Raise	5	6 or 4 / 0 or 2	7 or 5 or 4 / 0 or 2 or 3	Ex 1
	Seated Calf Raise	0			Ex 2

body should have sufficiently adapted to the stress and you can recover much quicker. By the time you have reached the advanced intermediate level the rest periods will be of an optimum length for stimulating the maximum amount of muscle fibers without over-taxing your body. The shortened rest periods will significantly increase the intensity of your workouts. As you might have guessed, the shorter rest periods will enable you to train the muscles more thoroughly.

But remember to shorten the rest periods gradually. Shortening them quickly can shock the muscles. Decrease the periods of the sets as illustrated in the following chart and you should have no trouble handling the transition to optimum rest periods. These rest periods will be of optimum benefit for the remainder of your body-building career. One suggestion is to vary these rest periods once in a while, because muscles always respond best to variety.

	Beg. Level	Beg. Int. Level	Int. Level	Adv. Int. Level
1. Quads & Lats	100 sec–2 minutes	95–110 sec	90–100 sec	90 sec
2. Pecs, traps, & delts	100 sec	90 sec	80–85 sec	75 sec
3. Biceps, triceps, hams, calves, & abs	80–90 sec	70–80 sec	70–75 sec	65 sec

The four-day split routine for naturals

The number of sets of the training routine at the beginning intermediate level is too high for you to continue to effectively train the entire body in one workout. There simply will not be the energy reserves for the last three or four muscle groups to train them effectively. Therefore, you will split the total body workout into two shorter workouts and will train half the body one day and half the next. This is technically called a split routine.

At the intermediate level, the frequency with which you train each muscle group will decrease slightly. Instead of training each muscle group once every three days on a consistent basis, you will now generally be training each muscle group twice per week. The schedule will be set up so that you have two days of rest after performing the first workout of the week for each muscle group and three days of rest after performing the second workout of the week for each muscle group. Since it will now be taking you two days to train every muscle group of the body instead of one and you have to train each muscle group twice per week, you will now actually be performing four workouts per week. These workouts are most commonly performed on Monday, Tuesday, Thursday, and Friday, with the first half of the muscle groups being trained on Monday and Thursday and the second half on Tuesday and Friday. This schedule satisfies the requirement that all the muscle groups be given two days' rest after their first workout of the week and three days' rest after their second workout.

The substantial increase in the overall workload and intensity level of your workouts at the beginning intermediate level and from now on taxes the recuperative capabilities of both the muscle groups and the body as a whole to such an extent that becoming chronically overtrained is imminent if you continue to train each muscle group once every three days on a consistent basis. It is basically the systemic stress placed upon the body which is the most important factor. You must consider the fact that if you continued to train each muscle group once every three days at the intermediate and advanced levels, you would actually be training two days out of every three instead of one day out of every three, as at the beginner level. This represents a 100 percent increase in the number of days the body as a whole is forced to endure the energy-draining effects of progressive resistance training. Over a prolonged period of time this added energy drain will lead to physical exhaustion in most natural individuals. One rest day out of every three for natural weight training at this level is simply not enough to allow sufficient systemic energy recuperation for anything more than a short period of time.

This is also applicable in terms of the individual muscle groups themselves. The progressive addition of sets, and progressive decrease in rest periods between sets through all three levels of the intermediate level will result in the individual muscle groups being trained at a level of intensity which will make it impossible for them to recover consistently from their workouts in 72 hours. This fact is even more apparent when you take into consideration that the additional systematic energy drain created from having to take two days to train the body at this level instead of one at the beginner's level, negatively affects the ability of the individual muscle groups to recover from their workouts. After all, it takes a lot of energy to rebuild muscle tissue, and as I previously discussed, the human body does not consider the development of additional muscle mass to be a necessity. As a result only the energy left over from normal functioning and normal growth and repair is used to build muscle tissue. Therefore, because of the energy drain caused by the additional number of workouts which need to be performed at this level, the body overall has less energy left over for muscle recovery than it did at the beginner level. The result, of course, is that the muscle groups need a little more time to recover than they did previously. By providing an additional day of rest every other workout, sufficient rest is provided both for the systemic energy level to be kept at a relatively high level and for the muscle groups to fully recover from the week's workouts. Adding this one day of rest per week to your routine will prevent a vicious cycle of systemic energy drain and muscle tissue breakdown from occurring, which will quickly lead to a chronically overtrained state.

You will be performing the first workout of the week for each muscle group with relatively heavy weights and low repetitions and the second workout of the week for each muscle group with lighter weights and higher repetitions. The reasoning behind this is that giving the muscles a 72-hour rest after the first workout of the week (the heavy one) will enable them to recover sufficiently so they can handle the second workout of the week, which is the lighter one. Then, by taking a 96-hour rest after the lighter workout, the muscle groups are given sufficient time to recover fully from the stress placed upon them by the two weekly workouts. Thus they will be maximally prepared for handling an all-out heavy workout on the first two training days of the following week. Setting up the schedule in this way also arranges things so that you will not be doing any workout at all for the two days prior to these heavy workouts. This will enable you to regain the systemic energy reserves which were drained during the week's workouts so that you will be fully recovered and have the high energy level necessary to get the most out of the two heavy workouts you will be performing to start off the following week's training.

What this all adds up to is that you will be 100 percent rested and fully prepared to get the most out of the first two workouts of each training week—the two heaviest, most intense, and most beneficial ones. Because of the tremendous physical and mental energy drain of the two heavy workouts you obviously will not have quite the same level of energy for the two lighter workouts. However, this will not negatively affect your ability to derive maximum benefit from these two workouts since they will not require near the energy output which is required for the two heavy ones. Despite the fact that the intensity level of these two workouts is not as high as the two heavy ones, the higher reps will stimulate different muscle fibers than the heavier workouts do and will provide all the muscles with a thorough workout, resulting in more full and complete development than would be possible if you just went heavy all the time. Of course, most importantly they will enable you to stimulate new muscle growth, while providing a sufficient break between the heavy workouts performed for each individual muscle group so you don't burn yourself out both mentally and physically. So make sure you resist the temptation to go heavy all the time. It will not benefit you in the long run.

Instinctive training

I must emphasize here that while everything I have just written here is true and applicable over the long run, the body does not react the same exact way to the same exact stress at all times. Your environment, work, personal life, biorhythmic pattern, emotional state and numerous other factors can have a dramatic positive or negative effect on your energy level and overall ability to cope with the stress that progressive resistance training places upon you. This will become clearly apparent as you attempt to program your mind and body to derive maximum benefit from different kinds of workouts on different days as required by the intermediate level of training. Because of the effect of these various stresses and the dynamic state of the human organism as a whole, you may occasionally find your body responding in what may seem to be an illogical manner when performing a workout.

For example, you may be perfectly rested for a heavy workout, walk into the gym and find that for some inexplicable reason your strength is so low that you have to reduce your exercise poundages by 20 or 30 pounds on each exercise in order to perform the prescribed number of repetitions. Another example which often occurs is that after performing two very heavy workouts at the beginning of a week, you walk into the gym for one of your lighter workouts later that week, and instead of being slightly burnt out and weaker, as should normally be the case after two such heavy workouts, you find that you are fully recovered, energetic, and unbelievably strong—even stronger than

you were on your heavy days. You may also find that you are incredibly energetic and strong or unusually fatigued and weak for a period of three or four workouts for no apparent reason. How should you respond to such situations? As you progress through the intermediate level and slowly gain an increased understanding of how your body as a whole and your muscles in particular are affected by every workout you engage in, and also learn the limitations of how much stress you can place on your body, you will eventually gain enough knowledge and insight about yourself to train almost totally by instinct by the time you reach the advanced level. In fact, I consider being able to train totally instinctively, according to what your body is telling you, to be the single most important characteristic necessary to be classified as an advanced bodybuilder. Following the training routines and principles exactly as they are outlined in this book will enable you to develop your physique to 70 to 80 percent of your ultimate natural genetic potential. However, since everybody responds slightly differently to any particular training routine, I can tell you that the only way you will ever develop your physique that extra 20 to 30 percent to its ultimate natural genetic potential is to listen to the signals your body is sending, and to act accordingly and ultimately to utilize advanced natural training methods. You, of course, must still stay within the boundaries of what training principles have been proven to work in terms of developing a strong, shapely, muscular physique naturally, but there is always a certain amount of room for flexibility in your training. In fact being flexible in your use of the training principles and programs outlined in this book is encouraged, and as I just stated, ultimately required for you to develop what you consider to be the ideal physique for you in terms of your genetic limitations.

So, keeping everything I have just said in mind and getting back to the question of how you should respond to unexpected situations when training, the answer is to listen to what your body is telling you, and to adjust your training as logically as possible. If you feel weak on a day when you are supposed to train heavy, reduce the poundages to the level where they feel comfortable, increase the reps, and train less intensely. If you're unusually strong on a scheduled higher rep, lighter weight workout, go for it and train heavy with lower reps. If you feel

strong and energetic for three or four workouts in a row and you've come to know the limitations of your recuperative abilities and are sure that you can handle a few heavy workouts in a row at that particular time, then do it. Of course, if you feel unusually weak or fatigued for a couple of weeks, then you should train much less intensely until you feel better. It's all basically common sense.

This type of instinctive training is applicable to virtually every other aspect of your training also. For example, as you gain an awareness of how hard each muscle group can be trained during a particular workout you will be able to adjust the number of sets and intensity level of each set accordingly so that each muscle group receives an almost perfect workout every time. By the time you reach the advanced intermediate level you will commonly be adding a set for a muscle group or doing one less set for another muscle group, according to how much work each particular muscle group can handle on any given day. This will also determine how close to an all-out effort you put into each set on any given day.

Then, of course, there's the subject of how many days to take off between workouts. There will occasionally be times when you'll know your muscles simply aren't ready to handle the second, lighter workout of the week 72 hours after the heavy workouts and that you'll need to give them an extra day's rest. There will also be times when you'll be fully recovered and ready to handle the first two heavy workouts of the following week only 72 hours after completing the two less intense workouts of the previous week and you'll end up training a day earlier. Once in a rare while you will also most likely find either your muscle groups recovering in 72 hours for three or four workouts in a row or requiring 96 hours to recover for a few workouts in a row. By the time you reach the advanced level you should be able to tell when your muscle groups are recovered with such precision that the four-day split routine outlined in this section will basically become obsolete. You will simply give the muscle groups either a 72- or 96-hour rest between each workout according to what you need. Later on in this book I will give you specific guidelines to follow which, combined with your own instinct, will make it easy to determine how many days' rest to give each muscle group and just how hard to train each muscle group.

Until you reach the point where you

have a complete mastery of all the training principles and routines outlined in this intermediate training section, you should alter your training routines only in response to those signals which are unmistakably obvious. Those signals include unusual strength or weakness, an abundance of energy or unusual fatigue, an unmistakable feeling of total muscle recovery a day earlier than usual or an obvious burned-out feeling in the muscles on a day they are scheduled to be trained, necessitating an extra day of rest. Any time your body sends you a signal which you have difficulty interpreting, perform your workout exactly as planned. Then, afterward analyze whether you made the right decision. If you conclude that performing the workout exactly as planned did not provide maximum benefit and you have an idea about what could have been changed, wait until that same signal presents itself again, as it most likely will sometime down the road, and give your idea a shot on that occasion. If that doesn't provide optimum results once again, analyze the situation and try something different the next time this subtle signal presents itself. Eventually by continually trying something new every time that signal presents itself, you'll discover either an alteration in your workout routine or a training technique which will provide optimum results each time that particular signal decides to present itself in the future. As you continue to progress in the sport and become more in tune with your body as a whole and your muscles in particular, you will more than likely become aware of a number of other subtle signals sent to your brain in certain training situations, which if interpreted correctly would result in your training becoming much more productive. By using the method of trial and error and careful analysis just outlined any time one of the signals particular to your own body presents itself, until you have discovered exactly what each one of them indicates and how to adjust your training so maximum benefit can be derived from them, you will ultimately master the instinctive training principle and open the door to any level of development you desire within the limits of your ultimate natural genetic potential.

How to best split up your training routine

As already discussed you will be splitting the entire body workout you performed at the basic level of natural training into two workouts of approximately equal length, to be performed on two consecutive days, in which approximately half the muscle groups will be trained on the first day and the remainder will be trained on the second. Considering the fact that there are so many different ways that the muscle groups can be apportioned between the two days, we must be concerned with placing them in the order which will best suit our training purposes.

As in the beginner section, we are most concerned with training all the muscle groups in the precise order which will allow each of them to obtain the maximum benefit possible without negatively affecting the training of the remainder of the muscle groups which have to be trained in the same workout. Furthermore we have to split the full body workout into two almost equal workouts which are divided so that the same thing is taken into consideration. While dividing and organizing the two workouts in the most efficient and productive way possible may appear to be an almost insurmountable task because of the practically limitless options available, I am happy to say that the optimum solution is actually quite simple and logical. To a large degree the setup at this level is based on the information which was presented in the logical progression of exercise section of the basic training level.

As previously illustrated the major muscle groups of the torso (pecs, delts, lats, and traps) are best trained together and in exactly that order. Being trained together and in this order allows each of them to be trained with maximum intensity and effectiveness. Each is simply so involved with and of major secondary support to the training of the others that breaking up this upper torso unit in any way would have too much of a negative effect on the training of each of these muscle groups. Also by training your abs with these muscle groups you will be training all of the muscle groups of the entire torso as one complete unit. This provides a couple of major benefits. First, because each of these muscle groups is so closely related with the training of the others, training them together will result in not only an increased ability to build muscle mass for each but also in more complete development of each, and better overall muscle shape of the torso unit as a whole. Training such closely related muscle groups together simply results in better muscle tie-ins between each other than would be possible if they were trained separately. So training the torso as a

unit is important both in terms of developing a shapely muscular upper body, and in terms of developing a massively muscular, perfectly tied together and well-shaped torso unit for competitive purposes.

The other advantage of training the torso as a unit is that you will be able to get a better pump in all of the muscle groups because each one of them is in extremely close proximity to all of the others. As a result, you will be able to localize the flow of nutrient- and oxygen-rich blood to each muscle group you are training more easily than if you were training muscle groups which were some distance away from each other. The increased blood flow will also result in a more efficient removal of waste products after each set. The result of these increased blood flow benefits is that each muscle group will recover more quickly from the stress of each set and will be able to generate greater intensity on each succeeding set. This will result in greater muscle growth stimulation than would be possible if the blood flow couldn't be so localized to an area in which a number of muscle groups in close proximity to each other would be all trained together. Localizing the blood flow so effectively also makes warming up each muscle group much easier than if the blood was concentrated in one area while training a particular muscle group and then had to be transferred to a different non-local area such as from the pecs to the biceps or the quads to the delts. This, combined with the fact that the training of each torso muscle group is organized so that the muscle to be trained next is thoroughly warmed up from the training of the previous one, significantly reduces the chances of sustaining an injury. Because of everything just outlined, the torso muscle groups will all be trained together as a unit on one of the two training days. This, of course, means that the muscle groups of the arms and legs will all be trained together on the other training day.

Because maximally productive training of the torso muscle groups requires that the arms be as fully recovered as possible and the reverse is totally unnecessary, the torso will always be trained on the first of the two training days and the arms and legs will be trained together on the second training day.

On the second training day the muscle groups of the arms will be trained before those of the legs in the same order as they were at the basic level and for the same reasons. Dividing the body over two days as suggested not only enables you to train the torso as a unit, but also enables you to train both the arms and legs as two distinct, although smaller, units. This workout schedule was specifically designed with this in mind, as it enables you to derive the same benefits from training your arms and legs as units as the ones just outlined for training your torso as a unit.

Although the arms and legs can themselves be trained as units, the arms are at one end of the body and the legs are at the other. If the muscle group units weren't so distinctly separated the benefits of unit training would be neutralized in this case. However, since they are so distinctly separated all you have to do is take a 15- or 20-minute break after training the arms before hitting the legs. This will give the arms sufficient time for their muscles to hold and take full advantage of the pump they have received, and for the localized heavy blood supply in that area to diffuse and return to a more evenly distributed level through the body. Then, when you train the legs, you will be able to pull maximum amounts of blood to the area without having to pull a large supply away from the arms, which would still be fighting to hold on to that extra blood for the first few minutes after they've been trained in an effort to replenish as much oxygen and remove as many waste products as possible.

Besides all the advantages associated with dividing your workouts in terms of units of closely related muscle groups, dividing the muscle groups exactly as suggested will provide the most even distribution of workload between the two days of any of the other common apportionments of muscle groups between the two days. The most common of these involves training the pecs, delts, triceps and abs on one day and the lats, traps, biceps, quads, hams, and calves on the second day. This routine is called a push/pull routine because all the pushing muscles of the upper body are worked the first day and all the pulling muscles of the upper body, plus the legs, are worked on the second day. This type of routine can occasionally be performed for a change of pace, but it has too many inherent disadvantages to be used on a regular basis. This routine has only one advantage over the torso, arm, and leg split. This advantage is that the biceps and triceps are each trained in combination with the two torso muscle groups in whose training they are strongly stressed. This means they are

not placed under any stress whatsoever on any other training day. Of course, this is the way it should be. Unfortunately, the one disadvantage, although not a major one, of the torso, arm, and leg split, is that both the biceps and triceps are quite strongly stressed during the torso workout and then they must endure a full workout the following day.

This is taken into consideration in terms of the number of sets recommended for the upper arms, muscles— always two less than for the torso muscle groups. By reducing the workload slightly to compensate for this stress, any added risk of overtraining is eliminated. It must also be emphasized, as in the logical progression of exercises section of the basic level which described a similar situation, that as long as this added stress is always taken into consideration and compensated for, there will be no detrimental effect in attaining maximum arm development. During the first couple of months on this routine your arms may be slightly fatigued on arm training day, but they will soon adapt to the stress placed upon them during the torso workouts, which really is not that severe. Your arms will soon respond on arm training day as if they hadn't done any kind of work at all the day before. As you gain experience and learn to direct virtually all of the stress of the torso exercise you are performing to the torso muscle you are trying to work, the arms will absorb less and less of the stress until their involvement in torso training becomes little more than superficial.

Except for this particular situation, the torso, arm, and leg split is flawless. It is by far the most logical and effective training split ever devised. The same obviously cannot be said for the push/pull split. Some of its disadvantages include insufficient use of unit training (only the legs are trained as a unit), and a totally uneven distribution of workload between the two days. With this routine, the three largest muscle groups of the body, the lats, traps, and quads, are all trained on the same day. Besides this, the hams, calves, and biceps are also supposed to be trained on this training day. By the time you get through training the lats, traps, and biceps with the amount of energy they require, there is absolutely no way you have enough energy left to train the leg muscles with the amount of intensity necessary to stimulate maximum muscle growth. You definitely would not have the energy necessary to handle the stress of heavy squatting at this time

(remember the workouts are much more intense at this level than at the beginner level) and even if you managed to drag yourself through some semblance of a squatting workout, you wouldn't have anything left afterward for even a light hamstring and calf workout.

With the torso, arm, and leg split you should find that overall, the torso workout is slightly longer and more energy-consuming than the arm and leg workout, although according to how hard you push your squats, you may find the second workout to be more energy-consuming. Overall, the second workout should be easier because five out of six of the muscle groups trained on that day are rather small in size and do not require much energy. But the one major one, the quads, requires more energy to train than two or three smaller muscle groups combined. It is the drain of quad training which almost equalizes the energy drain of both workouts. Otherwise the second workout would be much easier than the first. The torso consists of two large muscle group, the lats and traps, two moderate-sized muscle groups, pecs, and delts, and one small muscle group, the abs, making it more energy-consuming and difficult overall than the second workout, and you might find yourself dragging a little bit after lats. On the second day, getting through arms should provide absolutely no problem, but more than likely you will have to push yourself a little to get through hamstrings, calves, and lower back after those squats.

Training to failure

Training to failure means performing a particular set of all exercises until your muscles are so fatigued that you can't possibly complete another repetition, no matter how hard you try. Simply stated, it's an all-out effort. Going to failure guarantees you will stimulate the maximum amount of muscle fibers possible on any given set. Because training to total failure, especially when using heavy weights, constitutes an all-out effort, it represents one of the most intense forms of training you can perform. As a result of this intensity and the resultant stress placed on both the muscles and the body as a whole, going to failure too often will eventually result in overtraining.

It is therefore extremely important to know on what percentage of your workouts you should go to failure, and also how many sets of training to failure a particular muscle group can safely handle on a workout day in which the concept is to be utilized.

During the beginner level this concept was not discussed, even though each set was to be performed with a weight which would just barely enable you to complete the prescribed number of repetitions. On each one of these sets you were technically training to failure. However, because you did not have the ability to direct a major portion of the potential benefit of each set to the muscle you were working, and did not have a significant level of muscular endurance at this level, you were actually reaching the point where you couldn't perform another repetition before the muscles had been thoroughly worked. So in actuality, although you were consistently going to failure, at this level you did not have the ability to generate anywhere near the level of intensity which would result in overtraining.

You should also note that if you explicitly followed the beginning level section on warming up and applied it to the training routines outlined at each of the beginning levels, you could not possibly have gone to absolute failure on more than one set for each muscle group during any given workout. This only applies to the various beginner level and advanced beginner level routines in which you were performing three to four sets of one exercise per muscle group. As I clearly outlined at that time, you can't perform an all-out maximum effort set until at least the third set of any given exercise without greatly increasing your chances of sustaining an injury. This, of course, does not apply if you've already performed another exercise for a particular muscle group. In such a case the muscle group would be thoroughly warmed up by the time you got to the second exercise and you wouldn't have to perform more than one warmup set of the second exercise, before going to failure on it. This wasn't applicable during the basic training level since you only performed one exercise for virtually all the muscle groups, but it will be applicable at this level of training and henceforth.

Anyway, by the time you reach the intermediate level of training, you will have both a high enough level of muscular endurance and the ability to direct a large enough portion of each exercise to the particular muscle group it is supposed to work, that training to failure will come to be very intense, and the threat of overtraining from this training concept will become very real.

If it isn't utilized carefully, the risk of overtraining becomes even more obvious when you consider that you will be performing significantly more sets for each muscle group at this level than at the beginner level. That means there is a much larger number of sets which you could potentially go to failure on. Of course, the risk becomes greater within the intermediate level itself as you add sets to the workout at each of the three intermediate sub levels.

You should train to total failure on the average of one out of every two workouts you perform for each muscle group. Following the intermediate level program exactly as outlined, this will come out to be an average of once per week per muscle group. Furthermore, it is suggested than you train each muscle group to failure during the two lower-rep, heavier-weight workouts one week, and then during the two lighter-weight, higher-rep workouts the following week. Do this consistently on alternate weeks. This will enable you to obtain maximum benefit from both types of workouts without risking overtraining on either. In order to be able to go to failure on both types of workouts alternately on a consistent basis, you will have to go to failure two workouts in a row for each muscle group and then train at less than 100 percent capacity for two workouts in a row. This is fine. You will suffer no detrimental effects from going to failure two workouts in a row. As long as you don't go to failure for an extended number of workouts and the number of workouts performed to failure for any period of time comes out an average of one per week per muscle group, there will be no chance of overtraining from the use of this concept, and maximum muscle growth can be stimulated.

On the days that you are not training to failure, you should train at 80 to 90 percent of your maximum capacity. This means you will be using a lighter weight, which will allow you to do one or two more repetitions than the prescribed number. This will result in these sets being only slightly difficult to complete instead of an all-out effort, because you will only perform the prescribed number of reps, not the extra one or two.

Remember when following the guidelines just outlined to always listen to your body. On occasion, you may be scheduled to train to failure and find that your muscles just aren't recovered enough from the previous workout to handle it. Of course, you may also find yourself mentally and physically ready

to go all-out on a day when you were scheduled to take it easier. In such instances do what your body and mind tell you to do. As long as you follow these guidelines and properly balance the intensity of your workouts over the long haul, you're sure to make optimum progress.

Cheating principle

This is one of the two most misused training principles in bodybuilding. The definition of cheating, in terms of bodybuilding training, is any use of assistance muscle groups or momentum to complete a rep of an exercise beyond the normal amount of involvement such assistance muscle groups would normally have when performing that particular rep of that exercise in strict form. Cheating is not necessarily bad. Using a slight amount of cheating to get past the sticking point on the last repetition of a heavy set can be very beneficial when used sparingly. It allows you to complete a repetition you normally would not have been able to complete when using perfect form. In other words, you are actually training past failure. This, of course, means that, when used correctly, cheating can enable you to train at a very high intensity level, even more intense than when training to failure. To maximize the benefit of cheating you must use the minimum amount of help from assistance muscle groups to get past the sticking point and then not use momentum to throw the weight up during completion of the remainder of the rep. The maximum stress possible must be kept on the muscle you are training at all times during the performance of the entire rep, despite having to use a little cheating. This includes the first part of the rep before the sticking point, too. You are not to use momentum to get the weight started in an attempt to throw the weight up past the sticking point. In other words, you are only to kick in the minimum amount of extra assistance necessary from other muscle groups from the point constituting the precise instant you hit the sticking point to the precise instant you pass it. The entire rep except for this one point will be performed in strict form. Using the cheating principle in the exact way it has just been outlined is the only way to obtain a positive effect from it. Unnecessary use of momentum will completely neutralize any potential benefit this principle can provide to stimulate development of additional muscle mass.

The two most common ways to cheat are first, to slightly arch the back on exercises such as curls, and secondly, to bend at the knees slightly more than usual at the sticking point on such exercises as standing tricep extensions and standing presses and to then push up with your quads. This will give you just enough momentum to get through the sticking point. You should never arch your back on exercises which are performed while lying on your back, such as bench presses. You also are never to bounce the weight at the bottom of any exercise in an effort to get momentum for getting through a sticking point or for any other reason because of the damage such bouncing can cause to your knee, elbow, and shoulder joints.

Unfortunately, from what I've seen in the various gyms in which I've trained, virtually no one heeds these warnings, nor do they follow anything closely resembling the precise cheating principles in this section. These individuals are convinced that the only way to get massive is to use the heaviest weights on each exercise that they can possibly complete the prescribed number of reps with, using whatever means at their disposal. Basically, this means throwing the weights up to completion of each rep almost purely with momentum. Strict form is not a consideration, at all. As an example, I've seen 165-pound guys who have only been training for a year, curling 185 pounds, if you can call it that. They arch their back to the point where it appears ready to break and simultaneously swing the weight up into the completed position. By doing this almost all benefit the biceps muscle could potentially receive from the exercise is lost. In fact virtually everything else is being worked except for the biceps. Then these guys wonder why they're not growing. Of course, with such training, severe injury, particularly to the lower back, is imminent. Hopefully, any of you who are reading this and happen to train like this will realize the error of your ways and begin to use the cheating principle correctly before you sustain a serious injury.

Basically, during the intermediate level of training, cheating should only be employed when absolutely necessary. This means using cheating only on those days on which you are scheduled to train to absolute failure and then only if you happen to get stuck unexpectedly in the middle of the last rep of your heaviest all-out set. This means that when you barely complete a rep on any set and you know there is abso-

lutely no way you could perform the next rep of that set without incorporating some form of cheating you are to put the bar down and not even attempt to perform that next rep. This is true even when that rep occurs during a set two or three reps short of the prescribed number. Under no circumstances are you to cheat your way through the remaining reps as this would be too intense a stress for the muscles to handle and you would also end up cheating way too much by the second rep. When such a situation occurs, you are simply to take note of the fact that you used too much weight to complete the prescribed number of reps and adjust the amount of weight downward accordingly when performing the next workout so that you are then barely able to complete the prescribed number of repetitions for that all-out set. Slight miscalculations in the number of repetitions you can perform with various weights will occur with regularity because of the fact that the body's endurance and strength levels vary slightly from day to day. You will often slightly miscalculate and choose a weight which will enable you to complete either one rep more or less than the prescribed number. Constantly monitoring these miscalculations and adjusting the weights accordingly from workout to workout will ensure that they occur with minimal frequency, and that when they do occur the percentage of miscalculation will most often be insignificant. Being off by one rep now and then will have absolutely no detrimental effects on your bodybuilding progress.

Now that we know exactly when and how to incorporate the cheating principle, let's discuss exactly why it is used so infrequently at this level of training. Basically, it comes down to the fact that because the cheating principle enables you to train past failure, it dramatically increases the level of training intensity generated on any set in which it is employed. Because the increases in workload and training intensity at this level are designed to tax the body and muscles with the highest level of stress they can handle, any additional consistent stress will eventually result in a state of chronic overtraining. This is especially true in the case of any training principle which will enable you to train past failure.

Forced reps principle

Like the cheating principle, the forced reps principle is employed for

the purpose of completing a rep you don't have the ability to complete on your own, and like the cheating principle it is totally abused by natural bodybuilders at every level of training. As with the cheating principle, forced reps should be performed only when absolutely necessary at the intermediate level and for the same exact reasons.

A forced rep is a rep performed with assistance from another individual due to an inability to complete that rep solely with your own muscular strength in strict form. Forced reps are the method of choice for getting past sticking points on all exercises in which the cheating principle cannot be effectively employed, most notably various kinds of bench presses. In fact, I consider the use of forced reps to be superior to cheating even on the exercises in which the cheating principle can be effectively employed. The reason for this is that since forced reps are performed with the help of another individual, you don't have to worry about cheating the weight up in any way, and you therefore can maintain perfect form on every rep of every exercise. This ensures that the muscle you are trying to work receives the maximum amount of stimulation possible from every rep, even the ones you can't complete on your own. This is not the case with the cheating principle as a certain amount of the potential benefit to the muscle you are working is lost to assistance muscle groups.

How exactly does someone help you perform a forced rep? Assuming you have someone standing by prepared to spot you in case you need help, you should give the person a warning just before you begin to lower the bar in preparation for the rep you know will be difficult enough that you may require help to complete it. Your spotter should be watching you very closely as you attempt this rep. If the rate of ascent of the bar decreases noticeably during the course of the rep and it is apparent that the bar will come to a halt before completion of the rep because of insufficient strength to get through a sticking point and complete it, your spotter should apply just enough pressure under the bar so it continues to move slowly and steadily through the sticking point. That way the rep can be completed as smoothly as possible while maintaining the maximum amount of stress possible on the muscle.

From my experience the best way for the spotter to hold the bar when helping perform a forced rep is to face the palms of both of his hands toward the ceiling. Then he should hold his hands and forearms out in front of his body and place the index and middle finger of each hand under the bar, at equal distances from the exact middle of the bar. This ensures that it will be kept perfectly balanced. His upper arms should be partially along his sides and his forearms should be kept parallel to each other so that his grip on the bar he is spotting is approximately shoulder width. The grip is almost identical to the one he would use if he were performing curls instead of spotting someone else.

The person who is being spotted should never attempt a rep with a weight so far beyond his capacity that the spotter must use more than the force which can be generated by him with two fingers of each hand on the bar. As when using the cheating principle, you should never attempt another rep on a set if you have barely completed the previous one in perfect form, as there will be no way you'll be able to complete that next one without a lot of help. If you're not absolutely sure you'll be able to control the weight and provide at least 90 percent of the strength necessary to complete that final rep in strict form, don't even attempt it. By following this bit of advice, you'll practically eliminate the chance of being pinned under the bar when performing exercises such as bench presses. The willingness to use a weight which you know you will not be able to control, or to attempt a rep which you have absolutely no chance of completing simply because someone is there to spot you, besides providing absolutely no benefit to yourself and significantly increasing both your chances of overtraining and sustaining an injury, also shows no consideration for the individual who is kind enough to spot you. It isn't fair to make your spotter drag barbells off your chest or push practically the entire weight of your body up so you can get one last-ditch rep of chins. Remember, he has his own workout to perform, and there's no reason for him to waste his precious energy helping you when this energy could be much better spent ensuring that he has a maximally productive workout.

Of course, for some individuals, getting the bar moving in the first place constitutes their sticking point. This means that they can often get stuck at the bottom of the last rep of a set even though they follow the advice written here and make sure that they have at least 90 percent of the strength neces-

sary to get through that last rep in strict form. These special cases will be quickly diagnosed as just that by the person who happens to spot them, as a little pressure placed on the bar by the spotter will get it moving. Once the bar is moving, such individuals usually have little difficulty completing the remainder of the rep with little or no help. Of course, any individual who tends to have this difficulty should inform the person who is spotting him beforehand so that the spotter can be prepared and help get the weight moving with as little delay as possible. In fact, everyone should tell their spotters before a set of any exercise what their sticking point tends to be on that particular exercise, so the spotter can be as prepared as possible to help him. Of course, the first few times you perform a new exercise, you'll have to have your spotter watch you closely at all times as you won't yet know what your sticking point is.

At those times when the spotter's services are actually required, he must make sure that he applies just the right amount of pressure to the bar. As mentioned before, he must anticipate the point at which the bar is about to come to a halt during the course of an all-out last rep, and keep it moving at a slow steady pace through the sticking point. But just as important is the way the weight feels in his hands as he pulls it through the sticking point. This is hard to describe, but the spotter must concentrate on feeling the force the person he is spotting exerts on the bar as he reaches the sticking point. Just enough help is to be given by the spotter that he can feel the trainee exerting maximum force against the bar at all times as the bar is moved smoothly through the sticking point. If the spotter does not feel upward pressure against the bar from the person who is performing the rep, then he is helping too much. Just a little too much pull on the bar by the spotter will result in the trainee feeling as if the bar is being pulled from his grasp. The rep will be way too easy, and maximum benefit will not be derived from it. Inexperienced spotters often panic if they see an individual having any trouble whatsoever completing a rep and they grab the bar and pull it up to the completed position. These spotters seem to forget that the individual they are spotting is exerting maximum force against the bar at all times so that if the bar slows down during a rep it will only take a very slight amount of outside help to get it moving again.

Under no circumstances should a spotter wrap his hands around the bar and then exert sudden upward force against it. By doing this he will pull the bar out of the natural groove that the trainee is used to performing the exercise in. This will throw off the trainee's form and make it impossible for him to keep the maximum amount of intensity focused onto the muscle he is working. Remember, a spotter is only there to keep the bar moving smoothly, not to take over and alter its path.

Closely related to this is the fact that due to uneven arm strength, some individuals often have one arm lagging slightly behind the other when performing reps of certain exercises, and this lag tends to become more pronounced than usual under the stress of an all-out rep. Inexperienced spotters often panic and pull up harder on the side of the bar whose arm is lagging in an attempt to keep the bar as perfectly parallel as possible. What they fail to realize is that by pulling up harder on one side, they create a sudden imbalance which suddenly throws a much greater amount of resistance onto the other arm. This has an effect which is similar to what happens when the weight falls off one side of the bar as discussed earlier. There is a sudden jolt on the tendons and joints on one side of the body and then the other, resulting in a total loss of control of the bar and potentially serious injury, not to mention the fact that the set would be ruined. So, the spotter should never panic when an individual appears to be having a little trouble. Guide him through it and only take drastic action when normal spotting procedures have failed and the individual you are spotting is obviously losing control of the bar. Chances are he'll tell you if he's in serious trouble anyway.

Overall the forced reps principle is superior to the cheating principle. The only serious disadvantage of training to the point where you might have to employ it is that you have to rely on someone else to help you, and on top of this, that person has to know what he's doing if he's to be of any significant help to you. By the intermediate level it is strongly advised that you get a steady training partner for all of the reasons pertaining to safely training to the point of failure and effectively incorporating the forced reps principle.

The importance of a training partner

The first advantage of having a partner, and definitely the most important one, has already been discussed in detail. This, of course, is the fact that having a good partner always there to spot you will enable you to train at maximum capacity during those workouts in which you are scheduled to train to failure in complete safety. When training alone you always have to make sure you have enough strength to complete the last rep of an all-out set. You always have to train with this safety margin so there is no chance that you will miss the last rep of any set and get pinned under the weight, a situation which can result in severe injury on any exercise or even death in the case of various forms of bench presses. As a result, you cannot effectively train to 100 percent of capacity on your own, and you'll always have the mental trauma of worrying about making sure you can get that last rep on every set. No matter how carefully you calculate your safety margins, chances are you will eventually make a mistake and miss one of those last reps, with potentially serious consequences. A training partner will remove any risk of this happening.

The second advantage of having a training partner, and also of great importance, is that having someone to train with is extremely motivating. A well-chosen word of encouragement at the proper time can spell the difference between getting and not getting a final result-producing rep in a hard set.[10] A motivated and positive-thinking training partner can be instrumental in keeping you motivated to train over the long haul, as well as on those days you really don't feel like training. And you, of course, can do the same for him. The best training partners are very supportive individuals who care genuinely about the progress the other person is making. Constantly supporting each other and complimenting each other on the improvements you both are making will also keep the two of you extremely motivated. You and your steady training partner should eventually become very good friends. If you do not, the relationship will not be of maximum benefit to either of you. After all, if you don't really like and care about someone, you will not put 100 percent effort into supporting him or her. Because of the extreme importance of emotional support in bodybuilding training day in and day out, anything less than 100 percent commitment to each other's training will result in a less than maximally productive partnership.

The final advantage is that it is much more difficult to miss a workout if you have a training partner who is waiting for you at the gym. This fact is of particular importance for individuals who find it difficult to motivate themselves to go to the gym. Knowing that someone is waiting for you and that you will have someone to train with and support you during your workout will ensure that you go to the gym, unless, of course, you have no regard for others and no sense of responsibility to yourself.

The one major disadvantage of training with a partner is that either one or both of you will be forced to modify your training philosophies to some extent. No two bodybuilders train precisely the same way, so compromises must be made in order to come up with a training routine which you can both benefit from equally. However, it must be pointed out that even if you and your partner are willing to make certain compromises and manage to come up with a routine which will be of benefit to both of you, any compromises you make in your optimally productive workout will result in workouts which will provide less than optimal results. The more advanced you become the more true this becomes.

During the beginner level virtually everyone can make maximum progress from the same beginner's program as long as it is constructed along the guidelines outlined in the beginning training section. This is because progressive resistance training is such a new shock to the body that it can't help but respond optimally to any solid beginner's routine. By the advanced intermediate level, however, the body has become very adaptive to progressive resistance training and very choosy in relation to which combinations of sets, reps, and exercises it will respond to best. At this point, compromising your workouts and not performing the optimum training routine will hinder your progress noticeably. By the advanced level, your body is so adapted to training and so resistant to further muscular hypertrophy that making any compromises in your optimum way to train could easily result in a total cessation of progress. This is especially true in the case of natural bodybuilders, as they don't have the drugs helping them to overcome their body's resistance to further muscular hypertrophy. Because of this situation many intermediate and advanced natural bodybuilders, once they know exactly what works best for them, choose to train by themselves, myself included.

In my case, the major reason I find it impossible to train with a partner on a consistent basis is not so much my actual workout as it is the fact that I never know exactly how long it will take me to recover from each workout. Sometimes it takes three days and sometimes it takes four. There have even been a couple of times when I've recovered in only two days and a couple of others when it's taken as long as five. I don't care how long it takes. I simply refuse to perform the next workout for a particular muscle group until I know it is perfectly recovered. Training at the wrong time severely limits my progress, so I simply can't afford to do it. Because I don't know exactly when a particular muscle group will be recovered until the day I wake up and find that it is recovered, I literally can't plan my workouts in advance with any degree of accuracy. So it is virtually impossible for me to train with a regular partner. The same will be true for the majority of you by the time you reach the advanced intermediate or advanced level of training.

The question is, once you've reached the level where it isn't feasible to train with a steady partner, because of such variety in your routines, how do you best handle the fact that you'll still need someone to spot you on your heavy all-out sets even when training on your own? If you plan on training at home through the duration of your natural bodybuilding career, you really have no choice. You'll have to compromise with your training philosophy and train with a steady partner at all times. However, if you train in any kind of a commercial gym, which I highly recommend at this level of training for ensuring maximum progress, your best bet is to work out an arrangement with several other serious bodybuilders, to spot each other when either you or one of them needs help with a heavy set. Get to know enough individuals who train at the same time you do, so at least one of them will be in the gym on any day of the week your workout happens to fall. You can even work things out with three or four individuals, to call them on a day you will be training, until you find one who is also scheduled to train that day. Then set it up so you both meet at the gym and spot each other on the various exercises of your individual workouts. Of course, they should be encouraged to call you on a day they are scheduled to train to see if you'll also be training that day and can help them out. After someone has spotted you for three or four workouts he'll know exactly how to spot you so you obtain the most possible benefit from each set, and you'll be able to do likewise for him. Of course, the two of you should support and encourage each other just as if you were steady training partners. An arrangement like this with different individuals provides virtually all the benefits of a strong, very supportive partnership, and still enables you to perform your own individual workout. Once you've completely individualized your workout it's the only way to go. I've been training this way for years with maximum benefit.

Incidentally, virtually everyone in the gym will be willing to help you out if you just ask them. So, if by chance you are unable to make arrangements to train with someone during a given workout, just ask someone who knows what he's doing to spot you and he'll be more than willing to. Then just explain to him how you want him to spot you and chances are he'll be able to help you attain maximum benefit from your sets. It's an unwritten law in the gym that everyone will help each other out. Over the years I've never had trouble getting someone to spot me for a set and I've never turned down anyone else's request. In the process I've made a lot of friends and had a multitude of fabulous workouts.

However, during the beginner and beginner intermediate levels, you should definitely train with a steady partner, preferably someone slightly more experienced than you who can correct any basic mistakes you might make in terms of exercise performance and effectively utilizing basic training principles. During the two break-in levels, the two beginner levels, and the beginner intermediate level you should generally train with someone one to two levels above you. This is true at every one of these levels, except for the beginner and advanced beginner levels. By the time you reach these levels you will have completely mastered the beginning level exercises and training techniques and should therefore train with someone who is either at the same level you are or one or two below, so you can teach them what someone else has taught you.

The reason you can train effectively with someone one or two levels above or below you through the beginner levels is that the training routines performed at each of these levels are identical except for the number of sets which are to be performed on each exercise and the slight changes in the rep ranges. Because the exercises are virtually the same for each level, the only

disadvantage of training with someone one or two beginner levels above or below you is that he will be performing either one or two sets more or less of each exercise in the routine. Therefore, the individual who is at the lower level will have to wait for the individual at the higher level to complete the one or two extra sets he has to perform on each exercise, over and above the number of sets they both perform together. Each partner at different beginner levels is simply to take turns performing the prescribed number of sets of each exercise until the individual at the lower level has completed his sets. Then the individual at the higher level should complete the remaining number of sets he is scheduled to perform on his own, while his partner spots him. Training in this way will not detrimentally affect the training of the individual at the lower level since only one exercise is performed for each muscle group at these levels. He'll just have a few minutes more rest between each muscle group than he would normally have if he was training with someone at or below his own level. However, the benefit he will receive from training with someone more knowledgeable and more experienced than he is will make up for this small disadvantage many times over. The two best combinations I've found in terms of effective training partnerships at the four basic levels are someone from break-in level 1 and someone from the basic beginner level training together, and then someone from break-in level 2 and someone from the advanced beginner level training together.

During the two break-in levels, I cannot emphasize enough how important it is to train with someone more experienced than you are. The same thing is true when you progress to the beginner intermediate level. Because of all the new exercises and training techniques you will have to learn at this level, you should train with a more experienced intermediate natural bodybuilder, one who has mastered all the basics of intermediate level training, but hasn't yet progressed to the level of instinctive training where he is no longer utilizing the four-day split routine consistently. As previously discussed, once an individual has mastered the instinctive training principle and is constantly varying his routine, which usually occurs by the advanced intermediate level, he can no longer train effectively with a steady partner. However, until you reach this level, I strongly suggest that you train with a steady partner.

Finally, in case you have not already assumed this to be true, any training partner you choose to train with on any kind of steady basis whatsoever should definitely be a natural bodybuilder. Not only is a non-natural bodybuilder unsuitable as a steady training partner because his training philosophies and routines will differ significantly from the ones outlined in this book, but also because he will tend to have a detrimental psychological effect on you. Either the accelerated progress he will most likely make in relation to your own will frustrate and depress you, or even worse, training with someone who is taking steroids may tempt you to take them. This can occur both as a result of being frustrated over the fact that he is progressing faster than you, or because his casual attitude about drugs and willingness to risk his neck for some added muscle as if it's no big deal could eventually corrupt your own training and weaken your mental resistance. This is dangerous and could result in your giving in to the temptation of taking steroids. Therefore you should absolutely not train with a known steroid user under any circumstances, and if you happen to find out that the individual you are training with is taking steroids, you should seriously consider finding another training partner. You can still remain friends, but remaining training partners could definitely be dangerous to your health.

Intermediate level training programs

As I've already mentioned, there are anywhere from one to three different set schedules for the two exercises given for each muscle group at each intermediate level. In most cases you are given two alternative set schedules which are almost identical. The only difference between them is that in the first schedule you will be performing one set more of the first exercise and in the second schedule you will be performing one set more of the second exercise. Because these workouts are so similar, the heavy, light rep schedules will be presented only for the first choice of sets. When performing the second choice of sets, the same rep schedules will be valid except that they will apply to the opposite exercise they applied to in the first place. An excellent example of how the set schedules are reversed in such a case is the forearm routine presented in the advanced intermediate day 2 workout, in which the alternate set schedule is also presented. This exact reversal is applicable in all other similar cases.

In all remaining cases, the alternative set schedules are included, because they vary so greatly from the first choice that it would be too complicated to figure them out on your own. These schedules are very precise and complex. This is especially true when training the leg muscles at the advanced intermediate level, as you are given three alternative set schedules to perform for each of them on a rotating basis.

When training any muscle group with two exercises you will not require as many warmup sets before you can train heavy safely on the second exercise as you did on the first. This is due to the fact that the first exercise you perform for any muscle group, even though it will only warm up the muscle area it works most directly, will still provide a more general warmup for the muscle as a whole. As a result, you generally require only one moderately light warmup set on the second exercise before you can train with close to an all-out effort on the second set. You wouldn't be able to train maximally heavy or 100 percent all-out without there still being some risk of injury, but you can train hard enough on this set that it will be very productive. Combining this with only having to perform a moderately light first set, instead of a very light one as in the case of the first set of the first exercise, you will be able to thoroughly work the part of the muscle which the second exercise directly stimulates with only two sets of that exercise, instead of the usual three. I have only recommended your performing so few sets of an exercise either when absolutely necessary, as a result of having to perform a low number of total sets for certain muscle groups at certain levels, or because I consider it more beneficial to perform a disproportionately high number of sets of another exercise. Either way, I have set up the routines so that you will never perform only two sets of any exercise for two workouts in a row unless the section of the muscle which that exercise works is not supposed to be trained with more than two sets for an entire level. An example of this involves the forearm muscles. During the entire beginner, intermediate level you will only be performing two sets of wrist curls for the inner forearm and two sets of reverse wrist curls for the outer forearm. The same is true of the lower back and neck exercises at one or more levels.

Finally, you will note the addition of three muscle groups to the intermediate level routines which were not trained at the beginner levels. These muscle groups are the neck muscles, the lower back, and the rib box, which isn't exactly a muscle group. During the beginner levels of training each of these three areas received sufficient growth and strength stimulation indirectly from exercises which worked other muscle groups so they didn't require the performance of exercises which stimulated them directly. However, by the time you reach the advanced intermediate level you should have a training program for each one of these areas. Complete development of each one of these areas in combination with the remaining muscle groups is essential if you ever hope to obtain the most complete, proportioned, and shapely development of your physique. Full development of each of these three areas is of practical benefit, too, as we shall soon see.

In terms of appearance, few things look more ridiculous than having a strong muscular physique connected to your head by a pencil neck. It just doesn't look right. Having a thick, muscular neck gives you a rugged look. Also, on the practical side, having strong neck muscles will help to lessen the severity of a whiplash effect if you ever get in a car or motorcycle accident. The neck muscles require very little energy to train effectively, so you can train them with complete effectiveness with virtually no energy loss. The best time to train them is right after traps, as trap exercises such as shoulder shrugs strongly involve the neck muscles. Therefore, doing traps first provides a good warmup for hitting the neck muscles directly.

The second area is the rib box and serratus. Expanding your rib box is important for a number of reasons. In terms of appearance, a full, significantly expanded rib box will give your entire upper body a fuller, more shapely appearance. The appearance of your chest development will especially benefit as expanding the rib box will make the pecs look much thicker and fuller, and will add a whole new dimension of depth to your chest development. A full, deep rib box will also give your entire upper body an added dimension of thickness it did not possess previously and will give you a much larger differential between the width and thickness of your upper body and that of your waist. This, in turn, will give you a much more impressive V-taper, and a more symmetrical appearance overall. Besides the rib box itself, there are small surrounding muscles called the serratus which tie together the rib box with the lats. These muscles are on both the right and left side and are lined up in a row like small fingers. Developing these muscles will tie in the rib box with the chest, back, and abs in beautiful fashion, and will give the upper body a detailed, finished look. The serratus are best worked with various forms of bent-arm pullovers which also strongly stress the lats. Because of this, the serratus should be trained just prior to the lats. Since they are very small muscles, the most they will need is two sets at the intermediate level. In fact you will not begin training them until after the beginner intermediate level. Training your serratus just prior to your lats, as you will soon find out, will provide your lats with an excellent warmup.

Now let's get back to the rib box itself. There is one other major advantage which an expanded rib box provides besides that of improved appearance. An expanded rib box will result in increased lung capacity and more room for the internal organs. Besides the actual increase in lung capacity, you will also find that your breathing is fuller and deeper than it was previously. Simply stated, you will find yourself naturally taking in more air on every breath because of the increased size and flexibility of the rib box and the surrounding connective tissue which comes as a direct result of specialized rib box training.

An increased lung capacity, and an increase in the amount of air you inhale on every breath, means you will be taking in significantly more oxygen than you used to. This means that all the tissues of the body will be receiving more oxygen than they ever have before. The result of this should be a noticeable increase in energy levels and overall endurance. This is a benefit which will help make your training—and all other aspects of your life—both more productive and more enjoyable. The most important aspect of a productive rib box workout is controlled heavy breathing. Before you can train the rib box effectively you must place the body in a position where it is forced to start breathing heavily. Once the body is in this state it is very easy to maintain and control it so that you ensure maximally productive rib box workouts. Since nothing stimulates heavy breathing like training the quads, it makes perfect sense to train the rib box on day 2 after the quadriceps. This makes even more sense when you consider the fact that one of the most productive rib box expanding exercises you can perform is breathing squats. Breathing squats are performed with very light weights, so you will still be able to perform your regular quad workout without any risk of overtraining your legs. Quads, of course, will still feel very fatigued on the breathing squats because of the thorough workout they have just received, but their development will not be negatively affected. The other advantage of performing your rib box training at this time is that the workouts for the remaining muscle groups will not be negatively affected. Performing a squatting movement during your rib box training will ensure that the hamstrings retain the warmed-up condition which your regular quad workout provides them with.

The breathing squats, as I mentioned, will not be performed with heavy enough weight to stimulate a significant number of additional quadricep fibers. However, they will be more than sufficient for holding all the blood in the warmed-up hamstrings so that you can proceed with your usual hamstring workout immediately after training your rib box without any detrimental effects whatsoever. It should also be noted that the other exercise you will be performing for your rib box, which is a breathing pullover, is vastly different from the bent-arm pullovers you will be performing the day before your serratus and lats. Breathing pullovers, like breathing squats, are performed with very light weights. As a result, while breathing pullovers do place a slight amount of stress on the lats and serratus, it is so insignificant compared to that of bent-arm pullovers that you won't have to worry about either muscle group becoming overtrained. This is true despite the fact that you will, in essence, be performing one form or another of pullovers during every workout you perform. After training your hamstrings you can train your calves as usual. When I describe how to perform breathing pullovers and breathing squats in the exercise description section, I will describe a specific breathing pattern which should be utilized on each set.

Incidentally, breathing squats and breathing pullovers are the only two exercises which should be—in fact, must be—performed in superset fashion for maximum benefit. Remember that when training the rib box you are not trying to stimulate the development of muscle mass, but rather create a pro-

longed, controlled, heavy breathing effect. Superset rib box training is excellent for this purpose. Incidentally, when training the rib box you will always be performing some form of a breathing pullover supersetted with some form of breathing squat, in that order. The pullovers should always be performed first. There are no other exercises or exercise combinations which expand the rib box with anywhere near the effectiveness as the one just outlined. In fact, any other exercise besides breathing squats and breathing pullovers is almost totally useless for this purpose.

The final area which is added to the training routine at the intermediate level is the lower back, more specifically the lumbar muscles. During the beginner levels, the lumbar muscles were sufficiently stimulated by other exercises such as parallel squats. Also, the amount of weight that you were able to use on your exercises at the beginner level was not substantial enough to put undue stress on the lower back, as long as you consistently made use of the support provided by a weightlifting belt. However, by the time you reach the beginner intermediate level, the situation will be significantly different. By this time you will be using a lot more weight on your exercises, and the result will be a lot more stress on the lower back, especially when performing exercises such as full squats and bent-over rows. The addition of stiff-legged deadlifts will work the lumbar muscles hard enough to stimulate a more substantial increase in tone and strength than virtually all other non-direct lumbar exercises can provide. However, by this time they still require some direct work. For this reason, I have added a lower back exercise to the routine to be performed at the end of the day 2 workout at all three intermediate levels. Since the lower back muscles assist so much with the performance of other exercises, hitting them directly with more than three sets during any of the three intermediate levels will quickly lead to overtraining.

Now let's discuss the benefits of lower back training. In terms of appearance, well-developed lumbar muscles will probably not impress anyone except contest judges. Since most of you will not be concerned with competition, training these muscles for the sake of improved appearance will probably not motivate you very much. However, lower back training is extremely important for more practical reasons.

Number one on the list is injury pre-

vention. You will need a strong, well-developed lower back in order to safely support the amount of weight you'll be able to use on exercises, such as squats and bent-over rows by the time you reach the advanced intermediate level. The extra strength a few sets of direct lumbar training will give your lower back, in combination with consistently warming up properly, will virtually eliminate any chance of your sustaining a lower back injury. Since the lower back is generally a weak link, and therefore an injury-prone area, for most weight trainers, this is vitally important.

The other major benefit lower back training will provide is that it will give you added strength to move heavy objects which would normally be difficult to move. Lower back strength is especially important for individuals who have heavy labor jobs, such as construction for men and nursing for women.

Now let's discuss the reasons for training the lower back at the end of day 2. Basically, this time was picked by the process of elimination. First of all, you must always train your lower back last on whatever workout day you train it. Otherwise, the lumbar muscles will be too weak and tired after being trained to adequately support the weight which must be used on the exercises for the remaining muscle groups. For example, if you trained your lower back before your lats, the lumbar muscles would be so fatigued that they wouldn't be able to support the usual amount of weight you would use on bent-over rows later on in the workout. The fact is that training any muscle group after training your lower back is potentially dangerous because of the weakened condition and loss of support ability which occurs in the lumbar muscles after being trained.

The reason the lower back is trained on day 2 instead of day 1 is that the lumbar muscles would not sufficiently recover 24 hours after a day 1 workout to be able to adequately handle the stress placed upon them by the day 2 exercises, especially squats. Your lower back must be as fresh as possible in order to perform squats with maximum effectiveness and in complete safety. This means it's much better to train the lumbar muscles at the end of the day 2 workout. Training them at this time gives them at least 48 hours of recovery time before the next day 1 workout. This is sufficient time for their strength and support capabilities to return to the point where they can easily handle the support requirements the day 1 exercises place upon them. By the next day 2 workout, 24 hours later, they'll be fully recovered and ready to handle squats.

Overtraining—the most critical mistake

Throughout this book I have made numerous references to the condition known as overtraining and have discussed ways to prevent it. In this section I will discuss specific signs and symptoms of overtraining as well as other aspects of this condition not previously discussed in detail. Before discussing overtraining in depth, let's first clarify some pertinent background information.

As I've previously discussed, the only way to stimulate significant increases in both strength and muscular development is by consistently utilizing the overload principle. This principle, which underlies all other principles of physical training, is based on the following all-important fact: If the body is exposed to a slightly greater stress than it is accustomed to, it will respond by increasing its ability to withstand that stress.[13] Translated into bodybuilding terms this means that by slowly and progressively increasing the intensity of your workouts over an extended period of time, you will ensure that your body has a chance to respond with the necessary increases in both muscle mass and strength. In relation to such progressive increases is the amount of stress placed on the skeletal muscle system. The condition known as overtraining occurs in an individual when the body as a whole, and the muscular system in particular, is subjected to such rapid and significant increases in the intensity level and workload from an unreasonably intense workout schedule, or other intense stress, that the body can't cope with it for more than a brief period. Under normal circumstances the human body has a substantial energy reserve for use in unexpectedly severe energy-draining situations.

When an individual is training in the most productive way possible, he will be taxing the muscles and body to a point only slightly more stressful than they are used to. Thus, the drain on the body's energy reserves will be so slight that they can easily be restored to full capacity by the time of the next workout. Also, as previously discussed, the workload and intensity level placed on the muscles themselves should be increased gradually over a prolonged period of time so that the muscles are able to recover fully from workout to workout, and increase in both mass and strength at the most rapid rate possible. As I've already explained, at the intermediate level and henceforth you should only perform, at most, half of your workouts at maximum capacity to further ensure that the muscular system is not overtaxed.

When an individual overtrains he places a tremendous drain on his normal systemic and muscular energy reserves and recuperative abilities. The human organism considers the energy drain caused by overtraining to be a serious threat to its functional integrity. It uses its energy reserves to counteract these deleterious effects in an effort to maintain optimally functioning energy levels, to offset the stress placed on the systems of the body from overtraining, particularly the muscular, endocrine and nervous systems, and to maintain optimum functioning of the overall human organism as long as possible. While these energy reserves are being utilized, the body can be said to be effectively neutralizing the deleterious effects of overtraining. Therefore, it is quite possible for an individual to actually overtrain for a few weeks or so until all his energy reserves are completely drained without realizing what is happening. His actual energy level will still be maintained very close to normal until there are simply no more reserves to draw from. By the time the individual realizes what's happening he is totally burned out, both mentally and physically, and has to spend a prolonged period of time resting his body, replenishing his energy reserves, and repairing the damage prolonged overtraining has done to him in terms of his muscular development.

While the individual may not realize that he is overtraining, his body most definitely does. When any individual begins to overtrain on a consistent basis and the stress on the body becomes greater and greater, the body begins to send out subtle warnings and eventually more obvious ones as it becomes increasingly aware that it is in a perilous position.

These subtle warnings constitute the symptoms of overtraining. The first warning of an impending overtrained state is a general state of fatigue. Fatigue begins to develop and becomes more severe as the energy reserves are used up, and the body finds it increasingly difficult to maintain a constant high energy level. This condition, known simply as overfatigue, can also occur from insufficient sleep over a prolonged period of time or participating in an activity which places a tremendous energy drain on the body, similar to that of progressive resistance training. In fact, studies have shown that, in many cases, overfatigue and overtraining are the direct result of inadequacies in one's overall life style and not in the training program. These inadequacies include a lack of sleep (as just mentioned), inadequate nutrition, and physical and emotional stresses. Under the barrage of such a number of energy leaks, individuals have been known to slip into a state of overfatigue and eventually chronic overtraining while performing training routines which would normally provide optimum muscle growth. In such cases, it's as if the training load and intensity of the workouts is of secondary importance. However, if you do not recuperate sufficiently from the stresses of ordinary life, the training load and intensity becomes critically important in the development of overfatigue and eventually overtraining.[14] Having to cope with the energy drain of progressive resistance training on top of everything else is, in such cases, the proverbial straw which breaks the camel's back. And the muscles and overall body will ultimately become overtrained due to lack of sufficient energy to recover properly. Now that we know all this, let's list the specific symptoms associated first with overfatigue and then with overtraining. The symptoms of both are similar. Overtraining is basically just a more severe case of overfatigue. In fact, the only major difference between the two is that overfatigue is generally an acute, easily reversible condition, while overtraining is a chronic condition in which recuperation is generally slow.[15]

In the case of overfatigue, a decrease in training desire, decreased enjoyment of your workouts, a slight decrease in your ability to train hard, and increased fatigue are often the first signs of trouble. If ignored, these symptoms may be joined later by a decrease in appetite and sleep disturbances. These symptoms usually appear very gradually and may at first go unnoticed. Obviously, the more in tune you are with your body and its signals, the more apt you'll be to notice the appearance of these various symptoms, diagnose the condition and make the necessary adjustments in your training before your progress is substantially hindered.[16]

In cases where the condition is detected early, taking proper action will usually result in the elimination of all symptoms, a normalization of all mental and physical functions, and a total replenishment of all previous energy reserves to the level they were at before the condition existed within the space of a week or two. In cases where overfatigue manifests itself as a result of an inadequacy in one's life style, proper action is defined as giving the attention necessary for ensuring the institution of a proper program of work and rest and plugging the energy leaks with any means at your disposal. Temporarily reducing your training load and/or intensity may also help. In a case where the energy drain occurs as a result of having to perform a job (such as construction) which constantly requires hard physical labor, reducing your training load accordingly to allow for this necessary energy drain may be your only alternative.

In cases where there are similar complaints and symptoms, but no observable problems with the overall life style it's a sure bet that the overfatigued condition is the direct result of either too much physical or mental stress from the workout schedule you are following, or both. This is overtraining pure and simple, although, as previously discussed, it at first manifests itself as the condition of overfatigue. Only when the condition becomes severe is it technically classified as chronic overtraining. Still, the fact that the condition is classified in the early phases as overfatigue even when it is obviously the result of too intense a training load, does not change the reality that you are in essence overtraining, and that your only alternative is to significantly reduce the intensity level and workload of your workouts while increasing the rest days between workouts. How to effectively do this was previously discussed in depth. As in the case of overfatigue caused by an inadequacy in the overall life style, overfatigue resulting directly from too intense a training load can usually be corrected in a week or two if caught early enough.

Once your muscles and body as a whole have recovered from an overfatigued state caused by too intense a training workload, you can begin to make maximum progress once again. But, of course you can't train as hard as you did previously or you'll just overtrain again.

If the condition of overfatigue is not diagnosed and corrected within three to five weeks after the body as a whole and the muscular system in particular begins to be taxed beyond what it can effectively handle, a chronic state of overtraining will develop. Technically,

overfatigue becomes chronic overtraining at the point where either all the body's energy reserves are almost completely drained or the muscles themselves are so burned out from continuously being pushed far beyond their limits that gains in muscle mass and strength slow down significantly and eventually cease, and a sharp drop in work capacity also occurs. However, the actual transition from an overfatigued state to one of chronic overtraining is actually a relatively gradual process. The rapidity with which you gravitate from the first condition to the second depends mainly upon just how far you are pushing your body beyond the level of stress it can cope with most effectively. Obviously, the higher the level of stress, the greater the energy drain will be, and the faster you will slip into a chronically overtrained state.

Generally, the higher the level of energy drain and the faster an individual slips into a state of overfatigue and eventually chronic overtraining, the easier it is to diagnose. In such cases, the energy drain is so rapid that the symptoms of these two conditions appear very rapidly and are usually very distinct. You can actually feel yourself becoming more fatigued from day to day. In such cases, of course, the energy drain is so severe that it can be corrected only by drastic measures. Either a total revamping of your life style or a drastic decrease in workload or workout intensity must be instituted according to which aspect is responsible for the energy drain. Otherwise total physical exhaustion will quickly ensue.

However, in cases where the energy drain is only slightly greater than the body's ability to replenish its energy reserves from workout to workout, the onset of chronic fatigue is insidious. The depletion of the body's energy reserves is so slight and so gradual, the body itself often doesn't realize what's happening until its reserves are dangerously low. There are usually no sudden drops in energy nor quick onsets of fatigue until all energy reserves are completely drained. In fact, the various symptoms of both conditions usually appear so gradually and are so subtle in nature that the individual, unless he is totally in touch with his body, often does not notice a physically depleted condition until he is throroughly entrenched in chronic overtraining. The symptoms usually appear suddenly and are severe enough so the condition becomes unmistakably evident. This is usually at the point where total physical exhaustion occurs or just prior to that

point.

Similar effects are noted with the muscles themselves. There is usually little or no decrease in the ability of the muscles to recover from one workout to the next when performing workouts which tax their recuperative abilities only slightly for a prolonged period of time. At the point where these recuperative abilities become thoroughly exhausted, the muscular system often becomes completely burned out in the space of a couple of workouts. This is evidenced by a sudden drastic drop in the workload and training intensity the individual muscles can handle without becoming thoroughly exhausted, and is manifested in a loss of ability to pump.

There are specific symptoms indicative of a chronically overtrained state that occur in addition to the ones already described as occurring when overfatigue manifests itself. First of all, training enthusiasm continues to drop as the body is pushed deeper into a chronically overtrained state, until the individual reaches the point where he has absolutely no desire to train whatsoever. In fact, just the thought of walking into the gym may become repulsive. This is basically your body's subconscious way of telling you that it needs a rest. Therefore, anytime you lose your enthusiasm for training you should definitely analyze why. In many cases it may simply be that you are tired of performing the same workout day in and day out. As it turns out, monotony in training sessions has been found to be one of the factors most conducive to becoming overtrained.[17] After a prolonged period of time (four months or more of performing the same routine), the muscles have become so used to the routine that they can no longer derive substantial benefit from it, although this does not occur during the beginner level. As the workouts become increasingly less productive, the individual tends to become increasingly frustrated and eventually depressed about his training. Combined with the boredom which eventually sets in as a result of performing the same routine day in and day out, the ultimate result is total loss of enthusiasm and complete mental burnout. This results in such a mental energy drain, combined with eventual exhaustion of the endocrine system, that the individual can slip into a chronically overtrained state even though his muscles are more than capable of handling the workouts. This is why you should incorporate significant variations into your workouts after the beginner level every two months or so, such as switching exercises or trying a new training principle. In this way you'll continually shock your muscles, thus ensuring that your training is maximally productive while simultaneously preventing mental burnout and overtraining as a result of training monotony and endocrine system burnout. Keep in mind, however, that while training monotony is often the cause of a loss of enthusiasm, it usually occurs as a direct result of depletion in energy reserves and recuperative ability.

As you become more chronically overtrained, your sleeping patterns will tend to become increasingly disturbed. Eventually, you may find yourself feeling sleepy during the day and suffering from insomnia at night. Another symptom is sluggishness, and you may constantly feel like you are dragging a 50-pound weight around with you. There may also be a loss of appetite, a drop in work capacity and an increase in fatigue, as well as a decrease in the ability to pump.[18] Monitoring how well you pump from one workout to another is one of the most reliable ways of telling how hard to train your muscle groups without risk of overtraining them. The appearance of any or all of the symptoms just listed indicates a disturbance in normal functioning of the nervous system[19] and unquestionably establishes the fact that the individual is in a chronically overtrained state. Disturbances in proper nervous system function associated with chronic overtraining are one of the major reasons that recuperation from this condition is so slow. Generally, the more symptoms that are present and the more severe they are, the more severe is your state of chronic overtraining. If you are experiencing most or all of the symptoms listed above and do not both significantly decrease your training load and plug your energy leaks immediately, you will destroy practically everything you have worked for.

You will eventually reach the point where you just don't have the energy necessary to function correctly, and you will slip into a state of total physical exhaustion, as discussed previously. This will lower your defenses and make you very susceptible to illness. It can take three months or more to regain the energy to function optimally and also have enough left over to train effectively once you reach this level of energy depletion. Besides this, your nervous system will eventually be unable to handle any stress after enduring such a tremendous amount of stress for

so prolonged a time. The same thing will also happen to the endocrine system as the adrenal glands become totally exhausted and unable to cope with any more stress. Once these two systems are burned out, they can also require many months of minimally stressful existence to regain optimum functioning.

In terms of the muscles themselves, I've already mentioned that training them with greater intensity and more of a workload than they can recuperate from completely will drain their recuperative reserve abilities. As these reserves begin to deplete, the workouts will become increasingly less productive. This begins to happen soon after the onset of overfatigue of the muscles and the body as a whole. As the recuperative abilities of the muscles are totally exhausted, all gains in muscle mass and strength will cease. At this point, the muscles themselves are classified as being in a chronically overtrained state. This will normally occur in conjunction with more general symptoms, such as loss of enthusiasm and disturbance of sleep patterns. If corrective action is not taken at this time, the muscles eventually will be unable to recuperate at all, the body will slip into a negative nitrogen balance and you will actually begin to lose substantial amounts of muscle mass. The muscles will be so completely burned out by this time, that it will take a couple weeks to a month of complete rest from training, followed by three or four months of very low intensity training, to restore both a positive nitrogen balance and the recuperative abilities of the skeletal muscular system to the point where you will be able to regain the muscle mass you have lost. Only then can you resume training with the intensity which will enable you to once more gain additional muscle mass. Of course, you will have to make sure you don't train as hard as you did previously or you will once again become chronically overtrained.

If you take the necessary actions which will pull you out of the chronic overtrained state as soon as the symptoms indicate that you are in this state, you shouldn't suffer any severe complications. The symptoms you are experiencing will gradually disappear at the rate it took them to develop. For example, if you've been chronically overtrained for three weeks and were in a state of overfatigue for the previous four weeks, it will take approximately seven weeks before all the symptoms disappear and your systemic energy reserves

and the recuperative abilities of the muscles have returned to their previous optimum level. During this recuperation period you will often feel fatigued and find that you require a lot of extra sleep even though you may have completely plugged the energy leak. The fatigue, of course, is a result of the body being exceptionally drained of energy and the extra sleep is one of the most effective ways in which your body can replenish its energy reserves. During this period of time you should also not expect to gain any additional muscle mass or strength. Just be content to hold on to what you have. The low level of systemic energy will virtually ensure that there is not enough energy left over to build additional muscle mass. Only when the energy reserves are replenished can progress resume.

Before closing out this section, I am going to discuss a couple of specific factors which have been found to be particularly conducive to making an individual susceptible to slipping into an overfatigued and eventually a chronically overtrained state.

One factor is an especially large drop in body weight, which is defined as greater than 4 percent of your individual body weight. It doesn't seem to matter whether the drop occurs as a result of a long-term decrease in caloric intake or as a rapid drop, such as that necessary to get ripped for a contest, or make weight for a wrestling match, etc.[20] Anyone who is trying to tone up or build maximum muscle mass while simultaneously dieting to lose body fat should take this fact into consideration, and reduce the workload and level of intensity of their workouts accordingly. A slight decrease of both intensity and workload should be sufficient.

Advanced training principles and overtraining

Certain training principles and certain ways of training place more stress on the nervous system, endocrine system and the muscles themselves. Consistent use of any one of these principles will quickly result in a chronically overtrained state. Steroid users can effectively utilize the majority of these principles, but a natural bodybuilder has no tolerance for the stress these principles place on their systems. The following principles should be used sparingly and only at an advanced level.

The first principle is that of negative resistance training. This type of training involves resisting a weight as much as possible when lowering it from the completed position of a rep back down to the starting position of the next rep. You should take between 7 and 10 seconds to do this. This principle is based on the fact that resisting a weight when lowering it is much more intense and stimulates many more muscle fibers than the positive part of the rep in which you are raising the weight. This principle should not be utilized until the advanced level and then only on the last rep of the last set of each exercise you perform for each muscle group during the course of the two days it takes you to train your entire body. You should then wait at least two weeks before utilizing this principle again. Because of the muscle building potential of this principle, I am currently experimenting with advanced natural training programs based to a large degree on its use without resulting in the development of a chronically overtrained condition.

Another very intense training principle is supersetting. This involves performing a set of an exercise for a particular muscle group followed immediately, without any rest whatsoever, by a set of another exercise for that same muscle group. In other words, one set of two different exercises is performed for the same muscle group without any rest between them. This type of training is extremely intense. However, at least in the case of natural bodybuilders, it is not a very efficient or effective means of stimulating muscle growth. By the time you get to the second exercise your muscles are already so exhausted from the first that they cannot derive much, if any, benefit from the second. At the same time, the shock of performing a second set for the same muscle group without any rest puts tremendous stress on the nervous system and also on the endocrine system as adrenaline is released to enable the body to cope with such an intense shock. Since use of this principle will not significantly benefit you and it has great potential for hindering your natural bodybuilding progress, I suggest that you stay away from it altogether, including the variation of this principle known as pre-exhaustion.

Pre-exhaustion involves pre-exhausting a major muscle group like the pecs with an isolation exercise, and then following that up immediately with a basic exercise, in which the assistance muscle groups are utilized. An example of this is hitting the pecs with flyes, which does not involve the delts

and triceps, and then immediately following that with bench presses which utilize delt and tricep strength. Normally, when performing bench presses or any other basic exercise the assistance muscle groups (in this case the delts and triceps) will become fatigued and give out before the target muscle group (in this case the pecs) is thoroughly worked. Supposedly, by pre-exhausting the muscle group with an isolation exercise which does not involve the assistance muscle groups and then following it with a basic exercise, you will ensure that the target muscle group is thoroughly worked and will reach total muscular failure at or before the point the assistance muscle groups give out. This sounds good in theory. In actuality, things are slightly different. First of all, pre-exhaustion is simply too intense for natural bodybuilders and it puts even more stress on the nervous and endocrine systems than regular supersets. This is the major disadvantage. However, even with pre-exhaustion, as with supersets, it is extremely difficult to effectively control and utilize the second set of the superset. This results in this principle being much less efficient and, therefore, less beneficial than in theory. The reason for this is that assistance muscle groups are in actuality involved to a slight degree in the performance of isolation exercises, although not near the degree they are involved in the performance of basic exercises. As a result, the assistance muscle groups actually still often give out before the target muscle group, even when using pre-exhaustion. Because of the relative inefficiency of this principle in relation to the tremendous amount of stress it places on the body and the high predisposition it has to cause chronic overtraining, I strongly advise you to stay away from this principle completely during the intermediate level. The only time you should even consider trying it is when you are so advanced that you have developed the ability to withstand very high intensity training and also know your body so well that you know precisely how intensely you can train on any given day without overtraining.

Training to failure, combined with occasional use of the forced reps and cheating principles exactly as outlined, will provide you with the optimum level of intensity for stimulating maximum muscle growth in all your muscle groups. You are strongly advised to employ this method of training exclusively, at least through the intermediate

level.

Finally, the type of training which has been found to be the most conducive to overtraining involves performing too many single repetitions with maximum weight. No other method of training or training principle is nearly as stressful as the performance of an all-out single repetition with a maximum weight. The stress placed on the mind, the nervous and endocrine systems, and the muscles, tendons, and joints is unbelievably intense. The stress of an entire set is compressed into one all-out rep. To successfully perform an all-out single rep with maximum weight requires tremendous mental preparation. As the mind conveys to the body that an all-out effort will be required to lift the weight, the body reacts as if it is in an emergency fight or flight situation.

Tremendous amounts of adrenaline are released from the adrenal glands to prepare the body for an all-out effort. The rate of breathing increases and the muscles are charged with power as an increased supply of oxygen-rich blood flows into them. This all occurs in conjunction with the individual psyching himself up for the lift. At the moment when the mind is perfectly psyched and the muscular system is supercharged and fully prepared to spring into action as a result of the outpouring of adrenaline, the lifter makes his attempt with the weight. Often, he can perform it on his own, but sometimes he needs help which technically makes his all-out rep a forced rep. This results in his training past failure and puts even greater stress on his body and muscles. Because of the intense stress all-out single reps place on the mind and all the systems of the body, only one or two of them per muscle group will quickly lead to the complete mental burnout and total physical exhaustion which constitutes a chronically overtrained state in as few as three to four consecutive workouts. Therefore, they should only be performed at most once every two weeks and only by strength athletes such as weightlifters and powerlifters. Contrary to common belief, all-out single repetitions are of little, if any, benefit to bodybuilders at any level of training. Single max reps are excellent for building tendon and ligament strength, a necessity for strength athletes. However, they have been found to be virtually ineffective when it comes to stimulating muscle growth. In fact, significant muscle growth is not stimulated unless you use a weight which allows you to get at least five reps. As already discussed, 6 to 10 reps is optimum for most muscle groups when it comes to stimulating maximum muscle growth. A weight which will allow you to complete only 1 to 4 reps will mainly work the tendons and ligaments, and will therefore do virtually nothing in terms of developing your physique. The only possible way that the occasional performance of single reps can potentially benefit a natural bodybuilder is that the increase in tendon and ligament strength which their performance provides would give him the added strength which would enable him to lift heavier weights on all his exercises in every repetition range.

As an example, if he could only get 200 pounds for eight reps on the bench press, the occasional and proper use of single rep training might strengthen his tendons and ligaments so he could bench 250 for eight reps six months later. Of course, the heavier the weight you can use in strict form for the prescribed number of reps, the more muscle growth you will be able to stimulate. While performing one single all-out rep on each basic exercise in your training routine once every two weeks for a three- or four-month period each year after you've reached the advanced level can definitely help your bodybuilding in this way, I strongly advice you against utilizing it. The risk of overtraining combined with the possibility of an injury such as a muscle tear, a torn tendon, or permanent damage to your joints makes performing single-max reps much more potentially damaging to your natural bodybuilding training than potentially beneficial.

Training in the precise way I have previously outlined will enable you to become progressively stronger throughout your natural bodybuilding career at a rapid enough rate so you will be able to continually hit the muscles with heavy enough weights within the repetition ranges suggested for each muscle group, to stimulate the most rapid muscle growth possible. When you occasionally reach a point where your strength level does not increase for a number of months, and you find that your progress is slowing down as a result, you can train with slightly lower reps and heavier weights for a couple of months. This will enable you to increase your tendon and ligament strength enough and simultaneously shock your deep muscle fibers to the point where you can break your sticking point, and begin to once again use progressively heavier weights in the higher rep ranges, which are opti-

mum for stimulating maximum muscle growth. This is as effective for breaking strength sticking points as single maximum rep efforts and is without the associated risks of injury and overtraining. This type of training should still only be used at the advanced level. You do not need phenomenal strength in order to develop your physique to its ultimate natural potential. The most important thing is to work the muscle thoroughly during each workout, training slightly harder or easier from one workout to the next, according to the guidelines presented in this book with a continual increase in training intensity over the long haul. You must realize that progressively increasing your strength levels is only one way to increase the intensity of your workouts. Using forced reps, cheating, increasing the number of sets in your workout, and taking less rest between sets all effectively increase the intensity and productivity of your workouts when used exactly as outlined in this book. All will enable you to stimulate maximum muscle growth.

The reason I spent so much time putting the importance of strength in general and the use of single max reps in particular into the proper perspective is that many bodybuilders, especially the younger ones, are overly concerned with how strong they are. Either they believe you have to be tremendously strong to get big or they become obsessed with lifting very heavy weights to satisfy their ego. Virtually everybody wants to be the strongest man in the gym. This is especially true in the case of the bench press.

The first question the general public will usually ask a well-built male is "How big are your arms?" and the second will invariably be "How much can you bench press?" Since a 300-pound maximum bench press is the lowest amount generally considered to be a respectable bench press, the majority of bodybuilders and strength athletes are doing everything they can to bench the heaviest weight possible, regardless of the fact that this will not help their bodybuilding progress and may actually limit it. The ego of the bodybuilder is very strong. It's embarrassing to answer this question with something like, "I bench 180 pounds for eight reps in perfect form." Even if you know that you are training in the most productive way possible this just doesn't sound respectable to someone who doesn't know what bodybuilding training, especially natural training, is all about. So the tendency is to satisfy the public's

and the lifting community's definition of what respectable training is, and start doing all-out maximum reps so you can profess a heavy respectable max lift in all the basic exercises.

For a while I was caught up in this kind of training, as most everybody has been at one point or another during their lifting career. After a year of this kind of training my bench went from a max of 275 pounds to a max of 350. I was proud to finally have a reasonably respectable bench. My max lifts on all the other basic lifts also went up dramatically. I, of course, believed that as I got stronger I would get bigger, but I didn't make any appreciable gains in muscle mass and my joints began to bother me. Since my main purpose for training heavy was to get massively muscular, I was very disappointed. I finally came to realize how all this heavy training was just building tendon and ligament strength and simultaneously throwing me into a chronically overtrained state. I decided then and there to throw my ego out the window and train in the most productive way possible, no matter how light the weight I could use most effectively on each exercise happened to be. Once I did this, I began to make the most productive gains of my life. Hopefully, the detailed information and explanations just outlined will convince you to do the same.

Finally we come to the last training factor most conducive to overtraining. This factor differs from the ones just discussed in that it is not an intense training principle, but rather an improper way of training which is so stressful to the body that it will result in a chronically overtrained state and also dramatically increase the risk of injuries. This factor is exercising with heavy and maximum poundages without preparation, both in terms of not warming up sufficiently and simply not having a long-term training background.[21]

The proper way to gradually increase the intensity of your workout over a period of time in order to prevent this from happening has already been discussed in detail. So has the way to warm up properly. So there is no excuse for you to overtrain because of this factor. I do feel I should reemphasize the importance of warming up correctly. The danger of incurring an injury as a result of insufficient warmup has already been discussed. However, I have not previously discussed how insufficient warmup can result in overtraining. Basically, a thorough, gradual warmup ensures that you will be 100 percent physically and mentally prepared to handle the heaviest and most intense sets of each exercise. If you jump into your hardest sets without sufficient preparation, your body and mind will not be ready to handle it with maximum effectiveness. The sudden shock this will put on your muscles, tendons, joints, and nervous system will invoke an emergency response from the adrenal system, resulting in an outpouring of adrenalin in an effort to get blood to the muscles under stress as quickly as possible. The stress placed upon and responses of the body and mind are almost identical to that which results from the performance of a maximum single rep. So do yourself a favor and make sure to warm up thoroughly before training with maximum intensity.

Coax muscle growth—don't force it

If you analyze all the information thus far, you will realize that the natural bodybuilding training philosophy is basically one of coaxing muscle growth and not forcing it. It is true that you must progressively and gradually increase the workload and intensity of your workouts during the entire length of your natural bodybuilding career in order to continuously reach higher and higher levels of development. However, this does not mean that you are to attack your muscles during your workouts in an attempt to force them to grow. While this works for the steroid-using bodybuilder, for the reasons already explained, you as a natural bodybuilder cannot possibly get away with this without chronically overtraining in a very short period of time. So never get carried away and declare war on your muscles. Many bodybuilders treat their muscles as "the enemy" and attempt without success to bomb and blitz them into new levels of growth. This is simply not effective unless you're on drugs and know exactly what you're doing. As a natural bodybuilder, you will find that by treating your muscles as your friends, and treating them with respect, you will make the maximum progress possible.

Using the pump as a monitor to prevent overtraining

In the beginner section I briefly discussed the phenomenon known as the pump. As previously outlined, the pump is the phenomenon in which unusually large amounts of oxygen-rich blood are directed to the muscle you

are training. This extra blood supplies the working muscle with much needed oxygen and other nutrients and also facilitates the removal of waste products such as lactic acid. This allows the muscle to work much harder than it would normally be able to without the extra blood supply and as a result, your workouts are much more productive. As this extra blood concentrates in the muscle you are working, that muscle swells dramatically in size. Normally when a muscle is being trained correctly, the pump increases slightly on each set, becoming progressively fuller and tighter. The degree to which a particular muscle pumps in a workout is often an accurate indication of just how productive that workout has been for that muscle group. Generally, the better the pump, the better the workout. However, this statement has to be qualified as it is only accurate under certain precise conditions.

As I mentioned in the beginner section, beginning level bodybuilders rarely, if ever, experience a full pump in the muscles. The reason for this is twofold. First of all, it is a fact that the larger a muscle is, the more potential it has to attain a full, deep pump. Since beginners generally have no appreciable muscle mass, the individual muscles cannot hold very much extra blood and they therefore do not pump well. The other reason intermediate and advanced level bodybuilders get better pumps is that their muscles have a much more fully developed capillary network in proportion to the size of their muscles than beginners have in relation to the size of theirs. More specifically, as you continue to train and become more and more massive, the capillary system in each muscle will continue to become increasingly intricate and well developed. And the proportion of vascularity in relation to the size of the muscle will continue to increase. The result of this, of course, is that the more advanced you are, the larger the maximum volume of blood your muscles will be able to hold in relation to their size and the more potential they have to pump. During the beginner levels the insufficient development of the capillary network, combined with and in proportion to the lack of significant muscle, size results in a condition in which the muscles do not have the capacity to hold anywhere near the volume of blood which would constitute the attainment of a full deep pump. As you progress and your muscles mature you will progressively acquire the ability to pump so that by the

time you reach either the intermediate or advanced intermediate level, you will be able to attain a full enough and deep enough pump while training each muscle group exactly as outlined that you will be able to effectively use the pump as a gauge to tell just how hard to train.

How do you use the pump to monitor workout effectiveness? First, we must define exactly what a high-quality, growth-stimulating pump is. This is the type of pump you will be aiming to attain in each workout. Simply stated, this is the type of pump which occurs as result of performing the repetition ranges for each muscle group which have been found to thoroughly work the muscle and stimulate the maximum amount of growth possible. These optimum repetition ranges have previously been discussed in depth. The pump which results from this type of training will be full and deep and will remain in the muscle for an average of 15 to 30 minutes after it has been worked before decreasing markedly. Monitoring your pump from set to set and workout to workout when training in this way will provide you with an extremely accurate gauge for telling exactly when you've done enough work.

As I've already mentioned, each set you perform for a particular muscle group in any given workout will stimulate slightly more muscle fibers and result in a slightly fuller pump than the set before, and eventually a full, deep pump will result. Once you have achieved this maximum pump while training a particular muscle group, you must not do any more sets for that muscle group or you will transfer a perfect growth-stimulating workout into one in which you have overtrained. This is signified by the fact that any set you perform after the muscle has been optimally stimulated will result in a decrease in the pump. The moment that your pump starts to decrease when performing a set instead of increasing further, you know you've done too much and it's time to end the workout for that muscle group. It will take a while to develop the ability to know when your muscles have been optimally pumped during a workout, most likely until the advanced intermediate or advanced levels of training. Until you master this ability you will often miscalculate and cross the fine line of maximum pump. However, as long as you stop training a particular muscle group at the exact time it starts to lose its pump and begins to feel burned out, you will suffer minimal negative effects.

You can compensate for the slightly overtrained state this will create in the muscle group itself by training that muscle group with slightly less intensity during the following workout than you normally would. As you become more experienced you will become much more accurate in determining when you've attained a maximum pump. As a result, you will gradually perfect the ability to end the workout you are performing for a particular muscle group right at the point of maximum pump, and just prior to the set which would result in the beginning of an overtrained state and a decrease in pump.

At each level of training the number of sets and level of intensity outlined in this book will result in your attaining the fullest and deepest pump you can hope to achieve on a regular basis. However, as I discussed in depth in the instinctive training section, there are always exceptions to the rule, and times when it is advantageous to deviate from the recommended routines. Because monitoring the way your muscles pump in any given workout is such an accurate way of determining exactly how much to do during that workout and how productive the workout will ultimately be, you should concentrate on mastering an understanding of this informative tool as quickly as possible. By listening to your body and using the instinctive training principle as previously outlined, you will be able to determine exactly when to do a couple of sets more or a couple of sets less for a particular muscle group than is generally recommended. It should be pointed out that there will often be times when you can't get a full, deep pump, no matter what you do. The body sometimes just doesn't respond optimally. The reasons for this have been discussed previously. There are also times when you can't seem to get the proper groove on your exercises which would result in the attainment of an optimum pump. Because it is common to get a less than perfect pump, you will have to eventually develop the ability to tell when the muscles have been worked optimally as a reflection of the various ways in which you as an individual may pump from workout to workout. To do this effectively requires precise, long-term use of the instinctive training principle. It will take until the advanced level of training before you can analyze the various types of pump you personally experience in a muscle group from workout to workout with close to a high degree of accuracy, and

learn to adjust your workouts so you can maximize their productivity under various circumstances with close to complete effectiveness. During the intermediate level, as is the case with all other aspects of your training, when trying to attain an optimum pump you should vary your routine only when the signal your muscles are sending out is so clear that you are certain that the alteration you are planning will result in a much more productive workout and dramatically improved pump. In relation to obtaining the optimum pump possible, the following conditions are the only ones which warrant an alteration in the designated training routines at the intermediate level.

First, of course, you are to discontinue working a muscle group the second your pump starts to decrease, no matter how many sets this is prior to the designated number you should perform. There will more than likely be times when, for a few workouts in a row, your muscles pump to a certain level and then begin to lose it after performing only about half the normal number of sets. This is a strong indication that you are in an overfatigued or even a chronically overtrained state. The longer the condition persists, the more overtrained you most likely are. In such a case you should temporarily reduce the workload and intensity of your workout substantially. Once you begin to get full, deep pumps, you should once again gradually increase the workout to its former level and intensity as the muscles are capable of handling it.

Secondly, there will be times when your muscles are not fully pumped by the time you've completed the usual number of sets, but they've been slowly getting more pumped on each set you've performed and you are sure they would pump fully with a couple more sets. This often occurs when training at a time in which the body is not thoroughly warmed up, such as early in the morning soon after you've awakened. It's a result of the fact that either for this reason or some other one the body is unusually slow in delivering the usual amount of extra blood which constitutes a full pump to the muscle you are working. In such cases, you should go ahead and perform the extra set or two which will result in a full pump as long as you are sure the muscle can handle the extra workload without becoming burned out. Another side of this is that you will occasionally experience a dream workout in which your energy level is high, your muscles

feel fresh and on each succeeding set of your workout you are pumping up like a balloon. In such cases at the completion of your usual number of sets for some or all of your muscle groups you will be fully pumped, but with the way you've been pumping you're sure you could pump the muscle to an unbelievable degree if you did two or three more sets.

These are the very rare workouts in which everything responds perfectly and you can stimulate a tremendous amount of growth. You'll find that in such cases you will be amazed by the pump you'll get. The muscles will feel as if they can continue to pump forever, but don't push your luck. Stop after a few extra sets. As you become more experienced you'll discover exactly how many more sets you can do to pump to bursting without risking overtraining. By the time you get done with such a workout you'll feel as big as a house, and the full feeling in the muscles will give you an incredible kind of high. Normally, when you experience such a dream workout, the pump will last for hours giving you a type of long-term natural high. The high a bodybuilder gets from a full pump can be compared to the kind of high a runner gets. In fact, the feeling of the muscles becoming increasingly full and swollen with blood from set to set, even when you are pumping well but not phenomenally, is a very enjoyable experience. It is invigorating and puts you in touch with your muscles and your body as a whole in a way no other physical activity can come close to duplicating. Most people who are not familiar with bodybuilding training have a preconceived notion that it is all painful hard work and totally unenjoyable. They tend to think that the only reason anyone would even consider training with weights is for the purpose of reshaping their body. This simply isn't the case. Anyone whose been training for a while will tell you that feeling their muscles swell and pump from set to set makes their workouts both extremely satisfying and very enjoyable.

Following the training routines as outlined at each intermediate level, combined with proper use of all the training principles (especially the instinctive training principle), will ultimately enable the average individual to attain a full pump approximately 50 to 60 percent of the time with an occasional unbelievable pump from time to time. Of the remaining 50 percent a satisfactory to good pump should be experienced 30 to 40 percent of the time.

You should only experience an unsatisfactory pump at most 10 to 20 percent of the time, and this usually occurs either when the muscles are overtrained or when the body is occasionally sluggish and unresponsive. The more experienced you become, the more adept you'll be at getting your muscles to respond the way you want them to. The percentages presented above are, of course, optimum percentages. It will take most of you to the advanced intermediate or advanced level before you can train with such effectiveness. You'll have to start from scratch and work up to it.

What all this means is that you will ultimately find yourself experiencing the pleasurable feeling of enjoyment and satisfaction of the pump to varying degrees during 80 to 90 percent of your workouts. In fact, the achievement of a good pump is so satisfying that a large percentage of the people who train seriously with weights do so mainly because they enjoy the training and the way it makes them feel. Improvement in appearance is, in such cases, a secondary consideration. If you are willing to give bodybuilding training a fair chance, I'm sure you'll find it to be an extremely enjoyable form of hard work.

I must reemphasize here that while I consider the attainment of a full pump to be very important and a very accurate indicator of how productive your workout is, achieving a full pump does not necessarily guarantee that you will gain muscle. In fact, as previously mentioned, the only time the degree to which you pump can be used to accurately measure the productivity of your workouts is when you perform the range of repetitions found to be the most effective for stimulating maximum growth for each muscle group as previously outlined in this book. You must avoid becoming obsessed with getting a pump no matter what. Many individuals are under the false impression that if they don't get a phenomenal pump every single time, they won't make any progress. These individuals will often perform very high repetitions with very light weights on their exercises in an effort to gorge the muscles with blood. Such training will virtually always have exactly this effect. The extremely high number of reps will pump the muscle up like a balloon. This may at first appear to be very beneficial. However, such a pump is a superficial and totally nonproductive one. The reason for this is that high rep training, as previously explained, does not stimulate the muscle fibers to anywhere near the degree

necessary to produce a significant increase in muscle mass. Obviously when achieved in this manner, the pump is unrelated to the total productivity of the workout. The type of bodybuilders who train in this manner are called "pumpers" for obvious reasons. Pumpers who take steroids can often make reasonable gains in the measurements of the various muscle groups, as a result of a certain amount of blood remaining in the muscle for abnormally long periods of time (up to several days), combined with the fact that the superficial muscle fibers do hypertrophy to some degree. However, these gains are at best temporary. If the individual skips as few as one to two workouts for each muscle group, the amount of blood which has accumulated in the muscle from the previous workouts will have a chance to drain out and the muscle will decrease in size markedly. Then it takes several workouts to get that accumulation of blood back into the muscle again. With this type of training you will not be able to develop very far, and everything you do gain will be superficial and temporary, instead of long-lasting solid muscle. Because this type of training will ultimately lead you nowhere, you must avoid becoming overly obsessed with getting a blowup pump. This type of thinking could ultimately result in your becoming one of the pumpers.

Finally, let's discuss what you should do when you begin a workout and find that after a couple of sets for each muscle group one or all of them are totally unresponsive to getting a pump. Basically you have two choices, one almost the total opposite of the other. Often, failure of the muscles to respond and pump is the result of their not being fully recovered. In such cases you'll notice that instead of pumping up, your muscles will feel burned out and may actually start to go flat, almost from the first set. In such cases you should quit the workout and walk out of the gym before you burn the muscle out completely. Continuing to train in this state will often result in the muscle becoming so burned out and overtrained that it will lose mass. You'll have to spend the next several workouts trying to pull yourself out of an overtrained state while simultaneously trying to repair the damage you've done and regain the muscle that you've lost.

In other cases where your muscles are unresponsive to pumping but don't really feel burned out, the second alternative is usually the best. This involves shocking the muscles so dramatically

that they are forced to pump fully. In such cases you really have to feel out how the muscles are responding from set to set, and you will often find yourself making spur-of-the-moment decisions as you go along. The best way I've found to shock an unresponsive muscle into pumping is to replace all the exercises you were planning to perform for that muscle with different exercises. Even more specifically, I've found replacing all my barbell exercises with dumbbell exercises, and all my dumbbell exercises with barbell exercises to be extremely effective. For example, if I normally did barbell bench presses and incline dumbbell bench presses for my chest, and I found that my pecs weren't starting to pump after a couple of sets of bench presses, I would immediately switch to dumbbell bench presses for a shock, and then go on and perform barbell incline bench presses to complete the shock. Normally when doing something like this, I would get a fabulous pump. Then, according to what my instinct told me, I would either stick with the new exercises for a while or switch back to the old ones. Shocking the muscles in the most effective way possible will take considerable trial and error, but once you master it you will find it to be a valuable weapon in your muscle building arsenal, as it will usually enable you to turn a potentially disastrous workout into a very productive one. You must remember, however, not to attempt to shock a muscle when it feels burned out and flat after a couple of sets. In such cases, a shock routine will do as much or more damage in terms of further burning your muscles out as it would to continue on with your usual routine.

How to tell when your muscles are recovered

Since we've just discussed using the pump combined with logic and instinct to tell exactly how hard to hit your muscles in any given workout, it seems appropriate at this time to discuss the recovery process and how to tell exactly when your muscle groups are fully recovered from one workout and are fully ready for the next.

As already discussed, it will virtually always take between 72 and 96 hours for your muscles to recover from any given workout according to how hard you trained and how efficient your recuperative abilities are at any given time. What I will now do is discuss what your muscles will usually feel like from day to day as they recuperate from a workout, and how they will generally feel when fully recovered. Of course, while everything I am about to write will generally be true, nothing is a strict rule. Everybody is an individual, and the body is always in a state of constant flux. You will find that your muscles will hardly ever recover in the same exact way from any two workouts in a row. The following information will provide a very valuable guideline for assessing how quickly your muscles are recovering from any given workout, but ultimately you will have to rely on your own instinct and judgment as it is developed from the process of trial and error to tell exactly when your muscles are fully recovered and ready for their next workout.

In thoroughly covering the recovery process, let's pick up where we left off in the pump section—right at the termination of the workout. Previously, I mentioned that on the average you will retain close to the level of pump you've attained in any given muscle group for up to 30 minutes after you've completed training that group. The blood will slowly drain from the muscles until after about two hours, the entire pump will have left. At this time the muscle will normally look and feel rather flat and burned out. Generally, the more intensely you've trained, the more obvious this condition will be. Three or four hours later, assuming you haven't gone to bed yet, you will often find that the muscles look slightly more full. This is a good indication that replenishment of the glycogen supplies of the muscles has already begun.

Because the vast majority of growth and repair including that of the muscles happens while sleeping, you will notice that the most dramatic changes constituting the process of muscle recovery will occur from the time you go to bed to the time you get up in the morning. Incidentally, when you first wake up in the morning it is almost impossible to accurately assess the degree to which your muscles have recovered from the previous night. During sleep, blood tends to leave the skeletal muscles and concentrate in the internal organs. Because of this you'll normally wake up with your muscles feeling flat and unpumped and appearing flatter and smaller than they really are. As you wake up and get the blood flowing, the muscles will begin to fill out. After you've been awake for about two or three hours everything is usually functioning efficiently, and your muscles will have filled out to the point which accurately constitutes the degree to

which they've recovered from the previous night. So if you wake up looking flat, don't panic right away. Give your muscles a few hours to fill out upon awakening and you'll usually find that they do just that. Occasionally, for some inexplicable reason, they may not fill out at all. This should happen very rarely, but if and when it does, it usually indicates that the muscles were trained too hard during the previous workout and there weren't sufficient energy reserves in the body for them to continue with the recovery process, during the previous night. In such cases you will almost assuredly need to take at least one more recovery day than you normally would.

Normally the next day after your workout, which constitutes your first recovery day, your muscles will be somewhat fuller than they were soon after the workout when the pump left them, but they will still feel and appear rather small and burned out. If you have hit them just right they should also feel very mushy and kind of flaccid. In such cases, they will usually recover in 72 hours. If they feel very tight and dense to the touch, they have most likely been hit very hard and will require 96 hours to recover. If they are so dense, tight, and small that they both look and feel either stringy or like a little ball, then they have definitely been overtrained and may require five days to recover. This signifies that the muscle is still almost totally shot from the workout. According to how hard you trained, your muscles may also be achy. The achiness you experience can range in severity from very slight (in which there is just a slight tenderness in a localized area of the muscle) to very severe (in which the entire muscle is one big ache), with every move you make involving that muscle being very painful. The degree of achiness you experience in a muscle group is often an accurate indicator of how long it will take the muscle to recover. If you are only slightly achy and the muscle doesn't feel too burned out, it will usually recover in 72 hours. Such a slight degree of achiness doesn't usually indicate that the muscle was overworked. It usually occurs as a result of performing a different exercise or exercise variation than usual, which stresses the muscle from a slightly different angle than it is used to, resulting in certain fibers being worked more than usual and therefore becoming achy. However, since a simple exercise substitution does not normally constitute a significant increase in either workload or intensity for the

muscle as a whole, the recovery process usually proceeds unaffected. Therefore, the presence of slight achiness does not usually represent a significant alteration in the length of normal recovery time.

However, the presence of a moderate to severe degree of achiness is a different story altogether. If you are moderately achy the day after a workout you will likely require an extra day or up to 96 hours to recover completely. If you have shocked the muscles so severely that they ache from the slightest movement, you will require at least 96 hours for them to fully recuperate. In many cases, according to the state your body happens to be in at the time, you may even require five days or 120 hours to fully recover. In terms of achiness sustained from the performance of a workout, I've discovered a rule of muscle recovery which almost always holds true. This rule applies to natural bodybuilders and basically states that any muscle group which has become achy as the result of a natural bodybuilding workout will be completely recovered exactly two days or 48 hours after the day you last felt any achiness in the muscle whatsoever.

Generally, it will take you 24 hours to decrease your achiness by one level of severity. For example, if you were severely achy on the day after your workout, you would only be moderately achy on the second day, slightly achy on the third day, not achy at all on the fourth day and fully recovered on the fifth day. By matching up this rule with how achy you are from one day to the next after a workout, you can predict with relative accuracy how long it will take for you to recover completely from any degree of achiness. Of course, this rule only applies to cases in which you experience some degree of achiness after a workout, and there will be times when this achiness subsides either unusually fast or unusually slow. In such cases you must adjust your workout schedule and train totally by instinct. However, keeping in mind what I have just said about recovery from achiness and combining it with the information I am about to present on the specifics of how the muscles will generally feel on each of the remaining days of the recovery process will enable you to determine exactly when they are fully recovered. In fact the specifics of how the muscles should feel during each day of the recovery process holds true whether any achiness is present or not. For example, the muscles will feel flat and burned out the day after a workout as already described, whether they are achy or not. The major benefit of achiness is that it makes it obvious that the muscle has been worked very hard and that it cannot be trained until you have had at least one day of rest after which all achiness has subsided. You may occasionally need an extra day if your recuperative abilities happen to be unusually slow at the time, but this occurs very rarely. However, the following information will make it clear at which times to take an extra day of rest between workouts, even when no achiness is present.

At times when your muscles feel loose and flaccid on the first day, they should be a lot fuller on the second day although they will still feel kind of flaccid with a slight degree of underlying tightness. At this point you should only be 24 hours away from complete recovery. If your muscles felt very tight and burned out on the first day, they should be noticeably less tight and slightly fuller on the second. But they will still appear rather flat and feel moderately burned out. It will be obvious that they still require 48 hours more recovery time. If the muscle was so blown away during the workout that it felt small, dense, and stringy on the first day, there will usually be very little improvement on day 2. The muscle will feel slightly less dense, but it will normally not be any fuller than the day before. It will still feel very tight and completely burned out. When the muscles are blown away like this, their recuperative abilities are severely taxed and recovery is almost always exceedingly slow. Any time your muscles feel like this on day 2, whether it's because they were even more burned out on day 1 or because their condition has remained virtually unchanged from the previous day, it's a sure bet that you are in an overtrained state, and recovery will be unusually slow. In a case in which the muscles are no more recovered on the second day then on the first, or on the third than the second, etc., the major cause of the overtrained state is more than likely a systemic energy leak.

On occasions in which the muscle groups felt a lot fuller and only slightly loose and burned out on day 2, complete recovery will normally be realized by the evening of the third day. Complete recovery can be identified by the following criteria. First of all, the muscles will both feel and appear very full. In fact, they should be slightly fuller than they were after recovering completely from the previous workout. This will strongly indicate that

they have grown from the workout you have just done. Secondly all tightness and any sensation of being burned out will be totally gone. This will be replaced by a feeling of freshness in the muscles. The muscles will also feel rather loose, but it will be a full feeling of looseness which comes as a result of the muscle completely filling out, and not the looseness which is often experienced on the first day as a result of the muscles being flaccid and unresponsive from the workout. Besides this, there will often be a sensation of power in the muscles signifying that they are ready to hit the iron again. Finally, there is the mind–muscle link. On the days your muscles are not recovered you will notice that you really have no desire to train them. You'll just get this feeling that it's not the proper time. It's as if your mind is burned out as well as your muscles, and it just isn't mentally prepared to handle pushing those muscle groups through a workout when they aren't physically ready to handle it.

However, on the day that your muscles are fully recovered and ready to be hit you will often find that you are suddenly psyched to train them. This is a subconscious language between the muscles and the mind and it will usually take until at least the advanced intermediate level to become fully aware of it and to accurately tell the difference between when you just don't feel like training and when your mind is telling you not to train because you're not completely recuperated. There may even be times when you know your muscles are fully recuperated, but you still get the feeling you shouldn't train. In such cases your mind may be telling you that you just don't have the energy reserves to handle the drain caused by a workout. On the other hand, of course, it could be depression or just plain laziness. So until you've reached the level where you understand the link between the mind and muscles and can accurately analyze these feelings, you should stick with just the feeling in the muscles themselves from day to day to tell when you are completely recovered. Otherwise you'll simply become confused when your mind is telling you one thing and your muscles are telling you another. Most of the time you'll find that what your muscles are telling you is right, and that your mind is using its innately lazy nature to play tricks on you.

At times when the muscles still feel somewhat tight and moderately burned out on the second day and also still ap-

pear somewhat flat, you can expect the following improvements by the third day. The muscles will become somewhat fuller, most of the tightness will leave, and the muscles will often become somewhat loose and flaccid. They will also still feel slightly burned out and unresponsive, and any achiness that might have been present during the first couple of days will be completely gone. At times when the muscles feel like this after three days they are only one day away from recovery. There is normally dramatic improvement between the third and fourth day of a four-day recovery process. It's as if the muscle gains momentum on each recovery day. Between the third and fourth day the muscles suddenly fill out completely, and the burned out feeling leaves. By the afternoon of the fourth day they are 100 percent ready to be trained. At times when the muscles still feel very tight and totally burned out on the second day as a result of being overtrained, you should find that they begin to make noticeable improvements by the third day. By day 3 they will only be moderately tight and will often simultaneously become very flaccid. You'll feel as though you couldn't tense them if you had to. They will finally begin to fill out and they also shouldn't feel quite as burned out. By day 4 most of the tightness and any achiness which was formerly present should have left the muscles and they should only be somewhat flaccid. They should also be noticeably fuller, and feel only slightly burned out. By day 5 they should be completely recovered. However, they will not tend to be as full, fresh, and strong as they normally would have been if they hadn't had to recover from a blown-away condition. In fact, you will probably find that overall they have lost some mass. Also, because of the degree to which their recuperative abilities have been taxed, they will not be able to cope with the stress of a heavy workout again for a while. So train them very easy for at least two or three workouts.

Everything I have just written is a generalization of how your muscles will feel from one day to the next when requiring a three-day recovery period, a four-day period or even more time because of overtraining. By analyzing how your muscles feel on any given day and comparing them to the descriptions given, you will be able to accurately assess how far along you are in the recovery process from day to day, and whether you will require three, four, or more days to recover. It must be emphasized that since everyone is an individual and the body is always in constant flux, no two people will experience the exact same recovery characteristics nor will any individual recover in the same length of time or in the exact same way every single time. Everything I have just written is what most individuals at the intermediate and advanced levels will generally find to be true.

The most important thing to remember is not to hit a muscle until it has most or all of the characteristics of a fully recovered state which were outlined in this section. Also never train a muscle which feels and appears small, flat, and tight under any circumstances. The only real problem you may encounter when determining whether a muscle is fully recovered or not is differentiating between whether a muscle is loose and flaccid, meaning it's not recovered, or loose and full, meaning that it is. However, by closely analyzing the guidelines given in this section and combining them with instinct and continual analysis of how your own muscles feel from workout to workout, you should quickly gain the ability to differentiate between the two and to relate everything else I've written to your own case.

How can you tell when you have allowed a muscle too much time to recover? Basically, the muscle will go from being full and loose one day to flat and mushy the next. This signifies that the muscle is beginning to atrophy and lose mass. Therefore, anytime you've allowed a muscle at least 72 hours to recover, and you have decided to give it an extra day of rest because you're still not sure whether it has recovered, and you find that the muscle is smaller and mushy the next day, you'll know you gave it too much time to recover. Generally a muscle will begin to atrophy significantly 96 hours after it has last been trained. Therefore, you should never give your muscle groups more than 96 hours rest between workouts unless you have blown them away and are absolutely sure you have overtrained, and need the extra rest. Often, you will find yourself in a position where after 72 or 96 hours rest your muscles are not quite recovered from the previous workout, but you know that if you give them another day's rest, they will have too much rest and will begin to atrophy. In such cases you should definitely train them even though they aren't quite fully recovered. Simply modify your workout by reducing the workload and intensity of

your training somewhat to take this fact into consideration. In this way, you'll be able to have a productive workout while simultaneously ensuring that you do not overtrain them. In such cases you should not risk performing any more work than you are absolutely sure your muscles can handle, because of the vulnerable situation they are in. Taxing them beyond their limits in this state, to even the slightest degree, can throw them into an overtrained state.

How to train a lagging muscle group

By the time you reach the advanced intermediate level you will probably notice that one or more muscle groups are lagging behind the rest in terms of their comparative level of development. Unfortunately, virtually all bodybuilders have at least one underdeveloped muscle group, no matter how advanced their overall level of development. The perfectly developed bodybuilder will never exist simply because of the fact that human beings are not perfect. As discussed in the section on genetics, muscle groups which lag behind the rest normally are deficient in one or more of the following areas: Either there is a deficiency in the actual number of muscle fibers present; the muscle insertions are such that the muscle is unusually short in length; the muscle has an unusually high proportion of red muscle fibers, meaning there is a white fiber deficiency; or the neural efficiency for a particular muscle group is unusually low. The larger the number of deficiencies present and the greater the severity of each, the greater is the propensity of that muscle group to lag behind the rest. For an in-depth explanation of each of these factors refer back to the section on genetics.

The factor which is mainly responsible for a muscle group lagging behind the rest in the majority of cases is a deficiency in the number of muscle fibers present in the lagging muscle group, or groups, in proportion to the number of muscle fibers present in those muscle groups which do not lag behind. This is a very important fact as it forms the basis of the natural philosophy of how to train a lagging muscle group most productively. In fact, the difference between how a natural bodybuilder and a steroid user should train a lagging muscle group constitutes one of the most obvious discrepancies between the two groups in terms of training the most productive way possible.

The general consensus in the body-

building community is that the most productive way to train a lagging muscle group is to specialize on it and train it harder than those muscle groups which are growing at a nice pace. By beating the muscle group unmercifully one workout after another you will supposedly be able to force it to respond and eventually catch up. However, if you're a natural bodybuilder and you've read what I've written so far, especially the section on overtraining, you will realize that if anyone but a steroid user trains any muscle group in this way, much less one which lags behind the rest, he will quickly overtrain it. The only time a natural bodybuilder should ever train a lagging muscle group harder than he did before is if he has been loafing through the workouts he has been performing for that particular muscle group. There is no excuse for a muscle group lagging behind as a result of laziness. This demonstrates a total lack of commitment to your training. The prime example of this is calves. Very few individuals train their calves as hard as is recommended because they either don't consider calves to be that important a muscle group, or because they consider calf training to be boring, or both.

Assuming that you do not have muscle groups lagging behind as a result of laziness, what approach should you take to get them up? The natural philosophy of how to train a lagging muscle group is based on the fact that because of one or more deficiencies, a lagging muscle group is vulnerable compared to the other muscle groups. If a muscle is deficient in some way, how could it possibly handle the same workload as an optimally structured, optimally functioning muscle with anywhere near the same level of efficiency? More specifically, how can a muscle with a low amount of fibers, short fibers, or a low white fiber count (which all adds up to be an unusually low amount of overall muscle fiber mass) handle anywhere near the same workload or intensity level as a muscle which has an average or high amount of muscle fibers, moderately or unusually long muscle fibers, and an abundance of white fibers? The answer is, unless you are taking bodybuilding growth drugs, it can't. The growth drugs increase the recuperative abilities of the lagging muscle groups to the point where they can consistently recover from extremely intense workouts which would normally place them in a chronically overtrained state within the space of three or four workouts.

As a result of now being able to effectively recover from such intense workouts, they will make dramatic progress and can come very close to catching up with the remaining muscle groups. This, of course, assumes that the drug user is specializing in his lagging muscle groups and not training his remaining muscle groups with the same level of intensity. If he does this, his most responsive muscle groups will grow at least at the same rate as the lagging muscle groups, and because of their greater overall capacity for growth the gap in development may actually increase. This will do absolutely nothing for improving his proportion and, as I've demonstrated, may make the situation even worse.

Because a natural bodybuilder does not have artificially enhanced recuperative abilities, it is only logical that he take into consideration the deficiencies of his lagging muscle groups as just outlined and actually decrease the workload and intensity of the workouts he performs for these muscles accordingly. However, you must be sure to train with the maximum intensity that the lagging muscle groups can effectively recover from. Otherwise you will not be able to get them to come up. Having to decrease the intensity and workload of your workouts for these muscle groups is not an excuse to loaf. In the case of natural bodybuilders the major reason certain muscle groups lag behind the rest is that because of their structural deficiencies they cannot effectively cope with and recover from the stress placed upon them by a standard workout, even one which is specifically designed for naturals. This usually does not become evident until at least the beginning-intermediate level. At this point you may start to notice that one or more muscle groups are lagging behind the rest, and if you had not read this section you probably would not even consider that the suggested normal workload could be too much for certain muscle groups to handle, a major reason for their falling behind the rest. Fortunately, you are now aware of this, and armed with the natural training principles presented in this book, and especially the information presented on overtraining, instinctive training, how to tell when you've done enough work during a workout and how to tell when you are fully recovered from a workout, etc., you will be able to train your lagging muscle groups with maximum effectiveness, develop them to their ultimate natural potential, and keep them as well proportioned as possible naturally.

Keeping in mind that developing your physique as proportionately as possible is of utmost importance, whether you just want to look good or want to ultimately compete, it is just as important not to let your most responsive muscle groups get too far ahead of the rest of your physique as it is to do everything possible to prevent your least responsive muscle groups from lagging too far behind the rest. Everybody has at least one very responsive muscle group and it's always tempting to train the muscles hardest which grow the fastest. This temptation must be resisted. If one or more muscle groups start to pull noticeably ahead of the rest, train that muscle group with submaximal intensity so that it does not develop any further and the rest of the physique has a chance to catch up. Once you've done this and have reached the point where you can analyze your physique and determine precisely to what degree each muscle group should be developed for the attainment of optimally proportionate development, there is no excuse for those muscle groups which respond best to ever again get ahead of the rest of your physique. Of course, there is only so much you can do with those which lag behind, but if you are persistent and these muscle groups do not have ridiculously deficient potential, you can ultimately balance your physique to the point where these lagging muscle groups are hardly noticeable.

Leveling off your routine for maintenance

Each of you will have your own specific goals in terms of the level of physical development you wish to attain from your natural bodybuilding training. A few of you will want to develop yourselves to your ultimate natural muscular potential, but the vast majority of you will probably not want to become massively muscular. You will, instead, have as your physical ideal a physique which ranges in level of development anywhere from just being solid and toned up to being moderately muscular. Those of you who have as your ultimate physical ideal a physique which is only slightly to moderately muscular and well-shaped will, through persistent and consistent effort, and logical application of all training principles in this book, ultimately be able to achieve your goal, unless you have unusually poor genetic potential. The question is, once you've reached

the level of development which you consider to be optimum for you, how do you alter your training so you maintain this level of development and do not continue to progress past it? More specifically, how do you prevent the development of additional muscle mass you do not want, while simultaneously maintaining that which you have developed? Well, first of all, it needs to be established that it is proportionately much easier to maintain muscle mass. In fact it seems unfair that it is so easy to maintain what you already have, but that it requires up to twice the workload and level of intensity to build the muscle in the first place and even more to add just a little more to the level of development you have already achieved. But that's the way it is. The fact is, you will actually be able to reduce the workload and intensity level of your workouts by 40 to 100 percent and still maintain every ounce of muscle you have developed. Approximately a 40 percent reduction is usually optimum. There are two completely different approaches to maintenance training. One is far superior to the other for reasons which will be explained, but both methods will be described in detail.

The first approach involves reducing the number of workouts you would perform for each muscle group over any period of time by one half. For example, if you were at the beginner level, had toned up, and did not want to progress any further, you would reduce the frequency with which you would normally perform your workouts for each muscle group from once every three days to once every six days. At the intermediate and advanced levels, instead of training each muscle on the average of twice a week, you would reduce that to once a week on a maintenance schedule. However, since you would now only be training approximately half as often as you used to, the few workouts that you would be performing would have to be just about as intense as they were before.

The only difference would be that you would no longer train to the point where any set is a 100 percent all-out effort. Instead, you will terminate what would normally be your all-out heavy sets just short of the point of failure. This will ensure that the muscles will receive an intense and thorough enough workout, and that all their mass and density will be preserved during the five- to six-day rest period between each workout, but that they will not increase further in mass. For someone who wants to devote more time to other interests or does not particularly enjoy working out, reducing the number of actual training days by approximately half as a method of maintaining their present level of development may hold a tremendous amount of appeal, and overall may be the most beneficial of the two methods of maintenance training. However, training so infrequently has certain disadvantages which result in this method of maintenance being unquestionably inferior to the second method which I will soon discuss.

The reasons for this are as follows. Basically, all of the problems stem from the fact that after five or six days of rest, both the muscles and the body as a whole lose a significant portion of their adaptive capabilities in relation to the various stresses caused by progressive resistance training. After this length of time the formerly familiar stress of working out becomes unfamiliar to the body and muscles. Neuromuscular efficiency decreases dramatically after more than four days' rest so that it becomes impossible to isolate the muscle group you are trying to work with maximum effectiveness. In conjunction with this, the number of muscle fibers you can stimulate with any given workload or level of intensity decreases significantly from what would normally be possible. You will also notice an obvious loss of coordination in the muscles which will manifest itself in the performance of all your exercises. Execution of these exercises will be shaky at best. Of course, this means that you will lose your groove on all your exercises. No longer will the weights go up smoothly and in perfect form. Every set will feel uncomfortable. You simply will not be able to get your muscles to do what you want them to do. The mind–body link just won't be there anymore. Also, the muscles, tendons, and ligaments will all lose significant strength and flexibility after such a long rest and will not be properly prepared to handle the stress of heavy training. As a result of this and a decrease in coordination you will be much more vulnerable to sustaining an injury than if you were training more frequently. Besides this, after having not trained for so many days, performing your usual workout will shock the hell out of your muscles. They will simply have lost their ability to handle that level of stress. The same is true of the body. After so many days off, the systems of the body will have lost their ability to cope efficiently and effectively with what they would normally perceive as being just another workout.

Such a workout is now perceived as a shock. The stress on the endocrine and nervous systems is particularly great. Because the workout places such stress on the muscles, they will usually be completely blown away the next day and very, very sore. In fact, because of the shock of such infrequent workouts, recovery will usually proceed in the exact same way as if you were in a chronically overtrained state, and will exactly follow the five-day recovery plan as previously described. When you think about it, it's amazing that the body and muscles can lose such a large portion of their capacity to handle the stress of a workout which they had handled so efficiently in the past, in only six days.

Of course, training so infrequently plays havoc with the mind, too. It is extremely difficult to stay mentally committed to a training program when you are only training each muscle group approximately once a week. The mind needs to be exercised frequently just as the body does. By training so infrequently, the mind has a chance to become lazy. It becomes increasingly difficult to motivate yourself to train, and to maintain training enthusiasm. Training so infrequently eventually destroys your ability to discipline yourself into performing your workouts. In order to sustain discipline and commitment to your training, you must train consistently but more importantly you must train frequently. Then, of course, how can someone stay motivated, disciplined, and committed to his training when the workouts are performed so infrequently that every one of them puts the kind of stress on the muscles and body that was just described? How can such workouts possibly be enjoyable when nothing is responding the way it's supposed to? Such workouts are more of an ordeal than anything else, and you will quickly lose all desire to perform them. Because of all the disadvantages associated with training so infrequently, I strongly suggest you follow the approach to maintenance training which I will now outline.

As I believe I have clearly illustrated, allowing yourself to lose the groove of training is extremely detrimental and should be avoided if at all possible. Training inconsistently, even if the workouts you do perform are very intense, has a negatively stressful effect on the mind, body, muscles, and the overall productivity of your training. This would not be present if you trained much more frequently and consistently, but with a markedly decreased workload and intensity level. I there-

fore recommend that when you desire to maintain your present level of development but not stimulate any additional muscle growth, that you continue to train each muscle group as often as you did previously, but that you markedly reduce the workload and training intensity of each workout. In this way your mind, body, and muscles will remain completely adapted to the general stress that progressive resistance training places upon them, your neuromuscular efficiency will remain at optimum levels, everything will remain synchronized, and you will continue to derive maximum productivity from whatever level of intensity you continue to train at. More specifically, by continuing to train consistently so that the muscles do not receive anymore than a 96-hour rest (unless you are overtrained and need more rest), you will not lose the groove on your exercises, and your muscles, tendons, and ligaments will retain sufficient strength and flexibility from one workout to the next so there will be no increase in the risk of sustaining an injury, over and above that which existed when you were training hard enough and intensely enough to grow. In fact, because the overall intensity of workouts is significantly reduced on this type of maintenance schedule, any risk of suffering an injury as the result of training will be dramatically reduced to the point where it is virtually nonexistent.

There are also certain mental advantages when it comes to using this maintenance approach instead of the first one. First of all, the knowledge that you will no longer have to train with anything close to maximum intensity will more than likely result in the idea of training being a lot more appealing to you than it used to be. As a direct result of your workouts being much easier, they will become much more enjoyable, and your training enthusiasm will more than likely increase dramatically. At the same time, the fact that you are continuing to train frequently and on a consistent basis will keep you disciplined and mentally committed to your workouts. Besides this, continuing to train frequently will ensure that the mind–muscle link will continue to function at optimum levels. This is true even if you are training with very low intensity. In fact, the only prerequisite for keeping these nerve pathways to the muscle functioning with optimum efficiency is that you train the muscles frequently and consistently. The actual level of intensity at which you train them is of virtually no significance. Another benefit is that by keeping these pathways open, you will be able to increase the level of intensity of your workouts back up to their previous level or even beyond, very quickly, without totally shocking the muscle.

Now let's discuss the actual degree to which you should reduce the workload and intensity of your workouts when following this maintenance approach. In general, reducing the workload and intensity of your workouts by two training levels from the one at which you are presently training is optimum for maintaining the level of development you have thus far attained. Occasionally, you can get away with lowering it by three levels, but this is normally too low a level for most individuals to get away with if they plan on maintaining their present level of development. This approach is actually very simple as the following examples will clearly illustrate.

Let's say you have reached the advanced-intermediate level of training and want to maintain the present level of development you have attained. All you would have to do is reduce the workload and intensity of your workout by 2 levels so that you are once again training at the beginning-intermediate level. Basically, your new workout will be the exact same one you performed previously when you trained at this level, except that you may have discovered certain exercises which you prefer over the ones you used before. In such cases you can substitute these exercises in place of the ones you used while training at the beginner-intermediate level.

As another example, let's take someone who has reached the beginner-intermediate level and wants to maintain the level of development he has attained. In this case the level of training would be reduced to the beginner level. In the cases where reducing the level of your workouts by two puts you at one of the beginner levels of training, substitution of exercises as just discussed will be very common. After you've experimented with various exercises at the intermediate level of training, you may find that the one exercise you used to perform for each muscle group when you were formerly at the beginner level is not as productive as one you have used while training at your present level. In such cases when reverting back to beginner level training, you should use the exercise for each muscle group which you have found overall to be the most productive for that muscle group, independent of

whether you used it while at the various beginner levels or not. After all, at this level you will be performing only one exercise per muscle group at any given time. So you better make sure it's the one you have found to be most productive for you. For example, for the pecs you originally performed barbell bench presses when you were at the various beginner levels. But let's say, after advancing through one or more of the three intermediate levels and continuously rotating exercises every two months that you've found dumbbell bench presses to work better than barbell bench presses. In such a case you would incorporate what you have learned at the intermediate levels and would use dumbbell bench presses when switching back to one of the beginner levels on a maintenance schedule. Also, when reverting back to the beginner levels you should continue to incorporate the principle of rotating your exercises in order to maintain the more complete development of each muscle group which the variety associated with intermediate training had enabled you to attain. In fact, since you will be performing only one exercise per muscle group, it is advised that you rotate exercises very frequently, at least once every four weeks for most muscle groups. All should be rotated except for the five torso groups so that the muscles are continuously hit from different angles, thus ensuring that the level of complete development is maintained.

Rotation is especially important when training the torso muscle groups and is performed much more frequently. As you will remember from the chart outlined earlier in the intermediate section, all of the torso muscle groups have two dimensions of development. Starting at the beginner-intermediate level, one exercise is performed for each dimension so that the muscle can be developed as fully and as shapely as possible. In order to maintain your level of complete development and muscle shape at whichever intermediate level of training you had reached, it is best, when reverting to beginner level training, to perform an exercise which concentrates on the development of one dimension during one workout and then perform an exercise which concentrates on the other dimension during the next workout.

By alternating your exercises for any one of the torso muscle groups from workout to workout, you will ensure that the level of complete development you have achieved for each one of these muscle groups will be main-

tained. An example of this is when training the lats to perform an exercise which mainly develops width such as pulldowns during the first workout, and to perform an exercise which mainly develops thickness such as bent-over rows on the second. Then every four to six weeks you should replace the thickness exercise you are performing at the time with a different thickness exercise, and the same thing applies to the width exercise. In this way your maintenance workouts will constantly vary and will be as productive as possible.

When to take layoffs

Every bodybuilder should take some kind of layoff from serious training every once in a while. This section will explain how to tell when you need to take a layoff, how often you should generally take a layoff, and how long a layoff should generally last. I will also discuss the difference between partial and complete layoffs and how to tell when you should take each.

First, let's differentiate between a partial layoff and a complete layoff. A partial layoff is one in which you temporarily reduce the workload and intensity of your workouts significantly, but do not stop training completely. Partial layoffs are most frequently utilized by natural bodybuilders to maintain their present level of development while recovering from an overfatigued or chronically overtrained state. Such a partial layoff will usually last for anywhere from several days to two to three weeks, according to how severely overtrained the individual happens to be. A one- to two-week partial layoff also is commonly used as a means of giving the body, and especially the mind, a reprieve from the day in and day out grind of disciplined training, while simultaneously enabling the individual to maintain his present level of development until he's ready to charge ahead once again.

It's nice to be able to relax, and train rather casually for a week or two. It gives the body and mind the opportunity to relax for a little while and breaks the monotony of training. Also, taking a partial layoff periodically is an excellent preventive measure for protecting against overtraining. When used for this purpose, a partial layoff will enable you to replenish the drain which prolonged periods of moderate to heavy training inadvertently place on your energy reserves, before that drain becomes so severe that you become physically exhausted and mentally burned out and slip into a chronically overtrained state. Taking a one- to two-week partial layoff once every three to four months is optimum for this purpose. As a direct result of the replenishment in your energy reserves which a few weeks of partial layoffs will provide you with during the course of the year, the remaining 48 weeks or so will be more productive than they would have been if you hadn't taken any time off at all. In fact, taking four to six weeks of partial layoffs periodically during the year will result in the remaining 46 to 48 weeks when you actually train hard becoming so much more productive, that it would take you approximately 60 consecutive weeks of training hard and not slipping into an overtrained state to make the same amount of progress.

The major reason for this is that if you train hard every single week, and do not give yourself any sort of reprieve, your body will constantly be struggling to replenish and maintain its energy reserves. As a result of this, less energy will be put into building muscle tissue. Simply stated, by not taking partial layoffs you will be doing more work and getting proportionately less benefit from it than if you took an occasional reprieve. This is true even if you know your body so well that you are able to prevent it from slipping into a chronically overtrained state when training week in and week out. Just the fact that you are constantly pushing the body and muscles to the absolute limit of what they can handle on any given day, workout after workout, week after week, is enough to prevent them from responding in the most productive way possible. So don't be afraid to take it easy for a few workouts every once in a while, even if you feel you can handle more. In the long run an occasional reprieve from hard training will greatly benefit you.

On the other hand, abusing the privilege of taking partial layoffs now and then and taking them too frequently will definitely slow down your progress. It is an excellent idea to schedule your partial layoffs to coincide with any vacations you might be planning to take during the course of the year, as long as they are spaced well apart from each other. Nobody wants to train hard while on vacation. However, performing light workouts in the exercise rooms most large hotels and resort communities have can be a lot of fun. Most of these fitness rooms only have a Universal and maybe a small amount of free weights, but this is sufficient for

partial layoff training, and training casually in a relaxed vacation environment often doesn't feel like work. It's more like a recreational activity. If, by some chance, the hotel or resort you are staying at doesn't have any type of progressive resistance equipment, you can usually find some kind of fitness facility nearby which does. If not, you may be forced to take a complete layoff from training.

Now that we've discussed partial layoffs, let's discuss the best times to take a complete layoff from training. First, because of all the negative effects that not training for more than five days has on the individual muscles, the systems of the body, and the mind as described in depth in the previous section on maintenance training, I strongly suggest that you do not take a complete layoff from training unless absolutely necessary. Everything written there about how you will feel when performing a workout after five to six days' rest applies to taking layoffs.

It is very uncomfortable, both mentally and physically, to resume training after a one- to two-week complete layoff. The longer the layoff, the harder it is and the longer it takes to get back into the swing of things. Also, when you take a complete layoff the muscles begin to atrophy rapidly after approximately six days. The longer the layoff, the more they atrophy and the longer it will to take to restore your physique to its previous level of development once you resume training again. In fact, after taking a two-week complete layoff it will often take a natural bodybuilder three to four months to regain the muscle he has lost during the layoff and completely restore his physique to its previous level of development. Virtually every book on the market will tell you that after a one-week complete layoff it will only take you one to two weeks to get back the muscle tissue you have lost, and that after a two-week complete layoff it will only take you at most six weeks to get everything back. While it is true that it is much easier to get back lost muscle tissue which has been built previously, there is absolutely no way a natural bodybuilder can regain all the muscle tissue he will have lost during the course of a two-week complete layoff in only six weeks, unless he is a one-in-a-million genetic freak. Only anabolic users can regularly accomplish this feat. Since it is so difficult for a natural bodybuilder to build muscle in the first place and it takes so long to get it back after a complete layoff, I strongly suggest that you don't

take a complete layoff unless you absolutely have to.

The following situations are the only ones in which you should take a complete layoff. Such a layoff should not last any longer than a week unless you are injured.

You should take a one-week layoff if you are in a severe chronically overtrained state in which you are either physically exhausted or completely burned out mentally, or both. You should then work back up to your former workload and intensity very carefully and very gradually over a three- to six-week period.

You should take a five- to seven-day complete layoff after a bodybuilding contest. Preparing for a contest and actually competing is exhausting both physically and mentally and will most often leave you completely burned out. Once again, you should gradually restore your workouts to their former intensity level and workload over a four- to six-week period. Besides the energy drain associated with preparing for a contest it is common to suffer a slight, nagging injury or two because of the vulnerable state the body is in at that time. A short complete layoff will allow these to heal.[22]

As I've already mentioned, you may have to take a complete layoff while on vacation due to lack of access to training facilities. If you are forced into taking a complete layoff for this reason, do everything in your power to make sure it is for no longer than a week or you will be sorry when you get home. If worse comes to worse do pushups, dips, situps and pullups as well as some kind of strenuous athletic activity to maintain as much of your development as possible. It won't help much, but it's better than nothing. Incidentally, it is always good to remain physically active during a complete layoff as this will help keep your body somewhat used to the stress of physical conditioning.

Finally, you should take a complete layoff anytime you suffer a serious training injury. In such cases it may be several months before you can train again, and once you do resume training you will have to proceed with extreme caution.

The only other time you should take a complete layoff is if you ever reach the point where you are so sick of training that you can't stand walking into the gym anymore. In such instances, take off a week, don't even look at a gym or weight, and indulge in some other different, but exciting, physical activity, preferably a sport.[23] Incidentally, being completely sick of training is often a sign that you are on the verge of crossing over into a chronically overtrained state, so taking a one-week complete layoff at such times is often the best thing you can do. You should find your training desire beginning to return after three to four days, but in such cases it's advisable to wait a full week so that you reach the point where you can't wait to get back into the gym. Taking this approach will minimize the chances of your encountering this feeling of disgust with your training again for at least several months.

Training routines— intermediate level

Before we actually put down the intermediate level training routines, a few things must be clarified. First of all, you will be performing two different exercises for each one of the torso muscle groups (pecs, delts, lats, traps, and abs) at all three of the intermediate levels. As you will remember, earlier in this section there was a chart listing the two dimensions of each one of these torso muscle groups. All the intermediate level routines will be constructed so that the first exercise listed for each muscle group will concentrate on the first dimension of development which was previously listed for that particular muscle group on the dimension chart. The second exercise listed for each muscle group will concentrate on the second dimension of development of that muscle group which was previously listed on the dimension chart. Two exercises will also be listed for the arm and leg muscle groups. However, you will not always perform both exercises. Instead, you will sometimes perform the prescribed number of sets recommended for each of these muscle groups on just one exercise, and other times you will divide the prescribed number of sets between the 2 exercises listed. You will do this in rotating fashion as previously outlined. The alternative set schedules at each level for each muscle group will be listed under the set subdivision of each workout sched-

ule.

All the routines which will be outlined here will basically be sample routines insofar as the recommended exercises for each muscle group are concerned. However, the sample routines I present for each level are, in actuality, the ones I consider to be the most productive. After the routines, I will describe a number of exercises which will effectively work each muscle group. More specifically, I will describe two or three exercises which effectively work each dimension of the various muscles, except for the cases in which only one or two exercises work effectively. Since most muscle groups have two distinct dimensions of development which need to be worked on, this adds up to an average of four to six exercises being listed and described for each muscle group. Each one of these exercises should be incorporated into your routine at one time or another to provide variety and stimulate complete development. However, certain exercises provide more benefit than others in terms of development. The two to

Beginner intermediate level routine—sample
Day 1—pecs, delts, lats, traps, abs & neck to be performed on Monday and Thursday

Muscle Group	Exercise	Choice 1	SETS	Choice 2	Heavy (Based on Choice 1 Sets)	REPS	Light
1. Pecs	1. Decline bench press	3	OR	2	10, 8, 6		10, 9, 8
	2. Incline dumbbell bench press	2		3	9, 7		10, 9
2. Delts	1. Seated press behind neck	3	OR	2	10, 8, 6		10, 9, 8
	2. Dumbbell side laterals	2		3	10, 8		10, 9
3. Lats	1. Wide grip chins to front of neck	2	OR	3	10, 8		10, 9
	2. Bent-over barbell rows	3		2	10, 8, 6		10, 9, 9
4. Traps	1. Barbell shoulder shrugs	3	OR	2	10, 8, 7		10, 10, 9
	2. Upright rows	2		3	10, 8		10, 9
5. Neck	1. Front neck raise	1			15		20
	2. Back neck raise	1			15		20
6. Abs	1. Bent-knee situps	2			20, 15		25, 20
	2. Leg raises	2			20, 15		25, 20
7. Intercostals	1. Twists	2			50, 50		50, 50

Beginner intermediate level routine—sample
Day 2—biceps, forearms, triceps, quads, hams, calves & lower back
to be performed on Tuesday and Friday

Muscle Group	Exercise	1 SETS 2 3	Heavy	REPS	Light
1. Biceps	1. E-Z Bar curls	3	10, 8, 6		10, 9, 8
2. Forearms	1. Reverse curls	2	15, 10		20, 15
	2. Wrist curls	2	15, 10		20, 15
3. Triceps	1. E.Z. Bar Tricep extensions	3	10, 8, 6		10, 9, 8
4. Quads	1. Full squats	5	10, 8, 7, 6, 6		10, 9, 9, 8, 8
5. Hams	1. Leg curls	4	10, 8, 7, 6		10, 9, 9,
6. Calves	1. Standing calf raise	5	15, 13, 12,		20, 18, 16, 14, 12
	2. Seated calf raise		11, 10		
7. Lower back	Hyperextensions	1	15		20

three exercises I provide under each level of development will be listed according to their productivity. The most productive will be listed first, the next most productive second, etc. I will clarify all this when discussing the first muscle group. I will also list combinations of exercises for each muscle group which I consider to be the most productive, but I do not have the space to explain the reasoning behind my selection of these various combinations.

Incidentally, every time you add an exercise to your routine which you have never used before, you should start off with very light weights and concentrate on mastering the proper form for that exercise. Then gradually increase the weight until you can perform the prescribed number of repetitions with difficulty. Refer back to the section on training poundages if you have any questions about this.

As previously discussed, the routine presented at each level will be split into two parts, so that you train the torso muscles on the first day and the arm and leg muscles on the second day. You will normally be taking one day off after the first two training days, and two days off after the next two training days, although this will vary as you learn to train instinctively. Since the Monday-Tuesday-Thursday-Friday training schedule is the most common one used at the intermediate level, this is the one which will be in the sample workout

routines presented at all three intermediate levels. You will also alternately train heavy and light as previously outlined. In the rep section of each level of routines, I will present both the rep progression you should use when going heavy and the rep progression you should use when training lighter. The rep schedule for going heavy will be presented first and depicted by an H and the rep schedule for going light will be presented next and depicted by an L. No schedule of recommended exercise poundages will be presented with any of the training routines.

Start with a weight that will enable you to practice the exercises in perfect form until you have completely mastered their performance. You can, of course, adjust the poundages according to what feels best for you. Once you've mastered the form, you can increase the weight rapidly.

Advanced level training

There are two ways to define advanced training. One is simply to train with the maximum workload and intensity level that the body can ultimately handle on a consistent basis without overtraining, using the principles outlined in this book. The other is to be able to effectively utilize different types of advanced level training concepts and routines which require years of experience and complete mastery of the in-

stinctive training principle to be of benefit. Mastery and proper implementation of these principles will enable any individual at any level of development, who has been training for two to three years, understands his body, and has complete mastery of the instinctive training principle, to continue to progress indefinitely as a natural and to mold his body as close to his ideal of the ultimate physique as is possible. They will also add limitless variety to your workouts.

According to the second definition, every one of you technically will eventually become advanced natural bodybuilders, whether you are just attempting to build a moderately muscular and well-shaped physique or attempting to develop your physique to its ultimate natural potential. The only prerequisite is to have the complete mastery of the instinctive training principle which comes from years of experience. That way, you can apply the advanced training principles effectively to your own training, whatever the level of development you ultimately seek to achieve. This is the definition of an advanced bodybuilder that I consider to be most important and accurate.

Following the training programs and principles in this book, in combination with mastery of the instinctive training principle, will enable you to develop yourself to approximately 60 percent of your ultimate muscular potential by the time you complete the advanced intermediate level of training if you so desire, while simultaneously developing a symmetrical and shapely physique. By simply increasing the workload and intensity of your workouts gradually to the point where you are technically performing advanced level workouts, but are still just using the exercises, training principles, general training program structure, and nutrition outlined in this book, you will be able to develop yourself to approximately 80 to 90 percent of your ultimate muscular potential, and further improve the shape of your physique. Effectively utilizing advanced training techniques will provide you with the final 10 percent.

Now let's list the number of sets for each muscle group which constitutes advanced level training in terms of workload. Only individuals who want to develop themselves to their ultimate natural muscular potential will need to perform this many sets for each muscle group. Those individuals who have all the mass they desire and are only concerned with further refining and shaping their physiques need not add additional sets to their present training program. In fact, they will generally reduce the training workload and intensity as outlined in the section on maintenance training.

Sets per muscle group—advanced level

Pecs—(10–12)
Delts—(10–12)
Lats—(10–12)
Traps—(8–10)
Abs—(6–8)
Intercostals—(3–5)
Serratus—(3–4)
Biceps—(6–8)
Forearms—(6–8)
Triceps—(7–9)
Quads—(9–12)
Rib box—(4–6) (2–3 supersets)
Hams—(6–8)
Calves—(9–12)
Lower Back—(3–4)

Of course, when you've completed the advanced intermediate level of training and you decide it's time to increase the workload, you will not immediately begin to perform the number of sets recommended in the above chart. Instead, you will gradually increase the number of sets for each muscle group exactly as you did through each of the beginner and intermediate levels. Generally you will be performing one additional set for each muscle group every four to six months until you are in the range of sets recommended above. The workload for your arms will be increased at a proportionately slower rate.

Intermediate level routine—sample
Day 1—pecs, delts, lats, traps, abs & neck to be performed on Monday and Thursday

Muscle Group	Exercise	Choice 1	SETS	Choice 2	Heavy	REPS	Light
1. Pecs	1. Decline bench press	3			10, 8, 6		10, 9, 8
	2. Incline dumbbell bench press	3			10, 8, 6		10, 9, 8
2. Delts	1. Seated press behind neck	3			10, 8, 6		10, 9, 8
	2. Dumbbell side laterals	3			10, 9, 8		10, 10, 9
3. Serratus	1. Bent-arm pullover	1			10		12
4. Traps	1. Barbell shoulder shrugs	3			10, 8, 7		10, 10, 9
	2. Upright rows	3			10, 8, 7		10, 10, 9
5. Neck	1. Front neck raise	2	OR	1	15, 13		20, 17
	2. Back neck raise	1		2	15		20
6. Abs	1. Bent-knee situps	3	OR	2	20, 17, 15		25, 23, 20
	2. Leg raises	2		3	20, 15		25, 20
7. Intercostals	1. Twists	3			100, 75, 50		100, 75, 50

Intermediate level routine—sample
Day 2—biceps, forearms, triceps, quads, hams, calves, lower back & rib box
to be performed on Tuesday and Friday

Muscle Group	Exercise	Choice 1	SETS	Choice 2	Heavy	REPS	Light
1. Biceps	1. E-Z bar curls	4			10, 8, 7, 6		10, 9, 9, 8
2. Forearms	1. Reverse wrist curls	2			15, 10		20, 15
	2. Wrist curls	2			15, 10		20, 15
3. Triceps	1. E-Z bar standing tricep extension	4			10, 8, 7, 6		10, 9, 9, 8
4. Quads	1. Full squats	6	OR	4	10, 9, 8, 7, 6, 6, 0 | 10, 8, 7, 6, 9, 7		10, 10, 9, 9, 8, 8, 0 | 10, 9, 9, 8, 10, 9
	2. Hack squats	0		2			
5. Rib box	1. Dumbbell pullovers	1			20		20
	2. Breathing squats	1			20		20
6. Hams	1. Leg curls	5		3	10, 9, 8, 7, 6, 0 | 10, 8, 6, 9, 8		10, 10, 9, 9, 8, 0 | 10, 9, 8, 10, 9
	2. Stiff-legged deadlifts	0	OR	2			
7. Calves	1. Standing calf raise	6		4	15, 14, 13, 12, 11, 10, 0 | 15, 13, 12, 10, 15, 10		20, 19, 18, 17, 16, 15, 0 | 20, 18, 17, 15, 20, 17
	2. Seated calf raise	0	OR	2			
8. Lower back	1. Hyper-extensions	2			15, 12		20, 17

Advanced intermediate level routine—sample
Day 1—pecs, delts, lats, traps, abs, & neck to be performed on Monday and Thursday

Muscle Group	Exercise	Choice 1	SETS	Choice 2	Heavy	REPS	Light
1. Pecs	1. Decline bench press	4		3	10, 8, 7, 6		10, 9, 9, 8
	2. Incline dumbbell bench press	3	OR	4	10, 8, 6		10, 9, 8
2. Delts	1. Seated press behind neck	4		3	10, 8, 7, 6		10, 9, 9, 8
	2. Dumbbell side laterals	3	OR	4	10, 8, 6		10, 9, 8
3a. Serratus	1. Bent arm pullover	2			10, 10		12, 12
3b. Lats	1. Wide-grip chins to front of neck	3		4	10, 8, 6		10, 9, 8
	2. Bent-over rows	4	OR	3	10, 8, 7, 6		10, 10, 9, 9
4. Traps	1. Barbell shoulder shrugs	4		3	10, 8, 7, 7		10, 10, 9, 9
	2. Upright rows	3	OR	4	10, 8, 7		10, 10, 9
5. Neck	1. Front neck raise	2			15, 13		20, 18
	2. Back neck raise	2			15, 13		20, 18
6. Abs	1. Bent-knee situps	3			20, 17, 15		25, 23, 20
	2. Leg raises	3			20, 17, 15		25, 23, 20
7. Intercostals	1. Twists	3			100, 75, 50		100, 75, 50

Advanced intermediate level routine—sample

Day 2—biceps, forearms, triceps, quads, hams, calves, lower back, rib box to be performed on Tuesday and Friday

Muscle Group	Exercise	Choice 1	Choice 2	Choice 3	1	HEAVY	3	1	LIGHT	3
1. Biceps	1. E-Z bar curls	3	5		10, 8, 6	10, 8, 7, 6, 6		10, 9, 8	10, 9, 9, 8, 8	
	OR	OR								
	2. E-Z bar preacher curls	2	0		9, 7	0		10, 8	0	
2. Forearms	1. Reverse wrist curls	2	3		15, 10	15, 12, 10		20, 18, 15	20, 18, 15	
	OR	OR								
	2. Wrist curls	3	2		15, 12, 10	15, 10		20, 18, 15	20, 15	
3. Triceps	1. E-Z bar standing tricep extensions	3	5		10, 8, 6	10, 8, 7, 6, 6		10, 9, 8	10, 9, 9, 8, 8	
	OR	OR								
	2. E-Z bar lying tricep extensions	2	0		9, 7	0		10, 8	0	
4. Quads	1. Full squats	7	5	4	10, 9, 8, 7, 7, 6	10, 8, 7, 6, 6	10, 8, 7, 6	10, 10, 9, 8, 8, 8	10, 9, 9, 8, 8	10, 9, 9, 8
		OR	OR							
	2. Hack squats	0	2	3	0	9, 7	10, 8, 6	0	10, 9	10, 9, 9
5. Rib box	1. Dumbbell breathing pullovers	2	2		20, 20			20, 20		
	2. Breathing squats	2			20, 20			20, 20		
6. Hams	1. Leg curls	6	4	3	10, 9, 8, 7, 7, 6	10, 8, 7, 6	10, 8, 6	10, 10, 10, 9, 9, 9	10, 10, 9, 9	10, 9
		OR	OR							
	2. Stiff-legged deadlifts	0	2	3	0	10, 8	10, 9, 8	0	10, 10	10, 10, 9
7. Calves	1. Standing calf raise	7	5	4	15, 14, 13, 12, 11, 11, 10	15, 13, 12, 11, 10	15, 13, 12, 10	20, 19, 19, 18, 17, 16, 15	20, 18, 16, 14, 12	20, 18, 17, 15
		OR	OR							
	2. Seated calf raise	0	2	3	0	15, 10	15, 12, 10	0	20, 18	
8. Lower back	1. Hyper-extensions	3			15, 13, 12		20, 19, 17			20, 19, 18

——6——
PECTORAL EXERCISES

Barbell bench press

Comments—Barbell bench presses are often called the king of the upper body exercises because virtually every upper body muscle group is involved to one degree or another in their performance, with the pecs being the target muscle group, the lower and middle pec more so than the upper part. Only squats are considered a more beneficial exercise for overall development.

Equipment—You will be using a flat bench with a pair of uprights whose purpose it is to hold the barbell at approximately arm's length.

Starting position—Lie on your back with your head facing toward the uprights. Position yourself so that your head is a few inches from the top of the bench and your shoulders are approximately 6 inches shy of the uprights. This will put you in a position where you will have to reach back over your head a few inches to grab the barbell. Since this isn't the most advantageous leverage position for lifting the bar off the uprights, you should enlist the aid of a spotter to hand it to you when using moderate or heavy weights. The reason for making sure you are a good distance in front of the uprights is to prevent the bar from hitting either the safety catches at the bottom of the uprights or the uprights themselves while performing your bench presses. Hitting the uprights can throw off your form or cause you to miss a repetition alto-

START

FINISH

gether and end up with the weight stuck on your chest.

Once you've positioned your body correctly, the next step is to determine your grip. An excellent way of doing this is to first bend each arm at the elbow so that your forearm is perpendicular to your upper arm, forming a 90° L. Next, line up your elbows directly with your shoulders so that your arms are square with your shoulder girdle. Your forearms are pointing straight up and the palms of your hands are facing your feet. Your arms now look like the two bench uprights. Next, look up at the barbell which should be positioned a few inches above and behind your head. Then line up each hand with the part of the bar which is directly above it in your mind and just reach up and grab the bar at those exact two spots. Now, move both your hands in 1 inch from this position. From my experience, this is the best way possible to determine the perfect individual benching grip for you. This method is also applicable to finding the perfect grip on bent-over

barbell rows and overhead presses with only minor variations which will be discussed when describing the performance of each of these exercises. Back to bench pressing, the grip just described will place your pinky fingers approximately three to five inches from the inside collars, according to how long your arms are. It is a good idea to vary your grip either slightly wider or slightly narrower from time to time in order to stimulate the muscle fibers from different angles, but overall the grip just described should enable you to get the most out of your bench pressing. It will stimulate the most muscle growth and strength increases because of the fact that it provides maximum leverage for lifting the heaviest weights possible, while simultaneously allowing you to work the pecs through a full range of motion.

Exercise performance—Once you are in position the next step is to either reach up and back and lift the barbell off the uprights, or have someone hand it to you. As the bar is lifted off the rack, lock the weight out at arm's length and bring it into position directly over your chest. Once in position, make sure your arms and shoulders are squared before beginning the set, and keep them that way as much as possible when performing each rep. Since the elbows have a strong tendency to come forward and in closer to the body as the weights become heavier and the reps harder, you will have to make a conscious effort to keep your elbows back and square with your shoulders each time you bench. If you don't, much of the potential benefit of the exercise for the pecs will be lost, and the delts and triceps will receive most of the stimulation.

Keeping all this in mind you will actually perform your reps by lowering the bar all the way down to the point where it touches the lower part of your chest just about the nipple line. Pause for a split second and then push the weight back out to arm's length again. If possible, expand your rib box while lowering the bar to the chest. This will give the pec muscles an excellent stretch at the bottom of the exercise. When benching, you should always concentrate on feeling your pecs stretch at the bottom of each rep whether you are able to expand your rib box or not. You should also concentrate on feeling the pecs contract at the top of each rep. It is generally true when performing most exercises that the further you stretch the muscle at the bottom of a rep, the harder it will contract at the top of a rep. So the more you concentrate on getting a full stretch and a strong contraction on each rep of virtually all your exercises, the more muscle fibers and ultimately muscle growth you will stimulate.

Intermediate pectoral exercises

Lower pec exercises

1. Decline bench press:

Comments—Decline barbell bench presses develop the entire lower portion of the pectorals, especially the lower outer edge of the pecs.

Equipment—A decline bench whose angle of decline is between 20° and 30° (a 30° is standard) with built-in uprights.

Starting position—Exactly the same grip and starting position as with the barbell bench press, except that your upper body will be on an angle of descent. Because of the angle you will not have the leverage necessary to lift the barbell off the uprights and you will therefore have to have a spotter hand it off to you. Hold the bar at arm's length so that your arms are perfectly perpendicular to the floor. You will find that instead of being positioned over the middle of the pecs as when preparing to perform the bench press, the declined position of your body will necessitate your holding the bar directly over the lower edge of your pecs. If you don't hold the bar in this position, you will not be able to control it and it will be pulled back over your head, possibly resulting in serious injury.

Exercise performance—You will slowly lower the bar until it touches your lower pecs right on the nipple line. By keeping your elbows back throughout the entire movement, you will be able to lower the bar downward from the starting position in a perfectly straight line, while simultaneously ensuring that you maintain perfect control of the bar. After the bar touches your lower chest, immediately return the bar to the starting position by pressing it slowly and steadily upward in a straight line until it is once again at arm's length directly above the lower edge of the pecs.

START

FINISH

2. Dumbbell bench presses

START

FINISH

Comments—Like barbell bench presses, this exercise strongly stresses the lower half of the pec muscles. In fact, because of the much greater range of motion you can get on your bench presses when using dumbbells, dumbbell bench presses are actually superior to barbell benches in terms of thoroughly working the lower pecs and stimulating muscle growth. The only reason I suggested using a barbell at the beginner levels is that dumbbells are much more difficult to control and beginners do not yet have the coordination necessary to make effective use of dumbbell benching.

Starting position—You will sit at the end of a flat exercise bench, and will have two dumbbells in front of you on the floor, parallel to each other with the dumbbell bars pointing toward the wall like this: 11. Reach down, grasp the dumbbells with an overhand grip and swing them up so that the end of each dumbbell which was closest to your feet is resting on your upper thighs. Then carefully lie back on the bench and simultaneously bring the dumbbells up off your knees so that they are right against your chest at the point when you are lying completely flat on your back on the bench. Then carefully press them to arm's length directly over your chest while simultaneously turning your hands so that your thumbs are facing each other. This will mean that the dumbbells are lined up end to end, although they will not quite be touching. It will be just as if you are holding a barbell except that you will instead be holding two dumbbells.

Exercise performance—You will perform dumbbell bench presses almost exactly as if you were performing the barbell benches. The only major difference is that you will be lowering the dumbbells significantly farther than you lowered the barbell. In fact, you should lower the dumbbells as far as possible while still keeping them perfectly lined up end to end with your forearms perpendicular to the floor. This constitutes perfect form. If you lower your arms so far that the forearms are starting to angle away from the body and you can feel the dumbbells starting to pull away from your body, you know you've gone a little too far, and you must adjust how far you lower the dumbbells accordingly. Once you've reached the bottom of the movement, slowly press the dumbbells

back to the starting position without hesitation. Do not let them touch at the top of each rep. Once you've done the prescribed number of reps, sit up with the dumbbells against your chest, and carefully place them on the floor.

3. Parallel bar dips

START   FINISH

Comments—This exercise also strongly stresses the lower portion of the pecs and, like decline benches, especially works the lower outer edge of the pecs.[1] While they are an excellent lower pec exercise, dips are a complicated movement which requires perfect control for them to be of benefit. Many individuals have been known to have difficulty isolating the movement in their pecs. Besides this, dips put a tremendous amount of stress on the shoulder joints, which can either cause or aggravate a shoulder injury. For these reasons, I don't consider dips to be as beneficial as the two exercises just described for lower pec development. And if you have weak delts or a history of shoulder problems, I suggest that you stay away from them. This exercise strongly stresses the triceps so you

should reduce the sets you perform for your triceps by one when using this exercise.

Equipment—Parallel dipping bars.

Starting position—Grasp a pair of dipping bars with an overhand grip so that your thumbs are facing each other. Then jump up and press your upper body so that it is directly above the bars at arm's length.[2] Incidentally, the dipping bars should be close enough together that your arms will be, at most, 4 inches out to the side of your torso. This will ensure that you remain in a controlled, mechanically advantageous position when performing the exercise, and you'll be able to get the fullest range of motion possible. If your arms are too far out to your sides, excess pressure will be put on the shoulder joints; also, you will no longer be isolating your pecs effectively. Besides this you will lose your leverage advantage by keeping your arms too wide, and you will often find yourself getting stuck at the bottom of a rep way before your pecs have been thoroughly worked.

Exercise performance—Once your upper body is at arm's length, bend your head forward, bend slightly forward at the waist, and bend your elbows slightly so that your forearms remain stationary. Move your upper arms and entire upper body forward so that it is almost directly over your forearms, and you are looking downward almost straight at the floor. From this position, slowly lower your body between the dipping bars, moving your arms as far past the point where they make a 90° angle between the upper arm and forearm as possible.[3] Concentrate on feeling a good stretch in the pecs. Keep your head and body tipped forward at all times during the performance of this exercise. Once you've gotten the fullest stretch possible, slowly return to the starting position. Incidentally, the reason you must keep your head and body tipped forward at all times during this exercise is that that's the only way you'll be able to effectively isolate the pecs. If you dip with your body straight or leaning back, you will mainly work the triceps.

4. Flat dumbbell flies

Comments—This exercise works the lower pecs. Flies overall are more of a shaping exercise than a mass building exercise. However, because they duplicate so precisely the major function of the pec muscles (which is to bring the arms across the chest), they add a good degree of fullness to the chest. Also, because the flying exercise has a greater range of motion and gives the pecs a fuller stretch than any other pec exercise, they add a dimension of development to the pecs which you cannot get from any other pec exercise.

Basically, they give the pecs a shapely, full, completely developed look which various forms of benching do not provide. Therefore, everyone should perform either flat or incline flies from time to time at the various intermediate levels. For those of you who have developed just about all the chest mass you want, I suggest performing one benching exercise and one flying exercise in every workout from now on so you can perfectly shape the mass you have built while adding more fullness. As an example, you could perform decline benches and incline flies or flat flies and incline dumbbell benches. When performing a benching and a flying movement in a chest workout, it is usually preferable to perform the benching movement first, while the muscles are fresh, so you can stimulate the maximum amount of deep fibers possible, and to finish off the pecs with the flies. This is true even if you are performing an incline benching movement and a flat flie. The incline bench should be performed first.

Natural bodybuilders who want to continue to add significant muscle mass should still incorporate some form of flies into their training routine, but various forms of benching should dominate the routine. In such a situation you should substitute a flying exercise into the routine for a benching exercise for two months and then next time you alter your exercises, just replace them with a benching movement. Then next time you're ready to alter the routine again (in approximately two months), you can substitute another flying exercise, etc. It's wise to take turns substituting in a flat flie for a lower chest benching exercise and substituting in an incline flie for an upper chest benching exercise, as this will facilitate more complete and shapely development of the muscle.

Starting position—Sit on the end of a flat exercise bench with two relatively light dumbbells in front of your feet. Lie flat on the bench with the dumbbells exactly as if you were performing dumbbell bench presses. Then push them to arm's length, but do not rotate them so they are lined up with each other as when you were doing dumbbell benches. Instead, keep your palms facing each other so that the dumbbells are perfectly parallel to each other, but aren't quite touching.

Exercise performance—Keeping your palms facing each other, your wrists slightly flexed, and your elbow joints bent at about a 30° angle at all times, slowly lower the dumbbells in semicircles almost directly out from your sides, but with your elbows kept slightly back at all times so there is greater tension on the pecs during the movement. Lower the dumbbells until they are well below the level of your chest for maximum stretch.[4] When you reach the point where you would have to bend your elbow joints further than originally sug-

START

FINISH

92

gested in order to maintain control of the dumbbells, you'll know you've gone slightly too far and you should adjust how far you lower your arms accordingly. You should also never lower the dumbbells to the point where you feel any pain or severe pulling in the shoulders. All flies put a lot of stress on the shoulders so you must be careful. Always lower the weight slowly and under perfect control. At the bottom of the movement do not pause, but slowly return the dumbbells to the starting position in the exact same arc you lowered them in. At the top of the movement never let the dumbbells touch each other as this takes the tension off the pecs. Because of the stress flies put on the delts, it is a good idea to not quite lower the dumbbells all the way down during the first three or four reps of the first set. By lowering them about two-thirds of the way down on the first rep and a little further down on the next couple of reps so that you are doing full range reps by the fourth or fifth rep, you will give the muscles, joints, tendons, and ligaments three to four reps to gradually prepare for and adapt to the stress which the exceedingly full range movement of flies puts on them. This is also a good idea when performing other chest exercises such as dumbbell benches, dips, and dumbbell incline benches which also have exaggerated ranges of motion.

B. Upper pec exercises

1. Dumbbell incline bench presses

Comments—When it comes to upper pec exercises, this is the cream of the crop. This exercise strongly stresses the entire upper pec region and is definitely the best exercise for adding solid muscle mass to this area. Barbell incline benches of any type do not provide the full range of motion that dumbbells do.

Equipment—Incline bench, preferably adjustable and without uprights.

Starting position—Identical to that of dumbbell benches except that your body will be on a 30°–45° incline, necessitating your holding the dumbbells at arm's length so that they are positioned over the neck instead of over the middle of your chest. This will ensure their being held directly over the shoulder joint on an incline. Incidentally, when performing any type of in-

cline exercise, vary the steepness of the incline slightly from workout to workout within the range of 30° to 45°, with 40° being about optimum, to guarantee the most complete development of the upper pecs which is possible. Generally, the steeper the incline, the higher up on the pecs the benefit of the exercise is concentrated. Also, the steeper the incline, the more involved the front delt becomes in the exercise. Therefore, at times when you are performing steep incline benches of any kind, you should perform one less set for your delts.

Exercise performance—You will perform this exercise exactly as if you were doing dumbbell benches, concentrating on keeping your elbows back while lowering the dumbbells on each rep, so that the dumbbell bars themselves are directly over the insertion between the upper pecs and the neck at the bottom of the movement. You should feel a deep stretch across the upper pecs and the pec delt tie-ins when you lower them in this way. This will indicate that you are performing them correctly and working the muscles thoroughly. Once at the bottom of the rep you should immediately return the dumbbells to the starting position. Never allow the dumbbells to quite touch each other at the top of any rep.

START

FINISH

2. Barbell incline bench presses

Comments—This exercise is excellent for developing the upper pecs, although it is not quite as effective as dumbbell inclines. The one advantage of doing barbell inclines is that it is not as clumsy to handle as two dumbbells. As with dumbbell inclines, your angle of incline should range between 30° and 45°, with 40° being about optimum.

Equipment—Adjustable incline bench with uprights to hold the barbell.

Starting position—Exactly the same as for barbell bench presses including the exact same grip, except that you will be on an incline. You should have someone lift the bar off the racks with you as you will be at a mechanically disadvantageous position to do so yourself since the weight will be on the uprights a good distance behind you. Lift the weight off the rack with help and press it directly to arm's length so that your arms are perpendicular to the floor as is the case with all other benching exercises.[5] This should place the center of the bar directly over the base of your neck.

Exercise performance—Slowly lower the barbell in a straight line so that it touches your upper chest right where it inserts with the base of your neck. Keep your arms directly out at your sides and your elbows back at all times.[6] Hold your rib box up when lowering the weight so as to get the maximum stretch possible. Incidentally, you should lift your rib box as high as feels comfortable when lowering the weight on all your chest exercises, especially those performed with a barbell, as this enables you to get a much fuller stretch in the pecs at the bottom of every rep. Once you've lowered the bar to your neck, immediately press the weight back to arm's length in exactly the same way you lowered it.

START

FINISH

START

FINISH

3. Incline flies

Comments—This is an excellent exercise for filling in the area around the clavicles with muscle and developing the pec-delt tie-in which is so important for a shapely and completely developed upper body. They also contribute greatly to giving the pecs a high, full, shapely look. As is the case with flyes, incline flyes will not develop a significant amount of muscle mass, but as just demonstrated, they do provide numerous benefits and should be incorporated into your routine periodically.

Starting position—Exactly the same as with flat flies, including the grip, except that you will be on a 30°–45° incline. As such, the dumbbells will be held directly over your upper chest.

Exercise performance—Exactly the same as if you were doing flat flies except for the fact that you are on an incline. Remember to keep your wrists slightly flexed, and your elbows bent at a 30° angle and kept slightly back as you lower and raise the weight.

—7—
DELTOID EXERCISES

Beginning—
standing military press (barbell)

Comments—This exercise works the muscles of the entire shoulder girdle. Because this is a power exercise and heavy weights can be used on it, it is one of the best exercises for adding thickness to the delts, especially to the frontal delt and secondarily to the side delt. Most overhead shoulder press exercises do not work the rear head of the deltoid to any appreciable degree. For this reason a specialization exercise will be presented for this section of the delt at the intermediate level.

Equipment—Barbell and a squat rack to hold the weight at shoulder height if possible. With such a rack, you won't have to expend unnecessary energy moving the weight up to your shoulders from the floor before pressing it overhead.

Starting position—Assuming you don't have a squat rack, squat down, lean forward and take the exact same grip you used on your bench presses on the bar, with your palms facing away from you. Then, keeping your knees bent, your back straight, and the bar in close proximity, pull the bar up to your shoulders. Make sure your elbows are directly under the bar once you have brought it to shoulder level in order to keep the bar from pulling forward and falling back down to the floor. This process is known as cleaning the barbell and it is the starting position for military presses.

Exercise performance—Once the bar is in position at shoulder level all you have to do is press it straight overhead and then return it to your shoulders. When pressing the weight overhead, keep it close to your face and head as this will allow maximum control of the weight.[1] Also when completing the lift overhead, do not quite lock your arms out. Doing this puts too much pressure on the elbow and shoulder joints, and can eventually result in injury to these areas. Instead concentrate on the feel of the movement in the deltoids. If you do this you should feel the deltoids contract just before the elbow and shoulder joints are locked. This is the point at which you should end the movement. When lowering the weight, concentrate on getting a good stretch at the bottom of each rep, but don't lower the

START

FINISH

bar so far that you either feel the delt muscles straining or feel yourself losing control of the bar. It is also extremely important to keep your back as straight as possible at all times when performing this exercise. You must resist the urge to bend backward excessively especially as the reps become harder, and the weights become heavier, otherwise you're risking sustaining a severe back injury. Also, in relation to protecting the lower back, it is a good idea to keep your knees slightly bent at all times as this relieves a lot of pressure which would otherwise be put on the lower back during this exercise.

II. Delt exercises

A. Pressing movements

1. Press behind neck (barbell)

Comments—This is an excellent exercise for developing the entire delt muscle, especially the front delt. In fact, it puts more direct stress on the front delt than military presses.[2] Overall, I consider it to be the best exercise for adding solid muscle mass to the delts. The reason I did not recommend them at the beginner level is that they require a lot more coordination to correctly execute than military presses. This exercise is commonly performed seated on a specially designed bench called, obviously enough, a seated press bench. The advantages of performing either military presses or press behind the neck on such a bench is first of all that you do not have to waste excess energy cleaning the weight and pressing it overhead into the starting position. Since a seated press bench has two uprights to hold a barbell you can simply reach back, grip the bar, and have someone help you press it overhead into the starting position. The other advantage is that the movements tend to be more coordinated and concentrated when performed seated. You don't have to worry about balancing your body as much as you do when standing. The obvious disadvantage is that you need a spotter for all forms of seated barbell presses. If you don't have one, you have no alternative but to perform them standing up. If, however, you have access to both a seated press bench and a spotter, I suggest you perform them seated as the exercise is more productive when performed in this way.

Starting position—Same grip as for military presses. Push the bar overhead to arm's length so that the bar is held over the back of your head. You will be forced to keep your elbows slightly back to hold the bar in this position.

START

FINISH

Exercise performance—Keeping your arms out at your sides with your elbows way back, and your head bent slightly forward, slowly lower the barbell behind your head in a straight line until it rests across the top of your traps just below the base of the neck. Without pausing at the bottom, slowly press the bar directly upward behind your head, concentrating on feeling the delts contract. When you've completed the prescribed number of reps, lower the bar from over your head to the front of your neck, then carefully lower it to the floor, which is exactly what you should do when completing a set of standing military presses. Of course, if you are performing them seated, you need only have your partner help you place the bar back on the rack when you are done.

2. Dumbbell presses

Comments—Dumbbell presses stress the delts in almost the exact same way as barbell presses, mainly developing the front delt. The major advantage of using dumbbells is that you can stress the delts from a number of slightly different angles by turning your wrists inward to various degrees, something the use of a barbell does not allow. You can also get a slightly fuller stretch at the bottom of the movement with dumbbells. However, dumbbells are much more difficult to control when performing shoulder-pressing movements than barbells. Besides this, unlike the case of various forms of barbell benching for the chest, you can get a long enough range of motion on various forms of barbell shoulder presses that you do not require dumbbell shoulder presses to completely develop the delts. Because barbell shoulder presses require much less coordination than dumbbells, you can handle much more weight safely on them than you can in proportion to what you can use on the dumbbells. Therefore you can stimulate more muscle fibers and faster overall muscle growth while still being able to get a full enough range of motion to completely develop the delts. For this reason, various forms of barbell shoulder presses are superior to dumbbell shoulder presses for adding solid muscle mass to the delts, and should be used the majority of the time.

Starting position—Place two moderately heavy dumbbells in front of your feet. Grasp them with an overhand grip and clean and press them directly overhead to arm's length. Keep your knees slightly bent. Once overhead, rotate them so that your palms are facing forward and your thumbs are facing inward toward each other. This will line up the dumbbells end to end in exactly the same way as when you performed dumbbell bench presses. Incidentally, your feet should be kept a comfortable distance apart, approximately 6–8 inches in most cases when performing all your shoulder exercises. This will ensure optimum balance.[3]

FINISH

Exercise performance—Slowly lower the dumbbells along each side of your head down to the level of your shoulders, until you feel a full stretch in the delts. Then slowly return the dumbbells to the starting position making sure they do not touch at the top of the movement, concentrating on contracting them at the top of the movement.

B. Laterals

General comments—Laterals are more isolatory in nature than shoulder-pressing movements. However, certain variations do stimulate the development of significant muscle mass in those areas of the delts which presses do not directly stimulate, mainly the posterior and lateral heads of the delt. Their use is essential for anyone who desires completely developed, well-shaped delts. Since the front delt is so thoroughly worked by shoulder presses I will not present a version of laterals which will work the front delt.

1. Side lateral

Comments—This exercise strongly stresses the lateral head or side of the delts. It is responsible for giving the delts most of their width and an impressive melon-shaped appearance when utilized consistently. It is as such the most beneficial lateral exercise overall for developing the delts, and should be used more frequently than any other version of laterals.

Starting position—Grasp two light dumbbells with an overhand grip. Stand erect so that your arms are close to your sides. Your forearms are in front of your body, and your hands are holding the dumbbells right in front of you at the level of your hips. Your palms will be facing inward and your arms will be bent at about a 25° angle. You will also be leaning slightly forward, and your knees will be slightly bent.[4]

Exercise performance—From this position slowly raise your arms directly out to your sides in a semicircular arc until they are slightly above the level of your shoulders.[5] As you raise the dumbbells, concentrate on keeping your elbows slightly higher than your wrists at all times. This will direct more stress onto the side delts. At the top of the movement, hold for a split second. Concentrate on feeling the lateral delt contract and slowly lower the dumbbells along the same exact arc you raised them in.

START

FINISH

100

2. Bent-over laterals

Comments—This exercise develops the posterior head of the delt which is a weakness in terms of development for many bodybuilders. The muscles along the middle of the upper back are also stressed quite strongly.

Starting position—Grasp two light dumbbells with an overhand grip. Your palms will be facing each other and the dumbbell bars will be parallel. Keep your feet close together, no more than 4 inches apart. Bend your knees slightly, and bend over so that your torso is parallel to the floor. Hang your arms directly down from your shoulder joints[6] and bend them at a 25° angle.

Exercise performance—From this starting position, use the strength of your posterior delts to move the dumbbells in semicircular arcs directly out to the sides of your body and upward until your arms are parallel to the floor and the dumbbells are exactly at the level of your shoulder joints.[7] Pause for a split second at the top of the movement. Concentrate on feeling the rear delts contract, then slowly lower the dumbbells back to the starting position, just prior to the point where they touch.

Conclusion

All forms of shoulder presses and laterals can be performed either standing or seated. Ultimately, you have to determine your own preference for each particular exercise.

START

FINISH

— 8 —
LATISSIMUS DORSI EXERCISES

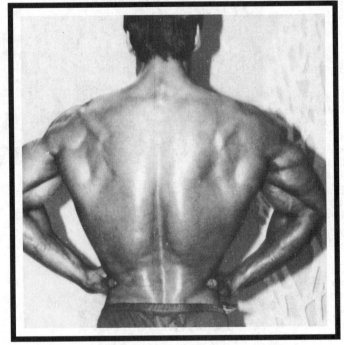

Latissimus dorsi— bent-over barbell rows

Comments—Overall, this is definitely the best upper back exercise you can perform in terms of adding muscle mass to the entire upper back. It primarily works the lats and is used mainly to add mass to and thicken this muscle group.

Equipment—Either a lightly padded flat bench with uprights or a block of wood approximately 4–6 inches high, 8–12 inches wide, and 2 feet or more in length. You may or may not want to use a chair for the purpose that will soon be discussed.

Starting position—Normally you will start with the loaded barbell on the floor. Your grip will be exactly the same as that of the bench press except that your hands will be approximately ½ inch narrower on each side. You will be bending over to pick up the bar and your palms will be facing your legs when gripping the bar. Before starting the exercise, place the barbell approximately 4–6 inches in front of your feet. Then bend over and take your grip. Make sure your feet are approximately 6–8 inches apart. Keeping them this close together seems to direct more of the benefit of the exercise to your lats. Also, keep your knees bent at all times when performing this exercise in order to keep undue pressure off your lower back. After grabbing the bar, you should lift it off the floor. Let the bar hang at arm's length a few inches off the floor and concentrate on pulling your shoulders upward and flattening or even slightly arching your back so that your torso is exactly parallel to the floor.[1] Your back will remain in this position during the performance of the exercise. The bar will still be hanging at arm's length a few inches off the floor. Adjust your center of gravity so that once you have the bar off the floor the weight does not pull you forward and off balance. You do this by concentrating on resisting the pull of the weight with your hamstrings and leaning slightly backward. Bent-over rows require careful balance and a high degree of general body coordination to perform them correctly. Anyway, what I have just described constitutes the correct starting position for bent-over barbell rows.

FINISH

START

Exercise performance—The next step is to use your arms to pull the weight up to your upper abdomen. As you do this concentrate on keeping your elbows slightly back as you raise them to your sides. At the top of each rep your arms and shoulders should be squared similar to the way they are when performing barbell bench presses. It is extremely important that you don't let your back become rounded at any time during the performance of the exercise. Absolute perfect form must always be maintained on bent-over rows or I guarantee you will eventually get hurt. When lowering the weight on each rep do not let your arms hang all the way down or the weight of the bar will put undue stress on your elbows. Even worse, the downward pull exerted by letting your arms hang all the way down at the end of each rep, especially if you don't maintain complete control of the bar and let momentum take over, can cause a separation to occur in the shoulder muscles, because of the extreme degree to which such pull stretches them. I therefore suggest that you lower the bar only to the point just prior to where the elbows totally unlock. This also allows you to better control the bar at the bottom of each rep and makes it easier to get the bar moving on the next rep. That's because the forearm and biceps muscles are still slightly flexed in this position, which allows you to use their strength much more effectively to pull the bar up than if you had to start each rep with them completely unflexed. When lowering the weight on each rep, concentrate on feeling the lats stretch. At the bottom of

the rep they should be fully stretched. As you start lifting heavier weight and using 35- and 45-pound plates on the bar, and as you gain an increasing amount of flexibility in the lat muscles and can lower the weight further and further, you will find that the loaded barbell will hit the floor before your lats are fully stretched. For this reason, once you have completely mastered performance of the exercise you should begin either performing it off a wood block or a minimally padded flat bench with uprights to make lifting the weight into the starting position easier. It requires more coordination to perform bent-over rows off either one of these pieces of equipment, but you will be able to lower the bar much farther without worrying about the bar hitting the floor, resulting in the fullest lat stretch possible and therefore the fullest lat development possible. When bringing the weight up on each rep, concentrate on pulling the bar right against the upper abdomen, holding it there for a split second, and feeling the lats contract before lowering the weight. It is easy to lose the feeling of bent-over rows working the lats unless you concentrate at all times.

When performing bent-over rows either off the floor or off a block you may find it helpful to lean your head against a chair or a high bench as a means of significantly reducing the pressure which this exercise places on your lower back. Some of you may have such a weak lower back that you may not be able to perform this exercise without risking serious injury. In such cases I recommend you experiment with using long-range cable rows as a possible replacement exercise for developing lat thickness.

103

A. Lat width exercises—introduction

Chins are better than pulldowns for widening the lats because hoisting around the dead weight of your body while performing chins will stimulate more muscle fibers than a smooth cable pulldown movement. Unfortunately, many individuals at the intermediate level of training don't have sufficient lat and arms strength to perform enough chins to derive maximum benefit from this exercise. They will be forced to use pulldowns exclusively for widening the lats, until such time as they gain strength. Those individuals who have the strength to perform chins should use various forms of chins instead of pulldowns approximately two-thirds of the time.

Another important fact about lat width exercises is that performing either pulldowns or chins to the front of the neck is more productive than performing either exercise to the back of the neck. The reason for this is that performing either exercise to the front of the neck precisely duplicates the function of the lats, which is to bring the arms down and back, thus stimulating them more effectively. When you do either exercise to the back of the neck you are only bringing the arms down, but not back.

1. Wide-grip chins to front of neck

Comments—This exercise takes into account everything I have just said and is by far the best exercise for widening the lats.

Equipment—Wide-grip chinning bar.

Starting position—Stand on a small stool so you can reach the chinning bar. If the ends of the chinning bar are bent you should grip it just past the bend on each side with an overhand grip. If the chinning bar is completely straight, take an overhand grip in which both hands are out 2–4 inches past shoulder width. In either case the grip will be quite wide. If your arms are unusually short or long you will have to adjust your grip accordingly. Anyway, once your grip is secure, kick the stool out of the way. Bend your legs at approximately a 50° angle, and cross your ankles for stability. Hang motionless from the bar.

Exercise performance—Being sure that your elbows move downward and backward, bend your arms and pull your body up to the bar until your upper chest at the base of your neck touches the bar.[2] Concentrate on using the strength of your lats as much as possible to reach the completed position, instead of just pulling up with your arms. As you perform the exercise, concentrate on keeping your back arched slightly as this will enable you to fully contract your lat muscles at the top of each rep.[3] At the top of each rep, pause for a split second, concentrating on tensing the lats, and then slowly lower yourself back to the starting position, concentrating on feeling the lats stretch all the way down, especially at the bottom of the movement. Once you've completed the prescribed number of reps, hang at arm's length, and carefully jump down to the floor. As you get stronger on chins, you can hang a dumbbell from your waist.

START

FINISH

2. Wide-grip pulldowns to front of neck

Comments—This exercise is second only to wide-grip chins for effectively widening the lats.

Equipment—Seated pulldown machine with a long bar attached to it.

Starting position—First adjust the pin on the weight stack to the desired weight. Then reach up and grip the pulldown bar with the exact same grip you used on wide-grip chins. Keeping the bar at arm's length, use the weight of your body to pull it down far enough that you can sit on the pulldown seat and place your knees under a built-in knee-restraining pad which will keep you from being pulled out of the chair when using heavy weights. Unfortunately, many pulldown machines do not have such pads and this will limit the amount of weight you can handle on this exercise. In such cases you should kneel down directly beneath the pulldown bar.[4]

Exercise performance—Starting with the bar at arm's length almost directly above your head, slowly pull the bar down to your upper chest at the base of your neck. Make sure you pull your elbows downward and backward so that you can most effectively duplicate the function of your lats. Also remember to arch your back slightly so you can get the lat muscles to fully contract. At the bottom of the movement, pause and concentrate on tensing the lats for a second, then slowly return the bar to the starting position, concentrating on feeling a good stretch in the lats.

START

FINISH

B. Lat thickness exercises

1. Long-range cable rows

Comments—This exercise is an excellent lat thickness builder, second only to bent-over barbell rows.

Equipment—Long-range pulley device with a parallel grip handle.

Starting position—Sit on the long pad of the long-range pulley apparatus. Place your feet on the built-in foot bar which these machines have at the end of the seat toward the pulley. Then lean forward and grab the parallel grip handle with an overhand grip so that your palms are facing each other during the movement.[5] Keeping your arms extended, push back with your thighs until you are sitting back far enough on the seat that your knees are only slightly bent. You will now be in a position where your upper body is leaning forward over your legs, your arms are straight, and your lats are fully stretched.

Exercise performance—From this basic starting position, bend your arms and use the strength of your lats to pull the handle toward your chest while simultaneously sitting backward until your torso is erect. Making sure that your upper arms are held in close to your body, pull the handle in so that it touches your upper abdomen just below your rib cage.[5] At the top of the movement, arch your back slightly lift your rib cage up, and concentrate on fully contracting your lat muscles. After a second's pause, slowly lean forward and return the handle to the starting position, concentrating on getting a full stretch in the lats. Incidentally, your back should remain straight throughout the performance of the exercise, even when leaning completely forward.

START

FINISH

2. T-bar rows

Comments—This exercise is superb for adding thickness to the lower lats and middle of the back. Unfortunately, it is known for putting a lot of stress on the lower back, and is therefore not suitable for everyone. This exercise must always be performed with absolutely perfect form because of its injury potential.

Equipment—T-Bar apparatus.

Starting position—T-Bars are shaped exactly like a T. The weight is put on the end of the bar and you grip the two smaller bars sticking out of each side of the main bar. The other end of the main bar will be securely fastened. There will also be some kind of block under the bar just prior to the place where it forms a T. After putting the desired weight on the end of the bar, you will stand up on the block. Next, you will bend at the knees, and bend over at the waist so that your arms are hanging straight down and you can take a close overhand grip on the two small bars. Your hands should be between 6 and 8 inches apart. Also, your back must remain flat and straight throughout the performance of the exercise. The reason you will be standing on a block is so you can get a full stretch in the lats at the bottom of each rep.

Exercise performance—Keeping your knees bent at about a 45° angle and your back completely flat, pull the bar in an arc toward your torso until the plates on the bar touch your chest. As you raise the weight, you will bend your arms and bring your elbows back while keeping your arms in close to your sides. Concentrate on pulling the weight up with the strength of your lats. At the top of the movement, arch your back slightly, lift up your rib box, and concentrate on fully contracting your lats. Then slowly lower the bar back to the starting position, just short of the point where the weight comes to rest on the floor, concentrating on getting a full deep stretch in the lats.

START

FINISH

—9—
TRAPEZIUS EXERCISES

Trapezius—barbell shoulder shrugs

Comments—From my experience barbell shoulder shrugs are the best exercise for developing and thickening the trapezius muscles as they allow you to hit them directly with very heavy weights. It is also one of the simplest of all the exercises to perform.

Starting position—To find the best grip, just let your arms hang down naturally at your sides. Then simply squat down and grab the barbell with both palms facing your legs. Your grip will be approximately shoulder width. Next, you will stand erect with the barbell, still at arm's length. It should now be resting against your upper thighs. Once again, keep your knees slightly bent to keep pressure off your lower back while performing this exercise. Also keep your back perfectly straight at all times for the same reason.

Exercise performance—To begin this exercise, sag your shoulders as far forward and downward as possible while still maintaining slight resistance against the bar with your delt muscles to prevent them from possibly pulling or tearing. Next, slowly shrug your shoulders upward and slightly backward through the full range of motion of your shoulder joints. Try to visualize your traps touching your ears at the top of the exercise.[1] Simultaneously, concentrate on contracting the traps at the top of the movement and hold them there for half a second. Then, of course, when lowering the weight, concentrate on getting as full a stretch in the traps as possible. Throughout the performance of the exercise, it is important to let your arms hang as straight as possible. Ideally, it is best not to bend them at all as the more you bend your elbows, the more your biceps become involved in the exercise. Unfortunately, this is unrealistic as it is impossible to use a sufficient amount of weight capable of stimulating the deep muscle fibers in the traps without bending your elbows and involving the biceps to some degree. There is also the fact that keeping your arms perfectly straight and your elbows locked while performing shrugs does not constitute proper body mechanics. The motion becomes unnatural as well as uncomfortable and you will feel undue pressure on both the elbow and shoulder joints which can eventually result in injury. You can vary your grip on shrugs, but refrain from taking too wide a grip as you will find it impossible to get a full stretch in the trap muscles.

FINISH

START

Traps

A. Shrugging exercises

1. Dumbell shoulder shrugs

Comments—This exercise is at least as good as barbell shoulder shrugs for adding mass and thickness to the traps. You can get a slightly longer range of motion with dumbbell shrugs than with barbell shrugs. As a result, this exercise is particularly good for tying in the traps with the pecs and delts.

Starting position—Place two moderately heavy dumbbells on the floor in front of you. Bend down and grab them with an overhand grip. Then stand erect so that your arms are hanging down at your sides, your palms are facing against your outer thighs, and the dumbbell bars are facing directly ahead of you.

Exercise performance—Keeping your elbows slightly bent, and without using the strength of your arms to assist you during the entire exercise, slowly sag your shoulders downward and forward as far as possible, concentrating on getting as full a stretch as possible in the traps. Then shrug your shoulders upward and backward as far as possible,[2] attempting to touch your traps to your ears. At the top of the movement, concentrate on contracting your traps, hold for a split second, and then slowly return to the starting position.

START

FINISH

110

2. Reverse dumbbell shrugs

Comments—This exercise is the exact opposite of the one just discussed. Besides being an excellent mass builder, it will contribute to giving your traps a high, full look.

Starting position—Exactly the same as for dumbbell shoulder shrugs.

Exercise performance—Sag your shoulders downward and backward as far as possible without arching your back; next, shrug your shoulders upward and forward as far as possible, concentrating on feeling your traps stretch and pull forward. Then sag your shoulders forward and downward, concentrating on stretching the traps and slowly return the dumbbells to the starting position.

MIDPOINT

B. Other trap exercises

1. Upright rows

Comments—Next to shrugs, this is the best exercise for adding thickness to the traps. The front and side delts are also strongly involved in this exercise, and it is often used as a shoulder exercise. In order to direct most of the benefit to the traps instead of the delts, you must concentrate on contracting the traps instead of the delts as you raise the weight.

Starting position—Bend over and grab a barbell with a narrow overhand grip so that your hands are approximately 6 inches apart. Make sure your hands are equidistant from the center of the barbell, so that it remains perfectly balanced during the performance of the exercise. Stand erect so that your arms are hanging down in front of your hips. Your hands will be facing your upper thighs and the barbell should be held comfortably across your upper thighs.[3]

Exercise performance—Keeping the bar close to your body at all times, slowly pull the weight upward until it touches the underside of your neck. As you raise the weight you must point your elbows outward and keep them above the level of your hands at all times.[4] As you raise the bar you will bend your arms progressively so that your forearms are almost parallel with your upper arms at the top of the movement. You should concentrate on squeezing your traps together as you raise the weight. At the top of the rep, you should especially emphasize keeping your elbows up[5] and concentrate on contracting the traps as hard as you can. After pausing for a moment, slowly lower the bar back to the starting position, concentrating on pulling the traps forward and stretching them as far as possible.

FINISH

START

2. Cleans from the waist to the shoulders

Comments—This is an excellent exercise for adding thickness to the traps, especially the lower portion of the traps and the middle of the upper back. While this exercise is not commonly used by bodybuilders, it is a staple of every serious weightlifter's routine and is mainly responsible for the massive trap development that these athletes possess.

Starting position—Starting with the barbell on the floor in front of your feet, take a rather wide stance (between 12 and 18 inches) for the purpose of improving your balance. Take an overhand grip on the barbell which is slightly wider than shoulder width and exactly the same as the grip you used on military presses. Then stand erect so that the barbell is resting against your upper thighs.

Exercise performance—From the basic starting position and keeping your knees bent at all times, bend your arms and, using the strength of your traps and upper back muscles as much as possible, instead of just momentum, swing the bar up in a semicircular arc until it is resting across your shoulders and upper chest at the base of your neck. Your elbows should be pointing directly out in front of you. Once at the top of the rep, pause for a second and then carefully swing the bar back down to the starting position, concentrating on stretching your traps as much as possible as you do so. It is extremely important when performing this exercise that you do not become carried away and use momentum to throw the weight around. It is also vital that when you swing the weight to your shoulders you arch your back as little as possible. You will have to lean back and arch

slightly, but it definitely should not be excessive.

Incidentally, the method I have just described to perform cleans is the same way you should clean a barbell or two dumbbells to your shoulders to perform exercises such as military presses and dumbbell presses. However, you do not have to concentrate on working your traps and upper back muscles when you use them for this purpose. This is also the way you should lower the barbell from your shoulders to your thighs after performing any of these exercises, before lowering the barbell carefully to the floor.

FINISH

START

—10—
BICEP EXERCISES

Biceps—standing E-Z curl bar curls

Comments—This is definitely the king of bicep exercises. It stimulates development of all portions of the bicep—outer, middle, and inner—and because of mechanical advantages it allows you to use more weight in strict form than any other bicep exercise. Thus, you can stimulate the deeper muscle fibers, resulting in your gaining more muscle mass and thickness than would be possible using any other bicep exercise or combination of exercises.

Starting position—Squat down and take a shoulder-width grip on the bar. The grip should be determined in a way similar to how you found your grip on shoulder shrugs. In this case, however, the palms of your hands will be facing forward away from your body instead of toward your legs. Also your grip will be affected by the fact that you will be using an E-Z curl bar. This is a bent bar and in almost all cases your grip will be taken along the length of the bar immediately after the first bend of the bar, which occurs closest to the inner outside collars on each side. When positioning the bar for proper grip make sure that the angle of these two outer bends is facing up in the air. When gripping the bar you will turn your wrists so that your thumb on each hand will be facing up and out, and your pinkies will be facing down and in. Except for turning your wrists outward so that your hands are in this position and therefore lined up with the length of angled bar you will have to grip, there will be absolutely no difference from performing straight bar curls. Once you've gotten the basic grip, adjust your grip along the bent length of bar you have to grab on each side so the grip is as close as possible to shoulder width.

The E.Z. curl bar is superior to a straight bar because it enables you to turn your wrists so that the full benefit of the curling exercise is directed right to the belly of the biceps. Using a straight bar forces you to rotate your wrists outward to such a degree that it tends to put a lot of pressure on the inner forearm, wrists, elbow joint, and major tendon which inserts the biceps muscle to the bone at the elbow joint. This pressure can eventually result in injury to one or all of these areas. Excessive wrist rotation also results in the bicep muscle being worked less directly than when using an E.Z. curl bar. With a straight bar, the inner bicep receives most of the stress, while the outer bicep receives almost no stimulation whatsoever. An E.Z. curl bar enables you to hold your hands in a much more natural position. As a result, the bicep muscle can be hit much more directly and the pressure exerted on the wrist, tendons, and elbow joint of the arm is eliminated.

Now that you have the proper grip, stand erect with the bar. The bar should be resting against your upper thighs and your elbows should be in as close to your sides as feels comfortable.[1] The belly of the bicep muscle will be facing directly in front of you. Once again, you will be keeping your knees slightly bent when performing curls to relieve pressure from your lower back.

Exercise performance—You will stand almost perfectly erect during the performance of the entire exercise, but not quite. I have found leaning slightly forward to be superior to standing perfectly erect. The reasons for this are that first of all, leaning slightly forward while raising the weight will prevent you from unconsciously arching your back or swinging the weight as it becomes progressively harder to lift. Sec-

ondly, leaning slightly forward throws more emphasis onto the bicep muscle and prevents the bar from falling into the shoulders at the top of each rep. More tension is placed on the biceps at all times. So, keeping this in mind, raise the bar in an arc from your thighs almost to your chin. Concentrate on feeling the bicep muscles contract fully at the top of each rep. Then stop, hold the bar in the top position for a split second and lower it again along the same arc back to the starting position.[2] Always remember never to let the bar fall into your neck or shoulders at the top of each rep. If you do this, all the tension will be removed from the muscle and it will be allowed too long a rest. Once you feel the bicep muscle contract, the bar should go no farther. Throughout the movement, your upper arms should not move appreciably and your elbows should be kept in at your sides at all times. When lowering the weight on each rep, never let your arm straighten fully and your arms unlock totally. Unlocking completely can put undue stress on both the insertion of the bicep tendon with the bone and on the elbow joint itself, so only lower the bar to just prior to full arm extension. The biceps will still get an extremely full stretch and all chance of injury will be eliminated.

FINISH

START

Basic biceps exercises

1. Barbell curls

Comments—Except for curls with an E-Z bar, this is the best exercise for adding mass and thickness to the biceps. I've already mentioned the inherent disadvantages of performing the basic curling movement with a barbell instead of an E-Z curl bar. However, this exercise provides an excellent change of pace from E-Z bar curls while providing similar mass building benefits. These two exercises should always form the basis of your biceps routine. At those times in the routine when I suggest performing only one exercise for the biceps it should be either E-Z bar curls or barbell curls. You should perform the E-Z bar curls approximately two-thirds of the time, however, because of their overall superiority over barbell curls and every other biceps exercise, too.

Starting position—Exactly the same as for E-Z bar curls. You will take a shoulder-width grip on the bar and keep your upper arms tightly against your sides at all times during the performance of the exercise.

Exercise performance—Exactly the same as for E-Z bar curls. It is advisable to experiment with various grips. When you take a grip slightly wider than usual, you will put more stress on the inner biceps and when you take a narrower grip, you will put more stress on the outer biceps.[3]

B. Combination mass building and shaping bicep exercises

The following exercises are to be used in two situations. The first is that they will be used alternately as a second bicep exercise at those times in the routines when you are instructed to perform two exercises.

Secondly, when you have reached the point when you are no longer concerned with adding large amounts of additional muscle mass to your biceps, but want to shape what you have built and add mass more slowly, you can use the following exercises interchangeably with the two basic curl exercises already outlined. The two forms of basic curls no longer need to form the basis of your biceps routine in such cases.

1. Preacher curls

Comments—This exercise is a good overall biceps mass builder, but it mainly develops the lower portion of the muscle. It also gives the muscle a thick, full and shapely look. Preacher curls give the biceps the high peaked development which every serious bodybuilder craves.

Equipment—A preacher bench, preferably a seated one. A preacher bench has an angled pad for you to rest your arms.

Starting position—Sit down in the built-in chair, and lean over a preacher bench so that the top edge of the bench pad fits snugly under your armpits. Your upper arms should hang straight over the angled pad, perfectly parallel to each other.[4] If you have a training partner, you should have him hand you the bar. If not, you will have to set up the bar on the built-in weight holder which most preacher benches have under the angled pad. In that case, simply reach over, grip the bar and hold it at arm's length. You should use an E-Z curl bar on this exercise for the same reasons you should use it on standing

FINISH

START

2. Supinating dumbbell curls

curls. You should take a rather narrow grip when performing preacher curls so that your elbows are not turned either in or out, and your arms are perfectly parallel to each other. In fact you should grip the E-Z curl bar on the same two inner bends you grip it on when performing standing tricep extensions. This grip will be explained in the tricep section. The only difference, of course, is that your grip will be reversed. Instead of taking an overhand grip on the bar, you will take an underhand grip.

Exercise performance—From the starting position in which your arms are hanging straight over the bench, slowly curl the bar in a semi-circular arc upward and toward your neck.[5] As when performing standing E-Z curls, stop at the point when the tension on your biceps starts to decrease. Do not let the bar fall into your neck. At the top of the exercise, pause for a second, concentrate on contracting the biceps, and slowly lower the bar back down to the starting position. As you lower the weight, concentrate on feeling a deep stretch in the biceps, especially in the lower part. Once back at the starting position, immediately begin the next rep.

Comments—The advantage to using dumbbells instead of barbells is that using dumbbells allows you to supinate your wrists as you raise the weight. Since part of the function of the biceps is to supinate the wrist,[6] dumbbell curls can give you a dimension of development which E-Z curl and barbell curls cannot provide. Dumbbell curls do not have quite the mass building properties that bar curls have, but they do shape and peak the biceps quite nicely.

Starting position—Basically the same as for E-Z bar curls except that you will be holding two dumbbells in your hands. You will have an overhand grip on the dumbbells, and your palms will be facing against your outer thighs.

Exercise performance—Slowly curl the dumbbells up to your shoulders as when performing bar curls. However, as you curl the dumbbells upward, slowly rotate the wrists of both hands outward so that by the time you reach the top of the movement, your palms will be facing directly up[7] and the dumbbells will be lined up end to end, although they won't be touching. At the very top of the movement, pause for a second and concentrate on peaking the biceps. Remember not to let the dumbbells fall into your neck at the top of the movement. When lowering the weight back to the starting position, reverse the curling and supination procedure and concentrate on feeling a good stretch in the biceps.

MIDPOINT

—11—
FOREARM EXERCISES

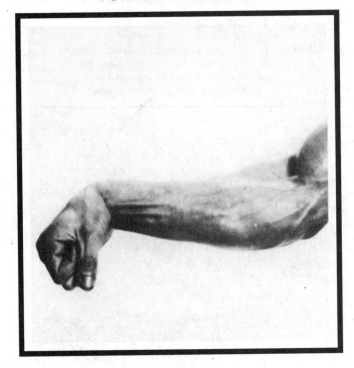

Inner forearms—barbell wrist curls

Comments—Barbell wrist curls are by far the best exercise for working all the muscles of the inner forearm.

Starting position—Sit at the end of a flat exercise bench with your feet in front of you. Bring your arms and your legs close together and parallel to each other, lean slightly forward, and place your elbows near the top of your upper thighs. Next, place your forearms along the length of your upper thighs. Hang your wrists and hands over your knees with your palms facing upward. Your hands will be approximately 6 to 8 inches apart. Next, lean forward and pick up a loaded barbell which you should have placed on the floor a few inches in front of your feet. Make sure your grip on the barbell exactly matches the distance your hands are apart when placed correctly hanging off your thighs and, of course, make sure your palms are facing up. Because your grip on the bar when doing wrist curls is relatively close compared to that of most other exercises, you should make sure that the length of bar extending from the outside of both hands is as even as possible. If it's not, you will find the bar extremely hard to balance and it will tend to tip to one side or the other while performing your reps. If you are fortunate enough to have a short-length barbell, preferably 4 ft. long instead of 5 or 6 ft., use it for this exercise as it is much easier to control than a longer bar. Once you have gripped the bar correctly, pull it up onto your legs so that your forearm and wrists are lined up with your thighs exactly, as previously discussed. If the bar is slightly off balance when brought into this position, which constitutes the starting position for this exercise, just slide your hands slightly to the left or right until the bar is comfortably balanced.

Exercise performance—Make sure you have a tight grip on the barbell at all times, then slowly curl your fists upward in an arc. Only your wrist joint will be involved in the performance of this exercise and you should concentrate on fully flexing the wrist and contracting the inner forearm muscles as you raise the weight. Once the wrist is fully flexed, hold the weight for a split second and concentrate on feeling the inner forearm muscles contract fully at the top of the rep. Next, lower the weight to the point where your wrists are fully extended. You should feel a good stretch in the inner forearm muscles at the bottom of each rep. If you feel an uncomfortable pull in the wrists or forearms at the bottom of your reps, it means that you are lowering the bar too far and you should adjust the range of your reps accordingly.

When doing wrist curls, many people recommend that you uncurl your hands and let the bar roll down to your fingertips at the bottom of each rep, then curl your fingers up again into a tight fist before actually flexing your wrists along the arc which constitutes the actual range of the rep. In my opinion, lowering the bar to the end of your fingers is unnecessary for maximum forearm muscle stimulation and is, in fact, counterproductive for a couple of reasons. First of all, lowering the bar to the tips of your fingers puts a tremendous amount of stress on the tendons and muscles of the wrist. The wrist and forearm muscles and tendons are simply stretched too far, and the result can eventually be injury. The other reason is that the amount of hand, finger, and wrist strength necessary to control the weight through such an extreme range of motion severely limits the amount of weight you can use during the exercise. As a result, the deep inner forearm muscles are not stimulated to contract during the range of motion which most directly involves them, which is the range in which the wrist itself actually travels. A sufficiently heavy weight simply cannot be used in such an instance.

Once you have mastered this exercise, you may try placing your forearms directly along a well-padded, flat exercise bench with your wrists hanging right over the edge instead of placing them on your thighs. The bench provides a much flatter and more stable surface than your upper thighs and it is therefore easier to control the bar and perform the exercise correctly. Consequently, you derive greater benefit from it when it's performed in this way.

Incidentally, because of the precarious balance involved and the necessity of keeping the forearms parallel during both wrist curls and reverse wrist curls (which are about to be discussed) don't vary your grip on either one of these exercises. In the case of these particular exercises, there is basically only one right way to grip the bar and that's using the information presented here on finding the proper starting position.

Outer forearms—
barbell reverse wrist curls

Comments—This is an excellent exercise for developing the outer forearm muscles. Except for one variation, it is performed in the exact same way as barbell wrist curls.

Starting position—The starting position is exactly the same as for wrist curls except that the palms of your hands will be facing the floor instead of the ceiling. As a result, you will be grabbing the bar with an overhand grip instead of an underhand grip.

Exercise performance—This exercise is performed through the exact range of motion and in the exact same way as wrist curls except, of course, for the fact that the grip is reversed. You will quickly find that in comparison to wrist curls you will be at a distinct mechanical disadvantage when performing reverse wrist curls. The outer forearm muscles and the tendons running along the back of the wrist do not have near the strength of their opposites. As a result, you will find you can use only about half the weight on reverse wrist curls that you can on wrist curls. Also, because of the difficulty involved in raising your wrist past parallel and fully contracting the outer forearm muscles on reverse wrist curls, you will find that they are a lot more difficult to execute correctly than wrist curls and therefore require a much higher degree of concentration.

The actual range of motion constituting a full-range rep of both wrist curls and reverse wrist curls is very short compared to most other exercises. Thus, there is a tendency to perform the reps so rapidly that the muscle is not sufficiently stimulated. This temptation must be resisted. The fact is that the forearms seem to respond best to reps performed at a slightly slower rate in proportion to their range of motion than is optimum for most other exercises. They should always be performed in a slow, strict, controlled manner with a solid one or two seconds spent both raising and lowering the weight with a slight pause at the top of each rep. While this is standard for virtually all exercises at the beginning level, close examination will reveal that this constitutes an extremely long period of time for performing the relatively short-range reps of wrist curls and reverse wrist curls compared to the other exercises.

A. Outer forearms

1. Reverse barbell curls

Comments—This exercise strongly stresses both the brachialis muscle, which lies underneath the biceps and separates the biceps from the triceps, and all the muscles of the outer forearm, especially at the point where the forearms tie into the biceps.[1] The biceps are also moderately stressed during the performance of this exercise, especially the lower part of the muscle. Overall, this exercise is far superior to reverse wrist curls, in terms of the developmental benefits it provides. Developing the brachialis as well as the outer forearm muscles gives the entire arm a more mature and completely developed look. The reason I did not recommend performing this exercise at the beginner levels instead of reverse wrist curls is that the biceps would not have been able to cope effectively with the extra stress reverse curls put on them. By the time you reach the intermediate level this extra stress is much less in proportion to the amount of work you are performing for your biceps than it was at the beginner level, and they can handle it effectively. If you feel you need to, you can slightly reduce the intensity of one or two sets of your biceps workout on days you perform reverse curls, to ensure that you do not overtrain your biceps. Also, a good rule to follow is never to perform preacher curls and reverse curls on the same day as they both strongly stress the lower biceps and can result in your overtraining this portion of the bicep muscle. Overall, you should train your outer forearms with reverse curls between 60 and 65 percent of the time and perform reverse wrist curls between 35 and 40 percent of the time.

Starting position—Exactly the same as for barbell curls except that you will have an overhand, otherwise known as a reverse grip on the barbell, instead of an underhand one. In other words, your palms will be facing downward toward the floor instead of upward.

Exercise performance—Exactly the same as for barbell curls except that you will have a reverse grip on the bar as you raise the weight. Concentrate on using just your outer forearm muscles and not your biceps. Your brachialis will assist naturally. At the top of the exercise, fully contract the outer forearm muscles, pause for a moment, and then slowly lower the weight back to the starting position, concentrating on getting a deep stretch in the forearm muscles.

START

FINISH

B. Inner forearms

Comments—Unfortunately, no other inner forearm muscle exercise is anywhere near as effective as barbell wrist curls. This exercise is in a class by itself when it comes to inner forearm development. The only other inner forearm exercise which has any value whatsoever is dumbbell wrist curls. However, this exercise has two major inherent disadvantages when compared to barbell wrist curls. Overall, barbell wrist curls should be performed at least 75 percent of the time for your inner forearms, and dumbbell wrist curls should be performed at most 25 percent of the time, and only for the purpose of providing a change of pace in your forearm training.

1. Dumbbell wrist curls

Comments—This exercise will work all the muscles of the inner forearm although not nearly as effectively as barbell wrist curls. There are two reasons for this. First of all, you cannot rest your forearms along your thighs parallel to each other, as you did when performing barbell wrist curls, because your arms will be so close to each other that the ends of the two dumbbells you are holding will bang into each other and you will not be able to perform the exercise. You will have to move your legs far enough apart so that your arms are apart far enough so the two dumbbells will not bang into each other. Since your lower forearms will be wider apart than parallel, your elbows and upper arms will be forced in relatively close together in front of your body. This will result in undue stress being placed on the elbows and shoulder joints. Besides this, your wrists are such small joints that it is very difficult for one of them to effectively support and control the weight of a clumsy dumbbell.

Employing a barbell allows you to use both wrists together to balance the total amount of weight they are being trained with much more effectively than if each has to support half the weight in the form of a dumbbell. Also, your legs are a much less straight and stable surface than a flat exercise bench. Since you have to rest your arms on your legs when using two dumbbells, this results in the exercise being even more clumsy and difficult to perform effectively. Many bodybuilders attempt to make up for this by performing the exercise one arm at a time by hanging one wrist and the dumbbell it is supporting over the edge of a flat exercise bench. But I don't suggest this as there is more pressure on the back of the wrist and more stress on the wrist joint itself when performing the exercise with a dumbbell in this way. Interestingly enough, the exercise is actually clumsier and more difficult to perform than when hanging one wrist and a dumbbell simultaneously over each knee.

Equipment—Flat exercise bench.

MIDPOINT

Starting position—Sit on the end of a flat exercise bench. Pick up two light dumbbells. Run your forearms along the top of your thighs so that your palms are facing toward the ceiling. Hang your wrists and hands over the top of your knees, and spread your legs apart slightly while keeping your arms in place so the dumbbells are end to end, but aren't quite touching.

Exercise performance—Exactly the same as for barbell wrist curls, except that you will be using two dumbbells.

━ 12 ━
TRICEP EXERCISES

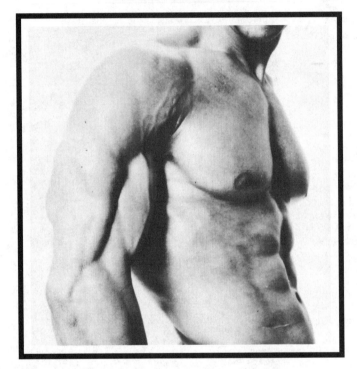

Standing tricep extensions

Comments—This exercise directly stimulates all three heads of the tricep muscle, especially the large inner head. Overall, I consider it to be the best exercise for thickening the tricep muscle and adding solid muscle mass to all portions of it. The reason is that although standing tricep extensions work the triceps in virtually the same way as the other excellent triceps mass builder, lying tricep extensions, the position of the body when performing the standing version will enable you, ultimately, to use much more weight in good form than on the lying version. That results in greater stimulation of the deep muscle fibers and, therefore, faster and more complete muscle development.

Starting position—As with standing curls, using an E.Z. curl bar on all forms of tricep extensions is superior to using a straight bar. That's because it turns the wrists and helps to line up the arms so that more direct stress is placed on the tricep muscle and the exercise is easier to control.

This exercise will be performed standing up. You will place the E.Z. curl bar on the floor in front of you in the following position. Basically the bar will be set in the exact opposite position as when performing standing curls. In this case the two bends in the bar closer to the inner-outer collars will be facing downward, and the other two bends—the ones closest to the middle length of the bar—will be facing upward. All forms of tricep extensions require a close overhand grip, with approximately 6 inches between your hands for maximum effectiveness. Using an E.Z. curl bar in the position previously described translates into gripping the outer part of the two inner bends of the bar directly on each side of the straight length. As with barbell curls you can slide your hand along the angled length of bar where you are taking your grip, but your hands should never be placed where the bar actually bends.

Once you have the proper grip, clean the bar to your shoulders and press it directly overhead to arm's length, as if you were doing standing military presses. Once the bar is in this position, bring your arms close together overhead so that your forearms, elbows and upper arms are parallel. The distance between your arms should match the distance between your hands. Your elbows will be pointing directly in front of you and up toward the ceiling. Your knees should be kept slightly bent during the performance of the entire exercise, and your back is to be kept perfectly straight at all times. Because you will be lowering the weight behind your head there will be a tendency to arch your back and bend backward when using heavier weights. Resist this tendency at all times as it can obviously result in a back injury.

Exercise performance—From the starting position just described, unlock your elbows and lower the bar in an arc behind your head. You will lower the bar until you feel a full stretch in the triceps, approximately down to the level of your neck. Then simply return it to the starting position and pause for a split second. During the course of the movement your upper arms will stay firmly in place pointing over your head, serving as a sort of pivot for your forearms, which will move in the aforementioned arc. Moving your upper arms will cause some of the benefit of the exercise to be shifted away from your triceps. Because of the leverage disadvantage associated with keeping your elbows in while performing this exercise, you will have a tendency to turn them outward, especially when struggling through the last couple of reps as a means of improving your leverage and making the reps easier to complete. Resist this temptation at all times as it will result in the loss of most benefits of this exercise to the triceps. Therefore, if you must turn your elbows out to complete your reps, simply reduce the weight so you can do it correctly.

In terms of injury prevention, never lower the bar so far that you feel an uncomfortable pulling where the tricep muscle and tendons insert into the elbow joint or discomfort in the elbow joint itself. Also, when extending the bar overhead, never lock your elbows. If you concentrate, you will feel the tricep muscle contract fully just prior to where the elbow joint is locked. Therefore, aside from the fact that locking the elbow joints can eventually damage them, it is not necessary to lock them to derive maximum stimulation to the tricep muscle. As previously discussed, this is also the case when performing military presses and is related to practically every other exercise. As a rule, locking any joint—whether elbow, knee, or shoulder—when performing bodybuilding exercises is both dangerous and unnecessary for maximum muscle growth stimulation.

START

FINISH

Basic heavy tricep extension exercises

1. Lying tricep extensions with E-Z curl bar

Comments—This exercise directly stresses all three heads of the triceps, especially the inner head.[1] Except for standing tricep extensions, for reasons previously discussed, it is the best exercise for thickening the triceps and adding solid muscle mass to all portions of it.

Equipment—Flat exercise bench.

Starting position—Take the same grip on the E-Z curl bar as you did when performing standing tricep extensions. Then lie on your back on a flat exercise bench, place your feet flat on the floor for stability and then press the weight to arm's length directly above your shoulder joints. More specifically, the bar will be directly over the middle of your chest. Your palms will be facing your feet. This starting position is almost identical to the one you used when performing bench presses.

Exercise performance—Keeping your upper arms firmly in place perpendicular to the floor during the performance of the entire exercise, bend your elbows slowly and lower the bar behind you in a semicircle until it lightly touches the top of your forehead.[2] Concentrate on feeling a full stretch along the back of the triceps muscle as you lower the weight. Immediately return the weight along the same arc to the starting position.[3] At the top of the rep, pause for a moment and concentrate on fully contracting the triceps muscles, then begin the next rep. You will use either this exercise or standing triceps extensions as the first exercise of every

START

FINISH

triceps workout, as outlined in the rotating schedule, until you have developed all the triceps mass you desire. Since standing tricep extensions are slightly more productive than lying triceps extensions, you should perform them during approximately 60 percent of your workouts and the lying version during about 40 percent of your triceps workouts. In those workouts in which a second exercise is recommended, you should use one of the following two exercises. Once you've developed most of the triceps mass you desire you can use all the tricep exercises described in this book interchangeably in the exact same way I recommended your using the exercises for the biceps.

124

Other basic triceps exercises

1. Tricep dips

Comments—This exercise strongly stresses the entire triceps, particularly the outer head. It is a good basic mass builder. However, it isn't quite as effective as tricep extensions because the pecs and delts are strongly involved in this exercise as assistance muscle groups. Because of this it is simply impossible to direct all the benefit of this exercise to the triceps. Nevertheless, you will get a thorough triceps workout from its use. Because of the nature of tricep dips, you will be able to get a more intense contraction in the triceps at the top of each rep than from any other tricep exercise. As a result, this exercise is superb for separating the three heads of the triceps and also giving the triceps better overall shape.

Equipment—Parallel dipping bars.

Starting position—Exactly the same as for chest dips except for some adjustments. Instead of leaning forward, your torso will be perfectly erect. Also instead of looking down at the floor, you will tilt your head slightly back, and you will concentrate on leaning back against your triceps so as much pressure as possible is on them instead of on your pecs.

Exercise performance—Exactly the same as for chest dips except that you will keep your torso as erect as possible while you perform the exercise, concentrating on keeping maximum tension on the triceps at all times. As you lower your torso between the parallel bars, concentrate on getting as full a stretch in the triceps as possible. When you return to the starting position, concentrate on contracting the triceps completely. Pause for a moment, and begin the next rep. The intensity of the contraction you will feel at the top of each rep on this exercise will be incredible if you perform it correctly.

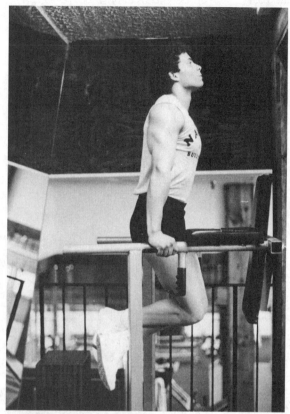

START

FINISH

2. Tricep pressdowns

Comments—This exercise works the entire triceps, but most directly stresses the outer head and lower portion of the triceps. This is more of an isolation exercise than a basic exercise and it is therefore more of a shaping exercise than a mass builder. However, it works the outer head of the triceps more effectively than any other exercise. It also stresses the hard-to-develop lower portion of the triceps near the elbow, and fills in this area more effectively than virtually all tricep exercises. The combination of these two benefits warrants occasional inclusion of this exercise in the triceps workouts of anyone attempting to build maximum triceps mass as well as for those more concerned with shaping what they have already built.

Equipment—Any freestanding lat machine or Universal lat machine, and also a short, straight triceps bar attachment, about 12 inches long.

Starting position—Stand in front of a lat pulldown machine, approximately 6 inches away from it. Reach up in front of you and take a narrow overhand grip on the lat bar so that your hands are approximately 6 to 8 inches apart and your palms are facing away from your body. Then pull the bar down in front of you so your upper arms are pinned against the sides of your torso,[4] and your elbow joints are completely bent so your forearms are pointing upward and outward in front of you. Then lean your torso slightly forward as this will result in maximum stress being placed on the triceps while performing the exercise.[5] This will be almost exactly the same as the completed position of a reverse curl.

Exercise performance—From this basic starting position, use the strength of your triceps to slowly straighten your arms. Your hands will travel in an arc downward and toward your upper thighs. At the point when your arms are completely straight, your palms with the tricep bar in them will lightly touch your upper thighs. At the bottom of the movement concentrate on contracting the triceps fully, especially the outer head. Remember, as in the case of all other exercises, never to lock your elbow joints. After pausing for a moment, slowly return your forearms to the starting position along the same arc in which you lowered it, concentrating on stretching the triceps fully at the point when your arms are completely bent.

I should mention here that many bodybuilders and weight training athletes are under the false impression that pushdowns are a basic mass building exercise. I must once again emphasize that they are not.

FINISH

START

126

—13—
QUADRICEP EXERCISES

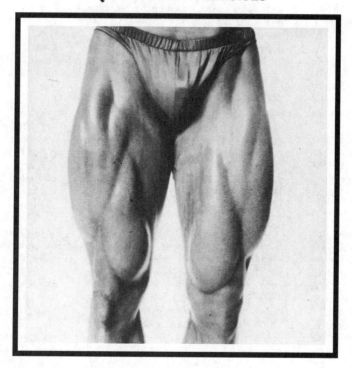

Parallel squats

Equipment—Squat rack.

Comments—Squats work the lower body as bench presses work the upper body. Most serious bodybuilders consider squats to be the most productive of all exercises. Squats provide the bodybuilder with a number of important benefits.

First of all, squats are indisputably the best exercise for developing the quadriceps muscles. They are the only leg exercise which hits the entire quadriceps muscle in the most direct way possible, while simultaneously providing the leverage to handle tremendous amounts of weights needed to stimulate the deep muscle fibers of the quads and, therefore, provide maximum gains in both muscle mass and strength. In fact, squats are such a superior exercise that it is next to impossible to build massive, muscular legs without them, unless you have fantastic leg potential and they respond to any kind of leg work whatsoever. Squats also stimulate the hamstrings and lumbar regions.

Contrary to popular belief, squats do not cause lower back and knee injuries. This is true only if you use sloppy form or try to use too much weight too quickly. If you attempt to bounce the weight at the bottom of the exercise, a bad form of cheating, you put a great deal of stress on the knee joint and the lower back, which will cause injuries.

Because it takes a couple of months for the muscles, joints, and tendons to become thoroughly accustomed to the unique stresses placed upon them by progressive resistance training, I suggest that in the case of squats, an exercise which requires a tremendous amount of coordination and has the potential to put an uncomfortable amount of stress on the lower back and knees, a less stressful variation of this exercise be performed during the beginning phase of training as a safety precaution. I therefore recommend that you perform parallel squats at first, instead of full squats. Parallel squats do not stretch the muscles of the lower back and the muscles and tendons of the knee to near the degree that full squats do. Therefore, performing parallel squats for the first few months provides an excellent way for these areas to gradually become accustomed to the type of stress the squatting movement places upon them, and to slowly gain the strength, flexibility, and coordination

necessary to perform full squats without any risk of injury whatsoever.

The final benefit of squats is that following a program of consistent heavy squatting has a positive effect on the metabolic processes of the body. It stimulates them so it becomes easier to gain muscular body weight, not just on the quads but on all the other muscle groups.[1] The body as a whole is stimulated to gain muscle faster. This is a fantastic benefit, for what it comes down to is that squatting can actually enhance the development of your upper body as well as your legs. Squats also benefit upper body development in another way: The heavy breathing associated with heavy squatting will eventually permanently expand your rib cage. An expanded rib cage is beneficial as it makes the entire upper body look thicker and fuller, especially the chest.

Starting position—Because of the amount of weight you will be using on this exercise you will need to place an empty bar on either an adjustable squat rack or a slanted, multilevel squat rack at slightly lower than shoulder level. You can then add as much weight as necessary to the bar. Once the bar is properly loaded and in position, duck underneath it and come up so that it rests across your shoulders and upper traps. Then step forward so that your weight is centered directly under the bar. Next, simply stand erect while simultaneously lifting the bar off the rack. Then carefully take a few steps backwards. Make sure when getting into position that you take a wide overhand grip on the barbell only a few inches from the plates on each side. Such a wide grip will best enable you to balance the bar on your shoulders. You should maintain a firm grip on the barbell at all times during the performance of this exercise, to ensure your maintaining total control of it. Before beginning the exercise, make sure that the bar feels comfortable resting across your neck and shoulders. If you place it too high on the neck, the bar can press against the cervical vertebrae which can cause noticeable discomfort and result in your being distracted and your concentration being broken when trying to perform the exercise. It is best to place the bar lower on your neck right across your trapezius muscles.[2] These muscles act as a cushion and therefore eliminate most, if not all, of the discomfort associated with having a heavy bar resting across your shoulders. If the bar still feels uncomfortable as it very well

may during the first few months or year of training due to lack of development of sufficient cushioning muscle mass on the traps and delts, you can either place a thick towel across your shoulders or wrap one directly around the barbell to ease the pressure. I've found the first method to be the better of the two.

Once the bar is comfortably on your shoulders and you've taken a couple steps back from the squat rack so you'll be sufficiently clear of it, stand perfectly erect with your lower back muscles tensed to provide support. Place your feet at approximately shoulder width.[3] Then point your toes out slightly at approximately a 30° v. Finally, focus your eyes on a spot on the wall in front of you which is slightly above eye level. Keep them focused on this spot throughout the performance of the exercise. This will force you to keep your head tilted slightly back, which will result in your keeping your back erect throughout the set.[4]

When performing squats, an option you should seriously consider is placing either a thin piece of wood or a couple of 10 lb. plates on the floor a couple of feet behind the squat rack and, after lifting the weight off, backing up so that the heels of your feet are positioned on the raised object. From my experience such a low board or other flat object about 2 inches high contributes greatly to improving your balance when performing squats. It enables you to keep your back almost perfectly erect during the entire squatting movement without losing your balance and falling backward. Without a block you will find that you will have to lean much farther forward during your squats in order to maintain your balance. As a result, there will be much more stress on your lower back, a much greater tendency to round your entire back during the course of your sets, and a chance of sustaining some sort of back injury. So give a board a try. It could do wonders for your squatting form.

Exercise performance—Keeping your back as straight as possible, bend your knees, let your butt drop, and slowly squat down to the point where the tops of your thighs are perfectly parallel to the floor. As you squat down, your knees should come forward and travel out somewhat over your feet.[5] However, you should concentrate on keeping your center of gravity as far back as possible without losing your balance during the course of the exercise; this helps you keep your back straight and

START

FINISH

also throws more stress directly on the quadriceps. You should also keep your thighs and knees as close to parallel as possible throughout the exercise, even though your toes are pointed out slightly. This throws stress on a greater portion of the quadriceps than is possible when having your thighs and knees pointed outward, instead of almost perfectly straight ahead. Anyway, once you've reached parallel, immediately stand erect again with the bar because pausing for any length of time at the bottom of a rep puts undue pressure on the knee joints. Despite not quite doing full-range reps you should feel a good stretch and a good amount of tension on the quads at the bottom of each rep. At the top of each rep stop just short of locking your knees, pause for a split second, and concentrate on contracting the quads. Then begin another rep.

Squats

1. Full squats

Comments—This exercise is the most productive quadricep exercise you can perform. It is better than parallel squats because in this version of the exercise, your quadriceps will travel through a full range of motion resulting in the development of more quad mass, more fullness, better shape, and more complete development of the muscle in every way. The reason I did not recommend performing full squats at the beginner level is that they stretch the lower back muscles, and tendons and ligaments around the knee, much more than parallel squats do. When you first begin training, these areas cannot be safely stretched to their limit while supporting the weight of a loaded bar. They simply don't have the flexibility to do so. You could probably get away with doing full squats right from the start if you really wanted to, but why take unnecessary risks. By performing parallel squats for a few months, you will give the lower back muscles and knee areas a chance to adapt safely to the stress that the squatting movement places upon them in general. They will gain progressively increased strength and flexibility so that by the time you have completed the beginner level of training, they will be able to safely handle the additional stress which the added range of motion of full squats will put upon them.

Most people who know something about weight training but don't know the full story believe that full squats will eventually destroy your knees. When performed correctly full squats won't damage your knees any more than tricep extensions will damage your elbows—generally not at all. In fact, full squats, when performed correctly, will increase the strength and flexibility of all the muscles, tendons, and ligaments around the knee joint.

The times that full squats can potentially damage your knee are in the following circumstances. First, of course, is if you do not perform parallel squats for a couple of months to prepare your knees for the added stress which full squats will place upon them. Second is if you either bounce or pause at the bottom of your reps. The stress which either one of these things places on your knee joints will eventually result in the tendons, ligaments, and connective tissue in that area being torn apart.

Always remember when performing any type of squat or leg press, especially full squats, to return immediately to the starting position without pausing or bouncing. Finally, full squats and other forms of this exercise can potentially cause damage to your knee joints if you either have an inherent weakness in that area or if you have a history of knee problems. In the latter case see an orthopedic specialist before incorporating full squats or any other exercise into your routine which puts an unusual amount of stress on the knee joint.

Starting position—Exactly the same as for parallel squats.

Exercise performance—Exactly the same as for parallel squats except that in this case you squat down as far as you can comfortably, without either putting undue stress on your knees or losing your balance. The back of your hamstrings will rest against the back of your calves at the bottom of the movement. Then slowly return to the starting position.

FINISH

2. Front squats (full)

Comments—This exercise actually hits the quadriceps a little more directly than full squats. It especially stresses the lower quads, right above the knees, an area of the quad which full squats do not stress that intensely. Because of this, front squats are potentially better than full squats when it comes to building massive, completely developed, and well-shaped quadriceps. Unfortunately, very few individuals are able to perform this exercise with maximum effectiveness because of two major disadvantages which hinder the ability to perform this exercise. These two disadvantages both stem from the fact that when performing front squats you have to support the weight of a heavily loaded barbell across the front of your neck and shoulders. Most individuals lack sufficient muscle mass in this area to hold the bar comfortably in this position, even when placing a towel under the bar. Besides this, when you squat down with a heavy bar held in this position, you will notice that a tremendous amount of downward pressure is placed on your rib box, which makes it more difficult to breathe air in. When you consider the fact that squats are such a demanding exercise that you will normally get out of breath by the time you finish performing a set, you can imagine how much more difficult it would be to breathe when having to contend with downward pressure on your rib box during the entire exercise. Because of this pressure most individuals run out of breath and have to terminate their sets of front squats before their quads have been thoroughly worked. As a result, this exercise turns out to be less productive than regular full squats. However, for those individuals who don't run out of breath too soon before the point where the quads have been thoroughly worked, this is still a very productive exercise, second only to regular full squats in benefit. It's just a lot more uncomfortable.

If you can perform this exercise, you should substitute it for regular full squats approximately one-quarter of the time. Unfortunately, a large percentage of you will find that until you reach at least the advanced intermediate level, you will not have sufficient muscle mass across the top of your shoulders to hold the barbell in the correct position. It will simply roll off your shoulders. Also, some of you will never be able to hold the bar comfortably in place because of the way you're built.

In both of these cases don't worry about performing front squats. If and when you reach the point where you feel relatively comfortable with them, incorporate them into your routine. If you never do, then stick with regular, full squats, and don't worry about it.

Equipment—Squat racks.

Starting position—Place a loaded barbell on a squat rack, just below the height of your shoulders. Lower yourself under the barbell with your arms extended straight out in front of you so it rests across the base of your neck, where it inserts with your upper pecs, and the top of your delts. Keeping your elbows up, fold your arms diagonally across the barbell so that the palm of each hand is resting across the opposite shoulder where the barbell is resting upon it.[6] Keeping your elbows up, lift the barbell off the squat rack and take a couple of steps back so you are clear of it. Take the exact same stance as you used for parallel squats and full squats, and make sure your back is perfectly erect.

START

Exercise performance—Exactly the same as for the other two forms of squats except that you will be holding the bar in front of your neck, instead of behind it. As a result of this, you will have to make sure you hold the bar firmly in place with your elbows pointing slightly upward at all times during the performance of the exercise so the bar does not roll forward off your shoulders. This could result in serious injury. Make sure you keep your back perfectly erect and never lean forward at any time during the performance of the exercise for the same reason.

FINISH

Other basic quad exercises

1. Leg presses (45° angle)

Comments—This exercise works the quads in almost the exact same way as squats (the movements are virtually identical). However, they do not stress the muscle fibers of the quads, especially the deep muscle fibers, as intensely as various forms of squats do. Therefore, while they are an excellent mass builder, they will not provide the same degree of full, massive leg development which consistent squatting will provide. Leg presses are most commonly performed on either freestanding lying leg press machines or 45° angled leg press machines, which are becoming increasingly popular. The Universal leg press machines are also quite popular.

The 45° angled leg press machines are superior to all the others. If you have access to more than one type of leg press machine in your gym and this type is one of your choices, I strongly suggest you make use of it. Angled leg presses are generally the most comfortable and smoothly functioning of all the leg press machines and they enable you to hit the quads very directly without putting undue stress on other areas. Universal leg press machines are excellent and make a good second choice. However, an uncomfortable seat and undue stress on the knees are two complaints commonly associated with these machines.

Lying leg presses, while they are one of the most effective varieties of leg presses in terms of improving leg development, are potentially dangerous and should be avoided if at all possible.

The first and most serious danger involves the fact that when you perform a lying leg press, your head is lower than any other part of your body. As a result, blood tends to pool in your head and there is an increase in intracranial pressure. This increase in pressure can become pronounced when straining to complete the final couple reps of a heavy set. Not only is this pressure uncomfortable, but it can commonly lead to the development of headaches. Then, to make things worse, there is a tendency to hold your breath somewhat under the stress of a heavy weight on lying leg presses. Even if you hold your breath for a brief second, the result can be disastrous, because of the increase in intracranial pressure which already exists.

This sudden increase in pressure can easily result in your fainting, which means all the weight you were using will come crashing down on top of you and either seriously injure you or kill you. You could also cause a stroke. So if you're going to use lying leg presses, make sure you breathe slowly and regularly at all times.

The other potential danger involves the fact that lying leg presses put a tremendous amount of undue stress along the back of the knee joint and hamstrings at the top of each rep. Therefore, if you're not thoroughly warmed up when you perform this exercise, you could very easily pull or tear your hamstring muscles, or the tendons and ligaments along the back of the knee joint.

Because of the potential danger associated with lying leg presses I am only going to describe 45° angled leg presses. If you're going to be using a universal leg press, perform the exercise with your feet on the top set of steps instead of the bottom set, as the bottom position puts more pressure on the knee joints than the top one.

Equipment—45° angled leg press machine.

Starting position—Sit in the machine so your back rests against the padded surface at the bottom of the machine, which is on a slight incline. There will be a corner where the back pad and the seat pad meet each other. Slide down and back so your hips rest snugly in this corner.[7] Place your feet against the sliding platform so that they are at approximately shoulder width. Your toes should be pointing outward at about a 35° angle to each side. Straighten your legs and release the stop catches at the sides of the machine so you can lower the weight.[8]

Exercise performance—Starting with your legs straight, slowly lower the weight platform. Bend your legs at the knee joint as fully as possible so your knees travel out over your toes exactly as they did when performing the squat. Without pausing, slowly press the weight rack back up to the starting position. Straighten your legs to within 5° of full lockout at the top of the rep so there is no undue stress placed on the knee joint. The quads should be fully contracted at this point. Pause for a split second, tense the quads, and begin the next rep. At the end of the last rep hold the sliding weight rack in the starting position so you can return the stop catches to the locked position.[9] Then lower the weight rack so it rests against the stop bars, and slide your legs out.

FINISH

START

2. Hack squats

Comments—This exercise strongly stresses the quads, especially the lower portion around the knee and the inner thigh. They provide both mass building and shaping benefits, as they fill in the area around the knee with muscle and give the quads a full sweep from top to bottom. They also tend to give the quads a separated and detailed look.

Equipment—Sliding back squat machine, preferably with shoulder pads.

Starting position—Place your feet on the slightly inclined platform at the bottom of the machine and place your back flat against the sliding platform of the machine so that your body, although slightly inclined, is in a perfectly straight line. When you lift the rack into the starting position, the heels of your feet will be approximately 6 inches in front of where your lower back rests against the sliding rack. Your heels should be placed approximately 6 to 8 inches apart and your toes should be pointing outward about 35° to each side.[10] Some of these racks have pads which rest on your shoulders and allow you to support the weight of the rack comfortably. With other versions, you have to support the weight of the rack by gripping two bars at the side of each leg. The first type is far superior, and it is the type I am describing here.

Starting with your knees slightly bent, press up against the shoulder pads so that they rest snugly on your traps and delts. Then straighten your legs so that the weight rack is lifted off the stop catch bars. Your body will now be in a perfectly straight line as previously mentioned. Then turn the stop catch bars out with your hands so the weight rack can travel downward.

Exercise performance—From this basic starting position, slowly bend your legs and lower your body until your legs are fully bent. As you lower your torso and the sliding platform, your knees will travel directly out over your feet. As a result of this your legs will spread apart as if you were a frog, when you bend your knees and lower the weight[11] instead of remaining perfectly parallel to each other, as when performing other forms of squats. As you lower the weight, concentrate on

getting a full stretch in the quads, especially along the inner and lower portions of the muscle. Without pausing, slowly return the rack to the starting position, and concentrate on fully contracting the quads, especially the inner and lower portions. As with leg presses, straighten your legs to within 5° of full lockout at the top of each rep. After pausing for a moment, begin the next rep. Complete the prescribed number of reps, then stand fully erect without jolting your knees, and turn the stop catches back in. Then lower the rack against the stop catches and slide out of the machine.

With the standard version of hack squats in which there are no shoulder pads, you have to start with the rack at the bottom of the machine and your knees fully bent, and then press it to the top position. With your legs fully flexed it is difficult to get the weight moving for the first rep, and there is a tendency

to bounce or jerk the weight to get it moving initially. That is one disadvantage of this apparatus. The second, and major disadvantage, is that since you have to support the sliding rack solely with grip strength, your grip will virtually always give out before your quads have been thoroughly worked, which makes this version significantly less than 100 percent effective. As a result, you will have to use wrist straps when you begin using heavy weights on this machine in order to keep your grip intact. Straps were discussed at the very end of the intermediate training section. For all of these reasons, I strongly suggest that you use the hack squat machine with shoulder rests if at all possible. Fortunately, most of today's modern gyms have this version of the hack squat machines as well as the superior 45° angled version of the leg press machine.

FINISH

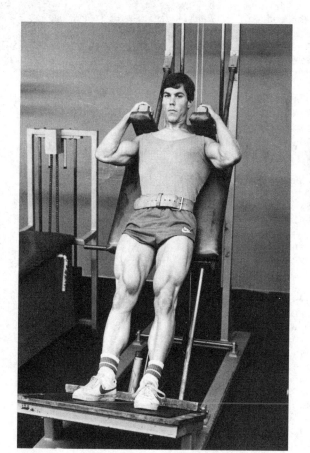

START

133

3. Leg extension

Comments—This exercise directly stresses all four heads of the quads. However, it is an isolation exercise and, as such, does not stimulate the deep muscle fibers with sufficient intensity to stimulate significant increases in muscle mass except for the lower inner head of the muscle which extends over the knee. This area is hit very intensely. Leg extensions are more of a shaping exercise and they are excellent for giving the quads a separated and completely developed look.

Equipment—Freestanding, Universal, or Nautilus machine. All three are virtually equally effective.

Starting position—Sit in the machine so that the backs of your knees are at the edge of the seated pad and the front of your legs are facing the padded, movable lever of the machine. Lean slightly forward and bend your legs at the knees so that your lower legs travel back and under the bench far enough so you can place the instep of your feet under the lower set of roller pads. (There will be only one set on the Nautilus machine.) So that you can keep your body steady as you perform this exercise, you should firmly grip either the handles provided at the sides of the machine or the edges of the padded seat on each side of your torso.[12] Then lean back in the seat so your torso is resting as comfortably as possible against the back rest. With some machines, the back rest is adjustable and can be moved either forward or backward.

Exercise performance—From the basic starting position, simply straighten your legs slowly. Your feet will travel in an arc as you raise the weight. At the top of the rep you should pause for a full second and concentrate on fully contracting all the muscles of the quads as hard as possible. Then slowly lower the weight back to the starting position, concentrating on feeling a full stretch along the top of the quads. At the bottom of the rep do not quite let the movable pad come to rest and the weight stack hit, so that there is no longer any tension on the quads. Once you feel a full stretch, immediately begin the next rep. In fact, the weight

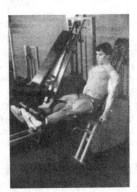

FINISH

START

stack should not hit at the bottom of a rep of any machine exercise you perform. Good examples are pulldowns, cable rows, and leg curls.

— 14 —
HAMSTRING EXERCISES

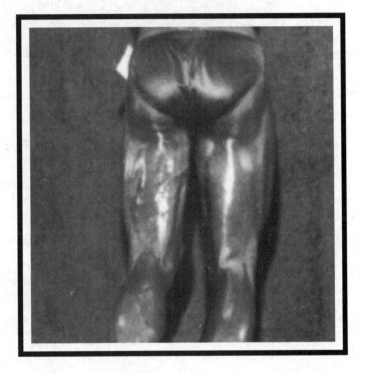

Leg curls

Comments—Compared to most of the exercises in this routine, leg curls are comparatively isolatory in nature. They place direct stress on the biceps femoris, the major muscle constituting the hamstring complex, with minimal involvement of other muscle groups. Only the glutes and calves are involved, and only to a slight degree. Leg curls are most commonly performed on either a plate-loading leg curl machine, a Universal leg curl, or a Nautilus leg curl. From my experience, I consider the Universal leg curl to be superior to all others. If you are fortunate enough to have access to one, take advantage of it. The smoothness of this particular machine and the intensity with which it isolates and stresses the hamstrings gives it a distinct advantage over all other leg curl devices in my eyes.

Starting position—The starting position for all variations of lying leg curl machines is as follows. Lie face down on the padded surface of the machine with your feet facing toward the padded lever at the lower end of the machine. Slide your body down along the bench so that your knees are resting right near the edge of the pad at the lower end. Most leg curl machines will have an upper set of roller pads approximately parallel with the padded bench and a lower set of roller pads close to the floor attached to the lever. You will slide your feet under the top padded lever so that your heels rest right against it.[1] Your legs will be almost perfectly parallel to each other. Your forearms should be placed on top of the padded bench, parallel to each other, and in such a way that your upper arms are pressed tightly against your upper body and you are propped up on your elbows. Your hands should grip the sides of the padded surface for support.[2] In conjunction, your entire upper back should be slightly arched and your neck should be flexed so that your head is lifted off the bench and your eyes are facing directly ahead of you. Doing this will help you keep your glutes down on the bench and result in the benefit of the exercise being directed almost exclusively to the hamstrings.

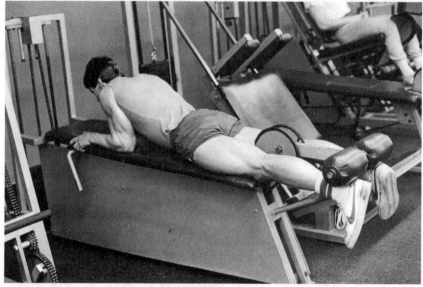

START

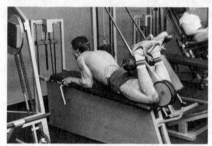

FINISH

Exercise performance—From this basic starting position, slowly curl your lower legs up toward your glutes. Your thighs should remain flat against the bench at all times. While curling the weight you should concentrate on feeling the hamstrings contract. Resist the temptation to lift your butt off the bench in an effort to provide added leverage for lifting the weight. This is one exercise in which the strictest of form should be maintained at all times. Once your legs are curled to the point where the hamstrings are in the fully contracted position, hold the weight there for a full second. Then slowly return the weight to the starting position, concentrating on feeling the hamstrings stretch fully all the way down. Once the rep is completed, immediately begin the next one without pausing. This exercise, performed in this manner, is the best thing you can do to fully develop and thicken your hamstrings.

Hamstrings—stiff-legged deadlift

Comments—For those of you who are beginning your training at home and do not have either access to a leg curl machine or attachment for a multipurpose bench, this exercise can serve as an excellent alternative for working the hamstrings. This exercise does stress the hamstrings strongly and provides them with a relatively good workout. However, it does not compare with leg curls when it comes to thickening the muscle and stimulating maximum muscle growth. Stiff-legged deadlifts simply do not isolate the leg biceps to near the degree that leg curls do. In fact, they work the lower back muscles almost as intensely as they work the hamstrings. As a result, I would normally recommend performing only stiff-legged deadlifts in conjunction with leg curls at the intermediate or advanced level as a means of efficiently finishing off the hamstring workout. It is when used in such a capacity that they are most effective. So keep this in mind when using them as your only hamstring exercise and don't expect to attain maximum hamstring development unless you find a way to do leg curls.

Equipment—A wood block 4 to 6 inches high, long enough and wide enough to stand on comfortably.

Starting position—Your starting position will be almost identical to that of shoulder shrugs except for a few minor variations. First, instead of standing on the floor you will be standing on either a wood block or an exercise bench. The barbell will be either on the floor in front of you when using a block or on the uprights when using an exercise bench. You will squat down, take a shoulder-width grip on the bar so your palms are facing toward your body, and stand erect with it so that it's resting against your upper thighs.[3] Your feet should be very close together, only 4 to 6 inches apart, so that your inner thighs are almost touching and your toes should be pointing directly in front of you. Also, in the case of this exercise your legs should be perfectly straight so that your knees are almost locked and your arms will also be kept almost perfectly straight throughout the course of the exercise.

Exercise performance—Keeping your legs and arms straight, slowly bend forward as far as you can, concentrating on feeling the hamstrings stretch. Being up on a block or exercise bench will allow you to lower the barbell much farther than if you were standing on the floor. As a result, you'll be able to get an incredibly full stretch in the hamstrings without worrying about the bar touching the floor prematurely and limiting your range of motion. Once you've reached the bottom position, immediately begin to stand up with the bar.[4] However, do not stand fully erect. Stop at a point approximately 30° short of the fully erect position, bend your knees about 15°, and tense your hamstrings. Hold for a split second, straighten your legs again and begin another rep. Stopping short of the fully erect position as just described keeps continuous tension on the hamstrings and is superior to standing fully erect for stimulating muscle growth. The top 30° of the movement strongly involve the lumbar muscles and involve the hamstrings to only a minor degree and therefore allow them too much time to rest. When performing the final rep you should simply either squat down and place the bar on the floor if using a block, or stand fully erect so you can easily step forward and place the bar on the uprights if using a flat exercise bench. Because of the mechanical disadvantage your lumbar region is at during the performance of this exercise and the resultant vulnerability to injury, it is essential that you both thoroughly warm up before going heavy on this exercise and that you use slow, perfectly strict form on every rep. During the first set of this exercise don't lower the bar all the way down during the first three or four reps, but lower the bar a little further on each of these reps so that the hamstrings have a chance to warm up and gradually adapt to being stretched. After three to four reps the hamstrings will be warmer, looser, and more flexible, and will be ready to handle a full stretch with no unusual discomfort. Doing this will act as an excellent safety precaution against sustaining an injury to this region such as a muscle or tendon pull or tear.

Leg curls and stiff-legged deadlifts, by far the two best exercises for developing the hamstrings, were already discussed in detail. No other exercise can compare with these two when it comes to strengthening and developing the hamstrings. Therefore, the only change in your hamstring workout at the intermediate level is that instead of performing only one or the other of these exercises as you did at the beginner level, you will now perform both. So if you're still training at home during the intermediate level of training, it's time to invest in a leg curl attachment for your multipurpose bench.

It should be mentioned here that from now on, through the remainder of your natural bodybuilder career, your hamstring workout will consist solely of leg curls and stiff-legged deadlifts performed in various set combinations. Since leg curls are the more productive of the two exercises in terms of adding solid muscle mass to the back of the legs, they should always be performed first. And since stiff-legged deadlifts do not hit the hamstrings quite as directly and are more of a shaping movement, they should be performed second. You will, of course, follow the rotating set schedule outlined at each of the three intermediate levels for the hamstrings. Because leg curls are far more beneficial than stiff-legged deadlifts overall, you will perform only leg curls for the prescribed number of sets of your hamstring workout once every two to three workouts consistently on a rotating basis, according to which intermediate level you are at. As already mentioned, you will be performing entire workouts of heavy basic curls for your biceps, heavy basic tricep extensions for your triceps and heavy basic squatting exercises for your quads in the exact same manner. You will also be performing entire workouts of standing calf raises for your calves as they are by far the most productive exercise for that muscle.

Hamstring workout

1. Leg Curls
2. Stiff-Legged Deadlifts

START

FINISH

—15—
CALF EXERCISES

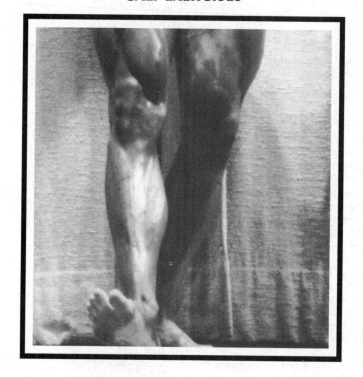

Standing calf raise

Comments—This exercise places direct stress on the entire calf muscle and because of the exceedingly heavy weights that can be used on it, it is definitely the best exercise for adding muscle mass and thickness to the calves. Standing calf raises work the large gastrocnemius muscle of the calf more so than the smaller, underlying soleus muscle. Specialization on the soleus with seated calf raises for complete development will be covered in the intermediate section.

Starting position—Standing calf machines are constructed with two long, thickly padded shoulder rests which make supporting the heavy weights you will be using relatively comfortable for your shoulders. These machines also have a thick wood block built into them so you can get a full stretch in the calf muscle. Proper starting position: Stand up on the raised block, bend slightly at the knees and slide your shoulders under the shoulder pads. (The shoulder pads are attached to the weight stack by an adjustable chain. You should adjust the chain so you will feel just as must tension at the bottom of each rep as you do at the top.) Adjust your feet so they are approximately 6 inches apart, your toes pointing straight ahead, and only the balls of your feet on the wood block. Once in this position, stand perfectly erect. This will lift the weight stack and put maximum tension on the calf muscles.

Exercise performance—From this starting position slowly rise all the way up on your toes as high as you possibly can. Concentrate on feeling the calf muscles contract fully. Pause for half a second and then slowly sag your heels as far below the level of your toes as possible,[1] concentrating on stretching the calves, to the maximum degree possible. Then immediately raise up on your toes again. Once you get to the level where you are doing three sets, you can perform one set with your toes pointed straight ahead, one with them turned inward (which directs more stress to the outer portion of the calf), and one with them turned outward (which directs most of the stress to the inner portion of the calf).

START

FINISH

One-legged calf raises

This exercise is recommended for those individuals who are training at home and do not have access to a standing calf machine. This exercise puts a great deal of stress on the calves. However, it is a slightly clumsy exercise and you will be appreciably limited in the amount of weight you can use on it. Nevertheless, you can make dramatic improvement in your calf development with this exercise, at least during the first few months to a year of training. After that, if you are serious about your training and of achieving balanced development, gaining access to a standing calf machine will become imperative.

As it stands right now, calves are the most often neglected muscle group in the bodybuilding world, even more so than the quadriceps. This is partly due to the fact that calf exercising is boring and partly because many bodybuilders simply do not consider calves to be an important muscle group. Calves are no more or no less important than any other muscle group and they should be trained at least equally hard as everything else. Despite its extremely repetitive nature, calf training requires very

little energy. As a result, calves are one of the few muscle groups which can be trained as effectively near the end of the workout, when energy levels are starting to drop, as during the beginning of the workout. Home trainers should not try standing calf raises with a barbell across their shoulders. It is very difficult to keep one's balance and therefore is unproductive and dangerous.

Starting position—The best place to perform this exercise is on a staircase in which the steps are at least three to four inches in height. It is preferable to stand on either the bottom step or one close to the bottom of the staircase in case you somehow happen to lose your balance so that you don't go tumbling down a full flight of steps. It is also essential that you choose a stairway which has either a railing or wall on both sides; you will need to brace your hands against the sides of the stairwell in order to keep your balance during the performance of the exercise. It is preferable to have a railing on at least one side, as gripping a railing is much more stable than bracing against a wall.

139

Anyway, to get into position, stand on one of the lower steps so your toes are pointing straight ahead and you are just standing on the balls of your feet. Next, place your arms out at your sides and slightly in front of you and grab the wall or railing on either side of the stairwell. Lean slightly forward, bending at the waist so that your center of gravity is slightly forward of your legs. This will prevent you from losing your balance and falling backward during the performance of the exercise. Finally lift one foot up off the stairs, bending your leg at the knee so that the foot has no chance of hitting the stairs during the performance of the exercise. This will throw all the resistance created by the weight of your body onto the other calf. You are now ready to begin the exercise. After you've done a complete set for the one calf, you will simply switch feet. When doing more than one set you will then wait a few seconds and train the first calf again, then the other one again, and so on.

Exercise performance—From the basic starting position slowly rise all the way up on the toes of the foot which is on the steps. Concentrate on feeling the calf muscle contract fully at the top of the rep. Pause for a half-second and slowly lower your heels as far below the level of your toes as possible. Use your arm to keep your upper body as stable as possible during the performance of the exercise. Also, during the course of the exercise, the foot of the calf you are training may shift slightly back because of the fact that your center of gravity will be slightly forward. When this occurs simply adjust your foot position accordingly. As you come to master the balance required for optimum performance of this exercise this will happen less and less frequently.

Because the minimum amount of weight you can use on this exercise is your own body weight there is a good chance that you won't have the calf strength necessary to complete the prescribed number of repetitions during the first few weeks of training. Eventually, however, you will gain the necessary strength and, in fact, you will ultimately reach a point where your body weight is too light for you to attain any significant muscle growth stimulation. It is at this time that the limitations of this exercise become readily apparent. Your alternatives are to move on to standing calf raises on the calf machine or to hold a weighted dumbbell at arm's length at the side of the body you are training. The only problem with this is balance. You only have one hand free to balance yourself.

Introduction to intermediate level calf exercises—As already discussed, standing calf raises are by far the most productive of all calf movements in terms of adding solid muscle mass to the calves. As a result of this they will always constitute the foundation of your calf training program and should be performed first in every calf workout you perform during your entire natural bodybuilding career. With this and all other calf exercises you should divide the total number of sets you perform at each level as equally as possible between the three toe positions previously described (toes straight, toes in, and toes out) so you can impart to the calf muscles a dimension of fullness, shapeliness, and complete development.

After performing standing calf raises, you will usually perform a second exercise during your calf workouts at the intermediate level and henceforth. The two best alternative exercises for finishing off the calves will be presented and described here. One is more effective than the other and is actually necessary for the most complete and shapely development of the calves to ultimately be attained. However, neither exercise is nearly as important or beneficial for overall calf development as standing calf raises.

Basic calf exercise

1. Standing calf raises

Comments—Perform exactly as previously described.

Other calf exercises

1. Seated calf raise

Comments—Seated calf raises develop the soleus muscle which underlies the gastrocnemius muscle of the calf. The gastrocnemius is the large muscle of the calf which is developed by standing calf raises. In order to directly stress the soleus muscle, you must perform toe raises with your legs bent at least 30°. Since your legs are bent at the knee at a 45° angle when performing seated calf raises this is the best exercise for developing the soleus muscle.[2] While the soleus is not a large muscle, developing it gives the calves a more separated, muscularly defined, and shapely look, especially the lower calf.

Equipment—Seated calf machine.

Starting position—Sit in the seat of a seated calf machine and position both your toes and the balls of your feet on the bar directly beneath your knees. Your lower legs will form a right angle with your thighs. Next, force your knees under the padded weight support bar by sagging your heels far enough below the level of your toes so you can slide your knees under the bar and rest it comfortably on your lower thighs. The height of the padded knee bar is adjustable. You can raise it or lower it by moving a metal weight pin. The pin actually attaches the knee pad securely to the machine.[3] This is important. If the pad is too low you will not be able to get your knees under it, no matter how far down you sag your feet. If it's too high, it will not be able to rest on your knees in the starting position and optimum resistance won't be placed on the calves during the exercise. Once your knees are comfortably in position, lift the padded bar off the stop bar of the machine by rising as high as you can on your toes, and simply push the stop bar forward and out of the way with your hand,[4] so you can lower the weight and perform the exercise.

START

FINISH

Exercise performance—From this basic starting position, slowly sag your heels below the level of your toes as far as possible, concentrating on getting a full stretch in the soleus muscle and the calf as a whole. Then, without pausing, rise up on your toes as high as you possibly can. At the top of the rep, pause for a second, and contract the calves—especially the soleus—as forcefully and completely as possible. Then begin the next rep. After performing the prescribed number of reps, return the weight to the starting position. Slide the stop bar back into place under the padded weight support bar which was resting on your lower thighs and carefully slide out of the machine. Divide the sets as evenly as possible between the toes straight, toes in, and toes out positions.

2. 45° Angled calf press

Comments—This is a good exercise for thoroughly working the entire calf, especially the gastrocnemius muscle. However, it does not stimulate the deep fibers nearly as effectively as standing calf raises and is, therefore, not nearly as productive in terms of adding mass to the calves. However, it is productive enough to occasionally be substituted into the routine as a second calf exercise for the purpose of adding variety to your calf training. However, seated calf raises should be used during approximately 75 percent of the workouts in which a second calf exercise is to be performed and 45° angled calf presses should be used only approximately 25 percent of the time. The reason for this, of course, is that it is much more important to perform an exercise which directly hits the soleus than to perform one which hits the calves in almost the exact same way as standing calf raises.

Equipment—45° angled leg press machine.

Starting position—Sit in the machine exactly as you did when performing leg presses. This time, however, place your feet toward the bottom of the sliding platform so that only the balls of your feet are actually on the platform. The back half of each foot will be protruding off the lower edge of the sliding platform. Your legs will be perfectly parallel to each other, and your feet will be pointing straight ahead. Your feet should be approximately 6 to 8 inches apart. Once your feet are placed correctly on the machine, press the sliding rack off the stop catches by straightening your legs. Then release the stop catches and bend your legs at the knee very slightly to remove undue stress from the knee joint. In the starting position, the angle that the top of your foot forms with the front of your lower leg should be 45°. This means your calves will not be overly stretched or flexed when you press the sliding weight rack into the starting position and prepare to perform the exercise.

Exercise performance—From this position, slowly sag your heels below the level of your toes, concentrating on feeling a deep stretch in the calves. Then slowly press the sliding rack with the strength of your calf muscles by pushing the balls of your feet against the rack until your toes are pointed as far as possible. Pause and concentrate on contracting the calves as hard as possible; then, after a moment, begin the next rep. After you've completed the prescribed number of reps, return the rack to the starting position, put the stop catches back into place, and slide out of the machine. It's a good idea to divide your sets as evenly as possible between the toes straight, toes pointed in, and toes pointed out positions.

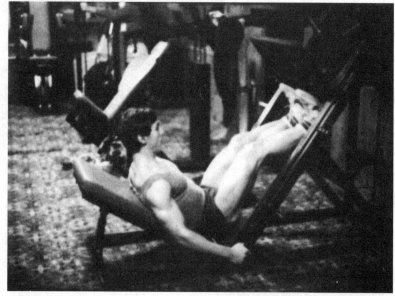
START

FINISH

— 16 —
ABDOMINAL AND INTERCOSTAL EXERCISES

Abdominals—bent-knee situps

This exercise puts direct stress on all the muscles of the frontal abdominal region, especially the upper abdominals,[1] resulting in increased muscle tone and thickness.

Starting position—Lie flat on your back on the floor. Hook your feet under either a sturdy piece of furniture or moderately heavy barbell in order to hold your legs in place and provide overall stability during the course of the exercise. Unlock your knees and slide your body down toward the bar until your legs are bent at the knee at approximately a 30° angle. This will take the pressure off your lower back during the performance of the exercise. Next, place your hands behind your upper neck and interlace your fingers to hold them securely in place during the performance of the exercise.[2] Bend your head forward so your chin rests against your chest.

Exercise performance—From this basic starting position, curl your torso up off the floor by lifting first your shoulders, then your upper back, middle back and lower back,[3] curl your torso upward and forward until your elbows touch your knees. Hold this position for a split second and then slowly uncurl your body and lower your torso to the point where your lower and middle back touch the floor. This is as far as you should lower your torso on each succeeding rep of the exercise. Your upper torso should remain slightly curled and your upper back and shoulders should never touch the floor during the performance of the exercise. Keeping your torso slightly curled like this keeps most of the pressure off the lower back, and keeps the abdominal muscles in a state of continuous tension—a state they seem to thrive on because of their unusually high endurance properties. Immediately begin the next rep. As you become stronger on this exercise, you can hold barbell plates behind your head as a means of increasing the resistance of the exercise.

START

FINISH

Upper abdominal exercises

1. Incline situps

Comments—This exercise strongly stresses all the abdominal muscles although it hits the upper abs much more directly than the lower ones. This exercise is more intense than bent-knee situps, which is why it is not recommended at the beginner levels, and will add significant muscle thickness to your abs. Incline situps are performed on an adjustable incline situp board. The steeper the incline, the greater the stress on the abs and the more difficult the exercise. Therefore, you should begin on the lowest incline level and progressively raise the level as your abs become stronger.

Equipment—Adjustable incline abdominal board, preferably a thickly padded one.

Starting position—Exactly the same as for bent-knee situps, except that your body will be on an incline.

Exercise performance—Exactly the same as for bent-knee situps, except that your body will be on an incline.

START

FINISH

2. Crunches

Comments—Although not quite as effective as bent-knee situps, this short-range exercise strongly stresses the upper abs and provides a good change of pace from situps.

Equipment—Flat exercise bench.

Starting position—Lie on your back, perpendicular to a flat exercise bench so that your calves are draped across the middle of the bench. Clasp your hands behind your head as if you were going to perform bent-knee situps.[4]

Exercise performance—This exercise is kind of tricky, and you must do a number of things simultaneously for it to be maximally effective. First, you must use your lower ab strength to lift your hips slightly off the floor. Secondly, you must use the strength of your upper abs, while simultaneously rounding your back, to force your shoulders to come up off the floor and travel as far forward toward your hips as possible. Finally, as you curl your torso toward your hips, you must breathe out forcefully while simultaneously tensing your abs as hard as you can.[5] If you do all of these things you will feel your abs, especially your upper abs, contract with maximum force.

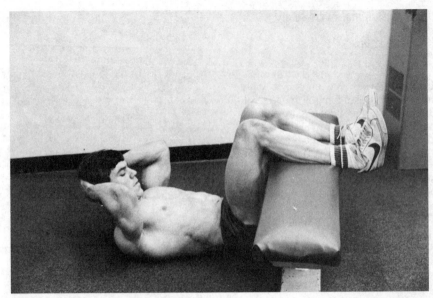

START

FINISH

Lower ab exercises

Introduction—At the beginner level, I presented the one exercise which works the entire abdominal complex most effectively overall, without being overly intense. That, of course, was bent-knee situps. At this time, I will present three different ab exercises which will strongly stress the lower abs. As you progress, many of you will find that you have a great deal of difficulty developing the lower abs to the same level as the upper abs, since the upper abs are stressed a lot more strongly on upper ab exercises than the lower abs are stressed on lower ab exercises. If you find your lower abs lagging behind, past the second intermediate level, it might be a good idea to perform an extra set or two of lower ab work during all of your ab workouts from now on.

1. Leg raises

Comments—This exercise strongly stresses all the ab muscles, especially the lower abdominal region.

Starting position—Lie on your back on a flat abdominal board with your head facing toward the foot strap on the abdominal board. Extend your arms behind your head and grab the ab-board strap in order to keep your body steady during the performance of the exercise.[6] Place your legs close together so that they are parallel to each other and the insides of your feet are touching. Bend your legs at the knee slightly in order to take undue stress off your lower back.[7]

Exercise performance—From this starting position, slowly raise your feet off the floor in a semicircle[8] up and back toward your head until your legs form a 55° angle with your torso. This means they will form a 35° angle with the floor, which constitutes the distance they should be raised. By not raising your legs past this point, you will keep continuous tension on your abs throughout the movement. At the top of the rep, pause for a second, tense your abs, and then slowly lower your legs. As you lower your legs, concentrate on feeling a deep stretch in the lower abs. Stop the descent of your legs when your feet are approximately an inch off the floor and then immediately begin raising them for the next repetition. This will enable you to keep continuous tension on your abs at all times. If you let your feet touch the floor after every rep, your abs will get too much rest. Remember to keep your legs slightly bent during the performance of the entire exercise. As your abs get stronger, you can hold a light dumbbell between your feet.

START

FINISH

2. Incline leg raises

Comments—Performing leg raises on an incline will enable you to concentrate the stress of leg raises on the lower abs much more effectively than is possible when performing them flat. In fact, this is by far the best exercise for thickening and separating the lower ab muscles. Incidentally, don't worry about your abs getting too thick. Abs look much more impressive when they are thick and separated than when the waist is completely flat. It is the obliques, the large muscles on each side of the waist, which look bad if they become thick, not the abs. Thick obliques will make your waist look too wide and destroy your symmetry.

Equipment—Adjustable incline abdominal board, preferably a thickly padded one.

Starting position—Identical to that of leg raises, except that your body will be on an incline.

Exercise performance—Identical to that of leg raises, except that your body will be on an incline.

3. Hanging leg raises

Comments—This exercise, while it does involve the entire ab region, also isolates the lower abs quite well. The advantage of this exercise over other forms of leg raises is that you will be able to raise your legs so that they form less than a 55° angle with your torso and still keep constant tension on your abdominal muscles. This means you will be able to work your abs effectively through a greater range of motion than is possible with the two lower ab exercises just discussed, which translates into more complete development of the abs, especially the lower abs. However incline leg raises are still significantly superior overall. This exercise also has two disadvantages which will be discussed after the exercise performance description.

Equipment—Chinning bar.

Starting position—Stand on a low stool and grasp a chinning bar with an overhand, shoulder-width grip. Your palms will be facing forward. Hang your body straight down below the bar and kick the stool out of the way. Then bend your knees slightly to take pressure off your lower back.[9] Keep your legs parallel to each other and close enough together so the insides of your feet are touching.

Exercise performance—From this basic starting position, slowly raise your feet in a semicircular arc in front of you until they are at the same height as your hips.[10] Your legs will be parallel to the floor at the completion of the rep. Concentrate on using the strength of your lower abs to raise your legs in front of you. At the top of the rep, pause for a split second, contract your abs as hard as possible and then slowly lower your legs back to the starting position, concentrating on feeling a deep stretch in the lower abs. When you lower your feet to the floor, stop just short of the point where your legs are hanging straight down. Then immediately begin the next rep. By keeping your legs and feet pointing slightly in front of you at the bottom of each rep, you will maintain continuous tension on the abs at all times.

There are two disadvantages of performing this exercise. The first is that your body will tend to swing back and forth as a result of raising and lowering your legs. This makes it difficult to effectively isolate your lower abs. However, the situation can be easily corrected by having someone stand behind you and hold your body steady while you perform the exercise. The second disadvantage is that because you will be performing high numbers of repetitions on this exercise, you may find that your grip on the chinning bar may give out before your abs do. This, however, can be corrected by using straps to secure your hands to the chinning bar.

START   FINISH

Intercostals

1. Side bends

Comments—This exercise will develop and tighten both the intercostals and the obliques. You must absolutely never use weight when performing this exercise, otherwise you will thicken up the obliques and make the waist appear thick and wide. This will totally destroy your symmetry. Performing this exercise with a high number of repetitions will give the intercostals and especially the obliques a tight, muscular appearance without the addition of significant muscle mass. Remember, the obliques are the only muscle group on your entire body which you will not want to increase in size. It is an unfortunate fact that numerous gym instructors and so-called bodybuilding authorities regularly advise trainees who want to tighten their waist and reduce its size to perform side-bends with a heavy dumbbell in each hand. Logic dictates that this couldn't possibly work. So, next time someone suggests you use dumbbells when performing side-bends—and sooner or later somebody will—inform him that he obviously doesn't know what he is talking about.

Starting position—Stand perfectly erect, with your feet relatively close together, about 6 inches apart. Interlace your fingers and place the palms of your hands directly on the top of your head. Your arms will be bent and your elbows should be pointing directly out from each side of your body.

Exercise performance—Without moving your legs, bend your torso at the waist directly to the right side. Concentrate on tensing and contracting the intercostals and oblique muscle on your right side while simultaneously stretching the same muscles on the left side of your body. You will tilt approximately 20° to 30° to the right side before you feel full contraction of the muscles on the right side and full stretch of the muscles on the left side. Once you've reached the point, slowly return your torso to the erect position and immediately bend to the left side in the same exact way. After you've bent to both sides and are once again standing erect in the starting position, you have completed one rep.

START

FINISH

Obliques—standing twists

Twists are usually done with a broomstick or bar held across the shoulders. However, I will present here my own form of this exercise which I have found to be superior to all others. Using a pole or bar across the shoulders diffuses the benefit of the exercise through the lats, as well as working the intercostals and obliques. The version presented here is specifically designed to isolate the intercostals and is most effective in doing so. This is an isometric exercise and it thickens and tones these muscles which, incidentally, are located along both sides of the waist. They tie together the serratus and abdominals in terms of appearance and give an impressive, tight look to the waist when developed.

Starting position—Stand erect, preferably facing a mirror. Your arms should be hanging comfortably down at your sides, your knees should be slightly bent and your feet should be slightly turned out. Keeping your upper arms hanging at your sides, bend your elbows and lift your forearms so that they are parallel to the floor. Then angle them in toward your torso. Bend slightly forward at the waist.

Exercise performance—From this basic starting position twist your torso to the right as far as you comfortably can. Your left forearm will come across the front of your torso as illustrated in the picture. As you twist, simultaneously crunch down on the intercostals on your left side and concentrate on tensing them. Then twist all the way to the left side in the same exact way and concentrate on crunching down on and tensing the intercostals on the right side of your torso. Twisting back and forth will indirectly work the oblique muscles, which will tone them up nicely. I must emphasize that it takes a good deal of concentration and a few workouts before most individuals find a groove which best allows them to isolate and stimulate development of the intercostals. So don't become discouraged if you can't feel the intercostals being sufficiently stressed during the first couple of workouts.

— 17 —
MISCELLANEOUS EXERCISES

Rib box

Introduction—The importance of specializing on the rib box was discussed previously. I also mentioned the fact that the rib box is the only area of the physique which responds best to superset training, instead of straight sets, as superset training encourages the development of a prolonged deep breathing effect much more effectively than the performance of straight sets. The rib box is most responsive to efforts to expand it from age 15 (the best age to commence training) to approximately age 21. By this age the rib box loses much of its flexibility and pliability as much of the cartilage connecting your ribs to your sternum turns to bone. The rib box can still be expanded to a substantial degree if you begin rib box training after age 21, but it will require much more of a prolonged and intense training effort to achieve the results you desire. You will not be able to expand it to quite the degree you would have been able to had you started at an earlier age.

As previously mentioned, you will always be performing the same two exercises in the exact same order for your rib box during your whole natural bodybuilding career. Stiff arm pullovers will be performed first, followed immediately by breathing squats. The only variables that will change are the number of supersets you perform at each level of training (ultimately you will perform 2 or 3), and the number of reps of each exercise you perform from workout to workout.

The reason pullovers are performed first is that they stretch the rib box very effectively. By pre-stretching the rib box you are able to utilize more effectively the very heavy breathing caused by breathing squats to induce a permanent expansion of the rib cage. The other reason is that of the two exercises, it takes more concentration to most effectively utilize the breathing pullovers, so it makes sense to do them first. If you do them last, when you are totally out of breath from performing breathing squats, you will find it extremely difficult to concentrate. At the top of each rep of each set you perform for both exercises, you will take two deep breaths before beginning the next rep. As previously discussed, the normal breathing pattern during the rep of any exercise is to breathe in when lowering the weight and breathe out when exerting the force necessary to raise it. During the performance of each of these two exercises, the breathing pattern on each rep will remain exactly the same. However, the two full breaths between each rep will be performed in the following way.

When you return the weight to the starting position after completing each rep of both breathing squats and breathing pullovers, you will have just completed the process of blowing air out. You will therefore pause at the starting position, take as deep a breath of air as you can, concentrating on lifting your rib box as high as possible, and then slowly breathe out. Immediately take another deep breath in the exact same way. After you finish breathing out, immediately begin the next rep, while simultaneously breathing in as you would normally do. Taking these two breaths exactly as just described after each rep of both breathing pullovers and breathing squats will dramatically increase the effectiveness of your rib cage expansion training. You should take three or four minutes rest between supersets so you can catch your breath somewhat.

1. Breathing pullovers

Comments—This version of pullovers is by far the most effective for expanding the rib box. This exercise does put a slight amount of stress on the lats, serratus, and lower edge of the pecs. However, because you will be using significantly less weight on this version of pullovers compared to the bent-arm version, you will not have to worry about stimulating these muscles with anywhere near the degree of intensity which would result in overtraining due to their being trained hard the previous day also. With this version of pullovers, emphasis is placed on completely stretching the rib cage on every rep and not on working the surrounding muscle groups.

Equipment—Flat exercise bench.

Starting position—Exactly the same as for bent-arm pullovers. Except that you will use a light dumbbell instead of a moderately heavy one. You will notice that I have recommended you perform both bent-arm and breathing pullovers with a dumbbell instead of a barbell. A barbell can be used in place of a dumbbell in both cases. However, a barbell is much more clumsy and difficult to control when performing all forms of pullovers than a single dumbbell is. When you extend a barbell back over your head so far, it tends to pull more to one side than the other, which can put undue stress on the shoulder and elbow joints. I therefore strongly suggest that you use a dumbbell instead at all times when performing various form of pullovers.

Exercise performance—Slowly lower the dumbbell in a semicircle downward and backward as far behind your head as possible. As you lower the weight, take as deep a breath as possible while concentrating on lifting the rib cage up and stretching it as much as possible. Once your arms are as far behind your head as possible and your rib cage is fully stretched, slowly return the dumbbell to the starting position without pausing while simultaneously breathing out. At the completion of the rep, pause and take two deep breaths exactly as previously described, then

commence the next rep. By the completion of the last rep you should be somewhat out of breath and breathing rather heavily.

START

FINISH

2. Breathing squats

Comments—As already mentioned, this is the best exercise for inducing the degree of heavy breathing which, combined with breathing pullovers, will result in a permanent and significant expansion of the rib cage.

Equipment—Squat racks.

Starting position—Exactly the same as for full squats, except that you will be using a much lighter barbell.

Exercise performance—The actual mechanics of this exercise are identical to that of full squats. The only difference in exercise performance is in relation to the breathing pattern. With breathing squats, you will take as deep a breath as possible while slowly lowering yourself into the full squatting position. You will simultaneously throw your chest out and lift your rib box up as high as possible. Without pausing, return to the starting position while simultaneously breathing out. At the top of the rep pause and take two deep breaths, exactly as you did on breathing pullovers, and then begin the next rep.

Lower back—lumbar muscles

Introduction—As previously discussed, having strong, flexible and well-developed lumbar muscles goes far toward protecting against lower back injury. The best single lower back exercise for providing all of these benefits is hyperextensions. Through the years, bodybuilders have generally considered heavy deadlifts to be the best exercise for strengthening the lumbar muscles. The reason for this is that the mechanics of deadlifting allow you to train the lumbar muscles with very heavy weights, which results in their becoming very strong.

However, deadlifts have a number of disadvantages. First of all, they compress the lumbar vertebrae of your spinal column.[1] This can potentially result in injury to the discs between the vertebrae. You can either slip a disc or rupture one (otherwise known as herniating a disc). Either one of these conditions is very serious and could spell the end of your natural bodybuilding career. Secondly, deadlifts do not work the lumbar muscles through a complete range of motion. Therefore, although the lumbar muscles will become very strong, when performing deadlifts they can also actually lose flexibility and become somewhat tight. This, of course, results in your lumbar muscles being more susceptible to muscle pulls and tears while performing other exercises or activities which involve the lumbar muscles. Also, just the fact that you are hitting the lumbar muscles with such direct heavy stress when performing deadlifts leaves you vulnerable to injury when performing this exercise.

Finally, deadlifting requires a tremendous amount of energy which could be better spent on other exercises. Deadlifts are as much of an energy drainer as squats. Because of all the disadvantages just outlined, I strongly suggest that you stay away from deadlifts and use hyperextensions instead. In actuality, this is the only lumbar exercise you will ever need to perform during the course of your natural bodybuilding career.

1. Hyperextensions

Comments—This exercise lets you train the lumbar muscles with direct stress and in relative isolation from the rest of your body. It allows you to train these muscles through a complete range of motion without compressing your spinal vertebrae,[2] and also does not require much energy. In other words, it has none of the disadvantages associated with deadlifts. Although you will not be able to build the kind of superpower into your lumbar muscles with this exercise that you can with deadlifts, you will be able to develop, strengthen, and increase the flexibility of these muscles to a degree which will be more than sufficient for enabling the lumbars to effectively handle the stress placed upon them by other exercises at the intermediate and advanced levels of natural training.

Equipment—Hyperextension bench.

Starting position—A hyperextension bench has two padded bars. One is much wider than the other and is padded on top. The other is much narrower and is padded on the lower surface. Stand between the two pads with your back toward the bar which is padded on the lower surface. This means you will be facing the larger of the two pads. Lean forward on this larger pad so the front end of your hips at about the belt line are at the front end of the padded surface. As you lean forward, the backs of your ankles should come up and rest against the bottom of the rear pad.[3] Some benches have two sets of pads for the feet close together so you can place your feet between them. This feature provides added stability during the performance of the exercise. Once your feet are in place, bend at the waist until your torso is hanging straight down and is perpendicular to the floor. Then place your hands behind your neck, interlace your fingers and hold them in this position.[4] As your lumbar muscles become stronger you can place weight on the floor in front of the bench, reach down and pick it up when your torso is hanging perpendicular to the floor and hold it behind your head during the performance of the exercise.

START

FINISH

Exercise performance—From this position slowly raise your torso in an arc, using only the strength of your lumbar muscles, until your torso reaches a position perfectly parallel to the floor. Pause for a second, concentrate on fully contracting the lumbar muscles and then slowly return to the starting position. At the top of the movement do not arch your back under any circumstances. Doing this will compress your vertebrae, especially the lumbar vertebrae and could result in serious injury.

Serratus exercise

1. Bent-arm pullover

Comments—This is the best exercise for developing and thickening the serratus muscles on each side of the torso where the lats insert with the rib box. This is also an excellent exercise for stretching out and warming up the lats for more direct work.

Equipment—Flat exercise bench, preferably well padded.

Starting position—Grasp a moderately heavy dumbbell with two hands so that your palms are against the inside plate of one side of the dumbbell and the dumbbell handle hangs directly downward.[5] The tips of your fingers should be wrapped around the outside of this plate to hold the dumbbell securely in place during the performance of the exercise. Swing the dumbbell up to your chest while kneeling down and leaning back against a flat exercise bench. Your body should be perpendicular to it. Next, lie across the bench so that only your shoulders and upper back are in contact with it, and extend your arms directly upward so that the dumbbell is held directly over the middle of your chest. Bend your arms at about a 30° angle. Keep your feet close together and bend your knees enough that your hips drop well below the level of your chest.[6] Keep your hips low and your arms bent at the exact same angle during the performance of the exercise. Concentrate on lifting your rib box as high as possible at all times, as this will help you to get a fuller stretch in the serratus and lats on every rep (see breathing pullovers-rib box exercises).

Exercise performance—From this basic starting position, slowly lower the dumbbell backward and downward in a semicircle as far behind your head as possible, concentrating on feeling a deep stretch in the lats and serratus. Then slowly return the dumbbell to the starting position along the exact same arc.

Neck exercises

Front neck raise

Comments—This is an excellent exercise for developing and strengthening all the muscles along the front of the neck.

Starting position—Lay on your back along the entire length of a flat exercise bench so that your head and neck hang completely off the one end. Your neck should be flexed so that your chin is resting on your upper chest. Your feet will be placed on the floor for support (in the exact position for performing a bench press).

Exercise performance—From this starting position, slowly lower your head in an arc until the muscles along the front of the neck are fully stretched, but not so far that the top of your head is hanging straight down to the floor, and/or you feel undue stress along the back of your neck or spine. Without pausing, slowly return your head to the starting position. Concentrate on contracting all the muscles along the front of the neck. As your neck muscles get stronger, you can add resistance by either holding a weight disc against your forehead or wearing a neck strap with weight attached to it.

Back neck raise

Comments—This is an excellent exercise for strengthening and developing the muscles along the back of the neck, as well as the upper traps.

Starting position—Lie on your stomach along the entire length of a flat exercise bench, so that your head and neck are completely off one end of the bench. Let your legs hang loosely along each side of the bench so that your knees are comfortably bent and your toes are resting on the floor. This will remove any undue stress from your lower back. Your head will be hanging off the bench so that your neck is bent at approximately a 35° angle and your chin is almost touching your chest.

Exercise performance—From the basic starting position, slowly raise your head in an arc until you feel the muscles along the back of the neck contract, but not so far that you feel any undue stress in this area. Then, without pausing, slowly return your head to the starting position, concentrating on stretching the muscles along the back of the neck. As your neck muscles get stronger, you can add resistance by either holding a weight disc against the back of your head or by wearing a neck strap with weight attached to it.

18

WOMEN'S NATURAL BODYBUILDING

Introduction

As we have progressed into the 1980s, women have become increasingly interested in developing a shapely, muscularly toned athletic figure instead of just becoming thin. As is the case with men, engaging in a natural bodybuilding training regimen is undisputedly the best way for a woman to develop an athletic type of physique. Whatever her ideal physique happens to be, any woman can effectively mold her body to the exact specifications she desires within the limits imposed by her genetic structure by the use of progressive resistance training. Women are beginning to realize this, as demonstrated by the fact that the number of women who have joined health clubs, spas, and gyms in the last few years has practically reached epidemic proportions. In fact, in many coed facilities, women members actually outnumber men.

The feminine ideal and natural bodybuilding

Every one has their own definition of what the ideal female physique is. Men generally prefer women to have a voluptuous, well-shaped figure which doesn't have an excess of body fat. The physique which women generally consider the ideal is one which is shapely, but slender. Neither gender, except for a few indviduals, considers a female physique which is extremely muscular, either in terms of muscle mass, definition, or both, to be an ideal physique to strive for.

The feminine ideal, according to the natural bodybuilding philosophy of this book, is that the female physique should be lithe and athletic in appearance. The entire physique should have a supple and definitely toned appearance as a direct result of progressive resistance training. Just enough muscle mass should be built to accentuate the natural curves of the female physique, to ensure the development of as proportionate and symmetrical a female physique as possible, and to shape each muscle group for as feminine and shapely an overall appearance as possible. The natural bodybuilding philosophy

does not encourage the development of an overly massive or muscularly developed physique. But it does encourage you to keep your body fat level between the range of 15 and 20 percent, which is slightly below the average of most women. Within this body fat range, you will not appear muscular, but you will appear optimally toned and well shaped. You will find that having this level of body fat will actually give you a supple, shapely and feminine appearance. If your body fat levels were to drop below 15 percent you would not only appear muscular, you would tend to lose a certain degree of your shape. On the other hand, if you exceed the 20 percent body fat level, you will begin to lose your toned appearance, and your shape may also be negatively affected. If you reach the 25 percent body fat level, you will find that you have a significant amount of extra body fat which will detrimentally affect your physical appearance. You can get a general idea of your body fat level by having a skinfold test done periodically. But while 15 to 20 percent is generally the optimal range at which to keep your body fat level, there are no specific rules. Therefore, let the mirror be your most important judge. If you look too fat in the mirror, chances are that you *are* too fat. The same is true if you look too lean. Diets to gain and lose fat while simultaneously gaining muscles, as well as more on body fat levels, will be discussed in the section on nutrition.

The fear of becoming too muscular

The vast majority of women who contemplate beginning a weight training program or are actively engaged in one are deathly afraid of becoming massively muscular and looking like a man. While a small percentage of women do seem to gain muscle mass relatively easily, the general rule is that it is extremely difficult for women to gain a significant amount of muscle mass, and literally impossible for them to attain anywhere near the level of muscular development that men can attain. The major reason for this is that woman only have approximately $\frac{1}{100\text{th}}$ the level of testosterone that men have. As already discussed, testosterone is the hormone which enables men to develop tremendous amounts of muscle mass in relation to women. Without high levels of this hormone, it is impossible to build a large amount of muscle mass, and women simply don't

have the necessary level. A few women have unusually high levels of testosterone naturally in comparison to other women, which results in their being able to gain muscle tissue in larger amounts and more quickly than most women. But compared to men, the level is still insignificant, and even the rate of growth of the fastest gaining women pale in comparison to the rate at which men gain muscle.

Besides having much lower testosterone levels than men, women also have significantly less muscle tissue to work with in proportion to their size than men do. Women simply do not have the number and density of muscle fibers that men have, so even if they had the same level of testosterone as men, they still wouldn't be able to develop as much muscle mass. This is especially true in terms of upper body development. Most of a woman's strength and muscle mass is located in the lower half of the body. Women's legs are particularly strong. In fact, studies have shown that in proportion to their size, women's legs are almost as strong as their male counterparts. Women also find it relatively easy to add shapely muscle mass to their legs. But the upper body is another story altogether. Women, as a rule, have little upper body strength and the potential for developing upper body muscle mass is also severely limited. In fact, your biggest challenge in trying to develop a shapely toned physique will not be preventing yourself from becoming too massive, but will actually be developing enough upper body muscle mass so that your upper and lower body are proportionately developed.

The general public is still under the false impression that anybody who picks up a barbell or does any kind of weight training whatsoever will automatically become massively muscular. I only wish it were so easy. In actuality, building muscle is a slow process for men, as I've discussed. For women, the process of building muscle tissue is even slower because of the two genetic disadvantages I cited.

Ultimately, you will have to decide how much muscle you wish to develop, and you will always have to adjust your training according to both how much muscle you ultimately wish to gain and how quickly you gain it. For example, if you happen to be one of the small percentage of women who gain muscle unusually quickly, but you only want to tone up and improve your overall shape somewhat, you may have to reduce both the number of sets you are performing and the intensity level of your workouts so that you do not gain a significant amount of muscle tissue. On the other hand, if you've always considered yourself to be too thin and you want to add a significant amount of shapely muscle to your frame, but find it difficult to gain that muscle, you should train heavier and more intensely for as long as it takes to gain the muscle tissue you desire.

A few of you may want to develop as much muscle mass and definition as possible and may ultimately want to compete in female bodybuilding contests. If that is the case, following practically the exact same training programs outlined for the men will enable you to develop yourself to your ultimate muscular potential. Of course, I am well aware that very few—if any of you—have this in mind.

Women and steroids

Since so few women wish to develop a massively muscular physique, the use of anabolic agents, especially steroids, is not nearly as widespread in the women's bodybuilding community as it is among the men. Even competitive women bodybuilders generally prefer not to become overly muscular and to remain as feminine as possible. However, many of the top women bodybuilders do take steroids, even though they claim otherwise.

Any woman who takes anabolic steroids is absolutely insane. They can actually destroy a woman's femininity. Remember, testosterone is essentially a male hormone which is responsible for the development of male secondary sex characteristics. Women normally have such a low level of testosterone that it has no adverse effect on their sexual development. However, when women take anabolic therapy the following side effects can occur: hirsutism (hairiness), male pattern baldness, deepening of the voice and clitoral enlargement as well as generalized masculinization. These changes, once they have occurred, are usually irreversible even after prompt discontinuation of steroid therapy. Menstrual irregularities are also common, and if the woman happens to be pregnant when she takes steroids, masculinization of the fetus can occur.[1] Besides this, women are subject to all the side effects that men are, including: liver damage, cancer, and heart disease, except for those which specifically involve the male sex organs. Why a woman would

risk destroying her femininity and risk her life to develop muscle for a female bodybuilding contest is beyond me. Even more so than in the case of the men, the potential benefit for women does not seem to be worth the risk. Fortunately, very few women wish to develop a muscular physique, and even fewer are willing to take the numerous risks associated with indulgence in anabolic therapy.

Practical benefits of natural bodybuilding training

Besides dramatically improving your appearance, natural bodybuilding training will have a couple of important practical applications to your daily lives. Because women do not have much upper body strength naturally, and because they have never been encouraged to engage in strenuous physical activity, women often find it difficult, if not impossible, to cope with situations in daily life which require some physical strength. These situations can range from carrying groceries to changing a tire. You never know when a little extra strength will come in handy. As women get older it becomes increasingly difficult for them to cope effectively with situations which require even a minimum amount of physical strength. Natural bodybuilding training will enable you to develop enough additional strength so you will find it much easier to handle situations which require more than the usual amount of physical strength. As is the case with men, natural bodybuilding training will also decrease your risk of getting injured, either as a result of physical strain or the progressive degeneration associated with the aging process.

Specific areas of concern of the female physique

While women who engage in natural bodybuilding training should strive to develop as proportionate and symmetrical a physique as possible, it is a fact that women, in general, are more concerned with the appearance of certain areas of their body than others. These areas include the bust, the waist, the glutes, and the thighs. Men are generally more concerned with developing a massive chest, big arms, and a wide back.

The first area is the bust. When dis-

cussing this area, the first thing that must be stated is that no amount of weight training will result in an increase in the size of the breasts themselves. Many women are under the false impression that training will have this effect. Unfortunately, the only way a woman can actually increase the size of her breasts is to have a breast implant or to gain excess fat. If you gain fat, chances are that some of it will deposit in the breasts, resulting in an increase in size. However, the deleterious effects which gaining excess fat will have on your physique as a whole will negate any positive effects which might occur in terms of registering an increase in breast size.

While progressive resistance training will not actually increase the size of the breasts, it will enable you to improve their overall shape and appearance by developing the pectoral muscles underneath them. As you develop these muscles, your bustline will tend to become higher and fuller, and your breasts will take on a more shapely appearance. Expanding your rib box in conjunction with developing your pecs will also contribute significantly to creating this appearance. Because you require a significant amount of muscle mass under the breasts to create this effect, the pectorals are one muscle group you should definitely concentrate on adding mass to. And you should also make sure to concentrate on expanding your rib box. You should use the same exact routine in terms of exercises and sets as recommended at the various beginner and intermediate levels presented earlier in this book. Changes in the rep scheme will be discussed later.

As far as the waist and all the other muscle groups of the upper body are concerned, you should perform the same exact routines at each level as outlined previously, except for the number of reps. With waist training, you will be performing a much higher number of reps on each set than the men performed. This will enable you to tone, flatten, and strengthen your waist without overdeveloping any of these muscles, especially the abs. This is important, for while deep, separated, and clearly defined abs definitely enhance the appearance of a man's waist, they do not enhance the femininity of a woman's—at least not in the eyes of most people. Incidentally, it is not uncommon for a woman's waist, even a well-toned woman's waist, to appear somewhat bloated during the time of her period each month because of the retention of fluid which tends to occur at this time. Keep in mind that this is only temporary and there really isn't anything you can do about it except to let nature take its course.

A prime concern of most women in relation to their physique is to have tight, shapely glutes. The glutes are strongly involved in all squatting movements, and many individuals believe that squatting will build a big butt. However, if you perform squats exactly as described previously and concentrate on directing the majority of stress to the quads where it belongs, you shouldn't have to worry about this happening, and you should, in fact, find that the squats work the glutes just enough to tighten and tone them. However, since squats do not work the glutes directly, I will add an exercise to the women's routine which will stress the glutes directly and with just enough intensity to tighten, tone, and shape them, but not so much that an excess amount of muscle will be added to them.

Finally we come to the legs in general and the thighs in particular. By adding a certain degree of muscle mass to your legs in the right places you will be able to enhance their shape dramatically. Most women are afraid that their legs, especially their thighs, will become too big. What they fail to consider is that by adding shapely muscle mass to their legs and improving their overall leg shape, the result will be that their legs will actually appear thinner. Women are noted for lacking muscle tone on the inner part of their thighs. Because of this I will describe an exercise later on which will directly stress this area of the thigh. Developing the sweep along the outer thigh which is worked most directly with back and front squats, and developing the hamstrings so that they sweep out somewhat from the back of the thigh will especially enhance the shape of your thighs. As far as the calves are concerned, you should definitely add enough mass to them to keep them in proportion with your thighs. Having beautifully shaped thighs and skinny calves doesn't give the legs an optimally proportioned and shapely appearance. This is as true for women as it is for men.

Body fat distribution

When discussing toning and shaping a woman's physique you can't help but take into consideration natural body fat distribution. Men tend to either have body fat distributed relatively evenly on the body or have it concentrated around their waist. However, women tend to hold most of their fat around their hips, glutes, and thighs. According to the way you are built, you may find it extremely difficult to lose fat from certain areas of your body. For example, I've seen women with extremely thin upper bodies, who had a large accumulation of fat in the thighs, hips, and glutes. Many of these women find it extremely difficult, if not impossible, to lose fat from these areas, no matter how much they exercise or diet. A major reason for this is that women, in general, have a much higher percentage of body fat than men. The essential body fat level of men is approximately 2 to 3 percent and for women it's about 10 percent. As a result, a woman's body tends to be much more resistant to losing body fat than a man's.

In cases in which a woman has a high concentration of body fat in a certain area as a result of her overall genetic structure, the body perceives that fat as being essential and, therefore, strongly resists every effort to eliminate that fat. What makes things worse is that since the metabolism of women is significantly slower than that of men, it is even more difficult to burn off this fat. If you happen to be one of those women who have large accumulations of body fat in certain areas and you've tried everything from aerobic exercise to following a healthy, scientific diet, without success, it may just be that you will always hold a certain amount of extra fat in these areas. Even if this is the case, natural bodybuilding training will enable you to optimally shape and tone your physique within the limitations caused by these fat deposits.

Unfortunately, no matter what anybody tells you, there is no such thing as spot reducing. If you train a certain area, you will not just burn fat from that area. While fat may not be evenly distributed on your body in the first place, it is a fact that whatever fat you lose comes off evenly from the entire body. As a result, you will not burn fat from those areas in which you tend to store fat any more quickly than from the rest of the body. The fat-storing areas will always tend to hold a greater proportion of fat in relation to the rest of the body, even after a prolonged diet. The only time these fat deposits will be completely burned up is when all other non-essential fat has been stripped from the body. Even then, as already discussed, according to the way you're built, you may not be able to eliminate all those fat deposits.

Of course, you're not to use what I just said as a cop-out. Only a small percentage of women have fat deposits which are virtually impossible to remove, and even if you happen to be one of them, you can make remarkable improvements in your physique with a combination of progressive resistance training, cardiovascular fitness training, and a sound, nutritionally balanced diet. And don't rule out the power of the mind.

The vast majority of you, while you may tend to hold slightly more fat in certain areas than others, still have the potential to develop a shapely, toned, well-proportioned, and attractive physique. But you're going to have to work to achieve your goal. In order to mold your physique as closely to your personal ideal as possible within the limits of your genetic potential, you will, overall, have to work just as hard as the men. While you will not be nearly as concerned with adding large amounts of muscle mass as the men, chances are you will have to work very hard to add the small amounts of muscle mass you will require to fill out and optimally shape your physique, because of the great difficulty women tend to have in adding this mass. You will also have to be sure to put the muscle mass on in just the right places to enhance your shape. Then, of course, there's the challenge of balancing your upper body development with your leg development, which requires a lot of hard work for most women to accomplish. In order to successfully accomplish each one of these feats and develop your ideal female physique you will have to master all the training techniques, learn how to harness the power of your mind, master the process of rest and recuperation, and master the nutrition principles outclined in this book exactly as the men had to do to achieve their goals.

Women's training routines

As I've already mentioned, the women's training routines will be almost identical to the men's. Both sexes will perform the same exercises for each muscle although the women will also perform the two exercises I will describe at the end of this section. The women will also perform the same number of sets for each muscle group at each level of training that the men will perform. However, there are a few differences in the way women should train in comparison to the men.

First of all, whether women are attempting to add muscle mass to some or all areas of the body or just trying to tone up, they should perform a somewhat higher number of reps on each set than men perform. According to one study, women actually gained strength faster and stimulated the muscles more effectively when using 10 to 12 reps than when using fewer reps. Besides this, women generally don't have the strength in their tendons, ligaments, or the muscles themselves to safely control and effectively utilize weights which only allow them to get 6 or 7 reps. They can't effectively direct the benefit of the exercise to the muscle they are trying to work when performing such low reps, and they also risk injury.

Keeping this in mind, at those times when a woman is attempting to gain additional muscle mass on a particular muscle group or groups, she should perform the exact same routine for those muscle groups as the men, except that she should adjust her weights so that she can get two more reps on every set than the number prescribed for the men. For example, if a woman is training at the advanced intermediate level and is performing bench presses to add mass to her pecs, on the first training day of the week, a heavy day, her rep plan on four sets would be 12, 10, 9, 8 instead of 10, 8, 7, 6. Every rep schedule for every exercise would be adjusted two reps upward. Also, on exercises

such as T-bar rows, bent-over rows, squats, etc., which put a lot of stress on the lower back, women should never perform less than 10 reps. Performing 10 reps on these exercises will still enable you to develop significant muscle mass while simultaneously minimizing the risk of putting undue stress on your lower back and sustaining an injury.

Women also do not have to perform as much trapezius work as men, and no neck work is necessary. What follows is an example of a good beginner and intermediate level woman's toning-up workout. These workouts are designed to enable you to tone and shape your body without adding significant muscle mass. The recommended starting poundage for women is given for each of the exercises of the beginner routine in terms of percentage of body weight. By the intermediate level you will be able to calculate starting poundages for the new exercises. As is the case with the men, you will commence your training by performing one set per muscle group and gradually increase the sets from one level to the next exactly as the men did. There is no point in presenting all the beginner routines and intermediate level routines because the only significant difference between them is the number of sets you perform for each muscle. Therefore I will present only one routine from the

beginner level and one from the intermediate level. By following the men's routines already listed you will know exactly when and where to add a set to the number you are performing for each muscle group as you advance from one level to the next. You will note that, as with the men, two rep schemas are presented for each workout. At the beginner level you will alternate between the two rep plans. At the intermediate level the lower rep schema, which constitutes a heavier workout, should be performed during the first workout for each muscle group each week, as is the case with the men.

With ab training, women should perform whatever number of reps feels comfortably difficult to them without using any additional weight. Fifty is really just a guideline number.

You'll notice that even women's natural bodybuilding designed specifically to tone and shape the physique consists almost exclusively of the basic exercises which are normally considered to provide the best gains in terms of muscular mass. The reason for this is that these exercises, because they involve the use of so many muscle groups working together, also happen to be the best for tying the muscle groups together and giving the entire physique a smooth-flowing, shapely appearance as well as giving the individual muscles a

Example   Women's beginner level tone-up routine to be performed once every three days

Muscle Group	Exercise	Sets	Reps H	Reps L	Percentage Poundage Body Weight
Pecs	Bench press	3	20, 17, 13	20, 17, 15	10%
Delts	Military press	3	20, 17, 13	20, 17, 15	10%
Lats	Long-range cable row	3	20, 17, 14	20, 18, 16	15%
Traps	Shoulder shrugs	2	20, 15	20, 18	15%
Biceps	E-Z bar curls	2	20, 17, 13	20, 17, 15	5–10%
Forearms	Wrist curls	2	20, 18, 15	20, 19, 18	5–10%
Triceps	E-Z curl tricep ex.	2	20, 17, 13	20, 17, 15	5–10%
Quads	Parallel squats	3	20, 17, 14	20, 18, 16	20%
Hams	Leg curls	2	20, 15	20, 17	5–10%
Calves	Standing calf raise	3	23, 20, 17	25, 22, 20	15–20%
Abs	Bent-knee situps	2	50, if possible	50, if possible	No weight
Intercostals	Twists	2	50	50	No weight

more shapely and completely developed look. Basic exercises should always form the basis of your routine, even if toning and shaping up are your primary goals. Besides this, performing basic exercises will, as already discussed, greatly improve your coordination since the various muscles are taught to work together as a unit. This benefit, of course, has many practical applications to all aspects of your life.

Example   Women's advanced intermediate tone-up routine   Day 1—to be performed Monday & Thursday

Muscle Group	Exercise	Sets	H Reps L	
Pecs	D.B. bench press	4 3	20, 17, 15, 13	20, 18, 17, 16
		or		
	Incline flies	3 4	20, 17, 14	20, 18, 16
Delts	Press behind neck	4 3	20, 17, 15, 13	20, 18, 17, 15
		or		
	Side laterals	3 4	20, 17, 14	20, 18, 15
Serratus	Bent-arm pullovers	2	20, 15	20, 18
Lats	Wide-grip pulldown to front of neck	3 4	20, 17, 14	20, 18, 16
		or		
	Long-range cable rows	4 3	20, 18, 16, 14	20, 18, 17, 16
Traps	Shoulder shrugs	4	20, 18, 16, 14	20, 18, 17, 16
Abs	Bent-knee situps	3	100	100
	Leg raises	3	100	100
Intercostals	Twists	3	100	100

Example   Women's advanced intermediate tone-up routine   Day 2—to be performed on Tuesday and Friday

Muscle Group	Exercise	Sets	H Reps L	
Biceps	Standing curls; E-Z curl bar	3	20, 17, 13	20, 17, 15
	Preacher curls	2	20, 15	20, 17
Forearms	Reverse wrist curls	2	20, 15	20,17
	Wrist curls	2	20, 15	20,17
Triceps	Standing tricep extension; E-Z curl bar	3	20, 17, 13	20, 17, 15
	Tricep pressdowns	2	20, 15	20,17
Quads	Full squats	5	20, 18, 16, 14, 13	20, 19, 18, 17, 16
	Adductor exercise	2	20, 15	20, 17
Rib box	Breathing pullover Breathing squats	2		
Hamstrings	Leg curls	4	20, 18, 16, 14	20, 18, 17, 16
	Stiff-legged deadlift	2	20, 15	20, 18
Glutes	One-leg kickback	3	20, 17, 15	20, 18, 16
Calves	Standing calf raise	5	23, 21, 19 17, 15	25, 24, 22, 21, 20
	Seated calf raise	2	20, 15	20, 18
Lower back	Hyperextensions	3	20, 17, 15	20, 18, 16

Specialization exercises for women

Muscle group—adductors
1. Adductor Machine Exercise

Comments—This exercise stresses the muscles of the inner thigh (known as the adductors), directly and in relative isolation from the rest of the quads. This exercise will tone and shape the adductors, giving the thighs a more shapely and completely developed appearance. This exercise is to be performed on a specialized adductor machine of which Nautilus and Polaris make excellent versions.

Equipment—Specialized adductor machine. Adductor machines have two movable padded extensions. The left extension supports your left leg and the right, your right leg. There is also a comfortable seat to support your upper body.

Starting position—The leg support extensions of the machine will be spread apart approximately 90 degrees in the starting position. This means, of course, that your legs will be spread apart 90 degrees. Each of the leg support extensions will have a number of support pads spaced along the inner part of each leg. The purpose of these pads is to hold your legs in place when you use the strength of your inner thigh muscles to perform the exercise. The starting position of this exercise constitutes your sitting comfortably in the chair of the machine and placing your legs on the leg support extensions so that your inner thighs are braced against the pads. The machines are designed so that your legs are bent at the knee at between a 25° and 45° angle, according to the particular make of the machine. This gives your inner thighs maximum leverage without putting undue stress on your knees. You should hold on to two handles at each side of the seat or hold on to the edge of the seat itself to stabilize your upper body during the performance of the exercise.

Exercise performance—Using just the strength of your adductor muscles, bring the leg support extensions as close together as possible. At the completion of the movement your legs will be almost perfectly parallel to each other. Once you've brought your legs together, pause for a moment. Concentrate on contracting your inner thigh muscles, then slowly return your legs to the starting position, concentrating on feeling as full a stretch as possible along your inner thighs.

Additional comments—This exercise should not only be performed as outlined in the women's shaping-up routine. It should also be performed from time to time when or if you are engaged in the mass-building routines. It must also be pointed out that while the adductor machine exercise just outlined is by far the best exercise for developing shapely muscle mass along the inner thigh, most gyms do not have them. Therefore, for those of you who do not have access to this piece of equipment, I am presenting an alternate adductor exercise.

FINISH

START

2. Duck leg presses, 45° angle

Comments—This exercise strongly stresses the quadriceps, especially the adductors. When lighter weights are used, this exercise will tone, tighten, and improve the shape of the inner thighs. When heavier weights are used, this is an excellent exercise for adding solid muscle mass to the inner thighs. Therefore, while this exercise is specifically recommended for women, male bodybuilders may find it useful for increasing the mass of their thighs and giving them a more completely developed and shapely appearance.

Equipment—Squat rack.

Starting position—Exactly the same as for 45° angle leg presses, except that your toes will be pointed out to each side at between a 55° and 75° angle. The farther your toes are pointed out to each side, the greater the stress you will be able to place on your adductor muscles during the performance of the exercise. Since your toes will be pointed out so far to each side, your heels will naturally be forced much closer together than they are when performing regular leg presses. In fact, they should only be between 3 and 5 inches apart.

Exercise performance—Exactly the same as for 45° angled leg presses, except for the position of your feet. As you lower the weight rack, your legs will spread wide apart because of the position of your feet. As you lower the weight, concentrate on feeling a full stretch along the inner thighs. Without pausing at the bottom position, press the weight back to the starting position, concentrating on contracting the adductor muscles. Then pause for a second and begin the next rep.

START

FINISH

Muscle group—glutes

1. Alternate one-leg kickback

Comments—This exercise directly stresses the glutes, especially the lower portion of the glutes and the glute-hamstring tie-in. Because this is an isolation exercise, it will not build a large amount of muscle mass onto the glutes, but it will definitely tone and tighten them up, and add just enough mass to optimally enhance their shape. Also, the development of the glute-hamstring tie-in will enhance the development of both muscle groups, giving them a more shapely and completely developed appearance, both individually and in combination.

Equipment—Flat exercise bench and ankle weights.

Starting position—Kneel down lengthwise on a flat exercise bench. Your arms will be parallel to each other and extended directly below your chest so that your hands grasp the side edges of the exercise bench firmly. The palms of each hand will be resting comfortably on the padded surface of the bench. Your arms will be almost perfectly straight except that they will be slightly bent at the elbow. Your knees and the frontal surface of your lower legs and feet will also be resting on the padded surface of the bench, so that your legs are parallel to each other and only a couple of inches apart. Your upper thighs will form a 90° angle with your torso, and your lower legs will form a 90° angle with your thighs. Your torso will be parallel to the bench. Your feet should be in an extended position so that your toes are pointing directly behind you.

Exercise performance—From this basic starting position lift your right leg up so that it is about 1 inch above the padded surface of the bench. It will still be bent at a 90° angle. Next, bring the entire leg slightly forward while simultaneously bending your leg at the knee completely. Your leg will be in a fully flexed position at this point. Now, gradually extend your leg directly out behind you until it is fully extended and your foot is a few inches above the level of your glutes. Your knee will be bent at approximately a 15° angle when the leg is fully extended. Your back will also be slightly arched. As your leg is extended behind you, you will feel an increasing amount of direct stress on your right glute. When complete leg extension is reached, pause for a second and concentrate on fully contracting the right glute. Then slowly return your leg to the position where the knee is fully flexed, concentrating on getting a full stretch in the right glute. Immediately begin the next rep. Once you have completed the prescribed number of reps for the right leg, place it back on the exercise bench in the starting position, and do the same thing for the same number of reps for the left leg.

As you get stronger, you can increase the resistance placed on your glutes by using ankle weights.

This exercise should be included in all of your training routines from the beginning-intermediate level on up, since the glutes are not hit directly by any other exercise.

START

FINISH

19

ESSENTIALS TO THE NATURAL BODYBUILDING LIFE STYLE

Cardiovascular fitness

One of the most important aspects of the natural bodybuilding life style is cardiovascular fitness. Cardiovascular training promotes optimum health by keeping the heart healthy and strong. No matter what level of natural bodybuilding an individual maintains, without cardiovascular training, one will not be fit.

Cardiovascular training raises a person's endurance and stamina. You will be able to train longer, more effectively and thereby more efficiently and more productively. It does this by providing a smooth flow of blood, and oxygen to all parts of the body.

Optimum cardiovascular activities are running, jogging, cycling, walking, hiking, swimming, skating, rowing, cross-country skiing, and skipping rope.

In order to derive the maximum benefits from your natural bodybuilding workouts, you should do as little cardiovascular fitness work as possible. This is important, because too much will increase your susceptibility to overtraining.

The following cardiovascular fitness program follows the guidelines of the American College of Sports Medicine.

Frequency

Three training sessions per week performed on non-consecutive days is optimum for natural bodybuilders. The reason for this is that the amount of improvement in maximum oxygen intake tends to plateau when the frequency of cardiovascular training is increased above three days per week.[1]

Duration and intensity

You should perform cardiovascular training for between 20 and 30 minutes at a moderate level. A moderate level means keeping your heart level between 70 percent and 85 percent of your maximal attainable heart rate.[2] Your maximal attainable heart rate is approximately 220 minus your age.[3] To find your exact maximal heart rate, have your doctor give you an exercise stress test.

As with the natural bodybuilding training schedules, you should build toward the 70 percent and 85 percent levels, beginning at 60 percent.

In order to make sure you are training at the right levels, it is a good idea to carry a watch. All you have to do is count your pulse for 15 seconds and multiply the number you get by 4. This number will be your pulse rate per minute. If you are lower than the target number, step it up. If it is higher, slow down.

In conclusion, before performing your 20 to 30 minutes of exercises at the target rate, you should warm up for 5 to 10 minutes so that your cardiovascular system and your body as a whole is not stressed too suddenly. Generally, it will take three to six months before you reach your level of optimal cardiovascular fitness. As for your choice of exercise you should engage in an aerobic activity which will stress your muscles as little as possible. The best choices are either stationary biking or cross-country cycling. My preference is stationary biking. With a stationary bike, you can ride anytime you desire without harm to your joints or muscles and do it during any kind of weather.

When performing a bodybuilding workout and a cardiovascular fitness workout on the same training day, it's always best to do the bodybuilding workout first. This is due to the fact that bodybuilding workouts require a tremendous amount of energy and concentration, and it's extremely difficult to get the most out of these workouts after doing cardiovascular fitness work. It's much easier to run or cycle when tired from a weight workout than the other way round.

Rest, sleep and recuperation

Sleep is without a doubt the keystone to the restructuring process associated with natural bodybuilding. A natural bodybuilder requires one to two hours of sleep more per night for optimum recuperation than required when not training. This extra sleep is required to rebuild the body's energy reserves, and to supply extra time for repairing and building muscle tissue. It is essential to get this extra sleep and also, to get your sleep in a consistent pattern. Any other way will markedly decrease your training efficency.

Rest is not as nearly as important as sleep, but it helps. It is a good idea to sit back and relax a few times a day for a few minutes each time. Rest and naps give both your mind and body a chance to relax and regain a significant amount of energy. These few moments give you a chance to get away from the mental stress which may pressure you every day.

Stress and negative emotions, such as anger and depression, deplete your energy supplies. It is essential to work out these mental energy deletors, or they will negatively affect your training.

Mental approach

Your mental approach toward your natural bodybuilding training will ultimately be the most important factor in determining how muscularly developed you become. You can have all the genetic potential, intelligence and training knowledge to be a champion, but if you are not totally committed to your training, or even worse, are not motivated—you will not make any progress. Besides being motivated, you will need to learn to visualize what you want to look like, to develop the ability to concentrate on your training, to effectively handle the pain you will experience, to enjoy your training, and to develop a positive attitude toward your training.

20
NATURAL BODYBUILDING NUTRITION

Introduction

Next to proper training, proper nutrition is probably the most important factor in attaining natural bodybuilding success. You must supply your body with the proper balance of nutrients in order to build solid muscle mass. You must also be able to properly balance your overall caloric intake so that you can either maintain or restore the optimum body fat levels which will give you a toned, shapely appearance. Then, of course, optimal nutrition is essential for the normal processes of growth and repair to be carried out, for the health of the organism to be maintained at optimum levels, and for providing the energy necessary for performing intense bodybuilding workouts and recuperating effectively from them. The human organism can survive on almost any type of diet, even one which is severely deficient in nutrients. However, if you plan on deriving maximum benefit from your natural bodybuilding training, you must approach nutrition as scientifically as you approach your training. The old saying "You are what you eat" has a lot of truth to it. Keep in mind that since your body does not consider muscle mass to be essential for survival, you will only be able to build muscle if you provide the proper nutrients your body needs to carry out the muscle building process over and above what is necessary for essential life-sustaining processes.

Something should be pointed out here. Many bodybuilders and supposed bodybuilding experts claim that proper nutrition is responsible for anywhere between 50 and 80 percent of bodybuilding success. While optimum nutrition and proper eating habits are extremely important, especially when attempting to build muscle and simultaneously lose fat, you cannot obtain your natural bodybuilding goals unless all the factors necessary for bodybuilding success are mastered and effectively implemented. Proper mental approach, rest and recuperation, nutrition, and of course training are all essential for natural bodybuilding success, and they are all interrelated. A chain is only as strong as its weakest link, and if you're weak in any of these areas, your progress will be greatly impaired, no matter how well you have mastered the other areas. So while optimum nutrition as a single factor is more important than most for promoting muscle growth, a weakness in any other area will virtually neutralize these benefits. Thus, nutrition is in actuality no more or less important a factor in achieving natural bodybuilding success than any other.

The four food groups

As is the case with every other human being, the best type of nutritional program for a natural bodybuilder is a well-balanced one. By following a well-balanced diet and eating a large variety of foods, you will ensure that you get all the nutrients in sufficient quantities necessary to maintain and promote optimum health. However, since you will require even greater amounts of these nutrients in order to build solid muscle mass I strongly suggest that each of you take basic nutritional supplements to ensure that your muscle building nutrient requirements are completely covered.

So in terms of the foods we eat, what constitutes a well-balanced diet? In 1956 the Department of Agriculture published the essentials of an adequate diet which described the four-food group plan.[1] This plan is an exquisitely well-balanced, health-promoting one, and it should form the backbone of your natural bodybuilding diet, with the exception of a few alterations which will be discussed soon.

The four food groups are

1. Cereals and grains—This group includes bread and flour products, cereals, and baked goods. This group is an excellent source of carbohydrates and minerals as well as some protein. Four servings daily is optimum.

2. Fruits and vegetables—Fruits and vegetables are an excellent source of vitamins, minerals and fiber. They are also an excellent source of carbohydrates. Some protein is also present in vegetables. Four or more servings daily is optimum.

3. The high protein group—This group includes beef, fish, poultry, eggs and vegetables such as nuts, dried peas, and dried beans. Besides being high in protein, these foods also provide B vitamins and iron. Unfortunately, some of these foods are also high in saturated fat. Two or more servings each day is optimum.

4. Milk and milk products—Milk and cheese form the basis of this group. Milk and cheese are high in protein, calcium, and riboflavin. Except for skim milk and fat-free milk, they are all high in saturated fats. Because of this, two servings or less is optimum.[2]

Balancing the three major nutrients—protein, fat and carbohydrates

Now that I've presented a well-balanced diet in terms of how much of each type of food you should generally eat in a day, let's take it one step farther and discuss exactly how you should balance your diet in terms of the three major nutrients—protein, carbohydrates, and fat. These three nutrients are the primary sources of energy in the body. Their energy potential is expressed in terms of calories. Calories are used to measure the amount of chemical energy which is released as heat when food is metabolized.[3] The average calorie value of each of the three major nutrients is known as its respective fuel factor. Carbohydrates and protein both yield 4 calories per gram and fats yield 9 calories per gram.[4]

The Senate Subcommittee on Nutrition recommends that our daily caloric intake should be comprised of 25 percent protein, 60 percent carbohydrates, and 15 percent fat.[5] For a natural bodybuilder who is not dieting to lose fat and is attempting to gain solid muscle mass, this distribution of calories between the three major nutrients is optimum. Later on, I will present the optimum distribution of calories between these 3 nutrients when dieting. I will also provide other necessary information on calories when discussing diet. However, what I will do now is provide an in-depth discussion on each of the three major nutrients.

Protein

Protein is of primary importance in the growth and development of all body tissues. It is the major source of building material for the muscles, blood, skin, hair, nails, and internal organs.[6] While it is used mainly for growth and repair, protein may also be used for energy when other energy sources are depleted.

Probably because muscle tissue consists primarily of protein, the majority of uneducated bodybuilders seem to think that tremendous quantities of protein are required to build muscle mass. Many bodybuilders take upward of 400 to 500 grams of protein a day, which is totally unnecessary and can actually be harmful. Any extra protein you take in above your caloric needs will be stored as fat. Even worse, processing large amounts of protein and eliminating the associated waste products puts a lot of unnecessary stress on the kidneys. Therefore, while it is true that an individual attempting to build muscle mass requires somewhat more protein than someone who isn't, the amount should still be kept in moderation. Recommendations on optimum protein consumption vary widely from 1 gram per kilogram of body weight (2.2 pounds) to 1 gram per pound of body weight. I recommend the second amount. It might be a little high, but when it comes to protein it's better to take in slightly too much than too little. So what this means is that if you weigh 150 pounds, you should consume 150 grams of protein a day. Taking in 1 gram of protein per pound of body weight will satisfy the requirement that 25 percent of your caloric intake be in the form of protein, with a couple of percentage points to spare.

A 1971 study confirms my belief that it's better to consume a moderately high level of protein. Of the three major nutrients protein is the only one which contains nitrogen. As already discussed, a positive nitrogen balance is essential for creating an anabolic effect. The 1971 university study determined that the average 150-pound man required approximately 2 grams of nitrogen every 24 hours for all the cells of the body to function normally. The key fact turned up by this study is that it will take more than 90 grams of protein a day from our diet to maintain that level. If you weigh more, you will require proportionately more and if you weigh less or are a female you will require proportionately less.[7] However, if you are attempting to gain muscle mass you obviously need significantly more protein than this, especially since you will be attempting to consistently maintain a positive nitrogen balance. When you consider this, an extra 60 grams of protein for a 150-pound man for the purpose of building muscle is not excessive, and it provides enough of a safety margin to ensure you make optimum gains. The body cannot effectively assimilate more than 30 grams of protein at one time and protein needs to be consumed periodically to effectively maintain a positive nitrogen balance. Thus, it is best to divide your daily protein consumption so that you are taking in 25 to 30 grams of protein every 3 or 4 hours four or five times during the day.

While the amount of protein you take in on a daily basis is very important, the quality of the protein you take in is even more vital. Proteins are made up of constituent unit building blocks called amino acids. Human protein is composed of 22 amino acids, of which 14 can be produced in the human body and are classified as nonessential. However, the other eight amino acids are classified as essential amino acids in the diet.[8] The eight essential amino acids are isoleucine, leucine, lysine, methionine, phenylalanine, threonine, tryptophan and valine.[9] In order for the body to properly synthesize protein, all eight essential amino acids must be present simultaneously and in the proper proportions. If just one essential amino acid is missing, or is at an unusually low level in relation to the others, even temporarily, protein synthesis will fall to a very low level or stop altogether.[10]

Any amino acid which isn't available in ample supply is referred to as a limiting amino acid because when it is used up no more human protein can be synthesized, even if all the other amino acids are available in ample supply.[11] Once an essential amino acid runs out, the remaining protein is virtually worthless.

Keeping all this in mind, the quality of any given protein is determined by the balance of the eight essential acids it contains. The better the balance, the higher the quality. This balance is measured in terms of the protein efficiency ratio. The highest protein efficiency ratio is 4.0. From 3.0 to 4.0 is considered high. Eggs have the highest P.E.R. of all foods. Milk, and all animal proteins (beef, pork, poultry, and fish) are also very high-quality protein and contain the ideal balance of amino acids.[12] Vegetables and nuts also contain all the essential amino acids, contrary to common belief. However, the balance is very poor[13] and as a result the P.E.R. is low. For this reason, vegetables and nuts are not an optimum source of protein. Since different vegetables and nuts have varying amounts of the eight essential amino acids, combining them in various ways will greatly improve the quality of the protein. However, you really have to know what you're doing to get this right and the quality will still not be as high as for meat, milk, eggs, etc. Also, since vegetables are not concentrated sources of protein, you have to eat tremendous quantities of them in order to get sufficient protein for musclebuilding purposes. Because of these two factors, I strongly suggest that any natural bodybuilder who is serious about making optimum progress not eat a strict vegetarian diet. However, a lactovo-vegetarian diet is satisfactory because of the high-quality protein supplied by eggs and dairy products. Vegetables have often been classified as incomplete proteins because of their poor balance of essential amino acids. However, this is, in actuality, an inaccurate classification since they do actually contain all eight essential amino acids. Unbalanced or poorly balanced are much more accurate descriptions for vegetables and nuts.[14]

Obviously, the individual bodybuilder or layman on a well-balanced diet should concentrate on getting his protein from eggs, various meats, and dairy products. However, since some of these sources are high in saturated fat we need to specify exactly which sources are best. Saturated fat in the form of cholesterol has been implicated as a contributing factor in the development of atherosclerosis and coronary heart disease, so while low to moderate amounts normally won't cause any problems, excessive consumption of saturated fats should be avoided. Therefore the best sources of protein are fish, chicken, and eggs. Fish has the lowest amount of fat of all balanced protein sources. Chicken is next. Most of the fat in chicken is in the skin so this skin should be removed before cooking.[15] Eggs normally have a high fat content and people tend to be afraid to eat them. However, it should be pointed out that the white of the egg contains most of the egg's protein and absolutely no fat. The yolk contains all the fat. So by throwing out the yolks of half the eggs you eat, you greatly reduce your fat intake and the taste remains virtually the same. For example, if you normally eat four eggs, have four whites and two yolks instead. Besides this, egg yolks themselves contain a fat-emulsifying agent, called lecithin, which neutralizes much of the potential danger of egg yolk cholesterol.

Milk is an excellent source of protein. However, it provides two major disadvantages. First of all, milk is high in fat unless it is either no-fat or skimmed milk. Even lowfat milk normally has a significant amount of fat. Therefore, milk as well as cheese should be consumed in limited quantities. Besides this, a large majority of men and women are at least mildly allergic to milk because of an inability to digest lactose, which is the sugar in milk. This is called lactose intolerance and it normally manifests itself in the form of various degrees of stomach discomfort.[16]

Pork is very high in saturated fat and should be eaten sparingly. No more than one serving per week should be consumed on a regular basis.

Finally, we come to probably the most misunderstood of all protein sources: beef. As of late, beef has gotten a bad rap because of its high content of saturated fat. However, beef is one of the most important protein sources for any individual who is attempting to add muscle mass naturally. For some reason which isn't quite understood, natural bodybuilders who consume beef on a consistent basis seem to gain muscle mass and strength more quickly and in greater amounts than individuals who do not eat beef and obtain all their protein from other sources. It's quite possible that the high levels of both hemoglobin and iron in beef could be responsible for this, at least in part, but no one really knows. Now this doesn't mean that you should consume large quantities of beef every day. However, consuming one serving of beef (4–8 oz., depending upon the individual) three to four days a week, preferably every other day, is recommended. From my experience, this is optimum. This amount of beef is of sufficient quantity to enable you to take advantage of any benefits it may provide, without taking in an excessive amount of saturated fat. Also, by purchasing the leanest cuts of beef possible, you can significantly reduce the amount of saturated fat you are consuming with your beef.

Fats

Since I've already discussed the content of fat in protein-rich foods, it makes sense to present my in-depth discussion of this major nutrient next. Since they contain 9 calories per gram—more than twice what protein and carbohydrates contain—they are the most concentrated form of energy in the diet.[17] However, carbohydrates are the preferred source of energy since the body finds them much easier to break down and utilize. Therefore, fat tends to be stored in the body as a reserve energy source. Fat also has two structural functions. It surrounds, protects, and holds in place the vital organs, and it insulates the body against rapid temperature changes and excessive heat loss.[18]

Obviously, since fats are so high in calories, consuming an excess amount of them will tend to result in your storing excess fat instead of using it as energy. However, besides that all-important fact, there is one other important thing about fat which all natural bodybuilders and other health-conscious individuals need to be concerned with. This is the fact that there are two types of fat, saturated and unsaturated. Saturated fats, which are usually solid at room temperature and which come primarily from animal sources,[19] are, as already discussed, the type which can be harmful to the body if a large amount is consumed. However, unsaturated fats, which include polyunsaturates, are derived from vegetable, nut, or seed sources. They are usually liquid at room temperature in the form of oil, and are actually beneficial to the body. In fact, three unsaturated fatty acids are essential to the body because it cannot produce them. These unsaturated fatty acids are necessary for normal growth and healthy skin, hair, blood, arteries, and nerves.[20] Besides this—and this is very important—they actually lower serum cholesterol.[21] This means they can neutralize some of the negative effects of saturated fats. Because unsaturated fats are actually beneficial while saturated fats are potentially destructive to the body, as much of your fat intake as possible should be unsaturated. In fact, a total intake of at least 1 tablespoon of vegetable oil is necessary each day in order to provide the benefits just mentioned. Any vegetable oil except for olive oil can be used. Some of this oil will come from the vegetables themselves, but it's always a good idea to include some vegetable oil in the form of salad dressing or cooking oil in your diet. The only saturated fat you should consume is that which inadvertently accompanies your optimal intake of ideally balanced protein. Incidentally, you should never fry meat because of the amount of saturated fat frying holds in. Always bake or broil your meat. Eggs can be fried in a no-stick pan without butter or margarine.

Carbohydrates

The prime overall function of carbohydrates in the human body is to provide energy.[22] In fact, because they are so quickly and easily metabolized, they are the body's preferred source of energy.[23] Carbohydrates also help to regulate protein and fat metabolism.[24] This fact will be pertinent to the section on dieting. Carbohydrates which are not used for energy are first of all stored as glycogen in the liver and muscles; anything left over is converted to and stored as fat.[25] Besides being consumed in the diet, some amino acids and the glycerol of fat can be converted to glucose for energy.[26] Incidentally, glucose is the only form of carbohydrate which the body can use for energy. So all forms of carbohydrates which are taken in, are converted to glucose before they can be metabolized.[27]

Carbohydrates are classified into two distinct categories. Simple sugars, such as those found in honey and fruit, are very easily digested.[28] Many health-conscious individuals and bodybuilders may find this surprising, since fruits are commonly classified as complex carbohydrates and table sugar is commonly classified as a simple sugar. In actuality, table sugar is a double sugar and requires some digestive action.[29] However, since it is broken down almost as quickly as fructose, which is the sugar in fruit, it can be and often is classified as a simple sugar.

The other distinct category is complex carbohydrates, the major constituent of which is starch. Starch is primarily found in whole grains, potatoes and other root vegetables, and legumes. Starches, like other complex carbohydrates, require a prolonged period of time to be completely broken down into simple sugars for digestion.[30]

Since complex carbohydrates take so long to be completely broken down they provide a long-term, relatively stable energy source.[31] Therefore, to ensure that your energy level is maintained at a high level as consistently as possible, the majority of the carbohydrates you consume should be complex carbs such as vegetables, cereal, and whole grain bread.

By consuming a high proportion of your carbohydrates from simple sugars, and especially concentrated sources of simple sugars, you run the risk of having markedly fluctuating energy levels. You also run the risk of consuming too many calories, which will be stored as fat.

What happens is this. When you consume a large amount of simple sugar in a brief period of time, your blood sugar rises so quickly and to such a high level that it triggers the release of insulin. Insulin allows the sugar to be transferred into the cells to be stored and, in most cases, converted to fat. As a result, the blood sugar falls. In fact, the insulin tends to overcompensate, and the blood sugar actually falls below the level it was at before you ate the high concentration of simple sugar. So while you will initially get a burst of quick energy which will usually last between 30 minutes and an hour, you will suddenly experience an even more dramatic drop in energy. This will often be accompanied by fatigue, dizziness, nervousness, or a headache, and since your blood sugar will now be lower than before, you will find yourself craving more sweet food.[32] If you eat more simple sugar, the same thing happens again, and as you can see, a vicious cycle can develop. Besides this, you'll actually gain fat, even though your body is craving sugar.

Now this isn't to say that you should never eat a candy bar or a sweet piece of fruit. Just don't eat two or more candy bars or a few pieces of sweet fruit, etc. at the same time so you don't invoke this response. Since you will require lots of sustained energy to have a productive workout, it's an excel-

lent idea to have a large portion of complex carbohydrates approximately two hours before you train. Then about 30 minutes before your workout have one piece of fruit. In combination with the complex carbs which will provide you with a steady energy source during the workout, the fruit will give you an added energy boost without being concentrated enough to trigger an insulin response. Then, on those occasions when you find yourself dragging during a workout, you can stop when you are halfway done, and if it doesn't upset your stomach (which it shouldn't), you can have another piece of fruit. Many individuals are dead set against training with any food in their stomach whatsoever, and they often won't eat for a couple hours before they train. By doing this, they increase their chances of running out of energy in the middle of their workout. Besides this, a number of individuals (including myself) find it very uncomfortable to train on an empty stomach because of the rumbling and feelings of hunger associated with it. It's hard to concentrate on your workout when all you can think about is eating dinner.

Nutrients

Vitamins

Vitamins are not components of major body structures. Instead, they aid in the building of these structures.[33] They are necessary in very small quantities for the performance of particular metabolic functions and for the prevention of deficiency diseases which are associated with a lack of their presence.[34] Vitamins also cannot be manufactured by the body and must therefore be supplied in the diet.[35] Vitamins also have no caloric or energy value.[36]

There are two distinct classes of vitamins. Water-soluble vitamins cannot be stored in the body for any length of time and must be replaced on a daily basis. These vitamins, including the B-complex vitamins and vitamin C, are usually measured in terms of milligrams.[37]

Fat-soluble vitamins can be stored in the body. In fact, taking in excessive amounts of a fat-soluble vitamin over a prolonged period of time can have a toxic effect. Many individuals are afraid to take vitamins because they believe this will happen. However, the doses you would have to take to cause a toxic effect borders on the ridiculous, so there's no reason to be overly con-

cerned about this happening. Fat-soluble vitamins—of which vitamin A, D, E, and K are the most common—are measured in units of activity known as international units.[38]

A well-balanced diet consisting of a variety of foods will provide the average person with enough of all the essential vitamins and minerals. However, since bodybuilders are not ordinary people and missing even one essential vitamin or mineral can hinder your progress, everyone engaging in natural bodybuilding training should take a multivitamin mineral supplement to make sure they're getting everything they need. Anyone who is not eating a well-balanced diet should also take such a supplement. These supplements and the reasons for them will be discussed more in depth in the section on supplements.

Vitamin C and the B-complex vitamins are two of the most important vitamins for natural bodybuilders, and are required in particularly large quantities. These vitamins are involved in one way or another with practically every aspect of normal functioning. They are often called the stress vitamins because they are quickly depleted when under stress, and large quantities of them tend to make the human body more capable of effectively dealing with various types of stress. Since natural bodybuilding training puts tremendous stress on the body in a variety of ways, the importance of these vitamins becomes evident. Also, since they are water soluble, you must be extra sure that you are consistently consuming adequate quantities of them for optimal functioning.

Minerals

Minerals are inorganic elements widely distributed in nature and many of them have vital roles in metabolism.[39] They are also constituents of the bones, soft tissue, muscle, blood, and nerve cells. Another important function they have is to maintain the delicate water balance inside and outside the cells.[40] Sodium and potassium are mainly responsible for this and are two of the most important minerals. Calcium is the most plentiful mineral in the body by far[41] and is closely associated with phosphorous. Both are found in large quantities in milk and both function together in the task of bone building.[42] All these minerals are extremely important to natural bodybuilders, and along with all the other minerals, can generally be found in adequate amounts for the normal person in a well-balanced diet. But once again, natural bodybuilders require more than the average person and should take a mineral supplement.

One way to determine whether you have a mineral deficiency is to have a hair analysis. The cost averages between $40 and $60. From analyzing the content of various minerals in your hair, an expert can accurately determine the amount of each mineral you have in your body.[41] Your medical doctor, if he's up to date on current nutrition research, will more than likely know of a company which will perform a hair analysis for you.

One mineral you will probably never have to worry about getting enough of in your diet is sodium. Normally, a human being requires approximately 1,000 mg. of sodium a day, which is present naturally in most diets. However, so many of our foods are laced with sodium to enhance their flavor, that the majority of us consume many times more sodium than we actually need. Since excessive use of sodium has been implicated as a cause of hypertension and heart disease, I strongly suggest that you eliminate as much unnecessary sodium from your diet as possible. The most obvious way to do this is to drastically curtail your use of table salt and eliminate it if possible. However, this is not enough since approximately half of the sodium we consume on a daily basis is hidden in the food we eat. [42] Of course, most of us love the flavor salt gives our food and we are reluctant to give it up. However, any steps you take in this direction will definitely benefit your health. Incidentally, sodium has a great affinity for water, so consuming an excessive amount of sodium will cause your body to retain large quantities of water and can give you a bloated appearance.

Fiber

Fiber is the part of the food which is not digested by the human body.[44] Cellulose, commonly found in the skins of fruits and the stems and leaves of vegetables, as well as seed and grain coverings[45], whole wheat bread and other virtually unprocessed grain products are all excellent sources of fiber.

Adequate amounts of fiber are necessary for the intestinal tract to function normally. A diet low in fiber has been associated with heart disease, cancer of the colon and rectum, diverticulitis, varicose veins, phlebitis and obesity.[46]

This blatantly points out the importance of fiber in maintaining and promoting an optimum level of health.

Junk food

Bodybuilding authorities generally recommend that natural bodybuilders and other health-minded individuals stay away completely from junk food. But the first thing that must be clarified is exactly what is junk food. My definition of a junk food is a food which has been processed to the point where the nutritional value that food provides in relation to its calorie content is insignificant. Such foods are said to contain "empty calories." A processed food is one in which most of the vitamins and minerals have been removed either in creating that food or in processing it for public consumption.[47]

So which foods can be classified as junk food? Well, since white sugar is processed to the point where it has practically no nutritional value, it is safe to say that just about any food which has a high content of processed sugar and also a very low nutrient level is junk food. Candy bars fall into this category as do doughnuts and cake. What about a cake, for instance, which is homemade, and contains lots of milk and eggs? Or what about ice cream which is also high in sugar, but contains milk which is high in protein? These foods aren't necessarily junk foods. Then there's fast food and pizza, which are generally considered to be junk food. Both foods have high levels of fat and sodium, but they also generally contain a reasonable amount of nutrients, especially pizza. Basically you have to define what junk food is to you and how processed a food has to be to fall into the junk food category.

The most important thing is to eat a balanced diet and make sure that you obtain sufficient amounts of all the essential nutrients without taking in an excess of calories. Once you meet your nutrient requirements, if you still haven't eaten the optimum number of calories for that day, there is nothing wrong with having a candy bar, a slice of cake, a slice of pizza, or anything else that would normally be considered junk food to supply the additional calories. Also, if you happen to be one of those individuals who have an unusually fast metabolism, you will be able to substitute as an occasional meal the extra quantities of pizza or fast foods which are necessary to provide your body with sufficient nutrients without worrying about the extra calories. Of

course, I'm not recommending that you make eating pizza and fast food burgers a regular part of your diet. Eating such high amounts of sodium and saturated fat on a consistent basis can have a negative effect on your body. But there's nothing wrong with having them occasionally. The same thing can be said for chocolate and doughnuts, etc. It's okay to have them occasionally. Even individuals who have difficulty watching their weight should occasionally leave room in their calorie intake to indulge in a normally forbidden food such as chocolate or pizza. Doing this once in a while won't deprive your body of the nutrients it requires to function optimally. It's when you make a habit out of it that the problems begin.

Some of you reading this may consider my views on so called junk food to be somewhat lenient for an individual who is presenting what he considers to be the ultimate fitness life style, but let's be realistic. Good-tasting food is one of the truly enjoyable things in life and the large majority of good-tasting foods are high in calories and low in nutrients. It's unrealistic to deny anyone the pleasure of occasionally partaking of these foods, unless it's absolutely necessary for health purposes. However, if you follow the guidelines in this section in relation to how often and how much of these so-called junk foods you can eat, neither your health, your body fat level, nor your natural bodybuilding progress will be negatively affected.

Water

Since water is an excellent body cleansing agent, and the human body itself has a very high water content, you should drink several glasses a day, at least 7 to 10. Since distilled water is completely free of impurities, it is preferable to tap water for drinking purposes. However, it is also obviously much more expensive so you will have to personally decide whether it's worth the expense. You can purchase distilled water in any grocery store.[48]

You should never let your body become excessively dehydrated. Since this is especially prone to occur during heavy bodybuilding training and other physically demanding activities, you should drink a few ounces of water at least every 15 to 20 minutes during your workouts. As soon as you feel thirsty, satisfy that thirst. Many people are still under the impression that you shouldn't drink any fluid when you are working out, and that doing so will cause your stomach to cramp up. This rarely, if ever, happens. Even if it did, the consequences of becoming overly dehydrated are much more severe and potentially dangerous. You can become weak and faint, and your body can overheat among other things. For a more complete list of side effects from dehydration refer to the section on diuretics and dehydration. Certainly, feeling weak and thirsty will, at the very least, hinder your workout performance.

During a workout it is preferable to drink plain water instead of juice or soda. Since juice and soda are high in simple sugars, their water content is more slowly absorbed than plain water. The reason for this is that 1 gram of sugar binds with 4 grams of water, so the sugar tends to hold the water in the stomach for a long period of time. A little sugar, such as that found in a piece of fruit, won't have a significantly detrimental effect on water absorption. But soda and fruit juices are very concentrated sources of simple sugars. In fact, one of the major reasons I recommended having a piece of fruit in the middle of your workout for a quick energy boost, instead of juice or soda, is because of the negative effect such liquids have on the absorption of water.

Optimal body fat levels

As I already mentioned, women who engage in natural bodybuilding training should keep their body fat level in the range of 10 to 15 percent for an optimally toned, shapely, and feminine appearance. Men should stay in the range of 10 to 15 percent, with the lower number being preferable, in order to appear muscular and optimally toned. You can have your body fat level measured with relative accuracy with a skin fold test. Or, for an extremely accurate measurement, you can have underwater weighing performed. However, this is much more expensive, usually costing around $100. By having one of these tests performed, you'll have a good idea how much body fat you have to gain or lose to fall within the ranges just outlined. While the vast majority will be concerned with losing fat, there will actually be a few of you who are so thin that you need to gain a few pounds of fat. Of course, simply by looking in the mirror you can get an excellent idea of exactly how much fat you need to lose or gain. The question is, once you have an idea of how much fat you need to lose or gain, how do you go about making the necessary adjustments in

the most scientific way possible? And if your body fat level is already where you want it, how do you go about keeping it at that level?

Metabolism

Metabolism is the sum of the physical and chemical processes in a living organism by which the basic substance of cells and tissues is produced, maintained or destroyed and by which energy is made available for the functioning of the organism.[49] More simply stated, your metabolism is the amount of energy it requires to keep your own individual body repairing itself, growing, and functioning at optimum levels. This energy is measured in terms of calories. The number of calories you require each day to maintain your body without gaining or losing stored energy in the form of fat is an accurate energy measurement of your metabolic rate.

Your total metabolic rate consists of the sum of your basal metabolic rate, and the number of calories you expend during physical, mental, and emotional activity on a daily basis. Your basal metabolic rate is the rate of internal chemical activity of resting tissue.[50] It represents the minimum energy requirement for day and night with no exercise or exposure to cold.[51] Different individuals have different basal metabolic rates. Some people have fast basal metabolic rates and have difficulty gaining or maintaining weight, while others have very slow basal metabolic rates and therefore have a great deal of difficulty burning fat. As far as activity is concerned, the more physically active you are, the higher your overall daily caloric requirements will be. Exercise is a major factor which accounts for individual calorie requirements. Calorie expenditure is also increased during agitated emotional states. Mental effort, such as that necessary to write this book or for studying, requires few if any extra calories.[52] Before you can successfully implement a program for either maintaining, increasing, or decreasing your present level of body fat while simultaneously gaining solid muscle mass, you will need as accurate an idea as possible of what your total metabolic rate is, in terms of your average daily calorie requirements. Of course, we don't perform the same exact activities for the same exact length of time every day so our total calorie requirements vary slightly from day to day. Therefore, what we are looking for is your average metabolic rate over a period of time. A

good length of time is a week. What I am going to do next is show you an excellent way of accurately calculating your average daily metabolic rate. This method is very common for calculating average daily calorie requirements. All you need is a calorie counter, which you can purchase in any grocery store.

What you do is this. Write down every single thing you eat for one week—seven days—and I mean absolutely everything. At the end of each day, sit down with your calorie counting book and add up the number of calories in each of the foods you ate that day. This will give you the day's total calorie intake. Do this on each one of the seven days. At the end of the week, add the seven daily calorie totals together. Then divide the number by seven. This will give you your average daily calorie intake. Weigh yourself on the morning of the first day you begin counting calories and then again on the morning of the eighth day. This will account for the seven days in which you are actually counting up your daily calorie intake. If you haven't gained or lost weight during the seven-day period, your daily average calorie intake will also be your average daily metabolic rate, and will be the number of calories you require to maintain your present weight. But what if you've gained or lost a pound or two? A pound of fat contains 3,500 calories. Keeping this in mind you can calculate your daily metabolic rate even if you've gained or lost weight. Let me give you an example. Let's say you gained one pound of fat during the seven-day period. That means you took in 3,500 calories more during the week than you required. By dividing 3,500 by 7 you will get 500. That means you took in an average of 500 calories more each day than your average daily metabolic rate. So if you had calculated your daily average calorie intake to be 3,000 calories, you would subtract the 500 calories from that number. This means your total average daily metabolic rate would actually be 2,500 calories instead of 3,000 calories.[53]

Once you know what your average daily metabolic rate is, it's relatively easy to determine how many calories to take in for the purpose of building pure muscle mass while simultaneously either maintaining, gaining, or losing body fat according to what your body fat levels happen to be, and what you ultimately desire them to be.

Maintaining body fat levels and building pure muscle mass

Contrary to popular belief in the bodybuilding community, you do not require a tremendous amount of calories over and above your average daily metabolic requirements in order to build muscle mass. Scores of individuals have attempted to bulk up in the belief that they would be gaining muscle. In actuality, most of what you gain when you bulk up is fat. Unfortunately, by the time most of these individuals realize this, they find themselves faced with the task of losing a large quantity of body fat.

You can make maximum muscle gains by consuming only a few extra calories more each day than your average daily calorie requirements, including those expended during your workouts. A pound of muscle contains only 600 calories.[54] The fact that muscle tissue is 70 percent water accounts for this.[55] What this means is that if you plan on gaining five pounds of muscle in a year—the most a natural bodybuilder can realistically expect to gain after the first couple of years—you would technically have to consume only 3,000 calories a year above the amount necessary for maintaining your present level of body fat. Dividing 3,000 by 365 days in a year, this means you would technically have to consume only 8 extra calories a day to gain this amount of muscle. That means if your average daily calorie requirement was 2,500 calories, you would have to consume only 2,508 calories a day in order to gain 5 pounds of muscle in a year. I'm not suggesting you be so precise, since calorie requirements fluctuate from day to day. But it's probably surprising to most of you that so few extra calories are required to build muscle mass.[56] So there's no reason to stuff yourself all the time unless you're terribly thin.

Of course, it requires energy to build muscle tissue, but this energy requirement was basically already accounted for when calculating the average daily metabolic rate. What you can do just to make sure all these energy requirements are accounted for is to experiment with consuming anywhere between an extra 50 to 200 calories a day above your calculated average daily calorie requirements. If you notice that you are gradually gaining fat, eliminate the extra calories and reduce your calorie intake an extra 100 calories a day until you are back to the way you looked previously. If, however, you don't look any fatter, chances are excellent that those calories are going into building muscle. By adjusting your calories slightly upward or downward for a few days when you notice that you are looking either a little pudgier or leaner than you would like, you can maintain optimum body fat levels while building pure muscle mass. Of course, your calories should be divided proportionately so that approximately 25 percent of your caloric intake is protein, 60 percent is carbohydrates, and 15 percent is fat.

Keeping in mind everything I have said about nutrition so far in this section, I will now present a typical daily food consumption menu for a year-round muscle-building, fat-level-maintenance diet. Eating along the following lines will enable you to build solid muscle mass without adding additional body fat. You will have to know the number of grams of protein, fat, and carbohydrates in each food you eat so you can balance your total daily intake of these three major nutrients according to the guideline previously presented. Of course, you will have to know how many calories are in the food you eat so you consume the optimum number of total calories on a daily basis which will enable you to build pure muscle mass without gaining additional body fat. Obviously, you will have to purchase some sort of calorie and nutrient breakdown table of common everyday foods so you can accurately determine exactly how much of each nutrient is in everything you eat, as well as the total calorie content of each. Carbohydrate gram-counting pamphlets are very common, but I've never seen a pamphlet listing the protein and fat content of these foods. This information is extremely important for anybody who is serious about nutrition and health, and if you're attempting to build muscle mass it becomes even more important. Some foods have the number of grams of fat, protein, and carbohydrates, as well as the total number of calories per serving listed on the package.

The most comprehensive tables of food composition I've ever found are in a book called the *Nutrition Almanac*. Over 2,500 common foods are listed in this table. All the information you could ever want to know about each food is presented, including the protein content, carbohydrate content, and fat content, which is subdivided into saturated and unsaturated fat content. This will help you to avoid saturated fat. The content of most of the vitamins and minerals including sodium is also listed for each food. So you'll be better able to avoid sodium. Even fiber is listed. I have found these tables to be invaluable when planning my daily food consumption. Now for some sample menus.

Year-round muscle-building, fat-maintenance sample diet

This is a typical example of a male natural bodybuilder's daily food intake. While the amount of food each of you actually consumes daily depends on your individual caloric requirements, women generally require approximately one-quarter fewer calories on a daily basis than men. Since the following is an example of a man's daily food consumption, women should realize that in order for this diet to be a representative example of what they should eat, the total amount of food listed here would have to be reduced by approximately 25 percent.

Daily food intake—example

Breakfast
1. 4 eggs less 2 yolks, poached, boiled, or fried in non-stick pan without butter or margarine
2. 2 slices whole grain bread with jam
3. 1/2 grapefruit or 4 oz. orange juice
4. Tea, coffee or water

Morning snack
1. 4 oz. lowfat cottage cheese or piece of chicken (broiled or baked)
2. 1 piece of fruit
3. Water, soda, diet soda, tea or coffee

Lunch
1. Roast beef, turkey salad, chicken salad, or tuna salad sandwich on whole grain bread with mayonnaise (regular or low calorie), lettuce, tomato or onion, if desired
2. Carrot or celery sticks to munch on
3. Water, soda, diet soda, etc.

Afternoon snack
1. Protein shake consisting of 8 ounces lowfat milk or orange juice, 1 rounded tablespoon protein powder, piece of fruit for natural sweetness; example: 1 small banana, a few strawberries, etc. Crushed ice

for an icy fresh taste (bring to work in thermos and shake well before drinking).

Dinner

1. 4–8 oz. chicken, fish, or lean steak (broiled or baked accordingly)
2. Tossed salad with oil and vinegar dressing
3. 1 medium baked potato or portion of rice or spaghetti
4. 1 portion of vegetables
5. 1 glass of non-fat or skimmed milk, or tea, coffee, soda, etc.
6. Dessert: ice milk or fruit

Late night snack

1. Unsalted, unbuttered popcorn or a piece of low calorie fruit

Pertinent points of interest

1. Unsalted, unbuttered popcorn is very low in calories and very filling, so it makes an excellent bedtime snack.
2. Certain fruits and vegetables are much higher in calories than others. Generally, yellow vegetables, the prime example of which is corn, are much higher in calories than green vegetables. Root vegetables, such as potatoes and beets, also tend to be high in calories. With fruits there are no general guidelines to follow. Some very sweet fruits, such as strawberries, are very low in calories and some not-so-sweet fruits, such as bananas, are quite high in caloric content. A list of relatively low and high calorie fruits follows.
   Low Calorie Fruit—canteloupe, strawberries, apples, peaches, grapefruit, and oranges
   High Calorie Fruit—Watermelon, figs, dates, bananas, cherries, and canteloupe
   Always check the caloric value of any fruit or vegetable before you eat it. Incidentally, fruits and vegetables are almost purely carbohydrates.
3. Steam vegetables instead of boiling them. When you boil vegetables, most of the vitamins and minerals they contain ends up in the water in which they are being boiled.

Weight-gaining diet

Certain individuals have a great deal of difficulty gaining body weight of any kind. This problem is not nearly as common as having trouble losing weight, but to those who face it, it is just as serious. Individuals who have a predominantly ectomorphic body type are especially prone to this problem since they tend to be both slender in build and have a very high metabolism. Many teenagers and young adults also face this problem because of the increase in metabolism which occurs as adulthood is attained. However, it can happen to anyone who, for one reason or another, does not consume enough calories for the body to either maintain or put on weight. Individuals who have very low body fat levels as a result of consistently taking in fewer calories than their average daily maintenance requirements tend to have an extreme amount of difficulty gaining muscle. The reason for this is that the body perceives it as an emergency when its fat reserves drop to very low levels. Since it becomes more concerned with storing and preserving energy in such a situation, it is less willing to part with the energy necessary to build additional muscle mass. This usually occurs in males when the body fat level drops below 5–7 percent and in females when it drops below 10–12 percent. Skinny people also tend to have an unhealthy and frail appearance. Therefore, individuals who are unusually thin tend to be as self-conscious about their appearance as individuals who are too fat. Individuals who are very thin should commit themselves to consuming extra calories consistently until their body fat level is in the optimal range previously outlined (10–15 percent for men and 15–20 percent for women). The extra body fat will give you a more filled-out and healthy appearance, as well as ensuring that there is enough of an energy reserve—that the calories you take in are used to build muscle mass at an optimal rate. I must emphasize here that adding fat in order to attain optimal body fat levels is not the same as bulking up.

Bulking up is when you deliberately attempt to gain additional body fat over and above your optimum body fat level in the belief that it will help you gain muscle. While a certain percentage of fat reserves is necessary for building muscle mass at an optimum rate, going over your ideal body fat level will not provide any additional help in this respect. In fact, if you gain too much fat it may damage your body, for no matter how you slice it, extra fat is extra fat. And as most of us are aware, being excessively fat puts a tremendous amount of stress on the body and is one of the risk factors associated with heart disease.

When attempting to gain weight, you should strive for a two-pound fat gain per week for as many weeks as it takes to reach your optimum body fat level. Since two pounds of fat is 7,000 calories, that means you will have to consume an average of 1,000 calories a day more than your average daily caloric maintenance requirements. Gaining more than two pounds of additional weight per week is not advised. If you gain weight too quickly you put undue stress on your body's systems, especially the heart and cardiovascular system. Gaining weight at the rate of two pounds a week is gradual enough so no undue stress is placed on the body.

So the big question is, how do you most effectively go about consuming these extra calories so you can gain that extra weight? Well, first of all you should eat more of everything. More specifically, you should make a conscious effort to eat foods which are concentrated sources of calories. This entails always eating high-calorie fruits and vegetables instead of low-calorie ones, eating pasta and rice more frequently and in larger quantities than usual, and eating foods such as pizza, ice cream, and fast food more frequently and in larger amounts than usual. However, you still shouldn't consume an excess quantity of junk food. When you're attempting to gain weight it's okay for fats to make up 20 to 25 percent of the total caloric intake, since they provide a concentrated source of calories. Consuming a slightly higher percentage of fat for a few weeks or months normally will not have any negative effect on the heart, cardiovascular system, and general health of the individual. It's when you consume a high percentage of fat for a long period of time that you risk seriously damaging your cardiovascular system and overall health. Still, it's a good idea to have your cholesterol level checked before you increase your fat intake. With the increase in fat, your total caloric level would be divided as follows: 20 percent protein, 55–60 percent carbs, 20–25 percent fat. Since you will be consuming so much more food, your protein intake will have to be only 20 percent of your total caloric intake or even less for you to be able to consume the one gram of protein per pound of body weight which is optimum.

One of the best ways to dramatically increase your daily caloric intake is to replace both your morning snack and moderate-caloried afternoon protein drink with a very high-caloried protein drink. Each of the two protein drinks should contain 12–16 oz. of lowfat or whole milk or orange juice, 2–3 heaping tablespoons of weight gain protein powder, 1 piece of high calorie fruit, and 2 scoops of ice milk or ice cream if desired. According to what you put into it, you can concoct a super-powered, high-calorie protein drink which contains 1,000 calories or more. Two of these a day will boost your caloric intake dramatically, and since this calorie boost is in liquid form, you won't have to worry about feeling stuffed or excessively bloated after consuming it.

Of course, if you're trying to increase your body fat levels while simultaneously building muscle you shouldn't be wasting your energy on unnecessarily physically demanding activities, especially sports. You should also keep your aerobic training to the absolute minimum that will produce optimal cardiovascular fitness. Besides the energy required for your job the only other significant amount of energy you should be expending is that required for your training. Of course, energy drain from stress and emotional turmoil should be kept to an absolute minimum. When an individual's body fat levels are low, the negative effects of any type of energy drain whatsoever on his muscle building progress is greatly magnified compared to an individual who has an optimal body fat level.

By following the guidelines in this section you should eventually be able to increase your percentage of body fat to an optimal level and your muscle-building progress should increase dramatically as a result. Once you get your percentage of body fat to the level you desire, simply reduce your calories just enough to maintain that level, being sure to reduce your fat consumption back to 15 percent of your total daily caloric intake.

Dieting to lose weight (fat)

First, let's discuss how *not* to diet. You should never follow any type of fad diet. Fad diets are nutritionally unbalanced, generally unhealthy, and are, at best, only temporarily effective. Some of these diets, if followed for prolonged periods of time, can actually be dangerous.

During the last several years, low car-bohydrate dieting has become the most popular of all fad diets. The low carb diet fad was started by such books as *Dr. Atkins' Diet Revolution* and *Doctor's Quick Weight Loss,* and recent books, such as *The Scarsdale Medical Diet,* have kept it in vogue. Soon everybody who wanted to lose body fat was counting carbs and apparently losing plenty of weight. This included the vast majority of competitive bodybuilders. Unfortunately, this diet isn't nearly as effective as it initially appears to be and a number of undesirable side effects accompany its use.[57]

The most attractive feature of this diet to people attempting to lose fat is that a dramatic weight loss occurs during the first week that it is used. This weight loss can be as high as 10 pounds and experiencing such a dramatic initial weight loss gives many people the incentive to continue with the diet. But these people don't realize that this initial weight loss does not occur as a result of burning fat, but as a result of the body losing a significant amount of water. Carbohydrates normally hold a lot of water in the body. In fact, one gram of carbohydrate binds with four grams of water.[58] When you severely restrict your carbohydrate intake, your body is forced to use up all the carbohydrate reserves you have. As these carbohydrates are burned for energy, the water they were bound to is released. Without carbs to hold them, the body can no longer retain this water, and it is flushed from the system. Once all the carbs are used up and all the carbohydrate-held water is flushed out of the body, the dramatic weight loss comes to a screeching halt. These carbohydrate reserves are normally exhausted within a week.

After this water is flushed from the system, future weight losses as a result of burning fat come very slowly. The reason for this is that low carbohydrate diets are as a rule very high in fats. Since fats are more than twice as concentrated a source of calories as either carbohydrates or protein, it becomes obvious that an individual on a low carb diet is actually consuming a lot of calories. In fact, because of the high fat content, these diets are usually too high in calories to allow body fat to be metabolized as energy.[59] Whether your calories are coming mainly from protein, fat, or carbohydrates is not the critical factor. It is the actual number of calories you consume in relation to your daily caloric maintenance level which determines whether or not you burn body fat. Biochemically, the body burns body fat only when you consume less calories each day than your body burns.[60]

Besides the all-important fact that it is extremely difficult to burn body fat quickly and in significant amounts, there are a number of other serious disadvantages associated with this diet.

Since carbohydrates are the body's preferred source of energy because of the fact that they are so quickly and easily metabolized, carbohydrate deprivation is extremely hard on the body.[61] Without sufficient quantities of carbs, your energy will drop to very low levels. This occurs as a direct result of low blood sugar levels. As the body struggles to normalize its blood sugar levels, small quantities of fat are burned. However, since fat burning is a very slow process, the body often turns to its protein stores as a source of energy. This is responsible for the significant loss of muscle tissue which most bodybuilders notice to their horror on a low carb diet.[62] Carbohydrates, unlike fat, have a protein-sparing quality because of the fact that they are the preferred source of energy. Even when burning both protein and fat the body finds it impossible to raise the blood sugar level significantly.

Because of the critically low energy levels which are a direct result of low blood sugar levels, you will find that you are constantly dragging through every daily event. You simply will not be able to function at anywhere near 100 percent. As a result your job, recreational activities, and especially your training will be negatively affected.

You will find it virtually impossible to train with anywhere near the intensity necessary to have a productive workout. After 15 to 20 minutes of working out, you will exhaust whatever small amount of sugar your body has been able to eke out of your fat stores and from breaking down your hard-earned muscle tissue. Once these reserves have been exhausted, the workout will become an ordeal.[63] After a few workouts like this, believe me, you won't want to work out anymore.

Besides its negative effect on the body, carbohydrate deprivation also has a serious negative effect on the brain. The brain requires a certain level of blood sugar to function normally. When the brain isn't provided with this sugar it becomes difficult to think quickly and clearly. Concentration is often impaired and mental confusion is also quite common. The tendency to make mental errors also increases significantly. Just try studying for and taking an exam on a low-carb diet and you'll see what I mean. Besides this, individuals on low-carb diets become prone to wild mood swings. Depression is especially common.[64]

A marked increase in irritability is also experienced by the majority of low carb dieters after the first few days of dieting. This occurs as a result of the extremely high phosphorus and low calcium content of animal protein (except for milk products). Normally, this wouldn't be a problem, but low carb diets have an unusually high content of animal protein compared to a balanced diet. Consuming so much phosphorus upsets the calcium-phosphorus balance that the human body normally has. As a result you get the "phosphorus jitters" which results in your being consistently nervous and irritable.[65]

Besides all of the negative aspects just mentioned, we also have to consider the damage that the high content of saturated fats in a low carb diet can do to your body. I've already mentioned that consuming a slightly higher percentage of saturated fat in your diet temporarily while attempting to gain weight will normally not be a problem. However, consuming a very high percentage of saturated fat for any length of time definitely has the potential to damage the cardiovascular system. It's not uncommon for about half or even more of the calories consumed on a low carb diet to be in the form of saturated fat according to what the individual eats. Low carb diets are also completely unbalanced. You deprive your body of numerous vitamins, minerals, and enzymes necessary for optimal health by eliminating most fruits and vegetables from your diet,[66] and because these foods contain carbs, you cannot consume adequate amounts of them when on a low carb diet. Vitamin and mineral supplements can replace most of these nutrients, but your main source of nutrients should always be the food you eat. Supplements are to be used as exactly that, supplements, not as a staple of your diet, and your major source of nutrients.

Finally, the bottom line is that low carbohydrate diets are ultimately doomed to failure. You will find yourself constantly craving carbohydrates in one form or another. Even those individuals with the toughest of wills and the greatest discipline will ultimately slip up and give in to the relentless hunger and cravings for sweets. The result will be a food binge in which you consume a tremendous amount of carbohydrates. Of course, this will trigger the

insulin response and you'll find yourself craving carbohydrates as much as ever within the space of a few hours. Eventually, you'll give in and binge again. And the cycle will continue indefinitely. Your body, when depleted of carbohydrates, considers binge eating to be virtually essential for its survival.[67] Of course, every time you binge, you will slow down or reverse whatever small degree of progress you have made in terms of losing body fat. As a result, you will become increasingly frustrated and will eventually give up on low-carb dieting. So do your body and mind a favor, and don't start one in the first place. Since a low carb diet has so many disadvantages, as do other fad diets, the big question is what's the alternative? Which diet is most effective?

Low-fat, low-calorie dieting

There's no question that a low-fat, low-calorie diet is the healthiest and most effective diet you can follow for burning fat while simultaneously maintaining or even slightly increasing your muscle mass. It should be pointed out that it is extremely difficult to build muscle mass when you are on any type of a restrictive diet. Since the body does not consider building muscle mass to be very important it tends to save whatever calories are taken in on a restrictive diet for more essential functions. Therefore you should not expect to build significant muscle mass even when on a low-fat, low-calorie diet. Your top goal should be to maintain the muscle mass that you have. And a low-fat, low-calorie diet is the best one for accomplishing this.

Since fats contain more than twice the calories of protein and carbs, the body needs only 10 to 20 grams of fat per day for optimum health,[68] and since carbohydrates are the preferred source of energy over fats, this diet is constructed so that a minimal amount of fat is consumed. By drastically reducing fat consumption and replacing it with the same amount of carbohydrates, you can significantly reduce your total caloric intake while still consuming approximately the same amount of food.

The balance between the three major nutrients on such a diet will be approximately 30 percent protein, 65 percent carbs, and 5 percent fat. Since you will be consuming less calories overall, protein must make up a slightly higher percentage of your total caloric intake. This will ensure that you continue to

consume the same number of grams of protein each day as you did when consuming a normal balanced diet.

Since even low-fat foods such as chicken breasts and fish have some fat in them (as do vegetables in the form of oil), you won't have to worry about consuming too little fat, only too much.[69] Even on a low-fat, low-calorie diet you should, however, continue to consume one tablespoonful of vegetable oil each day, just to make sure you consume enough of the essential fatty acids in unsaturated fat necessary for optimal health. You will also continue to consume small amounts of lean beef twice a week as a means of helping to maintain your muscle mass. This is because of the benefits which red meat seems to provide in terms of building muscle mass, as already discussed. Consuming a small portion of lean beef on occasion will not increase your overall saturated fat intake to a significant degree.

Unlike a low carb diet, careful analysis will reveal that a low-fat, low-calorie diet is actually quite well balanced and healthy for the body. After all, it provides just enough fat for optimal health and only slightly more protein and carbs than a normal maintenance diet. Since your calorie consumption will be much lower overall than that of a normal, well-balanced maintenance diet, the extra protein and carbs will not be stored as fat, but will be used for growth and repair, and preventing loss of muscle mass. On a low-fat, low-calorie diet, the protein-sparing benefit of carbohydrates can be fully utilized. The body can burn its fat stores and the extra carbs can be used to help the muscles repair and recuperate after each workout, and at least maintain their mass. Of course, that's assuming the calorie deficit is not too great. Another benefit of this diet has to do with the fact that the less saturated fat you consume, the better it is for the health of your heart and cardiovascular system. So even though a balanced diet (in which you consume 15 percent fat) isn't bad for you, a low-fat diet is even healthier. Of course, on a low-fat diet you also won't have to worry about your energy level, or any of the negative effects associated with not consuming enough sugar, such as those involving the brain, since with this diet you will be consuming plenty of high-energy carbohydrates. In fact, low-fat dieting isn't hard on the body as it puts no undue stress upon it.

Also you will not experience phosphorus jitters on a low-fat diet. There are two reasons for this. First of all, you won't be consuming very much red meat on this diet, and since poultry and fish are much lower in phosphorus than beef and pork, you will be consuming much less phosphorus. Besides this you can still consume one to two glasses of milk a day on a low-fat diet as long as it's non-fat or skimmed milk. You can also eat low-fat cottage cheese and an occasional yogurt as long as you take the number of calories into consideration in relation to your total daily caloric intake. By consuming a small amount of dairy products in the form just described, you will ensure that you consume enough calcium to keep the calcium and phosphorus levels in balance.[70]

Of course, the most important fact about the low-fat, low-calorie diet is that it works. With a little discipline, you can stick to it almost indefinitely. Since you will be consuming a relatively large number of carbohydrates, you won't have to worry about experiencing intense cravings for sugar all the time. You may get a moderately intense craving for a certain food at times, but it won't be anything you can't handle if you put your mind to it. You can usually eliminate it altogether by having a small portion of a sweet, low-calorie fruit such as strawberries. You may also find that you are often hungry when on this diet, even though you will be consuming a substantial amount of food each day. It's especially common to wake up hungry in the middle of the night. Munching on high-fiber foods such as carrot sticks, lettuce and celery stalks which have virtually no calories is an excellent way of curtailing this hunger without harming your diet. Except for severely limiting your intake of high-calorie foods, an occasional craving which can be satisfied, and a slight increase in the hunger you experience each day, which can also be satisfied, this diet has no other negative aspects that I can think of. On the other hand, the effectiveness of this diet for burning body fat is unparalleled.

To most effectively lose fat without burning muscle, you should consume an average of 500 calories a day less than your average daily caloric maintenance requirements. $500 \times 7 = 3,500$ calories. Since 3,500 calories equals one pound of fat, this means that you will burn one pound of fat per week on an optimally effective low-fat diet. If you attempt to burn more than a pound of fat per week by restricting your caloric intake, you run the risk of burning muscle tissue for fuel because of an inability to sufficiently meet the body's

energy needs. Remember that the body burns fats relatively slowly, and if you create such a large daily calorie deficit from restricting your food intake so drastically that the body cannot burn enough fat to replace this deficit, it will be forced to burn muscle tissue to make up for the deficit and provide the body with enough energy to carry on its essential functions.

So keep in mind that severely restricting your calories in an attempt to burn body fat more quickly will not have the desired effect. In fact, if you cut your calories too drastically, the body will read it as an emergency situation and implement a starvation alert. In such a situation, the body will attempt to lower its metabolic rate, burn muscle for fuel, and will actually attempt to increase its level of body fat. This is done as a safety precaution to prevent the body from starving to death for as long as possible. The body responds in this way because it has no way of telling that the only reason you are cutting calories so drastically is to burn body fat more quickly, and that you will eat more food as soon as you reach your desired level of body fat. All it knows is that it isn't getting enough calories to survive for long and, since it doesn't know when or if it's ever going to get more calories, it takes defensive action to preserve its energy. Since this effect is totally undesirable, especially for anyone attempting to lose body fat while maintaining as much shapely muscle mass as possible, do not cut your calories too drastically at any time when following any type of diet, even a well-balanced, low-fat, low-calorie diet. When it comes to the starvation response, it doesn't matter how balanced your diet is, only how great the calorie deficit is. If the calorie deficit is too great compared to your average daily requirements, the starvation response will be invoked. It's as simple as that. Whenever an individual goes on a restricted diet for prolonged period of time, even if the calorie deficit is optimal, his metabolism tends to slow down gradually to adapt to this deficit. Therefore, you may find that you have to decrease your total caloric intake slightly every few weeks in order to continue burning fat at an optimum rate.

To most people, losing one pound of body fat per week from dieting doesn't seem like much. You're just going to have to learn to be patient and realize that the body can burn body fat only so quickly without experiencing undesirable effects such as the burning of mus-

cle.

Since aerobic activity burns almost pure fat for energy, you can increase the rate at which you can safely burn body fat up to 1½ to 2 pounds per week by engaging in a regular cardiovascular fitness program as previously outlined.

When using aerobic activity for the purpose of burning body fat it's okay to perform slightly more than if you were just trying to develop optimal cardiovascular fitness. However, you must remember that it's very easy to slip into a chronically overtrained state when dieting because of the limited amount of calories being consumed. Therefore, if you do decide to slightly increase the amount of aerobic training you are performing while on a diet, you must be very careful not to overtax your energy reserves, and also be aware of any signs which indicate that you may be slipping into an overtrained state.

It might also be a good idea to simultaneously reduce the workload and intensity of your natural bodybuilding workouts slightly during the time you are performing an increased amount of aerobic work. By doing this you will reduce the risk of slipping into an overtrained state and you will still be training hard enough to retain your present level of muscle mass. In fact, whether you increase your aerobic training or not you will probably find that a restrictive diet will negatively affect your recuperative abilities to the extent that a slight cutback in the workload and intensity of your natural bodybuilding workouts is required anyway in order for the muscles to completely recover from one workout to the next.

For those who plan to increase aerobic workouts for the purpose of burning fat, I've found three to four days per week for 30–40 minutes to be optimum for this purpose. Since moderately intense running and cycling burns 600 calories per hour,[71] cycling or running for 40 minutes four times a week translates into 400×4 or 1,600 calories being burned. That translates into almost a half pound of fat being burned each week. Once again, don't get carried away with thought, "If some is good, more must be better."

If you perform any more aerobic activity than this while on a restrictive diet or even under normal circumstances, you will dramatically increase the risk of slipping into an overtrained state. Also, if you perform too much endurance work, your testosterone level tends to drop. This is true whether you're male or female. As a result of this, it becomes virtually impossible to retain all of your muscle mass while dieting. If you're eating normally, you will notice that gains in muscle mass either slow down dramatically or come to a screeching halt. So don't overdo the aerobic work. It's not necessary and is actually detrimental. In addition to everything just mentioned, losing more than two pounds of body fat a week as a result of dieting and aerobic work tends to put undue stress on the body as a whole, and the probability of also burning muscle tissue increases dramatically. It's always safer and healthier, as well as more effective in the long run, to lose fat gradually. Neither building muscle, nor losing fat, nor developing and shaping your physique to your ultimate ideal happens overnight. No matter what anybody tells you, there are no safe and effective shortcuts. If you plan on obtaining any or all of your fitness goals, you are going to have to learn to be patient and persistent.

Now that I've covered how to most effectively use low-fat, low-calorie dieting in combination with aerobic training to reduce body fat levels to optimum levels, I will now present a typical example of a low-fat, low-calorie diet. As was the case with the maintenance diet, this example will be typical of a male natural bodybuilder's daily food intake on a low-fat, low-calorie diet. To make this example representative of a female natural bodybuilder's typical daily food intake on such a diet, the amount of food, and total calories should be reduced by approximately one quarter. It must also be noted that it is generally more difficult for women to lose body fat than men, not only because they have more essential body fat and a lower metabolism than men, but also because they have high levels of the female hormone estrogen, which tends to hinder mobilization of body fat. This doesn't mean it's impossible, just more difficult, for women to reach their desired body fat levels.

Low-fat, low-calorie diet
Daily food intake—example

Breakfast
1. 4 egg whites with none or one yolk, poached, soft-boiled, or fried in non-stick pan without butter or margarine
2. 1–2 slices of whole grain toast
3. 1 piece of low-calorie fruit
4. Coffee, tea, or water

Morning snack
1. Chicken breast or 4 oz. low-fat cottage cheese
2. 1 piece of low-calorie fruit
3. Coffee, tea, diet soda, or water

Lunch
1. 4–8 oz. tuna packed in water with small amount of diet mayonnaise, large chicken breast, or white turkey meat
2. 2 pieces of low-calorie fruit
3. Diet soda, coffee, tea, or water

Afternoon snack
1. Protein shake consisting of 8 ounces non-fat or skimmed milk, or 6 ounces of orange juice 1 tablespoon of 95 percent protein powder and 1 piece of low-calorie fruit for sweetness

Dinner
1. Large chicken breast, turkey (white meat) or fish broiled or baked; 3 oz. of red meat (lean) twice a week (broiled)
2. Tossed salad (vinegar with herbs and artificial sweetener for salad dressing)
3. 1 portion of green vegetables
4. Small portion of pasta or rice, or a small baked potato
5. Water, tea, coffee, or diet soda to drink

Nighttime snack (no later than 2 hrs. before bed)
1. 1 piece of low-calorie fruit or bowl of unsalted and unbuttered popcorn

Low-fat, low-calorie dieting hints
1. As with maintenance and eating to gain weight, you must keep a record of how many calories you consume each day so you don't consume too few or too many.
2. Stay away from butter, cream, margarine, salad oil, chocolate, all nuts, peanut butter, all types of seeds, baked goods with shortening, highly processed bread such as white bread, sour cream, ice cream, and cream and creaming agents for coffee, since all of these items are high in fat content. If in doubt, check your nutrition tables.[72]
3. Always eat low-calorie fruits instead of high-calorie fruits.
4. Eat your baked potatoes plain. Adding butter and sour cream can double their caloric value. Believe it or not, plain baked potatoes actually taste quite good when you get used to them.[73]
5. Since your food intake will be restricted, you should definitely take a high-potency vitamin mineral supplement just to be sure you are getting adequate amounts of all the nutrients your body requires. Supplements will be covered in the next section.
6. Never fry meat or vegetables of any kind. The only food you can fry safely is eggs, but that's only in a non-stick pan without butter or margarine. Always bake or broil your meat.
7. When eating poultry such as chicken or turkey, always eat white meat instead of dark meat since dark meat is significantly higher in fat and calories.
8. If you have a choice, eat fish instead of chicken since fish is significantly lower in fat and calories. Remove the skin of chicken since it is almost pure fat.[75]
9. It's best not to eat anything within a couple of hours of going to bed, unless the food is very low in calories and is a small portion. The reason for this is that you tend to burn calories at a slower rate in the evening as you relax and prepare for sleep. Therefore, if you consume a large quantity of calories at this time chances are you won't be able to burn them all off by the time you go to bed. As a result, there is an increased chance of converting these calories to fat for storage as you sleep. I found this practice to be very effective for encouraging the burning of fat. Of course, denying yourself food for a couple of hours before going to bed will often result in your feeling hungry by the time bedtime rolls around. This situation can easily be rectified by munching on carrot sticks, celery stalks, or a chunk of lettuce before going to bed, since these foods are very low in calories and quite filling.
10. Eat a minimal amount of junk food. It's okay to have a small amount once a week, just so you don't feel that you have to deny yourself every tasty treat. Just don't eat too much and take the extra calories into consideration when planning your food consumption for that particular day.

By following all of the guidelines here, you'll be able to gradually lose as much fat as it takes to reach optimum body fat levels. The key to sticking to this diet is the same as for sticking to your training: You must have a specific reason for dieting and a clear-cut picture in your mind of how you ultimately want to look with optimal body fat levels. Of course you should set long-term and short-term goals. If you do this, and resist the temptation to diet too strictly, you won't find the diet too difficult to handle, and you'll be able to follow it almost indefinitely until you reach your body fat level goal.

Supplements

Most nutrition experts believe that by consuming a well-balanced diet Americans will receive adequate amounts of all the nutrients necessary for optimal health, growth and repair, and optimal body functioning. They, therefore, do not generally recommend the consumption of food supplements.

However, I believe that anyone who engages in natural bodybuilding training should consume vitamin, mineral, and protein supplements.

First of all, natural bodybuilders are not average individuals. They put their bodies under a tremendous amount of physical and mental stress during workouts in an attempt to build muscle tissue. While other athletes do train very hard, bodybuilders are the only group of athletes who train specifically to effect drastic changes upon their physiques. In order for the body to carry out these changes, and add additional muscle tissue as quickly as possible, an optimal amount of all nutrients must be present. Because of the stress of training and the extra building material required for growth of additional muscle tissue, the optional amount of nutrients is significantly higher than that required by both average individuals and other athletes.

Taking vitamin and mineral as well as protein supplements ensures that you as a natural bodybuilder get optimal amounts of all the nutrients you need to achieve your natural bodybuilding goals as quickly as possible.

The importance of taking food supplements becomes even more apparent when you consider the fact that very few people, including bodybuilders, consume a well-balanced diet consistently. Our fast-paced society forces many people to grab what they can and eat on the run. It's very difficult to find

the time to prepare optimally balanced meals on a consistent basis. While the average person can often get away with consuming a less than perfectly balanced diet for extended periods of time, anyone who is attempting to build muscle mass most definitely cannot. Without compensating in some way by taking food supplements, you will not be able to offset any dietary inconsistencies on a daily basis. This does not mean that food supplements should replace a well-balanced diet. It simply means that you should eat as nutritionally balanced a diet as you possibly can and make up any nutritional deficiencies in that diet by subsidizing it with food supplements. It's like having an insurance policy just to be sure you've covered your nutritional requirements.

Finally, I must point out that even if you somehow managed to consume what on paper looks to be an optimally balanced diet, it's very unlikely that you would actually be receiving anywhere near the nutrient value which your supposed perfectly balanced diet is purported to contain. Fresh fruits and vegetables, which are the best sources of almost all the vitamins and minerals essential for optimum functioning, tend to lose a lot of their nutritional value during shipping and storage. Certain vegetables begin losing their vitamin and mineral content as soon as they are picked. The longer they sit in the store, the more nutrients they lose.

Then, of course, there's cooking. As already mentioned, the only way to cook vegetables without causing them to lose a significant amount of vitamins and minerals is to steam them. Even with steaming, there still tends to be some loss of nutrient content.

Cooking has an even greater detrimental effect on protein itself. It's a fact that cooking protein-rich food decreases its protein availability by 40 to 80 percent. An article in *Nutrition Review* reported that up to half of the essential amino acids lysine, arginine, tryptophan, and histidine are destroyed by cooking.[75] This results in protein sources such as beef and eggs that have an excellent balance of essential amino acids and a high P.E.R. in an uncooked state sustaining a marked decrease in that P.E.R. after being cooked. Generally, the longer you cook protein, the larger the amount of essential amino acids that are destroyed, the lower the P.E.R. becomes, and the less value that protein has for normal growth and repair and muscle growth.

This doesn't mean that you should

eat your meat and eggs raw. Some meats such as fish and pork simply have to be cooked because of the risk of infection from parasites. If you don't cook pork, you can get trichinosis, and raw fish may contain worms.[76]

Also, eggs should not be eaten raw for two reasons. First of all, raw eggs are hard to digest, and secondly, eating raw eggs interferes with the assimilation of biotin which is a B vitamin.[77] The best way to cook eggs is to poach or soft boil them. If you only like eggs scrambled or sunny-side up you have the option of frying them, but keep in mind that heating eggs excessively also makes them difficult for the body to digest.[78]

As far as milk and milk products are concerned, raw milk, yogurt, and cheese are better for you than their pasteurized versions because they contain all the enzymes necessary to aid digestion. Pasteurization kills most of these enzymes[79] and, because it is a process involving heat, it also tends to destroy a certain percentage of the four essential amino acids previously mentioned. However, keep in mind that milk is pasteurized for health reasons, and it is quite possible for harmful micro-organisms to grow in raw milk. Raw milk has a significantly shorter shelf life than pasteurized milk and if it isn't stored correctly or used quickly, the potential for harmful micro-organism growth is even greater.

As far as beef is concerned—for example, steak and hamburgers—you should cook them as rare as possible. Well-done beef has a much lower P.E.R. than beef which is rare or medium rare, so refrain from cooking your beef until it looks like a burnt cinder.

Nuts, seeds, fruits, and vegetables are sources of raw protein. However, as previously discussed, they have very low P.E.R.'s compared to meat, eggs, and dairy products, and have to be eaten in tremendous quantities and complicated combinations in order to supply a significant amount of reasonable quality protein. Therefore, I don't consider these foods to be practical sources of protein.

So how can you be assured of consuming adequate amounts of high-quality protein? Well, besides cooking your eggs lightly, and cooking your beef as rare as possible, you should consume a high-quality powdered protein supplement once or twice a day, in the form of a protein shake, as previously described. There are a wide variety of protein powder supplements on the market. Some are of great value to natural bodybuilders and others aren't.

For a protein supplement to be considered of optimum value it must have the following two characteristics.

First, the eight essential amino acids must be present in optimally balanced amounts, which means that the P.E.R. must be high.[80] Milk and egg protein powders generally have the highest P.E.R.

Secondly, the supplement must contain a very high percentage of protein in relation to all other elements present. These other elements include the amount of carbohydrates and fat, which should be present in very low amounts. The best milk and egg protein supplements are 90 to 95 percent protein, contain only a few grams of carbohydrates, and little if any fat.[81] These high-quality protein supplements are more expensive than lower quality ones, but they are worth the extra money. There's no point in purchasing a low-quality protein which the body can't make maximum use of.[82]

The only time you should purchase a protein powder which has a lower percentage of protein and a large amount of carbohydrates and fat is if you are too skinny and have extreme difficulty gaining weight, both fat and muscle. Special weight-gain protein powders have been designed in just this way for individuals with weight-gaining problems. Combined with ice cream, milk, and high-calorie fruits such as bananas in shake form, these protein powders provide a concentrated source of calories. Even though such protein powders are designed so they have a lower percentage of protein than those which should be consumed by individuals who don't have trouble gaining weight, there's no excuse for the amount of protein which is contained in these supplements having a low P.E.R. The amino acid balance and P.E.R. must still be optimally high.

Besides having a high P.E.R. and a high percentage of protein, the protein powder you use should also taste good and be easy to mix.[83] Although these are not essential characteristics, consuming a horrible-tasting protein which doesn't dissolve well and floats in clumps on your shake is not at all enjoyable. Unfortunately, most protein powders do not mix well and taste either bad or awful.

One of the few protein powder supplements which meets the three criteria above in outstanding fashion is Multipower Formula 90. This protein has a biological value of 97 out of a possible 100. This means that the essential amino acids contained in the product are so perfectly balanced that 97 out of every 100 grams is completely utilized by the body. This translates into a P.E.R. of over 3.9 out of a possible 4.0 which is incredibly high. In terms of percentages, this is a 90 percent protein with only a trace of carbs and virtually no fat, making it an extremely high-quality protein. Very few, if any other, milk and egg protein supplements can boast such numbers. In addition, this protein supplement has a reputation in the bodybuilding community for mixing easily and being one of the best tasting of all protein powders. For obvious reasons, this protein supplement has come to be considered among the best by knowledgeable members of the fitness and bodybuilding communities. Multipower also makes a high-quality weight gain protein supplement, 70 percent protein and vegetable protein for vegetarians. They also market a number of other high-quality supplements for health-minded individuals and natural bodybuilders alike. More information on these supplements can be obtained from writing to the address listed at the end of this book.

Vitamin and mineral supplements

As I've already discussed, it's virtually impossible for anyone engaged in natural bodybuilding training to obtain optimum amounts of all necessary nutrients from food sources. Therefore, I recommend that you take a complete multivitamin mineral supplement on a daily basis. Women should also consume 15–30 mg of additional iron daily. You can get 15-mg. iron tablets separately. As with protein supplements, there are virtually dozens of different vitamin and mineral supplements on the market. Most multivitamin mineral supplements are very similar in nature. Some have higher potencies of certain vitamins and minerals than others. The only way to tell if one supplement is superior to another is to compare the price of both relative to the vitamin and mineral content of each.[84] Recently multipacks have become very popular. Each multipack contains a number of individual vitamin pills. Anywhere between one and three packs can be consumed on a daily basis, according to how hard you're training, as a means of getting a well-balanced supply of vitamins and minerals. If you don't like multipacks you can simply consume one or more multivitamin mineral tablets which contain a good balance of all these nutrients. Virtually all these supplements have directions on the package recommending the optimum number of tablets or packs to consume on a daily basis.

There are a few things you should be aware of when purchasing vitamin-mineral supplements. First of all, because B-complex vitamins are relatively expensive, their content tends to vary widely from vitamin to vitamin.[85] Look for those supplements which contain the highest concentrations of B-complex vitamins per tablet or per pack.

Besides this, all vitamin-mineral combination tablets must be chelated and all multimineral tablets in the vitamin packs must also be chelated. Chelation is a process by which protein molecules are chemically bonded to inorganic minerals, resulting in their being much more easily and efficiently assimilated by the human body than unchelated minerals.[86]

For optimum results, all vitamin and mineral supplements should be consumed with meals. These supplements are more efficiently assimilated and utilized by the body when consumed with foods.[87]

Also, vitamin and mineral supplements which are time released are more easily assimilated and effectively utilized by the body than those that aren't.

Virtually all multivitamin mineral supplements have two major disadvantages which severely limit the potential benefits they can provide. The human body can absorb only 5 to 10 percent of most supplemental forms of vitamins and minerals. That means if, for example, you consume 10,000 I.U. of vitamin A in supplement form, you will, in the case of virtually all vitamin supplements, be able to absorb only 500–1000 I.U.

Besides this, many vitamins and minerals work against one another. For example, iron tends to rob your vitamin E stores, and vitamin C tends to limit the usefulness of vitamin B-12. Many other vitamins and minerals work against each other, too. You could try purchasing each vitamin and mineral separately, but you have to practically be a scientist to decipher at exactly what time and in which combinations you should take your daily vitamins and minerals for optimum results. Besides this, buying each vitamin and mineral separately ends up costing a lot more than buying them combined in one tablet or in a pack. Fortunately, there is a viable alternative which effectively compensates for the two disadvantages just discussed.

This alternative is Super-Spectrum, an amazing vitamin-mineral supplement developed by Dr. Anthony Pescetti. This supplement provides maximum vitamin and mineral absorption, 100 percent as opposed to the 5 to 10 percent of virtually all other vitamins.

This supplement is cold-processed over a 40-day period and the minerals are chelated. Since some vitamins are heat-labile, which means they can be destroyed by heat, the process used to manufacture virtually all vitamin and mineral supplements results in certain amounts of these heat-sensitive vitamins being destroyed. The cold processing used in producing Super-Spectrum prevents the structure of the molecules of these heat-sensitive vitamins from being destroyed.

Besides this, each Super-Spectrum tablet is so precisely time-released over a 12-hour period that the vitamins and minerals all work together synergistically. They are released at the precise time, and in the precise combinations, necessary to provide optimum utilization of each one of them. Also, while Super-Spectrum, according to its label, contains a lesser amount of vitamins and minerals than most other supplements, the fact that it is 100 percent absorbed actually results in an equal amount of Super-Spectrum being 10 to 20 times more potent than these other supplements. As a result, Super-Spectrum actually is much more potent than these other supplements. For these reasons, Super-Spectrum has come to be considered by biochemists and members of the bodybuilding community alike as the ultimate vitamin-mineral supplement.

21

STAYING NATURAL MY STORY

I began bodybuilding in the spring of 1976. It began when I decided to make a commitment to get into decent physical shape, and I had decided to go out for spring track.

Before this, I was your typical 98-pound weakling. Last to be picked for any team, a miserable and ridiculed loner. My only consolation was that I was an excellent student.

When I began track, I noticed that my arms felt like dead weight every time I rounded the last turn of a race. My track coach recommended that I do some light upper body weight work. Luckily for me, my father had been into weightlifting and powerlifting for sometime. He had set up a small gym in the garage. He gave me a light routine and suggested that I look through his *Strength & Health* magazines for training tips. It was then that I saw my first pictures of bodybuilders. Immediately, something clicked. I said to myself, "Hey, I'd really like to look like that." After reading several articles on training and seeing some more pictures of the top bodybuilders, I was hooked.

I bought all the magazines I could, and eventually set up what I thought was a good training schedule. I did all barbell exercises one day and all dumbell exercises the next, three sets of ten reps on each exercises. Needless to say, I was overtraining, although not too badly since I was always doing light workouts.

When I began training in May, I was 5-foot-5, 118 pounds; by September, I was 5-6, 140 pounds. Despite running four to five miles a day in preparation for cross country, I gained twenty-two pounds of muscle.

During the next year I concentrated on my studies and my training. I experimented with many different exercises and training programs, and I finally developed a good basic training routine consisting of almost all heavy basic exercises such as the bench press, squats, and bent-over rows. I trained six days a week, working each body part three times a week. Again despite the fact I was overtraining, I was able to make great gains. By fall of 1977, I was 5-6½ and 157 pounds.

The wrestling coach talked me into going out for the team. I felt that I might

as well use my newfound muscle and strength for something other than show, and wrestling seemed the perfect sport. I also felt the experience would help me grow as a person and that it would increase my chances of getting into a good college.

I wrestled at the 165-pound weight class because we did not have enough big guys. This, combined with a lack of killer instinct and a lack of experience, resulted in an unimpressive 2-7 record. Besides, practicing until 6 P.M., then trying to do productive bodybuilding workouts at night was slowly exhausting me. My bodybuilding progress slowed drastically. I was sick three times during the season, then during the last match I sprained my wrist so badly that I lost an easy win, but, more importantly, was unable to train my upper body for a week.

This occurred mid-February 1978. Soon afterwards, I heard about the teenage Mr. Westchester contest which was slated for Saturday, March 11. I had

vowed never to compete, but now I was curious about how I would stack up against other bodybuilders, so I decided to enter, if my wrist healed. It did and I managed to gain back the upper body mass I had lost.

I was nervous and did not know what I was doing. I analyzed pictures of bodybuilders in the magazines and tried to imitate the poses. It was not working out and I knew I needed help. Fortunately, Pierre Asselin, a friend of my father's, happened to be into bodybuilding and had attended a number of contests. We combined our limited knowledge and came up with a respectable routine.

The day of the contest I was a wreck, especially when I was called out to do my individual posing routine. Once I got going, the nervousness left and I began enjoying myself. It felt good being the center of attention and hearing the audience clapping in appreciation during my routine. I did not win the contest, but I finished a respectable fifth. A couple of teenagers were really massive and I just was not in their league. I vowed that next year this title would be mine. The only thing that bothered me about the contest was they only gave trophies for the first four places. Usually it is the first three or the first five. I had never won a trophy in my life and I wanted one badly.

The day after the contest I could barely move, I was totally exhausted, both physically and mentally. It took me a week to get my energy level back to normal and I did not resume training for five days.

I trained as hard and as heavy as possible all spring and summer and continued to make good gains. Then in September, I ripped a muscle in the right lower lumbar region while doing shoulder shrugs. It did not improve as fast as I thought it would and I made the mistake of resuming my training prematurely and attempting to train around it. Because of this, it never had a chance to heal and my condition slowly deteriorated in the months ahead, as I pulled more and more muscles and refused to quit training.

In November, I entered the open Mr. New York City in order to gain more competive experience. I placed 10th out of 12 in my height class, and since, at the age of 18, I was the youngest competitor, I was happy with my placing. It was at this contest that I first met Bob Gruskin, a national physique judge, physique photographer, and contributing editor for many of the muscle magazines. This was an extremely important meeting for me. Bob became the individual primarily responsible for successfully guiding my bodybuilding career and enabling me to achieve the high level of competitive success I have attained.

The day after the open Mr. New York, I was flat on my back in a lot of pain. The posing had irritated my back injury. It was a week before I could train again and I had to work my way back to heavy training by working out on my high school's Universal.

In the following months, I began preparing for the upcoming teenage Mr. Westchester slated for February. I dieted to drop my weight from 169 pounds to 158 pounds. My back still hurt, but I wanted to win the title, so ignored my pain. I would soon pay for my foolishness.

With Bob Gruskin's help, my contest preparations were going well. He was an expert in posing technique and taught me how to best present myself. On his suggestion, I entered the junior Mr. Metropolitan championships one week before the Westchester, in order to gain further contest experience. It was a tough contest and I was happy to place eighth out of 24.

The Friday before the Mr. Westchester, Bob came up and helped me with the final preparations. This included additional posing tips and a couple of extra coats of evenly applied Sudden Tan. On Saturday, February 17, 1978, I was in fantastic condition. At 5-7, 157 pounds, I was muscular, perfectly symmetrical and deeply tanned. This condition, combined with an almost flawless execution of my poses, resulting in my winning the teenage Mr. Westchester over a couple of monsters, and placing a close third in the novice. I was ecstatic.

My back continued to get worse. Finally, I quit training in March and went to a chiropractor for help. Unfortunately, this guy did not know what he was doing and his treatment put more pressure on my back. The pain became unbearable and I was admitted to the hospital in a state of near shock. The tests showed I had a herniated disc in the lumbar region of my spine. The doctors expected me to be able to get around relatively pain free within a couple of months, but my bodybuilding

career looked over. I spent the next month in traction with varying amounts of pain.

I had always been an agnostic, not really knowing whether God existed, and not really caring. I had always considered going to church and reading from the Bible a bore. So when my uncle sent me a book called *Prison to Praise* about a messed up guy who found Christ, I threw it in the cabinet. My mother told me it would mean a lot to my uncle if I read it, so I reluctantly agreed. As I read, it occurred to me that God could work today as he did 2,000 years ago and that he could heal my back. In my hospital room, I quietly accepted Jesus as my personal Lord and Savior and put my life in his hands.

I was discharged on April 29, 1979, in considerable pain. My uncle had invited me to a healing service to be held by Father Ralph Diorio in Worcester, Massachusetts, on May 3 and that morning we left for the service.

What I saw that night blew my mind. As people were called forth and were healed, I lay on my pew as pain wracked my body. Near the end of the service, Father Diorio told my uncle to bring me up front. My uncle had to help me up the aisle to the altar as I was still in severe pain. Father Diorio placed one hand on my forehead and one on my lower back and straightened me up. The pressure on my disc was excruciating. He sat me down on a chair and had me extend my legs in front of me. He

placed his hands on my shoulders and began to pray. A couple of minutes later he told me to stand up. Then he told me to touch my toes. I bent over and was able to touch my toes without pain for the first time in eight months. He told me to lift the chair over my head and I did this without any pain, and I knew that my disc had been healed. By healing my back, God had given me back the one thing that meant the most to me—bodybuilding—and from that day on, I dedicated my bodybuilding to the Lord.

Several days later, testing revealed no disc abnormalities and almost 100 percent restoration of normal nerve function. The doctors were at a loss for an explanation.

I resumed training a couple of weeks later. Carefully I reeducated my back muscles. By the beginning of September my upper body was better than ever, and by the beginning of October, my legs were in hot pursuit.

At this time Bob suggested I enter the teenage Mr. Appalachia on October 14. Everything fell into place and I entered the contest in better shape than I was for the Mr. Westchester. I was the best teenager in the short class, but the judges ripped me off and awarded me second place. The winner called me a few weeks later to say I deserved to win.

Seven weeks later I competed against the same bodybuilder in the teenage Super Mr. Gemini and Mr. Gemini contests held in Baltimore. When he stripped down to his posong trunks for prejudging, I could not believe the dramatic improvement he had made in his physique. He had put on 13 pounds of solid muscle since the Appalachia. We were now dead even in development. The judges could not make up their minds, so they awarded him the teenage Super Mr. Gemini, and me the Mr. Gemini, a novice level contest.

After the contest, I got to talking with this bodybuilder. He told me he had been taking decadurabolin, an anabolic steriod, for the last six weeks, and he attributed most of his improvement to the drug, not his training. Although I had heard of steriods from time to time in the past, this was the first time that I had actually met someone who admitted taking them, and had seen firsthand the benefits they provide. I suddenly realized how come so many other teenagers I had competed against were abnormally huge for their age. I thought I had been training wrong, now I knew better.

Up to this point I had been able to compete successfully against steroid users at the local level—should I try steroids and get huge quick? After careful deliberation, I chose to stay natural. I was doing okay as a natural; besides, the side effects of steroids were a health risk—cancer, and there was my commitment to God. For these reasons, I decided to become the best teen bodybuilder on the East Coast without using drugs. I continued to train and to grow. I entered the teenage Midwest Open in Chicago and took fifth place, instead of the second I deserved. Then three more regional contests where I continued to get ripped off. I was in the best shape ever and kept losing because of bad judging. I entered a couple of more contests and did okay. Then on June 21, I entered the teen Atlantic States in great shape. I deserved fourth place, but was awarded sixth. This was the first time in 14 contests that I did not get a trophy.

All the contests, low carb diets and dehydration had worn me out. My college studies in nursing were suffering. I was weak and unable to concentrate. My training was going badly. I landed in the hospital with back spasms. Nothing was working out. I knew that if things did not work out soon, I would walk away from competitive bodybuilding forever. I decided to give it one more shot and began to train slowly. It took a month before my back was ready. My progress continued to be discouraging and once again I thought about steroids.

Bob and I talked and decided that I would enter the teenage Eastern America slated for November 22, 1980. I decided that if I did not win my height class, I would quit or use steroids.

The day of the contest arrived, and I entered in excellent shape. I won my class by an unjustifiably close 4-3 decision, then lost the overall to a big drug monster. Still I was ecstatic, I had just won my class in the most prestigious teenage competition in the eastern half of the country. The following week I won the teenage Super Mr. Gemini and almost beat the reigning Mr. Maryland in the overall.

In December, I won my first teenage overall title, the teenage North Atlantic Cup. By May of 1981, I had won ten straight and established myself as the best middleweight teenager in both Canada and the U.S.A. by winning the Teenage Canadian American Bodybuilding Championship.

Then on May 31, 1981, I turned twenty. I knew it would be at least a

year before I could compete and that I needed to put on at least ten pounds of solid muscle before I could consistently win open-level steroid contests.

During September I resumed my nursing training. As the school year progressed, I began training less and less. My lower back was aggravated by moving patients and this, combined with an increasing lack of motivation, assisted in my discontinuing my leg training in October. My progress kept slowing down and then in April 1982 I quit training altogether. Bodybuilding no longer gave me the satisfaction it once did. I took the next twelve days off, which felt great and did some soul searching. I decided to resume light training in order to keep in shape. Unfortunately, I developed a severe case of asthma during the workout and eventually had to go to the hospital. I had been an asthmatic since I was three, but had no problems the last three years. I spent five days in the hospital after having three more severe attacks and there I decided to resume my training. Somehow the training helped me physically and mentally.

I soon graduated from my nursing program and took the nursing boards, which I passed. I was now a registered nurse.

I began working seriously again. Soon after I regained almost all of my previous muscle mass, I reached a plateau I could not seem to break. By July I

was fed up and began to investigate steroids seriously. I prayed to God for something to come up that would prevent me from taking the drugs. A few days later, almost as an answer to my prayer, it was announced that the Natural for Life American Apollo Bodybuilding Championships would be held on February 5, 1983. This would be the first Natural for Life contest ever held. I immediately decided to stay natural and enter it.

A few days later a Natural Mr. America contest was announced for October of 1982, but I decided to pass this year and see how I did in February. Then in August, I heard the Natural for Life contest had been canceled. It was going to be hard, but I was going to try for the natural Mr. America.

I drove up to Utica with a friend on Friday, October 8, 1982. In the morning, all the contestants took lie-detector tests to verify that they had not used any muscle growth drugs. I, of course, passed. The next morning, I woke up in excellent condition at 170 pounds. I was more massive than ever before, and very cut. When I saw the lineup of the 19 competitors, I knew I was in for one of the toughest battles of my bodybuilding career. I thought I should place fourth or fifth, but when they did not call me out for body part comparisons, I was concerned that I had not placed in the top five. When they listed the top seven in each class, I found that I had made it through the first cut. When I was announced fourth in my class, I was ecstatic. I was now one of the top twelve natural bodybuilders in the country. Was I motivated to stay natural!

At the Natural Mr. America, I met the promoter who was supposed to run the Natural American Apollo. He told me it was still on for February 5, 1983. This was Natural for Life, not for one year. I knew I had an excellent chance of winning it.

Between contests, my asthma was acting up, but I was not going to let it stop me. I kept on dieting and by February 3, I was incredibly muscular. However, I also looked flat, so Bob told me to carb up. When I woke up on February 5, I was full, vascular and even more shredded. I felt I was in the best shape of my bodybuilding career.

As it turned out, I was. I was so far ahead of the rest of the competitors that I was not even called out for comparison posing during prejudging. That night I gave the best posing exhibition of my life and had the audience on its feet. I was awarded the title of Natural for Life American Apollo by unanimous decision. By winning this title, the first Natural for Life contest, I had made natural bodybuilding history.

I resumed training hard and in December 1983 I entered and won the Natural for Life East Coast by unanimous decision. The following January, I decided to enter the W.P.C. Intermediate (Jr.) U.S.A. slated for April 14, 1984, to see how I'd stack up against steroid users at the national level. By the day of the contest I was an unbelievably lean and incredibly muscular 154 lbs., the lightest I had ever competed at. Amazingly, I was able to pull a major upset and win the lightweight class championship. It was the happiest and most satisfying day of my natural bodybuilding career. I had proved once and for all that a natural bodybuilder could win at the national level against steroid users. The following day I won my weight class and the overall 1984 Northern States championships, a big regional, now natural, contest. Finally, the following week I completed my two-year domination of the Natural for Life contest circuit by winning the 1984 Natural New York State. The major reason I entered this contest was to prove I was natural at the time I won the W.P.C. Jr. U.S.A. the week before. This was my last contest. I have not competed since and have no plans to in the near future. I have accomplished all of my bodybuilding goals and more. In total I have won 22 bodybuilding championships. Nineteen of these were won in nonnatural competition against steroid users, most of them at the regional level or above. In recognition of my accomplishments, I was voted Natural Bodybuilder of the Year for 1983–1984. A couple of months after winning the Jr. U.S.A. I was also recognized by top bodybuilding officials as being the most competitively successful natural bodybuilder of the last decade, the most drug-filled decade the sport of bodybuilding has ever seen. I've proved that a natural bodybuilder can accomplish incredible things in terms of both muscular development and competitive success if he or she so desires, and I hope my story and accomplishments inspire each one of you reading this book to strive for and accomplish all your goals of physical development.

Although I am no longer competing, I am training for the purpose of staying healthy and fit while simultaneously maintaining a lean, shapely, and moderately muscular physique.

I'm keeping busy spreading the natural bodybuilding philosophy and training methods to individuals and groups through lectures, seminars, high school assemblies, and personalized training instruction. I want to help as many people as possible accomplish whatever goals of physical fitness and physical development they so desire and believe with all my heart that the information presented in this book and by me personally will enable them to do so.

I want you all to know that I have drawn from seven years of research, experience, and plain hard training to try to make this book the most complete and accurate training guide available on bodybuilding naturally, for the ultimate in health, fitness, and physical development. Everything I have written is straightforward and totally honest. I have not withheld any information that could possibly be of value to you during the beginner and intermediate levels of natural bodybuilding training. And a tremendous amount of the information will help you train and progress at the advanced level. Unfortunately, because of the depth with which I covered beginning and intermediate natural training, as well as how to develop what I consider to be the ultimate fitness life style with natural bodybuilding, I simply did not have room in this book to cover advanced natural bodybuilding training and nutrition principles or preparing for competition naturally.

There is no question in my mind that if you faithfully follow the guidelines presented in this book, you will make the most rapid possible progress within the limits of your genetic potential. Of course, for you to follow what I have written will require that you be willing to put a certain amount of trust in me. I have gone to great lengths to back up everything I have written about training, diet, etc., with logical reasons and to further validate what I have written with scientific facts wherever possible. I truly believe that if an individual is willing and able to back up his views with flawless logic and scientific fact, that he is worth listening to. I have, therefore, taken this approach to make my views on natural bodybuilding as credible as possible.

Finally, I have tried to make it clear that to derive the many benefits a natural bodybuilding life style can provide, you will have to be motivated, patient, persistent and willing to work hard. Anyone who tells you that there is an easy way to build and reshape your physique, or lose body fat, is lying to your face. Nothing worthwhile in life comes easy. This is especially true when it comes to improving your physical appearance. So when it comes to building and reshaping your physique, do it logically, do it scientifically, do it patiently, and most importantly, do it naturally, according to the guidelines set forth in this book.

22 Bodybuilding Titles and 1 Bodybuilding Award:

1. 1979 - Teenage Mr. Westchester, 1st Overall
2. 1979 - Mr. Gemini, 1st Overall
3. 1980 - Teenage Mr. Hercules, 1st Short Class
4. 1980 - Teenage All East Coast, 1st Short Class
5. 1980 - Teenage Eastern America, 1st Short Class
6. 1980 - Teenage Super Mr. Gemini, 1st Overall
7. 1981 - Teenage North Atlantic Cup, 1st Overall
8. 1981 Teenage Mr. Suburban, 1st Short Class, 1st Overall
9. 1981 - Teenage Mr. Supercolossus, 1st Overall
10. 1981 - Mr. Supercolossus, 1st Overall
11. 1981 - Teenage Atlantic Coast, 1st Overall
12. 1981 - Teenage Keystone State, 1st Short Class, 1st Overall
13. 1981 - Teenage Mr. Eastern Seaboard, 1st Overall
14. 1981 - Mr. Eastern Seaboard, 1st Overall
15. 1981 - Teenage Canadian American Bodybuilding Championships, 1st Middleweight Class, Most Muscular
16. 1981 - Teenage All Atlantic Seaboard, 1st Short Class, 1st Overall
17. 1983 - Natural American Apollo, 1st Overall
18. 1983 - Mr. Suburban, 1st Lightweight Class, 1st Overall
19. 1983 - Natural Mr. East Coast, 1st Overall
20. 1984 - N.P.C. Intermediate (Jr.) U.S.A., 1st Lightweight Class
21. 1984 - Mr. Northern States, 1st Middleweight Class, 1st Overall
22. 1984 - Natural Mr. New York State, 1st Overall

Also voted N.P.O. Outstanding Natural Bodybuilder of 1983

How to order products discussed in book

1. For more details including price and ordering information, on Super-Spectrum multivitamins, multi-power protein powders and other supplements, top-quality leather lifting belts, knee wraps, and triple-stitched leather lifting gloves, write to:

   R.T.O Enterprises
   P.O. Box 33
   Taylor, PA 18517

2. For more details including price and ordering information for Meeko Power Grips, write to:

   Power Grips
   Department A
   P.O. Box 1
   Catasauqua, PA 18032

3. The following companies produce an exceptional line of home gym equipment at affordable prices. For more information including prices, contact:

   Jubinville Health Equipment
   Dept. N, P.O. Box 622
   Holyoke, MA 01040

   Pro Gym Systems
   Dept. P
   2250 Plainfield Ave. North
   Piscataway, NJ 08854

   J.K. Gym Equipment
   Dept.—Home Gym
   6 Franklin Ave.
   Mt. Vernon, NY 10550

NOTES

1. Introduction

1. Sprague, Ken, and Bill Reynolds. *The Gold's Gym Book of Bodybuilding.* Chicago: Contemporary Books, 1983, p.6.
2. *ibid.,* p.6.
3. *ibid.,* p.4.
4. *ibid.,* p.3.
5. Weider, Joe. *Bodybuilding, The Weider Approach.* Chicago: Contemporary Books, 1981, p.21.
6. *ibid.,* p.22.
7. Sprague, *loc. cit.,* p.3.
8. Weider, *op. cit.,* p.24.

2. Natural Bodybuilding

1. Massey, Freeman, Manson, and Wessel. *The Kinesiology of Weightlifting.* Iowa: Wm. C. Brown Co., 1973, pp.42–44.
2. *ibid.,* p.53.
3. *ibid.,* pp.42–44.
4. *ibid.*
5. Smillie, Tom. "Potential, What Is It? Do You Have It?" *Muscle Training Illustrated* (Dec. 1982).

3. Drugs in Bodybuilding

1. Wright, James E. "Steroids, Shortcut to Disaster." *Muscle,* vol. 40, no.9 (October 1979):51.
2. Todd, Terry. "The Steroid Predicament." *Sports Illustrated,* vol. 59, no.5 (August 1983):69.
3. Morey, Stanley W., and Ken Passariello. *Steroids.* U.S.A.: Morey & Passariello, 1982, p.10.
4. Wright, James E. "Steroids, Shortcut to Disaster." *Muscle,* vol. 40, no.9 (October 1979): 212.
5. *ibid.,* p.121.
6. Morey and Passariello, *loc. cit.,* p.10.
7. Rodman, Morton J., and Dorothy H. Smith. *Pharmacology & Drug Therapy in Nursing.* Philadelphia: J.B. Lippincott Co., 1968, pp.413–417.
8. *ibid.,* p.417.
9. Wright, *loc. cit.,* p.121.
10. Todd, *op. cit.,* p.66.
11. *ibid.*
12. *ibid.,* p.64.
13. *ibid.*
14. Morey and Passariello, *loc. cit.,* p.10.
15. Todd, *loc. cit.,* p.66.
16. Wright, James E. "If You Must Use Steroids." *Muscle & Fitness,* vol. 42 (January 1981):52.
17. MacDougal, Duncan. "Drug Symptom—Anabolic Steroids." *The Physician & Sports Medicine,* vol. 11, no.9 (September 1983):97.
18. Todd, *op. cit.,* p.70.
19. *ibid.,* p.71.
20. *ibid.*
21. *ibid.*
22. *ibid.*
23. *ibid.,* pp.71–72.
24. *ibid.,* p.71.
25. American College of Sports Medicine, Position Statement on "The Use and Abuse of Anabolic Androgenic Steroids in Sports," p.1.
26. Wright, *op. cit.,* p.167.
27. *ibid.,* p.1.
28. *Physician's Desk Reference,* 27th edition, "Dianabol," p.664.
29. *ibid.*
30. *ibid.*
31. *ibid.*
32. *ibid.*
33. *ibid.*
34. *ibid.*
35. *ibid.*
36. MacDougal, *op. cit.,* p.99.
37. *ibid.*
38. *Physicians Desk Reference, loc. cit.,* p.664.
39. MacDougal, *op. cit.,* p.98.
40. Todd, *op. cit.,* p.70.
41. MacDougal, *op. cit.,* p.98.
42. Goldman, Bob. "Liver Death." *Muscle,* vol. 47 (February 1980): 105.
43. American College of Sports Medicine, Position Statement on "The Use and Abuse of Anabolic Androgenic Steroids in Sports," p.2.
44. Goldman, *loc. cit.,* p.158.
45. *ibid.,* p.158.
46. American College of Sports Medicine, *loc. cit.,* p.2.
47. *Physicians Desk Reference, loc. cit.,* p.664.
48. Brunner, Lillian, and Doria Suddarth. *Textbook of Medical Surgical Nursing.* Philadelphia: J.B. Lippincott Co., 1980, p.225.
49. Ashpaugh, Bill. *Powerlift.* Nashville: Impact Books, 1981, pp.104–105.
50. *ibid.,* p.137.
51. *ibid.,* p.139.
52. *ibid.,* p.142.
53. *ibid.,* back cover.
54. *ibid.,* p.85.
55. Kerr, Robert. "S.T.H.—Tomorrow's Anabolic Drug for Today." *Muscle Digest,* vol. VII (March 1983):16.
56. *ibid.,* p.16.
57. *ibid.,* p.52.
58. *ibid.*
59. Kerr, Robert. "S.T.H., The Growth Hormone." *Flex,* vol.1, no.3 (June 1983):30.
60. Kerr, *loc. cit.,* p.16.
61. Wright, James E. "The G.H. Factor," *Muscle & Fitness,* vol.44 (January 1983):193.
62. *ibid.,* p.193.
63. *ibid.,* p.194.
64. *ibid.*
65. *ibid.*
66. Kerr, *loc. cit., Flex,* p.30.
67. Kerr, *loc. cit., Muscle Digest,* p.52.
68. *ibid.,* p.52.
69. Kennedy, Robert. Editorial: "When Will It End?" *Muscle,* no. 39 (December 1983):6.
70. Wright, *op. cit.,* p.195.
71. Bergerson, Betty S., and Andres Goth. *Pharmacology in Nursing.* Missouri: Mosby Co., 1979, p.568.
72. Wright, *loc. cit.,* p.195.
73. Mentzer, Mike. "5th Caveat Emptor." *Flex,* vol. 1, no.3 (June 1983):30.
74. Wright, *loc. cit.,* p.195.
75. Mentzer, *loc. cit.,* p.30.

76. *ibid.*, p.30.
77. Wilbourn, Claudia. "Why Bodybuilders Are Dying to Win." *Muscle & Fitness*, vol.44 (March 1983):193.
78. Dobbins, Bill. "Thyroid, Nothing to Fool With." *Muscle & Fitness*, vol.42 (August 1981):62.
79. Wilbourn, *loc. cit.*, p.193.
80. Dobbins, *loc. cit.*, p.62.
81. Sprague, *op. cit.*, p.223.
82. *ibid.*
83. *ibid.*
84. Dobbins, *op. cit.*, p.120.
85. Bergerson, *op. cit.*, p.576.
86. *ibid.*, p.576.
87. Sprague, *loc. cit.*, p.223.
88. Bergerson, *op. cit.*, p.333.
89. Taylor, W.W. "Amphetamines: Useful Bodybuilding Medication?" *Muscle Digest*, vol. VII (July 1983):50.
90. Bergerson, *loc. cit.*, p.333.
91. Columbo, Dr. Franco. "Will Amphetamines Jazz Up Workouts?" *Muscle & Fitness*, vol.42 (May 1981):69.
92. Bergerson, *loc. cit.*, p.333.
93. *ibid.*
94. *ibid.*, p.334.
95. Wilbourn, *loc. cit.*, p.193.
96. Bergerson, *op. cit.*, p.333.
97. Columbo, *loc. cit.*, p.69.
98. Wilbourn, *loc. cit.*, p.193.
99. Pirie, Dr. Lynn. "Diuretics." *Muscle & Fitness*, vol.44 (February 1983):97.
100. Wilbourn, *loc. cit.*, p.193.
101. *ibid.*
102. Pirie, *op. cit.*, p.96.
103. *ibid.*, p.97.
104. *ibid.*
105. *ibid.*, p.96.
106. *ibid.*, p.97.
107. *ibid.*, p.157.
108. *ibid.*, p.96.

4. Prerequisites for Training Naturally

1. Schwarzenegger Arnold, and Douglas Kent Hall. *Arnold: The Education of a Bodybuilder*. New York: Simon & Schuster, 1977, p.151.
2. *ibid.*, p.152.
3. Weider, *op. cit.*, p.28.
4. *ibid.*
5. *ibid.*, p.30.
6. *ibid.*, p.29.
7. *ibid.*, p.30.
8. *ibid.*, p.29.
9. *ibid.*, p.28.
10. Sprague, *op. cit.*, p.27.
11. *ibid.*
12. *ibid.*
13. *ibid.*, p.101.
14. *ibid.*
15. *ibid.*, p.12
16. *ibid.*, pp.13–14.
17. *ibid.*, p.26.

5. Fundamentals of Natural Bodybuilding

1. Sprague, *op. cit.*, p.21.
2. Massey, *op. cit.*, p.53.
3. *ibid.*, p.54.
4. *ibid.*, p.53.
5. Sprague, *op. cit.*, pp.11–12.
6. *ibid.*, p.26.
7. *ibid.*
8. *ibid.*, p.27.
9. *ibid.*, pp.34–35.
10. *ibid.*, p.293.
11. *ibid.*, p.84.
12. Wright, James E. "Overtraining—the Symptoms and the Remedy." *Muscle & Fitness*, vol.41 (August 1980):74.
13. *ibid.*, p.75.
14. *ibid.*
15. *ibid.*
16. *ibid.*
17. *ibid.*, p.105.
18. *ibid.*
19. *ibid.*
20. *ibid.*, p.75, 105.
21. Sprague, *op. cit.*, p.27.
22. *ibid.*, p.156.

6. Pectoral Exercises

1. Sprague, *op. cit.*, p.111.
2. *ibid.*
3. *ibid.*, p.112.
4. *ibid.*, p.53.
5. *ibid.*, p.52.
6. *ibid.*

7. Deltoid Exercises

1. Sprague, *op. cit.*, p.55.
2. *ibid.*
3. *ibid.*, p.117.
4. *ibid.*, p.56.
5. *ibid.*
6. *ibid.*, p.120.
7. *ibid.*

8. Latissimus Dorsi Exercises

1. Sprague, *op. cit.*, p.50.
2. *ibid.*, p.109.
3. *ibid.*, p.110.
4. *ibid.*, p.49.
5. *ibid.*, p.50.
6. *ibid.*, pp.50-51.

9. Trapezius Exercises

1. Sprague, *op. cit.*, pp.45–46.
2. *ibid.*, p.108.
3. *ibid.*, p.44.
4. *ibid.*, p.45.
5. *ibid.*

10. Bicep Exercises

1. Sprague, *op. cit.*, pp.56–57.
2. *ibid.*, p.57.
3. *ibid.*
4. *ibid.*, p.122.
5. *ibid.*
6. *ibid.*, p.121.

7. *ibid.,* p.122.

11. Forearm Exercises
1. Sprague, *op. cit.,* p.127.

12. Tricep Exercises
1. Sprague, *op. cit.,* p.61.
2. *ibid.*
3. *ibid.*
4. *ibid.,* p.62.
5. *ibid.*

13. Quadricep Exercises
1. Sprague, *op. cit.,* p.38.
2. *ibid.*
3. *ibid.*
4. *ibid.*
5. *ibid.,* p.39.
6. *ibid.,* p.107.
7. *ibid.,* p.40.
8. *ibid.*
9. *ibid.,* p.41.
10. *ibid.,* p.105.
11. *ibid.*
12. *ibid.,* p.42.

14. Hamstring Exercises
1. Sprague, *op cit.,* p.44.
2. *ibid.,* p.45.
3. *ibid.,* p.109.
4. *ibid.*

15. Calf Exercises
1. Sprague, *op. cit.,* p.66.
2. *ibid.*
3. *ibid.*
4. *ibid.*

16. Abdominal and Intercostal Exercises
1. Sprague, *op. cit.,* p.68.
2. *ibid.*
3. *ibid.*
4. *ibid.,* p.131.
5. *ibid.*
6. *ibid.,* p.69.
7. *ibid.*
8. *ibid.*
9. *ibid.,* p.131.
10. *ibid.*

17. Miscellaneous Exercises
1. Sprague, *op. cit.,* p.47.
2. *ibid.*
3. *ibid.*
4. *ibid.*
5. *ibid.,* p.181.
6. *ibid.*

18. Women's Natural Bodybuilding
1. *Physicians Desk Reference,* 27th edition, "Dianabel," p.664.

19. Essentials to the Natural Bodybuilding Lifestyle
1. American College of Sports Medicine Position Statement on "The Recommended Quantity and Quality of Exercise for Developing and Maintaining Fitness in Healthy Adults," p.1.

2. Zohman, Lenore R. *Exercise Your Way to Fitness and Heart Health.* C.P.C. International, Inc., 1974, p.14.
3. Zohman, *ibid.,* p.15.

20. Natural Bodybuilding Nutrition
1. Mentzer, Mike. "Nutrition for Pure Muscle Mass." *Muscle & Fitness,* vol.43 (September 1982):96.
2. *ibid.*
3. Nutrition Research, Inc. *Nutrition Almanac.* New York: McGraw Hill Book Co., 1979, p.7.
4. Williams, Sue Rodwell. *Nutrition & Diet Therapy.* Missouri: C.V. Mosby Co., p.69.
5. Mentzer, *loc. cit.,* p.96.
6. *Nutrition Almanac, op. cit.,* p.9.
7. Pardee, Richard. "How Much Protein? Consider the Gorilla." *Muscle & Fitness,* vol.44 (November 1983):157.
8. *Nutrition Almanac, loc. cit.,* p.9.
9. Williams, *op. cit.,* p.49.
10. *Nutrition Almanac, loc. cit.,* p.9.
11. Hyland, Carl. "The Truth About Amino Acids." *Muscle & Fitness,* vol.43 (March 1982):93.
12. Coe, Boyer. "Advanced Bodybuilding Nutrition." *Muscle & Fitness,* vol.42. (January 1981):42.
13. Hyland, *op. cit.,* p.11.
14. *ibid.*
15. Bressler, Susan. "The Low Fat Miracle Diet." *Muscle & Fitness,* vol.42 (January 1981):140.
16. Coe, *loc. cit.,* p.42.
17. *Nutrition Almanac, op. cit.,* p.42.
18. *ibid.,* p.8.
19. *ibid.*
20. *ibid.*
21. Williams, *op. cit.,* p.33.
22. *ibid.,* p.15.
23. Coe, *loc. cit.,* p.219.
24. *Nutrition Almanac, loc. cit.,* p.7.
25. *ibid.*
26. *ibid.,* p.8.
27. *ibid.,* p.7.
28. *ibid.*
29. *ibid.*
30. Williams, *loc. cit.,* p.15.
31. *Nutrition Almanac, loc. cit.,* p.7.
32. *ibid.,* p.8.
33. *ibid.,* p.11.
34. Williams, *op. cit.,* p.79.
35. *ibid.*
36. *Nutrition Almanac, loc. cit.,* p.11.
37. *ibid.*
38. *ibid.*
39. Williams, *op. cit.,* p.30.
40. *Nutrition Almanac, loc. cit.,* p.12.
41. Williams, *loc. cit.,* p.131.
42. *ibid.,* p.136.
43. Gouvart, Frances. "Crystal Clear, Salt and the Bodybuilder." *Muscle & Bodybuilder* (July 1983): 42.
44. *Nutrition Almanac, op. cit.,* p.186.
45. Williams, *op. cit.,* p.15.
46. *Nutrition Almanac, loc. cit.,* p.186.
47. Coe, *loc. cit.,* p. 219.
48. Sprague, *op. cit.,* p.28.
49. Williams, *loc. cit.,* p.26.
50. *ibid.,* p.73.
51. *Nutrition Almanac, op. cit.,* p.245.

52. Williams, *op. cit.,* p.76.
53. Mentzer, *loc. cit.,* p.96.
54. *ibid.,* p.94.
55. *ibid.,* p.95.
56. *ibid.,* pp.95–96.
57. Bressler, *op. cit.,* p.140.
58. *ibid.*
59. *ibid.*
60. *ibid.*
61. Coe, *op. cit.,* p.221.
62. Bressler, *loc. cit.,* p.140.
63. *ibid.*
64. Coe, *op. cit.,* p.223.
65. Bressler, *loc. cit.,* p.140.
66. *ibid.*
67. Coe, *loc. cit.,* p.223.
68. Bressler, *loc. cit.,* p.145.
69. *ibid.*
70. *ibid.*
71. Zohman, *op. cit.,* p.21.
72. Bressler, *op. cit.,* p.160.
73. Coe, *loc. cit.,* p.220.
74. Bressler, *loc. cit.,* p.160.
75. Benton, Mike. "Protein, The High Cost of Cooking." *Muscle & Fitness,* vol.43 (August 1982):55.
76. *ibid.*
77. *ibid.*
78. *ibid.*
79. *ibid.*
80. Centrella, Bernard. "Nutrition-Boost Your Progress with Protein Supplements." *Muscle & Fitness,* vol.44 (March 1983):15.
81. *ibid.*
82. *ibid.*
83. *ibid.*
84. Sprague, *op. cit.,* p.84.
85. *ibid.,* p.85.
86. *ibid.*
87. *ibid.,* p.29.

BIBLIOGRAPHY

American College of Sports Medicine Position Statement on "The Recommended Quantity and Quality of Exercise for Developing and Maintaining Fitness in Healthy Adults."

American College of Sports Medicine, Position Statement on "The Use and Abuse of Anabolic-Androgen Steroids in Sports."

Ashpaugh, Bill, with Holly Miller. *Powerlift.* Tennessee: Impact Books, 1981.

Benton, Mike. "Protein, The High Cost of Cooking." *Muscle & Fitness,* vol.43 (August 1982):55.

Bergerson, Betty S. and Dr. Andres Goth. *Pharmacology in Nursing,* 14th edition. Missouri: Mosby Co., 1979.

Bressler, Susan. "The Low Fat Miracle Diet." *Muscle & Fitness,* vol.42 (January 1981):140.

Brunner, Lillian and Doris Suddarth. *Textbook of Medical Surgical Nursing,* 4th edition. Philadelphia: J. B. Lippincott, 1980.

Centrella, Bernard. "Nutrition-Boost Your Progress with Protein Supplements." *Muscle & Fitness,* vol.44 (March 1983):15.

Coe, Boyer. "Advanced Bodybuilding Nutrition." *Muscle & Fitness,* vol.44 (April 1983):42.

Columbo, Dr. Franco. "Will Amphetamines Jazz Up Workouts?" *Muscle & Fitness,* vol.42 (May 1981):69.

Dobbins, Bill. "Thyroid, Nothing To Fool With." *Muscle & Fitness,* vol.42 (August 1981):62.

Freeman, Manson, Massey and Wessel. *The Kinisiology of Weightlifting.* Iowa: Wm. C. Brown Co., 1973.

Goldman, Bob. "Liver Death." *Muscle,* vol.41 (February 1980):105.

Goulart, Frances. "Crystal Clear—Salt and the Bodybuilder." *Muscle and Bodybuilder* (July 1983):42.

Hyland, Carl. "The Truth About Amino Acids." *Muscle & Fitness,* vol.43 (March 1982):93.

Kennedy, Robert. "When Will It End?" editorial, *Muscle Mag,* no. 39 (1983):6.

Kerr, Dr. Robert. "S.T.H.—Tomorrow's Anabolic Drug For Today." *Muscle Digest,* vol.7 (March 1983):16.

Kerr, Dr. Robert. "S.T.H., The Growth Hormone." *Flex,* vol.1 (March 1983):30.

Mac Dougall, Duncan. "Drug Symposium—Anabolic Steroids." *The Physician & Sports Medicine,* vol.11 (September 1983):97.

Mentzer, Mike. "Nutrition For Pure Muscle Mass." *Muscle & Fitness,* vol.43 (September 1982):96.

Mentzer, Mike. "S.T.H. Caveat Emptor," *Flex,* vol.1 (March 1983):30.

Morey, Stanley W. and Ken Passariello. *Steroids.* U.S.A.: Morey and Passariello, 1982.

Nutrition Research Inc. *Nutrition Almanac.* New York: McGraw Hill Book Co., 1979.

Pardee, Richard. "How Much Protein? Consider the Gorilla." *Muscle & Fitness,* vol.44 (November 1983):157.

Physicians Desk Reference. "Dianabol," 27th edition, p.664.

Pirie, Dr. Lynn. "Diuretics." *Muscle & Fitness,* vol. 44 (February 1983):97.

Reynolds, Bill and Ken Sprague. *Golds Gym Book of Bodybuilding.* Chicago: Contemporary Books, 1983.

Rodman, Morton J. and Dorothy W. Smith. *Pharmacology & Drug Therapy in Nursing.* Philadelphia: J. B. Lippincott Co., 1968.

Smillie, Tom. "Potential, What Is It? Do You Have It?" *Muscle Training Illustrated* (December 1982):40.

Taylor, W. W. "Amphetamines, Useful Bodybuilding Medication?" *Muscle Digest,* vol.7 (July 1983):50.

Todd, Terry. "The Steroid Predicament." *Sports Illustrated,* vol.59 (May 1983):69.

Weider, Joe. "Sleep." *Muscle Builder,* vol.40 (November 1979):43.

Weider, Joe. "Stress." *Muscle Builder,* vol.40 (December 1980):147.

Weider, Joe. "Those Meddlesome Moods." *Muscle Builder,* vol.41 (February 1980):91.

Wilbourn, Claudia. "Why Bodybuilders Are Dying To Win?" *Muscle & Fitness,* vol.44 (March 1983):193.

Williams, Sue Rodwell. *Nutrition and Diet Therapy.* Missouri: Mosby Co., p.69.

Wright, Dr. James E. "If You Must Use Steroids." *Muscle & Fitness,* vol.42 (January 1981):52.

Wright, Dr. James E. "The G.H. Factor." *Muscle & Fitness,* vol.44 (January 1983):193.

Wright, Dr. James E. "Steroids, Shortcut to Disaster." *Muscle,* vol.40 (September 1979):121.

Zohman, Lenore R. *Exercise Your Way to Fitness and Heart Health.* C.P.C. International, Inc., 1974.